Emily Allen-Hornblower
From Agent to Spectator

Trends in Classics –
Supplementary Volumes

Edited by
Franco Montanari and Antonios Rengakos

Scientific Committee
Alberto Bernabé · Margarethe Billerbeck
Claude Calame · Philip R. Hardie · Stephen J. Harrison
Stephen Hinds · Richard Hunter · Christina Kraus
Giuseppe Mastromarco · Gregory Nagy
Theodore D. Papanghelis · Giusto Picone
Kurt Raaflaub · Bernhard Zimmermann

Volume 30

Emily Allen-Hornblower

From Agent to Spectator

Witnessing the Aftermath in Ancient Greek Epic and Tragedy

DE GRUYTER

ISBN 978-3-11-057818-8
e-ISBN (PDF) 978-3-11-043004-2
e-ISBN (EPUB) 978-3-11-043009-7
ISSN 1868-4785

Library of Congress Cataloging-in-Publication Data
A CIP catalog record for this book has been applied for at the Library of Congress.

Bibliographic information published by the Deutsche Nationalbibliothek
The Deutsche Nationalbibliothek lists this publication in the Deutsche Nationalbibliografie;
detailed bibliographic data are available on the Internet at http://dnb.dnb.de.

© 2016 Walter de Gruyter GmbH, Berlin/Boston
This volume is text- and page-identical with the hardback published in 2016.
Logo: Christopher Schneider, Laufen
Printing and binding: CPI books GmbH, Leck

♾ Printed on acid-free paper
Printed in Germany

www.degruyter.com

Preface

This monograph started out as my PhD Thesis in Classical Philology, which I wrote at Harvard University, and submitted in 2009. I wish to express my warmest thanks and admiring gratitude to my advisor, Gregory Nagy, as well as to my committee members, Albert Henrichs and Gloria Ferrari, for their attentiveness, wisdom, and the many illuminating exchanges they generously made time for. I wrote the thesis in *"cotutelle"* with the université de Paris IV–Sorbonne, and defended it before a *"jury"* of readers, all of whom gave me valuable feedback: Paul Demont, Christine Mauduit, Ioanna Papadopoulou, Philippe Rousseau, and Monique Trédé. I had the opportunity to revisit and rework the manuscript thanks to a semester-long research fellowship from the Center for Hellenic Studies in Washington, DC, and one that I received from the Loeb Classical Library Foundation. I am extremely grateful for both.

I had the great fortune of receiving encouragement, stimulation, suggestions and advice of various kinds over the years from a number of colleagues and friends, most notably Lowell Edmunds, Doug Frame, Renaud Gagné, Giulio Guidorizzi, Marianne Hopman, Richard Martin, Leonard Muellner, Kirk Ormand, Silvia Romani, Seth Schein, Laura Slatkin, and Eirene Visvardi. Several sections of this book were presented in earlier versions at a number of conferences and lectures. I want to express hearty thanks to all those who participated in these events and raised important questions, as well as to the two anonymous readers for the Press, for their insightful observations. The editors of *Trends in Classics*, Franco Montanari and Antonios Rengakos, were immensely helpful and provided valuable guidance in bringing this book through to its final stages.

I also wish to express deep thanks to those who inspired me to devote my life to the Classics in my early years: mademoiselle Rousseau and Jean Gruber, both outstanding teachers and inspiring figures. *In fine,* there are no words that can adequately express my gratitude to my family for their continuing love, support, and patience.

This book is dedicated to Calypso, who sat by me as I wrote every word, heaving only an occasional sigh as the time for a walk came around.

Contents

Introduction —— 1
    The powerless spectator: Witnessing the limits of the human condition —— 5
    Voicing their vision: Emotional response and character —— 6
    Time, knowledge, and power —— 8
    Narrative in tragedy, tragedy as narrative —— 11
    Perceptions and values —— 12
    Chapter Outline —— 15

Chapter One: The Helpless Witness: Achilles, Patroclus, and the Portrayal of Vulnerability in the *Iliad* —— 18
    Methodology —— 22
    Watching through the eyes of *philoi* —— 23
    Seeing and pitying —— 25
    Helpless spectators, mortal and immortal —— 29
    Zeus's helplessness: Regarding the death of Sarpedon —— 31
    Looking on from the walls of Troy: The death of Hector —— 36
    The Death of Patroclus —— 44
        No witness, no pity? —— 44
        You, Patroclus —— 46
        Calling out to the threatened warrior: The *Patrocleia* and Patroclus's doom —— 49
        Apostrophes and turning points: danger or death —— 55
        The downfall of Patroclus —— 64
        Negativity and absence —— 65
        Apostrophes and the poetics of helplessness —— 71
        Absence and presence: The Voice of the Helpless Spectator —— 74
        Achilles' delayed vision —— 81
        Mortal Achilles —— 87

Chapter Two: Spectatorship, Agency, and Alienation in Sophocles' *Trachiniae* —— 94
    Watching through Deianeira's eyes —— 98
    Pity and Vulnerability —— 107
    From spectator to agent: Playing Aphrodite —— 117
    Watching Deianeira watch Heracles burn —— 127
    The divine agent and spectator: Cypris —— 140

Watching Deianeira die —— 145
Watching Heracles die —— 149
The silence of Heracles —— 158
Divine agents and spectators —— 166

Chapter Three: From Murderer to Messenger: Body, Speech, and Justice in Greek Tragedy —— 171
Part One: The Murder of Agamemnon: Imagery and vision —— 177
Clytemnestra's moment of truth —— 177
Part Two: Matricide: Speech and the Body —— 199
The Death of Clytemnestra in Aeschylus: The Tyranny and the robe —— 201
Sophocles' *Electra:* Viewing Clytemnestra's body through other eyes —— 210
Euripides' *Electra:* Motherhood destroyed —— 224

Chapter Four: Neoptolemus Between Agent and Spectator in Sophocles' *Philoctetes* —— 247
The healing presence of a witness and interlocutor —— 255
Pain and its perceiver —— 261
A blind eye and a deaf ear: The averted gaze and selective hearing of Odysseus —— 273
Watch yourself, young man —— 283
The sounds of Neoptolemus's moral awakening —— 285
How to "act?" —— 300

Bibliography —— 311

Index —— 327

Introduction

> "The man of action is always free of conscience;
> the only person with a conscience is the observer."
>
> (*Der Handelde ist immer gewissenlos,
> es hat niemand Gewissen als der Betrachtende.*)
> — Goethe[1]

For nearly every figure accomplishing a major deed or enduring a great blow on the Homeric battlefield or on the tragic stage, there is someone looking on – a witness, watching and reacting to the actions and misfortunes unfolding before his eyes. In both Greek epic and Attic tragedy, a wide variety of internal spectators, divine or mortal, present events to their audience from a specific vantage point, through which the audience sees events unfold. Countless examples of such witnesses come to mind, such as the rarely compassionate, often detached, and at times downright sadistic divine audience, or the Chorus, which sees, reacts to, and comments on the action in a role so complex and varied that critics still struggle to pinpoint or define it. Greek tragedy is rife with messengers (usually anonymous or secondary characters such as nurses, tutors, children, heralds, and the like) who give subjective eyewitness accounts of what has occurred offstage.[2]

These internal audiences are central to both of the genres under consideration in the present book, and have already received abundant attention.[3] The bibliography on the Greek Chorus is considerable.[4] The divine audience and its responses (or lack thereof) to a situation are a pervasive point of interest for critics concerned with questions of responsibility and justice, whether in epic or tragedy.[5] Studies devoted to vision and the gaze across genres have con-

---

1 Goethe 1985–8, 17, 758 (no. 241).
2 Several monographs have been devoted to those minor figures of Greek tragedy that deliver messenger speeches, including recently De Jong 1991; Karydas 1998; Barrett 2002; Markantonatos 2002; Yoon 2012.
3 I use "audience" to refer both to the Homeric audience of listeners and to the spectators of Greek drama. The differences in each of their experiences, based on the nature of the performance before them, will become apparent in the specific analyses that follow.
4 On the Chorus's functions, see e.g., Calame 2005. Regarding the Chorus as "intermediary between various levels of reference," see Gagné and Hopman 2013 (for the quotation see the introduction to the edited volume, p. 2). Visvardi 2015 provides an original and much needed examination of the *collective* emotion the Chorus gives voice to, with substantial bibliography; see also Rutherford 2012, ch. 6.
5 See for instance Lloyd-Jones 1971 and Griffin 1980.

sidered in depth the role that internal observers and their subjective points of view play in narrative and drama.[6] The study of characters' individual perspectives and reactions hinges on an important, related question: the nature of the relationship between internal and external audiences, which has been an object of scholarly interest since Antiquity. In Greek tragedy, that relationship is central to the place of pity and fear in the elusive process of *catharsis* as Aristotle defines it in the *Poetics*.[7]

This book covers new ground: it deals with a specific subset of characters whose relationship to the action is distinct from the internal audiences mentioned above. We tend to associate the act of witnessing primarily with bystanders who play no active role in the events they are watching. The present monograph takes a novel approach: it considers characters in Homer's *Iliad* and Greek tragedy that are looking on and reacting — in word, or in deed, or both – *to their own actions*. What I propose to do in the present inquiry is to look at the effect of the action, not on *any* given set of characters, but on a particular subset of characters that forms a category of its own: those figures who have committed an act of significant consequence and are (by way of circumstance and the poets' ingenuity) relegated to the status of spectator to (and, often, commentator on) that act, and shown in the process of reacting to its aftermath.[8] As these characters become spectators, they go from acting to reacting; the audience, in turn, goes from watching them act to watching them watch and react. Their reaction may be manifested through strong emotional responses, words, further deeds, or any combination of the three. This agent-turned-spectator stance usually lasts for a limited amount of time – often a single scene, or even just the length of a speech – but every instance is of tremendous importance, not only to our understanding of the characters in question, but also to the articulation of themes that are essential to the poetic works within which these characters and their reactions are thus prominently featured.

In his article "The Pursuit of Hector," Samuel Bassett notes that, "in Homer almost as much as in Attic tragedy the vehicle of emotion is not primarily action, but rather the *emotional effect* of action on the characters, revealed by their own

---

[6] On the epic gaze in particular, see Lovatt 2013 (with substantial bibliography concerning the gaze across genres and periods). On the role of focalization within the Iliadic narrative, see De Jong 1987; on the role of sight and the mediation provided by internal characters' gazes within the Homeric *Iliad*, see Slatkin 2007, 19–34.

[7] See e.g., Nussbaum 1986, Belfiore 1992, Segal and Easterling in Silk 1996, Halliwell 2002, Konstan 2005, Munteanu 2012.

[8] Going forward, I sometimes refer to these characters as "agents-turned-spectators" for shorthand.

words or by the words of others."⁹ Featuring the emotional effect of the action on characters is without a doubt a powerful "vehicle of emotion" for the audience. Whenever the Homeric poet and the Greek tragedians make the audience see an event from the specific vantage point of internal spectators (divine or mortal) and foreground these characters' reactions to the action, they provide a measure of the action's gravity and momentousness for the audience. The action's emotional impact on the audience is particularly strong when the witnesses through whose eyes they see the events have a close relationship with the loved ones whom they see falling victim to suffering or death.¹⁰

The specific spectators to a given action and its aftermath that I am interested in here form a sub-category of their own: they are also the perpetrators of the action whose effects they are watching. Bassett's point remains true in their case as well: those who have committed the deeds offer up reactions that are no less pronounced (and are in fact perhaps even more so) than those of witnesses standing by; whether their reactions involve regret, ambivalence, horror, or delight, they contribute to heighten the impact of the events on the external audience.¹¹ When the audience members watch characters shift to the status of witness and see through these characters' eyes what they have done, they may experience some form of emotional contagion by espousing these characters' gaze.¹²

My goal, however, is not to offer an investigation of the nature and modalities of the relationship between this particular sub-category of internal audience and the external audience, nor is it to explore the emotional mediation that the former can (and, undeniably, often does) provide for the latter.¹³ The relationship

---

9 Bassett 1930, 130. Italics mine.
10 See ch. 1 for examples from the *Iliad*, including the death of Hector as it is seen by his parents, Priam and Hecuba, pp. 36–41. As audience members, we experience the events with greater intensity because of the sense of emotional immediacy and proximity that is created by these internal witnesses, and the events' relevance to (and devastating impact on) them.
11 As is to be expected in the genres from which the examples that I consider have been selected, the actions that the agents-turned-spectators consider involve the infliction of suffering, death, or both (whether deliberately or inadvertently).
12 It is important to bear in mind the possibility of a disparity between the internal and external audience's responses, in lieu of a direct or straightforward form of emotional contagion. The external audience does not always or necessarily simply mimic and condone or condemn and reject the emotional reactions of the characters in question. In the most interesting and tragic cases, the audience is made to feel something in between.
13 Regarding the emotions in ancient Greek history and culture, see the volume edited by Chaniotis 2012, as well as Chaniotis and Ducrey 2013 (which also includes a study of the emotions in ancient Rome).

between internal and external audience is extremely important to our understanding of how emotions are evoked within any poetic work, especially since we are looking at genres that were performed before an audience, and they are a consideration in what follows; but the aim of the present exploration is different.[14] It is another relationship that interests me here: that between characters and their actions, and their (often shifting) relationship to their own selves (and the actions they have taken) when they shift from the stance of agent to that of spectator. I ask what effect is achieved when, time and again, poets put their *principal* characters who have committed drastic acts (deliberately or not) in the position of observers to their own deed, witnessing and reacting to its aftermath. What is the purpose of having the audience zero in on these central characters' visions of and responses to their past actions, and of making the latter an equal if not greater point of focus than the actions themselves?

There is more at play in foregrounding characters' visions of and responses to their own deeds than the creation of greater emotional immediacy and involvement for the audience. My aim here is to bring to light the other unexplored yet essential functions – poetic, dramatic, and thematic – fulfilled by these agents-turned-spectators' reactions to their deeds. I pay careful attention a) to the language, and (in some cases) gestures with which the characters under consideration (and others) convey their reactions and b) to the particular (and often novel) perspectives on their actions that these verbal or physical testimonies express. What do agents-turned-spectators "see" from this other standpoint? Does their shift to the status of observer bring about changes in perspective and new insights for these characters, and if so, how are these changes reflected in their words, actions, or emotions (if they are at all)? What focalized, subjective vision and version of the events and of themselves do these characters give the audience a glimpse of? What new insights do the characters in question gain concerning their actions, and the audience concerning them? In some cases, the characters do not gain new insights at all: they remain blind or ignorant to a large degree; in such cases, the point seems precisely to highlight their restricted and biased knowledge with what the external spectators are able to know and see for themselves.

---

[14] Vickers 1979 ch. 2 discusses the centrality of "seeing" and "feeling" in the experience of the spectator to Greek tragedy. On Greek tragedy's "indirect comment on its desired emotional response" by way of the depiction of emotion onstage, see Segal 1993, especially ch. 2.

The powerless spectator: Witnessing the limits of the human condition

The relationship between spectator and object of spectacle, or between audience and character, is often seen as comprising an important power differential:[15] the power and security of the spectator is contrasted with the suffering and vulnerability of the character that is the object of the spectator's gaze.[16] The characters that are of interest to me here are not merely objects of sight, however, and they complicate the scheme described above. Since they are themselves cast in the role of spectators to their own actions, they are both spectators and objects of spectacle. In this situation, does the power differential between spectator and object of spectacle change?

I argue that it can and often does, designedly so. By featuring central characters in the act of watching the outcomes of their actions, the poets are able to make the audience perceive the powerlessness inherent to the status of spectator, a status that the audience shares with the characters. The characters I am concerned with look upon the consequences of their action as a spectacle, in relation to which they are relegated to the role of onlooker and no more: it is either too late or beyond their power to backtrack.[17] Their new role as spectator to the aftermath of their deeds is marked by a tension between their powerless gaze, on the one hand, and their inability to intervene and change the outcome that they provoked (should they desire to do so), on the other. As they shift from the status of agent to that of mere witness, characters straddle the line between power and helplessness and waver between accepting responsibility for their acts and acknowledging subservience to powers beyond them (including the divine). These protagonists, *qua* spectators to the consequences of their actions, give voice to, dramatize, and enact the tragic motifs of human helplessness and mortal fallibility that lie at the core of Homeric epic and Greek tragedy and that define the human condition, in a manner that leads the audience looking on to ponder their own.[18]

---

15 This differential is seen as the very basis of tragic pleasure and an important component of *catharsis* as defined by Aristotle. On tragic emotion, *catharsis*, and the theatrical experience, see e. g., Belfiore 1992; Halliwell 2002. For a discussion of scholarly disagreements concerning how to read Greek tragedy and the possible over-emphasis on its relevance to its immediate context, as opposed to the centrality of the emotional experience of the audience, see Gregory 2002.
16 I discuss this further in ch. 2.
17 The only two exceptions are Clytemnestra (ch. 2) and Neoptolemus (ch. 4).
18 In his reflection on the source of *pathos* in tragedy, Redfield considers the specifically pathetic nature of suffering that characters inflict upon themselves (inadvertently), and the painful

Voicing their vision: Emotional response and character

When characters step back and view their action from the stance of a spectator, the audience members' attention turns from their action to their reaction, and from what they have done to their retrospective vision of what they have done as they face the deed's aftermath. That response and that vision are in most cases expressed in the characters' own voices; they may also, albeit more rarely, be articulated by other characters, or by other poetic means, which suggest or imply the characters' reactions rather than express them directly.[19] The characters are not just spectators: they are *a posteriori* focalizers of their own action and its outcome. In most cases, they are also the narrators of their action, relating and reacting to the impact of their past action in the here and now of performance. In considering characters' visions of their own deeds and the words that they use to describe them, my approach to the poetic texts of the *Iliad* and Greek drama combines a number of analytical tools and methodological approaches – mainly those of philology and literary criticism, but others come into play as well, including the tools of narratology and considerations of stagecraft (in my analyses of tragedy).

Narratologists distinguish between a first-person narrative (homodiegetic, in Genette's parlance) and a third-person (heterodiegetic) narrative.[20] A third-person narrative is a story told by a narrator who does *not* play a role in the events that he reports. The poet's voice in Homeric epic is often given as a typical example of such a heterodiegetic narrator: the Homeric narrator is an omniscient speaker, who is endowed with knowledge (from the Muses) that the characters do not possess, and is exterior to the world of his characters (extradiegetic). A first-person narrative, on the other hand, is presented by a narrator who is also a character in the narrative that he is recounting; that speaker *participates*

---

alienation that comes from the realization that they are both doer and sufferer: "The source of *pathos* is not in the sufferer; *pathos* is inflicted on the sufferer by others, by chance, or even by his own act, in which case he will appear alien to himself. A central question in tragic drama is the question: How could I have done this to myself?" (Redfield 1975, 80).

19 Such is the case with Achilles, in the scene of greatest impact and relevance to him in the entire *Iliad* that I examine in ch. 1. The case of Achilles is also exceptional in that it is not exactly a retrospective vision that we are presented with in his case, nor even an actual vision; it is, rather, an implicit gaze: see below, pp. 44–86.

20 Genette *Figures* 1980. For bibliography concerning theoretical literature on the first-person narrative, see De Jong 1991, 2 n. 2.

in the events that he represents to the (internal and external) audience. As he tells his story, he fulfills the roles both of narrator and of focalizer.²¹

The scenes I examine predominantly involve characters that offer up first-person, homodiegetic accounts of their own past actions. Within the accounts that they provide of their actions after the fact, the audience can see their deeds through their eyes and hear them give voice to their reactions. In their report, the characters describe their action (that is, their particular vision of it) and their reaction in their own words, in a focalized account that is colored and restricted. It is the very subjectivity of these accounts that makes them a critical part of the arsenal of poetic tools used by the epic poet and tragedians to characterize the *dramatis personae* in question: it gives the audience an opportunity to see and even embrace the characters' views of their own actions, for a brief period of time.²²

One dominant subcategory of speeches that I consider within Greek tragedy are the narratives that characters provide of actions that they have committed offstage – primarily murders. These speeches are variations on the traditional, set type of the messenger speeches that abound in the genre. Normally, the messenger speech is delivered by anonymous or secondary figures.²³ The passages that I consider are unusual in that the main characters are the ones that report the murderous deeds that they have perpetrated (rather than someone else doing so). What is true of messenger speeches in general is true *a fortiori* of these characters' speeches as well: as first-person narratives, they are subjective perspectives of an event. When the protagonists are put in the position of being *a posteriori* homodiegetic narrators and focalizers of their deadly act, they are given a chance to observe and comment on their own actions. These lenses and accounts are biased, limited, and hence revealing, especially of the characters' moral partiality. As such, these first-person accounts are functional and dramatically effective. In both of the cases of murderers-turned messengers that I examine, moreover, there is an additional layer of complexity for us to consider as we watch the characters respond onstage to the act they have committed offstage, because the

---

21 De Jong 1991, ch. 1, offers a helpful typology of first-person narratives (within messenger speeches) and an overview of their characteristics, including, primarily, restriction and bias.
22 On the notion of "perspective" and the non-sensory filters that the notion encompasses (going beyond the strictly visual), see Hopman 2013, especially 59–60, with bibliography.
23 Just because they are delivered by anonymous or secondary characters that are somewhat removed from the action does not mean that messenger speeches in general are factual and objective. In her study of Euripidean messenger speeches, De Jong 1991 has convincingly shown that there is considerable subjectivity and bias, even in accounts given by marginal participants in the action. Barrett 2002 and Goward 1999 have corroborated her important insights.

characters in question also act out (at least parts of) their deed (physically) as they recount it (verbally), thus introducing an additional, visual (and biased) depiction of their deed for our consideration.

Time, knowledge, and power

One major question that arises as we examine agents-turned-spectators' verbal accounts of their past actions and reactions to them, is that of their agency and responsibility. It is not the question of the audience's (or the poet's) assessment of a given character's guilt (or lack thereof) that I am concerned with here.[24] Rather, I ask, how do these characters see themselves, and how do they assess their own place and role in their action, explicitly or implicitly?[25] Since they are *a posteriori* spectators of their action, they often see their action through a different lens in the present from the one through which they viewed it when they were committing it in the recent past. When they look back at and narrate what they have done, how they relate to their act as spectators and how they relate to and perceive their earlier, acting selves can vary tremendously.[26] Their perspective on their past action may also change in light of what they actually see of its aftermath — in tragedy, it is often lying before them in the tangible form of a corpse (see the following section, titled "Perceptions and values").

Most frequently (logically enough), agents-turned-spectators observe the aftermath of their deed *after* the fact. In these cases, the linearity of time is respected: characters look back on their action with (as the case may be) regret or *Scha-*

---

[24] The questions of agency and responsibility are narrowly interconnected; see e.g., Adkins 1960 and Williams 1993.

[25] In some cases that I consider, we are faced with a slight variation on this scheme, as the characters' vision and assessments of their deeds are put into words not by the characters themselves, but by others (the poet or other characters).

[26] In a sense, we might say that, in the figures of agents-turned-spectators, we are given to see "the discovery of the mind" (Snell's phrase, 1953) at work, as characters themselves face the task of disentangling their own individual human personality and subsequent actions from the responsibility of the gods for these actions. Winnington-Ingram 1965 discusses the complex nature of archaic thought and the place the Greek tragedians (Aeschylus and Sophocles especially) grant to human agency and free will, within a conceptual framework whose underlying premise is recognition of the fact that "our deliberate acts are themselves in large measure the product of innumerable causes in the past over which we have no control" (W.-I. 1965, 126 and *passim*). W.-I. also discusses Plato's criticism of the place afforded the gods in the tragedians' thought system, and the limits of that criticism.

denfreude. Occasionally, however, poets use ingenious poetic devices that topple the chronological linearity I have just described: they make their characters observe the outcome of their initiative *while* it is playing out or even, in some rare cases in which a form of foresight is granted to them, *before* it actually occurs.²⁷ Whether they foresee the outcome of their actions, or are otherwise given a means of envisioning that outcome before it actually plays itself out, or watch it as it is occurring, or look back on it after the fact – regardless, in every one of these cases, when protagonists transition from the status of actively engaged participant to that of observer, a shift occurs, and it is that shift that I am interested in. The shift may lie in their perspective on their action, or in some newly acquired knowledge or understanding of the nature or implications of that action, which emerges as they step back and observe what they have done, taking in the full consequences.

Poets often convey the limitations of a given character's vision and knowledge by playing up the disparity between what characters can see, from their restricted and biased perspective, and what the audience is given to see and know, either by an omniscient, third-person narrator (in Homeric epic) or by other characters and the Chorus (in tragedy).²⁸ In the works that I consider, however, it is the shift of characters to the stance of onlooker and the insights that this shift provides, either for these characters or for the audience, that serves to express and reveal their mortal limits – especially when they are allowed to gain the painful lucidity that enables them to see that disparity themselves. When they go from being participants in the action to being external onlookers, viewing the action from the outside, the characters' stance changes: from active to passive, from that of doer to that of observer. As their status changes, so does their viewpoint. The retrospective lens of the observer introduces a distance between characters and their actions (and, often, a disparity between aims and outcomes); and in this removal, the powerlessness, remorse, or alienation experienced by the characters in question can emerge and find full poetic expression.

For some characters, adopting the vantage point of an observer brings newfound lucidity. That lucidity often stems from a crucial element of knowledge that they have acquired only too late, when the concrete and tangible spectacle before them puts the harm that they have done before their eyes. Such is the case

---

27 Both the Homeric poet and the tragic dramatists have various poetic means of making their characters (fore)see the aftermath of their initiative *before* the consequences actually play themselves out, or before they have certain knowledge of that outcome: such is the case with Achilles in relation to Patroclus's death, which I deal with in ch. 1, and Deianeira in connection with Heracles', which I deal with in ch. 2.
28 On tragedians' use of irony in connection with this disparity, see Rutherford 2012, ch. 8.

with Deianeira in Sophocles' *Trachiniae*, as well as with the matricidal Orestes and Electra in Euripides' *Electra*, all of whom come to recognize and see what it is they have done only at a point when no remedy or change is possible anymore.[29] However, lucidity is not always what the stance of spectator brings. Sometimes, the point of casting protagonists in the role of spectators lies elsewhere: namely, in the gap between what the audience members know, and the limited vision (and knowledge) of the characters in question. In such cases, while they embrace the restricted viewpoint and lens of the characters, the spectators are the only ones who are in a position to recognize the tragic limitations of these characters; it is the audience member as spectator who can fully see, not just the harm that the characters have caused, but their incapacity to measure it or truly see it for what it is.

Achilles (in the Homeric *Iliad*) and Clytemnestra (in Aeschylus's *Agamemnon*) are interesting examples of the above. In Achilles' case, the audience witnesses the outcome of his initiative (the death of Patroclus) as though they were viewing it through his eyes, while the hero himself only actually learns of his best friend's doom (for which he blames himself) later. In that disparity (between Achilles' merely virtual vision of the event while it occurs, and the time when he actually learns of it, only too late) lies great pathos. It is the fullest poetic expression in the entire *Iliad* of its main hero's helplessness in the face of death. Clytemnestra's case is different; in her post-factum report and vision of her deed (the murder of her husband, Agamemnon), her character does not recognize her fallibility or restricted vision. This very lack of recognition is a means of underscoring Clytemnestra's incapacity to fathom the nature of her deed. The audience members are the only ones who can gage these limitations, while she remains trapped, as it were, in her subjective and restricted viewpoint.[30] In fact, poets often manipulate their characters' ability to grasp the full impact of their deed by delaying or otherwise impeding their capacity to witness or understand its outcome. They see and know too little too late – and in some cases, they never come to understand their actions and their impact fully at all.

Most important of all considerations in my examination of agents-turned-spectators is the defining fact of their relationship to their deed: these are figures who can only look on and react. Though they may be granted some form of be-

---

[29] On the tragedy inherent in the motif of "learning too late" and the crucial dramatic turning point that the acquisition of knowledge marks, see Di Benedetto and Medda 1997, ch. 6.
[30] At the same time, intervowen within the blind biases of Clytemnestra's vision are insights into the complicated network of forces that have come into play in leading her to take the action she has committed. I discuss the complexity of human agency as Aeschylus presents it in her speech at some length in ch. 3.

lated knowledge, they are not in a position to intervene. Through these characters, the audience is given a sense — indeed, a vision — of the limits of human knowledge and agency, particularly in the face of broader, unseen forces, including the divine. The agents-turned-spectators are paradigmatic of the helplessness and fallibility intrinsic to, and defining of, the human condition, which constitutes a key theme in each of the poetic works under consideration.[31] They illustrate what Whitman calls "the whole Greek association of action-suffering-learning ... and the theme of life penetrated and illuminated by time ... One only knows what one has done. Act and suffer, suffer and know."[32] It hardly bears stressing that the Greek verb οἶδα, "I know," is the verb ὁράω in the perfect tense: "I have seen," therefore "I know." Characters who observe and assess their own actions are an interesting variation on the learn-through-suffering motif tersely encapsulated by Aeschylus in his *Agamemnon*, πάθει μάθος (177). They learn by seeing (and, often, feeling the impact of) the suffering that they have inflicted on others.

Narrative in tragedy, tragedy as narrative

I deal with two different genres in this book: epic and tragedy. Tragedy does not have an external, omniscient narrator as Homeric epic does. This has led to vivid debates regarding whether the only actual narratives in tragedy are the speeches of messengers.[33] One of the major categories of characters that interest me clearly formulate a narrative of their actions: those who, though they are not messengers, nonetheless serve the purpose of a messenger as they report on the deed that they have just committed *in lieu* of the traditionally anonymous and secondary characters to whom such a task habitually falls. I agree with Markantonatos and De Jong's criteria for establishing an inventory of first-person reports: these can and should be expanded to include the speeches spoken by protagonists, including the type of speech that I examine here.[34] In chapter 3, all of the

---

31 For a cross-cultural comparison of tragic view of the human condition in Greek and Shakespearean tragedy and ancient epic, see Lourens 2013.
32 Whitman 1951, 105 and 112. Though this statement is used in reference to the bitter themes of middle-period Sophoclean tragedy, it applies equally well, as we will see, to the case of Achilles.
33 For this debate, see Roberts 1989; more recently Barrett 2014, 877–82 offers a good summary, with bibliography. Regarding the question of narrative and point of view more broadly, see Chatman 1990 and Chatman and van Peer 2001.
34 See Markantonatos 2002, especially 16, and De Jong 1991. For a different perspective, see Dunn 2012b.

agents-turned-spectators that I consider are murderers-turned-messengers who deliver first-person narratives of their own deeds.

Another important debate surrounding narrative and drama that comes into play in my analyses of tragedy is the debate concerning whether or not drama as a whole can be considered narrative. Because, outside of the reported narratives described above, drama *shows* rather than *tells*, employing *mimesis* rather than *diegesis*, some have argued that the absence of an external, heterodiegetic narrator to whom a play as a whole can be attributed precludes us from considering drama as narrative. Yet the narrator function *can* be performed through other techniques within drama, and an entire drama can thus be considered a narrative – a position recently endorsed by Goward 1999 and Markantonatos 2002 in their studies of narrative in Greek tragedy, which I also embrace and apply in the case studies I have selected. That is, I consider the playwright to be the equivalent of the Homeric poet, "the invisible consciousness that shapes the narrative," the "guiding *nous*" and "omnipotent artistic figure behind the tragic narrative."[35] This consideration is especially relevant because I do not only examine agents-turned-spectators who report their deed but also those who voice a response to it in other ways, including through silence, exclamations, or deliberate and marked gesture. All of the latter can function as a means by which the dramatist "shows" us in a manner that tells. In considering the first of the murderer-turned-messenger speeches in chapter three (Clytemnestra's report of the death of Agamemnon), I suggest that the complex layers of imagery within the queen's speech function as a metanarrative, by "showing" us connections (mainly by establishing important thematic and causal parallels) that the speaker herself never explicitly articulates, and of which she remains largely unaware.

Perceptions and values

The characters from Greek tragedy that I examine are homodiegetic speakers of a narrative put in the unusual situation of reporting their own deed to the audience. As they describe their action, they give voice to their view of and their emotional response to their deed and its aftermath in a first-person narrative, making the audience listen to them shape their version of their action and reaction, as they put it into their own words (and sometimes gestures as well). When the audience members listen to an agent-turned-spectator's vision, a form of complicity

---

[35] All quotations from Markantonatos 2002, 6.

between them is created, as the motivations and reasoning underlying that character's deeds are revealed to the audience firsthand.

Yet agents-turned-spectators need not be entirely lucid about their actions. On the contrary, a given protagonist's perspective on her own deed and her emotional response to it, along with the motives that her words reveal as she takes stock of the deed, are not necessarily intended to serve as a model response to be imitated by the audience. The audience may be led to embrace and appreciate the character's vantage point, but this does not mean that they necessarily condone it. Viewing and hearing characters' perspectives on their own actions can actually highlight the emotional, moral, psychological, or perceptual shortcomings that may have clouded their judgment and led them to act in a morally, socially, or otherwise reprehensible manner, whether the characters recognize these shortcomings or not. A close-up, insider's view of a character's perceptions and responses may invite the spectators to adopt the character's point of view, but they can also alienate the audience from the character because of the obvious limitations of his or her perceptions and the disturbing, perverse, or otherwise inappropriate nature of his or her responses.[36] In dealing with scenes in which characters are the focalizers through whose eyes the audience sees their deed, I examine how the characters' accounts and perspectives match up or contrast with others' accounts of and perspectives on their deed. Highlighting the relationship between their own and other characters' (and the Chorus's) accounts is one means by which poets expose their epistemological limitations.

Characters' depictions of their own deed and their (related) reactions to those deeds are also an important source of information regarding the processes — mental, but also concretely perceptual – that shape their assessments of their actions. It is of great interest to see the connections between characters' "vision," in a figurative sense, with their actual points of focus in a literal sense. Even the retrospective gaze that they cast on their past action, or (as the case may be) the gaze that they cast on the aftermath of that action in the here and now of performance (in drama) are telling, to the extent that a character's preconceptions and values can influence his actual perceptions, and these perceptions – their actual, literal vision, or what we might call their "visual perception" – in turn may influence their responses to and judgment of their actions, before, during, or after they have committed them. Watching (or listening) is not innocent; how and what a character sees is a reflection of underlying values, biases, motives, and other defining traits that make up that character's persona.

---

[36] Regarding the lack of any direct correspondence between the values of characters and those of the audience, see Cairns 2005.

In the process of watching characters watch, the audience is made acutely aware of the place and role that is played by the characters' preconceptions and priorities, and of the influence exercised by their principles in shaping and influencing their perceptions, and vice versa.[37]

The audience members' less restricted perspective — what they may be able to see onstage or envision and know through the supplemental information provided by the omniscient poet-narrator or other tools (such as imagery in drama) – can significantly contribute to their understanding of what a given character's viewpoint reveals or conceals, and includes or excludes. How does an agent-turned-spectator's viewpoint or account square with the actual spectacle of misery that lies before them either literally, in the case of theatrical works, or with the mind's eye, in the case of Homeric epic? I take into account a variety of possible comparanda and alternatives that the poets provide to the agents-turned-spectators' visions and versions of their deeds, including internal (verbal and visual) echoes, intertextual references, and, in the case of tragedy, what Revermann calls the "inter-performative" connections[38] – that is, the (visual and thematic) connections the audience would be led to make between the performance they were viewing and performances of other tragedies (especially of similar scenes in other tragedies). Even the audience's broader mythological competence and knowledge would come into play in their assessment of a given character's viewpoint and its limitations. We must understand every speech, gesture, or scene in light of what the dramatists presupposed to be the audience's knowledge and past experience of a given scene or myth.[39]

---

[37] The rich and complex meaning of the term "perspective" and the importance of considering its breadth beyond the realm of the strictly visual into the emotive, cognitive, and ideological domains has been explored by Chatman 2001; see Hopman 2013 (above, n. 22), with bibliography.

[38] Reverman 2006, 10.

[39] On the audience's knowledge as an important component to bear in mind in our reading of the Greek tragedies as instantiations of long-standing myths, see e.g., Roberts 1989 and Revermann 2006. As Roberts 1989, 162, writes, "A play's story (its plot) is part of a larger story (the encompassing myth), but [it] also is the intersection of other and different stories, the stories of its characters." Markantonatos 2002, 24 uses the short-hand "spectators' encyclopaedia" to refer to "the reservoir of knowledge and presuppositions that each member of the audience brings with him in order to make sense of the performance." Of course, our ability to fathom the knowledge and experience that poets would be drawing on is limited, given the fragmentary nature of our evidence.

Chapter Outline

This book is divided into four chapters. It does not aim to be exhaustive or to provide a comprehensive survey of every instance in which an agent is put in the position of a spectator in Greek epic or tragedy, and no doubt the choices that have been made will in some respects appear limited or arbitrary. I selected works in which the poetic function fulfilled by the agents-turned-spectators is essential to our understanding of the works as a whole.[40] In all the instances that I examine, whether in the *Iliad* or Greek tragedy, the shift from participant in the action to observer of their action enables the characters to serve as tragic paradigms for aspects of the human condition in which both internal and external audiences share, and which these characters enact and foreground *qua* spectators: human powerlessness, fallibility, and mortality.

While the order of the chapters is (roughly) chronological, it does not seek to reflect any particular chronological progression or evolution. Rather, it illustrates the thematic continuity that connects all of the works. I start with epic and turn to tragedy in a manner that shows the important archaic undercurrent that defines the thought-world of the tragic plays of the fifth century.[41] Such an approach does not question the importance of examining Greek epic and tragedy with an eye to their contemporary contexts (performative, civic, political, ritual, cultural, and so on), an importance brought to light by scholars ever since Vernant and Vidal-Nacquet's initial publications drew attention to it. The book does, however, participate in what has been called a "counter-movement"[42] by refocusing our attention on "questions of the role of the gods and fate in human action; of the justice or otherwise of the gods and of the world over which they preside; of the causes of human suffering and of the stability, indeed of the nature and possibility of human happiness," as Cairns's edited volume on

---

[40] I also focused on works that had not yet received due scholarly attention with respect to such agents-turned-spectators. Pentheus' enlightenment after he embraces the standpoint of observer in Euripides' *Bacchae* and the related question of the play's metatheatricality have already been thoroughly examined; see e.g., Foley 1975, 1981; Segal 1982; also Dunn 2012a, with bibliography.
[41] Regarding aspects of the archaic world-view that remain central to the Greek thought in the fifth century and particularly in tragedy, Dodds 1951 remains a reference; see also Winnington-Ingram 1965. Lloyd 2013 provides a useful overview of sources that prominently feature the helplessness and insecurity central to the archaic outlook, based on its two complementary tenets: the disjunction between human effort and achievement, and the fundamental role of the gods in all matters.
[42] The formulation is Gregory's in her 2014 review of Cairns 2013 in *CJ* 109 (4), 506–9.

Greek tragedy and archaic thought recently has done.⁴³ The backbone of the line of archaic thought that underlies each of the works under consideration is encapsulated in the agents-turned-spectators that I examine: protagonists who serve as a channel through which the audience is led to consider the limited nature of human knowledge and the degree to which human action is affected by hidden forces and fate, which mortals cannot grasp, or do so only when it is too late. In recognizing or illustrating these hidden forces, these characters make the vanity of human effort shine forth, as they stand back and take stock of their own limitations.

I include below a brief outline of the chapters. For ease of reference, there is also a short summary of my argument at the start of each chapter.

In chapter one, I begin with the mortality of the hero, the core theme of Homeric epic: it is this mortality that the audience is given to contemplate throughout the *Iliad*, including as viewed and vicariously experienced through the eyes of its principal, semi-divine hero: Achilles.

In chapter two, I turn to Sophocles' *Trachiniae*. The play's date is uncertain, but its theme and style have led critics to believe Sophocles composed it early in his career; at the very latest, it appears to have been one of his middle plays. There is something distinctly archaizing in the way Deianeira comes to "see," from the position of spectator to the horrendous outcome of her only initiative in the entire play, the limited range of human agency and the restricted knowledge that inevitably defines every mortal's existence.

In the third chapter, I examine the Aeschylean conception of mortal blindness due to the penumbra of forces underlying every human act, an idea that is also archaic (and typically Aeschylean) in nature and that is clearly brought out with each new murder in the *Oresteia* – never more so perhaps than in Clytemnestra's partially lucid vision of her own place and role in killing her husband, Agamemnon. The unusual portrayal of Clytemnestra's death at the hands of her children in Euripides' *Electra* continues in this vein, as the matricidal children come to realize what their Aeschylean and Sophoclean counterparts did not, or refused to see: how much they are "a plaything of the gods

---

43 The quotations are from Cairns's 2013 edited volume with the evocative title, *Tragedy and Archaic Greek Thought* (Cairns 2013, ix–x). As Cairns notes, one must be careful not to exaggerate the gulf between the two approaches, nor overlook the presence (and influence) of scholarship paying heed to such an archaic undercurrent (see e.g., Winnington-Ingram 1965), even as Vernant and Vidal-Naquet paved the way for new directions (see Vernant, Vidal-Naquet 1992). Concerning the latter and their continuing influence, see Goldhill and Hall's 2009 edited volume on Sophocles, especially the introduction. On tragedy and the early Greek philosophical tradition, see Allan 2005a.

and fate" who have carried out an action that is personally, morally, and socially devastating for all concerned.[44]

In chapter four, the final case I examine is slightly different from the preceding ones. Neoptolemus in Sophocles' *Philoctetes* is the one character that I consider who is able to revert back to action after being in the position of observer for the greater part of the play, and to rectify the ultimate outcome of his endeavor, after adopting the stance of silent observer. When he embraces a spectator's stance (to Philoctetes' pain, and to the consequences of his own actions on the sufferer and their relationship), Achilles' son discovers the full effect of his participation in Odysseus's scheme, and takes action accordingly.

---

[44] The quote is from Mac Donald 1978, 114, where she discusses an evolution within Euripides' plays, from those in which the protagonists appear to have a choice, to those in which man increasingly appears to be driven (and even manipulated) by divine forces as well as misguided by human error and delusions.

Chapter One: The Helpless Witness: Achilles, Patroclus, and the Portrayal of Vulnerability in the *Iliad*[46]

> "Farewell, too little and too lately known,
> Whom I began to think and call my own;
> For sure our Souls were nearly ally'd; and thine
> Cast in the same Poetick mould with mine.
> One common Note on either Lyre did strike,
> And Knaves and Fools we both abhorr'd alike;
> ...
> O early ripe! To thy abundant store
> What could advancing Age have added more?"
> — Dryden, "To the Memory of Mr. Oldham"
> (1684)

This first chapter foregrounds the essential role played by Patroclus's death in the *Iliad*, and particularly the lens through which it is viewed, in developing the themes that are central to the epic as a whole: human helplessness, vulnerability, and mortality. The case study I focus on presents an interesting variation on the agent-turned-spectator pattern. In the scenes from the Homeric *Iliad* that I consider (mainly, the death of Patroclus at the end of book 16), the spectator (Achilles) is not actually present and watching the consequences of his actions. It is also not actually his voice that we hear narrating and reacting to the death that he has caused — at least not directly. Rather, the poet resorts to an unusual poetic device: a voice calling out Patroclus's name at various crucial turning points. With the repeated use of narratorial apostrophes, through which he addresses one of his characters by name, the poet enters into the universe, time, and place of his characters. These instances of *metalepsis* are a deliberate and significant violation of the traditional boundary between the world of the narrator and the world of his characters. Each instance of *metalepsis* at the time of Patroclus's demise is a source of patent tension and pathos: it enables the poet to make Achilles' voice heard and his presence felt throughout the scene, the better to underscore his absence at a pivotal time, when the one dearer to him than life itself meets his doom.

Both the particularity of the poetic voice calling out to Patroclus and the subjective focalization that this voice introduces into the scene convey what is never actually portrayed within the narrative itself: the powerlessness of the poem's greatest hero, Achilles, in the face of his *alter ego*'s death — a death that foreshadows, and even enacts, his own. As the audience watches Patroclus die, it is led to experience and envision Achilles' death as well (which never occurs within the limits of the *Iliad* proper) as though they were watching it through Achilles' eyes.

---

[46] All citations of the *Iliad* are from the *OCT* text of Monro and Allen. The translations of the Greek in this chapter are largely based on Lattimore's translation of the *Iliad* (Lattimore 1951, with minor changes), as well as Lombardo's more recent, highly evocative rendering of the epic poem (Lombardo 1997).

For every major heroic deed or death in the *Iliad*, there is a witness looking on. Whenever a significant hero's life is threatened, another character is present, watching as a potentially fatal wound is being inflicted. As these witnesses look on, they display powerful emotional reactions to the action unfolding before them. In fact, the greatest emotional effect for the audience is often achieved through and mediated by a shift in focus within the narrative, from the action itself to the emotional responses that this action elicits from those looking on.[47] Time and again, the poet of the *Iliad* prominently features those who watch the theater of war and the countless deaths it causes, whether these witnesses are fellow warriors, gods, or even, in some particularly emotionally charged cases, kin (who may also be divine). In the case of the greatest heroes, those who watch them as they fight and kill (or get killed) are given at least as much importance as the heroes accomplishing the heroic feats: the perceptions and reactions of these internal spectators provide a measure of the significance of each warrior's death for others, *philoi* and *echthroi* alike, and contribute to highlighting the heroes' stature and importance, whether the spectators express grief at the loss of the hero, fear at the consequences of his death for themselves, or relief at seeing a major enemy vanquished.[48] The momentousness of the wounding or death of the greatest heroes is thus brought out by the reactions of witnesses (sometimes several of them) looking on, particularly the reactions of those who care for the victims (who are their *philoi*). The witnesses' grief heightens the glory (*kleos*) of the hero by stressing the human cost at which it comes. These internal audiences and their powerful emotional reactions are what make the *Iliad* a formidable war epic — it sings the glory of heroes, while tragic undertones form its very core.[49]

Slatkin pays close attention to the prominent place given to "the experience of viewing" in the *Iliad*:

---

[47] This was noted by e.g., Bassett 1930, 130; see the introduction, p. 3.

[48] There are, of course, witnesses who are hostile to those whose plight they see and who rejoice in the opportunity to gloat over a fallen warrior; for multiple examples and their contexts, see Muellner 1976, 89–97; on warrior vaunts in Homer, see Kyriakou 2001. I consider the Homeric poet and the narrator to be interchangeable throughout this chapter; the obvious exception to this is when the narrator is one of the characters, in which case we have an embedded narrative.

[49] In his *Poetics*, Aristotle puts forward the emotional effect of a poetic work on the audience as the criterion for the ideal tragedy, stating that, "any one epic makes several tragedies" (*Po.* 26.13). The *Iliad* certainly fits (and illustrates) such a definition, and scholars ancient and modern have pointed to Homer as the father of tragedy; see e.g., Finan 1979, especially 72–3.

> The *Iliad* is a poem of shocking visions. Drawing attention throughout to what its characters perceive, to their experience of viewing, the poem dwells on the impact of the sights that confront them and on the act of seeing itself ... At such moments, what they are seeing we are seeing; the audience shares their line of vision.[50]

One of the important points mentioned by Slatkin here, in connection with the prominence given to the act of watching in the *Iliad*, is the poet's ability to hone in on the *impact* of events or actions on those who are watching, whose gaze and emotional lens the audience is led to embrace.[51] Those who watch (from within the narrative) do so because they care about the outcome of a given conflict (and are often prompted to take action themselves in response to what they see). Because they are involved emotionally in the action and directly affected by its outcome, their concern heightens that of the audience members who, by viewing the events through the witnesses' eyes, experience the impact of the action with greater immediacy and intensity.[52] This is why I speak of an "emotional lens:" the onlookers' strong responses are a means of drawing attention to the thematic, emotional, and overall import of a given scene. In fact, the emotional impact of the action thereby takes on equal importance to, or in some cases even greater importance than the deed being watched.

The helpless gaze of *philoi* in particular — caring friends, dear ones, often next of kin — is an important feature in the scenes depicting the deaths of each of the central heroes of the epic: the poet adds pathos to the scenes and glory to the deaths by prominently featuring the grief of those watching it happen.[53] The deaths of such great heroes as Sarpedon, Hector, and Achilles are anticipated, foreshadowed, watched, and lamented by those who care for them

---

50 Slatkin 2007, 19. On the central role of the Homeric poet and Muse-narrator's manipulation of perspective and point of view throughout the *Iliad*, see Rabel 1998. For an approach to the visual poetics of the *Iliad* that involves the insights of cognitive psychology and discusses the ability of the poet's narrative to make itself visible and turn its audience into spectators, see Strauss Clay 2011.
51 Regarding the narrator or performer's posture as eyewitness to the events within Homer's epic narrative, see Bakker 1993.
52 On the linguistic markers that contribute to the Homeric vividness (*enargeia*) stemming from the audience's viewing the action as though they were spectators watching it rather than mere listeners, see Bakker 1997 and Bakker 2005, chs. 5–9. See also below, n. 127, and p. 72.
53 On the place of *philoi* and the prominence of patterns of care, including parental care, as a source of pathos in the *Iliad*, see e.g., Griffin 1976, 1980; Lynn-George 1996; Mills 2000; Slatkin 1991, 2007. On tragic patterns in the *Iliad* whereby a man is obliged to relinquish something dear to him, see Rinon 2008.

most.⁵⁴ At times, the witnesses are in a position to take action and prevent (or avenge) the harm done to those who are dear to them; in other instances, they must simply endure the sight of their loved ones' demise. Thus, the goddess Thetis, despite her divinity, spends the entirety of the *Iliad* envisioning and lamenting the imminent death of her son Achilles, which she knows to be inevitable and which she remains helpless to prevent.⁵⁵ The father of gods and men himself must grudgingly stand back and look on as Patroclus takes the life of his beloved son Sarpedon in book 16, the bloody, tear-like drops he sheds a clear cosmic sign of the extraordinary pain that he endures at the sight. In book 22, Hecuba, Priam, and finally Andromache look on from the walls of Troy as Achilles takes the life of their son and husband Hector, bulwark of Troy, and not one of them is able to rescue his corpse in order to administer a proper burial (yet).

What about Patroclus? Who witnesses the death of the hero that arguably has the greatest impact on the entire plot of the *Iliad*, as it puts an end to Achilles' anger at Agamemnon and makes him reenter the fray in a destructive rage against Hector and all the Trojans? Seemingly, no one: no protective god is present; no fellow warrior or hero stands close by and pities Patroclus's demise or attempts to take action, as happens with the deaths of all the other major Trojan and Achaean heroes. Why is Patroclus so completely isolated, so hopelessly alone at the time of his death?

In what follows, I take a close look at the poetics of the scene of the hero's demise. It is a unique one in the present exploration of agents-turned-spectators. First off, the agent behind the death in question is only the agent in his own eyes: though the gods and fate loom large in the narrative, Achilles blames himself.⁵⁶ Second, the act of watching from the spectator's standpoint is not actually done by the character through whose lens we view the death of Patroclus, at least not in a literal sense. Instead, the poet makes the narrator (that is, the poet himself) and the audience the primary witnesses to the hero's death, while multiple elements within the scene's structure, diction, and traditional formulas make the listener view it as though they were watching it through Achilles' eyes. In what follows, I bring to light how and why this particular lens and the particular voice that we hear throughout the scene are essential

---

54 Achilles' death is never actually narrated within the epic, but it is envisioned by Thetis throughout the poem, and especially after Patroclus's death, as we will see.
55 On the paradoxical combination of the power and helplessness of Thetis in the *Iliad* and other epic traditions, see Slatkin 1991.
56 Regarding the question of Achilles' responsibility in causing Patroclus' demise, see below, p. 83.

to our understanding of its direct relevance to Achilles, and of its importance within the epic as a whole.

Methodology

Throughout the present chapter, I approach the *Iliad* from the angle of oral poetics; one of the main accepted premises of my argument is Milman Parry and his student Albert Lord's demonstration that Homeric poetry is both oral and traditional. It follows certain rules, which are both essential to, and a result of, its composition in performance, and which give rise to certain specific poetic characteristics. Repetitions (thematic and formulaic) and any parallels (verbal and structural) are a reflection of this mode of composition, and significant, as are variations within these repetitions and parallels.[57]

The oral and traditional character of Homeric poetry is not in question. However, scholars still debate the date and manner in which the Homeric epics reached a fixed, written form. As I have stated elsewhere, my arguments stand whether one believes that recurring formulas and themes are the work of one poet, or whether one thinks (as I do) that they are characteristic of and intrinsic to the "traditional and constantly self-referential system within which the Iliad was composed."[58]

---

[57] That is, I adopt the view that these repetitions are features of the oral, traditional nature of Homeric poetry; see Parry 1928 and Lord 1960, 2000 (2nd ed.). On my approach and method when it comes to Homeric poetry and my adoption of Nagy's evolutionary model of Homeric poetry, see Allen-Hornblower 2014, 29–30, especially n. 21, with bibliography. There is a useful discussion of repetitions and what Bakker calls "interformularity" within Homeric poetry in Bakker 2013 (in the epilogue). B. coins the useful term "interformularity" (preferring it to 'intertextuality') because interformularity does not presuppose that textual fixity is necessary for repetitions to be significant (Bakker 2013, 157–69). Regarding the Homeric question and the relation between Neoanalysis and Oral Theory in 21st-century scholarship, see Montanari, Rengakos, and Tsagalis 2012.

[58] For an overview of the consequences of Parry and Lord's concept of *traditionality* and bibliography, see Dué 2002, 1–5 (quotation p. 5). Scodel 2002 puts forward the interesting argument that the Homeric poet creates the illusion that his material is entirely traditional, even in the necessarily innovative process of composition-in-performance.

Watching through the eyes of *philoi*

Before examining the particular case of Patroclus, I propose that we begin by looking at other examples of how the Homeric poet uses the vision and response of those who watch the action unfolding within the poem as a way of shaping the audience's vision and experience of that action, especially in moments of central importance to the poem's plot.[59] I am especially interested in those scenes that involve the gaze of individual characters who are bound to those whose suffering or demise they witness by a personal relationship. A brief glance at a singular instance in which the Homeric poet introduces an anonymous, "imaginary spectator"[60] provides an enlightening point of comparison for the effect produced by having personally involved spectators be a point of focus (and, in some cases, a focalizer as well).

At 4.539–44, an unusual and fascinating figure enters the ferocious struggle between Greeks and Trojans – "a man" who has not (yet) been wounded and remains immune to the battle's dangers as Athena leads him through the ranks and averts all spears from him. Even *that* man, we are told, would not have made little of the fighting, so fierce was the engagement on both sides:

> Ἔνθά κεν οὐκέτι ἔργον ἀνὴρ ὀνόσαιτο μετελθών,
> ὅς τις ἔτ' ἄβλητος καὶ ἀνούτατος ὀξέϊ χαλκῷ
> δινεύοι κατὰ μέσσον, ἄγοι δέ ἑ Παλλὰς Ἀθήνη
> χειρὸς ἑλοῦσ', αὐτὰρ βελέων ἀπερύκοι ἐρωήν·
> πολλοὶ γὰρ Τρώων καὶ Ἀχαιῶν ἤματι κείνῳ
> πρηνέες ἐν κονίῃσι παρ' ἀλλήλοισι τέταντο.
> (4.539–44)

And there no longer could a man, having entered the field, have made little of the fighting, (a man) who, not hit nor pierced by sharp bronze yet, would rove around in the middle (of the fighting), and him Pallas Athena would lead, having taken him by the hand, and she would avert from him the rush of the spears.

The bT scholia remark (*ad* 4.541) that "the poet has created a spectator of the battle for himself ... in order that he might take an undisturbed look even amidst the

---

[59] It has been well demonstrated that the third-person narrator is not "objective," one reason being that hints of individual characters' viewpoints can be embedded within the third person narration. De Jong's work (especially De Jong 1987 and 1991) on the Homeric narrator has been crucial in dissipating the long-held view that the Homeric narrator is "objective." On the third-person narrator in other genres, including prose, see for instance Rabel 1997.

[60] The expression is Leaf 1900, *ad* 13.343–4; in that passage, the poet invites the audience to feel sorrow by calling the man who would *not* feel anything on seeing the fierceness of the battle that is unfolding "stout-hearted," (μάλα κεν θρασυκάρδιος εἴη).

fighting and to behold (everything) in detail."[61] Eustathius comments on the function of this anonymous internal spectator along similar lines, but also introduces the notion that this imaginary spectator might take pleasure in looking on without partaking in the misery that he observes, just as he imagines that the audience does: "Such a spectator might have been the hearer of the poet, who does not partake in the misery of the war, but who enjoys in his mind the splendid spectacle of these war stories."[62] De Jong discusses both of these assessments of the figure that she prefers to call the "anonymous focalizer." Her interpretation of the role played by this spectator is quite the opposite from that imagined by Eustathius. To her mind, the focalizer does not give the external audience a chance to "enjoy" the spectacle with a detachment reminiscent of the occasional enjoyment that the Olympian gods take in the spectacle of human suffering. On the contrary, she argues, "the anonymity of the focalizer ... invites the ... historical hearer/reader to identify himself with him and to share his feelings of awe ... about the intensity and fierceness of the battle."[63]

De Jong stresses that the *anonymity* of this figure facilitates the transmission of his feelings onto the audience members: it is because of his lack of any differentiating qualities that the audience readily identifies with him. I would submit that the audience's involvement in a given scene is even greater if they view that scene through the eyes of a specific individual who is directly affected by it. Everyone knows what it is to love and to wish to protect a loved one; everyone also knows the bite of failure (to protect) and the grief of loss. These are the universal emotions experienced by the internal, caring spectators of the *Iliad* when they see a loved one fall and cannot fend off his or her death. It is the universality of these emotions, and the universality of the interpersonal attachments and ties from which they stem, that makes the use of *philoi* as spectators of their loved ones' demise such a powerful means of involving the audience in the action and, in turn, of channeling their emotional response. Whether the gods are watching (and whether they care) or not, the demise of a hero is made more

---

61 θεατὴν ἑαυτῷ ἀνέπλασε τῆς μάχης, B(bce3)T ὑπὸ θεῶν ὁδηγούμενον, T ἵνα ἀθορύβως σκοπῇ καὶ ἐν μέσοις τοῖς μαχομένοις, καὶ ἵνα ἀκριβῶς θεῷτο, B(bce3) T (TLG transcription of Erbse's edition of the *Iliad* scholia available online in Kahane and M. Mueller's Chicago Homer, *ad loc*, through the associated website Eumaios; see http://homer.library.northwestern.edu/). Translation based on De Jong 1987, 58.
62 τοιοῦτος δ' ἂν εἴη θεατὴς ὁ τοῦ ποιητοῦ ἀκροατής, ὃς οὐ τῶν τοῦ πολέμου κακῶν μετέχει, ἀλλὰ τοῦ τῶν πολεμικῶν διηγήσεων κατὰ νοῦν ἀπολαύει καλοῦ θεάματος (Eust. 506, 6–8, quoted by De Jong [see previous note]; also discussed in connection with the Aristotelian notion of *catharsis* in Bouvier 2002, 45–8.
63 See De Jong 1987, 58–9. For this and similar examples, see her analysis of "signs of the 'you'" in the Homeric *Iliad* at 54 ff.

poignant when the personal cost of the loss of that warrior to his (sometimes divine) *philoi* is foregrounded.

There are countless examples of witnesses who watch and react to the sight of one dear to them being harmed in the *Iliad*. In what follows, I turn to specific death scenes in which the demise of a hero is watched by spectators, both divine and mortal, for whom the death is of particular emotional import. Three broad categories of what we might call "caring witnesses" can be established: those who see their *philos* harmed and are able to intervene and do so successfully; those who see their *philos* harmed and attempt to intervene but fail; and the most pathetic, those who see their *philos* harmed and are unable to intervene, left with nothing to do but look on in horror as the demise of their dear one unfolds before their eyes. For our present purposes, I will limit myself to a selection of representative examples that will allow me to bring to light the uniqueness of the scene portraying the death of Achilles' best friend and *alter ego*, Patroclus. One of the unique features of the death of Patroclus is immediately obvious, and bears mentioning from the start: while the other examples I look at involve spectators looking on at deaths of *philoi* that they did not cause, in the case of Patroclus's death, the emotional intensity of the scene is all the greater as the audience is made to anticipate Achilles' searing pain on realizing that his initiative — allowing Patroclus to go to battle wearing his armor — is what led to his dearest friend's death.

After a rapid overview of death scenes and of the different sorts of roles that witnesses play within them, I will turn to two conspicuous heroic deaths, Sarpedon's and Hector's, that are especially relevant to our understanding of the portrayal of Patroclus's: the central motif in both is the helplessness of their *philoi* to intervene, whether they are mortal and weak (Priam and Hecuba are aged; Andromache is female and not a warrior) or as powerful as can be (Zeus, father of gods and men). Accordingly, I give these scenes due attention, particularly to how they compare with the first category of the three categories of death scenes (with caring witnesses) that I described above, in which witnesses see loved ones in danger and *are* able to intervene. The unique features of the deaths of such major figures as Zeus's and Priam's sons will serve as a segue to the crux of my argument regarding the death of Patroclus, to which I will devote the last and longest section of this chapter.

Seeing and pitying

First, then, let us examine some instances in the *Iliad* in which witnesses look on as those dear to them are wounded or killed, and are able to take action in some way. The emotional charge that comes with the act of watching a loved one suffer (or die) is directly apparent in the phraseology of the *Iliad:* such recurrent formulaic diction as τὸν δὲ ἰδὼν ἐλέησε and its variants (τὸν δὲ πεσόντ' ἐλέησεν) narrowly connect the act of seeing (ἰδὼν) with an immediate emotional response (ἐλέησε[ν], pity) and subsequent action attempted or words spoken as a result of the emotion evoked by the act of viewing.[64] Witnessing the distress experienced by a *philos* arouses pity and demands action, not just from fellow warriors but also from protective gods, when there are any who care enough for the mortals suffering down below.[65] There are two principal sorts of action taken by warriors when a companion is wounded or killed. In the case of a wound, they protect him from death; if death was not preventable, they seek to protect the corpse from being despoiled of its armor. In both instances, if the circumstances allow, they lash back at the enemy in anger (and grief) at their friend's death and seek to obtain revenge.[66] The gods present a wide range of stances when it comes to human suffering. At times, they sit back and rejoice in the spectacle of human strife; in such cases, they point up the gap between divine detachment and the pity that the suffering inherent in mortality calls for on the part of humans, who share in the mortal condition.[67] Conversely, the gods sometimes are heavily emotionally involved in the human theater beneath them, whether they are con-

---

[64] The connection between pity and *philia* in the *Iliad* has been brought to the fore by Kim 2000; on seeing, pitying, and ensuing action, see 41–6 in particular. From here on, I will use the shorthand "seeing-and-pitying" to refer to those typical sequences in which a warrior or divinity witnesses a friend being killed or despoiled, pities them, and then takes action (successfully or not). Sometimes, verbs of sight are not actually used; at other times, no specific emotion (pity or fear for a beloved) is mentioned; but the general pattern of seeing, reacting (with an emotion), and attempting to take action is implicit in all cases, even when the usual phraseology does not appear.

[65] On the interdependence of anger and pity and how the latter prompts subsequent action, see Most 2003. Regarding exceptional scenarios in which a suffering character seeks to elicit pity from *echthroi* (and sometimes succeeds in doing so, as Priam does with Achilles in book 24), see for instance Burkert 1955, Kim 2000, Most 2003, and Pagani 2008 (407–15). Gods tend to feel pity when their own divine offspring or protégés are involved, but not only then: in book 13, Poseidon pities (all) the Greeks. For near-death scenes in which gods intercede, see De Jong 1987, 70–1. For various examples of divine interventions preventing dire events, see Louden 1993, 184 n. 8.

[66] Such mortal interventions to protect fellow warriors' lives, bodies, or armor are abundant. See Kim 2000, 41–2 for a list of occurrences that include the seeing-and-pitying sequence and variations; also Most 2003, 55–6, and Marks' discussion of divine rescue scenes in the *Iliad* (Marks 2010, *passim*).

[67] See e.g., Athena and Apollo sitting on the tree of Zeus in the shapes of birds and "rejoicing in [the spectacle of] men" (ἀνδράσι τερπόμενοι, 7.61).

demning a mortal's actions or experiencing pity (or a combination of both).⁶⁸ The gods who are of interest to me here are the ones who look on as their mortal favorites fight and face potential death.

Some caring gods are able to rescue their mortal loved ones. Take Aphrodite, for instance. In a crucial scene near the beginning of the *Iliad*, Helen's Trojan lover Paris and Helen's rightful husband Menelaus have agreed to face each other in a duel. That duel's outcome could bring an end to the Trojan War, now in its tenth year, without any further losses on either side. But when the goddess of love catches sight of Paris on the verge of being killed by Menelaus in the one-on-one confrontation, she snaps the chinstrap of her protégé at a key moment, leaving the Atreid holding an empty helmet. As the Greek king then prepares to deal the final blow to the foe who stole his wife, Aphrodite whisks the Trojan prince away in a thick mist and drops him off safely in his bedroom, where he makes love to Menelaus's wife, Helen.⁶⁹ A similar *in extremis* rescue is successfully carried out by the goddess of love during the so-called *Diomedeia* of book 5, where Diomedes goes on an extremely effective killing rampage (his *aristeia*).⁷⁰ At one point, he smashes Aeneas's hip with a huge slab of stone, and an ominously dark night descends over the wounded Trojan's eyes. The imagery marks Aeneas as close to death, but Aphrodite has been watching the whole interaction.⁷¹ She has "had this all in sharp focus" (ὀξὺ νόησε Διὸς θυγάτηρ Ἀφροδίτη) and rushes to the scene, wraps her white arms around her son, covers him with her ambrosial robe, and protects him from the Greeks' spears.⁷²

---

68 The gods convene to express their disapproval of Achilles' excessive rage and savage mistreatment of Hector's corpse at the start of book 24 and to deliberate action, thereby heightening the audience's sense of the injustice and violation at hand. On pity within the divine audience of the *Iliad*, see Burkert 1955, 147; on its role as a model for the real audience and its relation to "real religion," see Griffin 1978. Konstan 2001, ch. 4, discusses divine pity in Greek literature across genres and periods (both Greek and Roman).
69 3.380–2.
70 I discuss the wounding of the gods and the *Diomedeia* at greater length in Allen-Hornblower 2014, with bibliography.
71 The metaphor of night or darkness covering a warrior's eyes is commonly used to describe death; compare e.g., 5.659.
72 The translation here is Lombardo's, *ad* 5.312 ff. Fenik 1968, 39 notes the extraordinary nature of Aphrodite's epiphany in Book 5 and of the method of salvation to which the goddess resorts, citing the more typical occurrences where a cloud of darkness or mist is cast: 3.381, 5.23, 5.344, 20.444, and 21.597. Aphrodite herself subsequently gets wounded by Diomedes and lets Aeneas fall in her pain: 5.311 ff.

Athena is another protective divinity who frequently intervenes on behalf of her mortal favorites on the battlefield. During a truce between Greeks and Trojans, following her father Zeus's orders, she disguises herself as Laodocus and convinces the archer Pandarus to aim one of his arrows at Menelaus. Antenor's son obligingly complies, in search of glory and gratitude from his fellow Trojans (especially from Paris, who faces potential death at the hands of Menelaus). The arrow is headed straight for Menelaus's bare flesh when Zeus's daughter steps in and redirects it toward his belt with the ease of a mother waving a fly away from her sleeping child.[73]

The effortlessness of such interventions by the divine on behalf of their protégés, offering protection with sometimes no more than a flick of the hand, contrasts with mortal warriors' attempts to protect a *philos* or his corpse and armor, a cause to which they must devote all their might, often without success.[74] One example of divine intervention particularly spotlights the contrast between mortal helplessness and divine power in the face of adversity and death. The context is the following: the Greeks are being routed back to their ships by the Trojans, who have scaled the wall protecting the Greek encampment. Zeus leaves the Greeks to their misery, "turning his shining eyes away" (αὐτὸς δὲ πάλιν τρέπεν ὄσσε φαεινώ, 13.3), but Poseidon the Earth-Shaker "is not keeping a blind man's watch" (οὐδ' ἀλαοσκοπιὴν εἶχε κρείων ἐνοσίχθων, 13.10). Following the familiar pattern, he sees them, pities them (13.15), and takes action immediately, leaping down from the high crest of Samos (αὐτίκα δ' ἐξ ὄρεος κατεβήσετο, 13.17) and driving his horses straight to the Achaean ships, where he makes his way to the two Ajaxes in the guise of Calchas and fills them with renewed strength (13.59–61). Poseidon's seeing-and-pitying is followed by action. The mortal Achaeans, by contrast, simply despair when they see the swarm of Trojans clambering over the walls and driving toward them in droves: they are helpless spectators, looking on (εἰσορόωντες) with heavy hearts at the seemingly irrepressible wave of Trojans coming straight at them:

καί σφιν ἄχος κατὰ θυμὸν ἐγίγνετο δερκομένοισι
Τρῶας, τοὶ μέγα τεῖχος ὑπερκατέβησαν ὁμίλῳ.
τοὺς οἵ γ' εἰσορόωντες ὑπ' ὀφρύσι δάκρυα λεῖβον·
(13.86–8)

---

[73] 4.130–3. I return to this scene below.
[74] The entirety of book 17 is devoted to the zeal with which the Greeks attempt to protect Patroclus's body and Achilles' armor, which the fallen hero is still wearing at the time of his death, before Hector makes it his own.

And great pain came to their hearts as they saw the Trojans,
Clambering over the walls in droves.
They watched helplessly, with tears in their eyes.[75]

Helpless spectators, mortal and immortal

Even the powerful gods, however, are not always able to protect their mortal favorites. Equally noteworthy and even more central to the present inquiry are the scenes of wounding or death that include caring divine witnesses who see the harm being done to their *philoi* but remain entirely helpless to intervene. Divine inability to save a beloved human stresses the ineluctability of death for all mortals, even (indeed, especially) for the greatest of heroes: the hero is fated to die, and no human or divine power can change that.[76]

Nearly all of the heroes of the *Iliad* are given an audience at the time of their death that includes caring divine figures; Patroclus is the telling exception, as we will see. Even immortal onlookers are condemned simply to endure the sight of a beloved mortal's demise. Their presence and emotional response enhance the pathos of the scene, as they aggrandize the hero by showing the pain that his loss brings to them, divine though they may be. The discrepancy between their strong emotional reaction to what they see, which is explicitly foregrounded, and their inability to take any action to prevent or heal the harm being done, is a source great dramatic tension.[77] The gods cannot intervene because they must not, in the face of a death that is fated.[78] It is a similar tension that we will find in the scene of Patroclus's death; only there, the witness is not divine,

---

[75] Translation here based on Lombardo 1997.
[76] The ineluctability of death for the heroes of the *Iliad* distinguishes them from those of the poems of the Epic Cycle, in which, by contrast, it *is* within a divinity's power to save a beloved mortal. The Iliadic heroes must die to receive *kleos*. On the inescapability of human mortality as a central theme of the Homeric *Iliad*, see Glaucus's speech to Diomedes at 6.145–9 and Apollo's words to Poseidon at 21.462–7. Regarding the tragic core of the *Iliad* in connection with the centrality of the theme of mortality within the poem, see e.g., Redfield 1975, Griffin 1977 (esp. 42–3 regarding immortality as a specific feature of the Cycle poems in contrast to the mortality for the heroes of the *Iliad*), Griffin 1980, Rutherford 1982, Schein 1984, Slatkin 1991, ch. 1. On *kleos* and the death of the hero, see Nagy 1979 *passim* and Nagy 1990, 223–62.
[77] Griffin 1978, 196 n. 5 notes how the gods' "presence and attention also serves as a device to heighten for us the emotional significance of terrible events."
[78] This is particularly apparent in the debate between Zeus and Hera over the death of Sarpedon, to which I return in greater detail below (16.440 ff.). Protecting a hero from death would also mean "denying him a heroic life" (Slatkin 1991, 45).

but a mere mortal: Achilles, who, were he present on the battlefield, could easily face down any Trojan to protect his beloved friend, Hector included.

The more central a hero is to the plot, the more witnesses are present at his demise, and the more these witnesses' care and desire to aid and protect the hero's life and body are stressed. At the same time, the more prominent the hero, the more powerless his onlookers are to protect him, whether divine or mortal. This is true for at least two reasons. Firstly, the stakes are higher when a great hero's body and armor are in a vulnerable position, and the battle for them on the part of (often equally) great opponents is all the fiercer. Secondly, as mentioned above, the hero's death is necessary: it is the very condition of his glory.[79] There are various degrees and stages of powerlessness among these witnesses, ranging from the inability to step in and protect a hero before his death to the most extreme cases, in which the caring *philoi*, looking on, are unable even to protect the corpse of the dead *philos* and prevent it being despoiled of its armor.

Two examples involving major heroic figures illustrate these points clearly: the death of Sarpedon in book 16 and that of Hector in book 22. Both are prominent heroes who meet their doom despite the explicitly voiced divine will of Zeus to intervene and protect them from their deaths. I discuss these examples below, before turning to the death of Patroclus, the particularities of which will be made apparent by comparison and contrast with the other two. All three of the great heroes' deaths share elements of language and theme that draw attention to their commonalities as essential and interconnected milestones of the *Iliad*'s plot.[80] I wish to concentrate on the place and role played by *witnesses* in each of these deaths, and on the similarities and contrasts that these witnesses point up.

---

[79] At 17.140–68, Glaucus goads Hector into action by pointing out just how much is at stake in fighting for Patroclus's body: he is so dear to Achilles (17.164–5) that if they gained possession of his body, the Trojans would then be in a position to get Sarpedon's armor back, and carry his body into Troy.

[80] The structural, thematic, and dictional parallels have been noted previously, and only a cursory overview is necessary here; see e.g., Kirk 1985, *ad loc.* and Griffin 1980; Leuzzi 2008 (especially regarding Patroclus and Hector). Regarding the patterns of great heroes' deaths, and Diomedes' survival by contrast, see Allen-Hornblower 2014.

Zeus's helplessness: Regarding the death of Sarpedon

When heroes that are dear to him are threatened, Zeus – as is to be expected of the most powerful of the gods – is often in a position to intervene on their behalf, mainly by directing other gods to act (or desist) as he sees fit.[81] We witness an example of this at the beginning of book 15 when the father of gods and men emerges from his tryst in the clouds with Hera, to which she lured him with the help of Aphrodite and Sleep in order to draw his attention away from the battlefield so that the Greeks could gain the upper hand. Zeus looks down and immediately takes stock of the situation: he sees the Greeks on a killing spree, and the Trojans in dire straits (ἴδε δὲ Τρῶας καὶ Ἀχαιούς, 15.6). The supreme god quickly zeroes in on Hector (Ἕκτορα δ' ἐν πεδίῳ ἴδε κείμενον, 15.9), who is lying on the Trojan plain, vomiting blood, after Ajax has hit him in the chest with a huge stone.[82] Zeus immediately has Hera order Apollo to go and breathe renewed strength into the Trojan hero, rousing him to forget his pain and fight so that he can drive the Achaeans back to their ships. Zeus's concern is to keep his promise to Thetis: that the Greeks should suffer from Achilles' absence from their ranks, as the son of Peleus had requested.[83] The Olympian god thus intervenes in a manner that tips the scales back in favor of the Trojan camp, by preventing the other gods (mainly Hera and Athena) from providing any more aid to the Greeks, and by reviving Hector *in extremis,* at a time when death seems near.[84]

Yet the ineluctability and necessity of death for mortals is such that even Zeus is sometimes powerless to intervene. By the middle of book 16, things are going poorly indeed for the Trojans. Clad in the armor of Achilles, Patroclus sends the Trojans running back toward Troy, killing many of them as they flee.[85]

---

81 For instance, in book 8, Zeus catches sight of Athena and Hera heading straight for the battle scene, eager to intervene on the Greeks' behalf, and sends Iris to stop them with threats of extreme violence in reprisal: the wounds from his thunderbolt would not heal for ten years, he says: 8.404–5.
82 15.4–13.
83 15.59–62. Athena reminds us of Zeus's promise to Thetis at 8.370–3. On Zeus's commitment to his promise, see also 15.72–7.
84 Ajax wounds Hector at 14.418, and the consequences are severe. He subsequently vomits blood and loses consciousness at 14.436–9. He is still wounded and vomiting blood again at the beginning of book 15 (15.9–11). The gravity of his wound is further emphasized by the fact that Zeus witnesses his pain and pities it, turning angrily on Hera who (he now realizes after the fact) seduced him so as to allow for a Trojan setback. Regarding wounded heroes, see Neal 2006 (on the significance and variety of wound narratives, see especially 33–44); for a typology of wounds in the *Iliad*, see Saunders 1999 and 2004.
85 On the Trojan flight, see 16.373–6.

At this point, the narrative zooms in on one figure: the Lycian hero and Trojan ally Sarpedon. The encounter between Sarpedon and Patroclus occurs while the latter is reaching the culminating point of his *aristeia*, mowing down Trojans by the dozen after successfully routing them from the Greek ships.[86] Sarpedon steps down from his chariot and prepares to face Patroclus. Zeus, the father of gods and men, is watching and feels pity, according to the recognizable pattern of seeing-and-pitying (τοὺς δὲ ἰδὼν ἐλέησε Κρόνου πάϊς ἀγκυλομήτεω, 16.431):[87] it is his own son that he sees heading straight toward death. He wonders aloud to his wife Hera whether he should intervene and spirit Sarpedon off to his native Lycia rather than allow him to die at the hands of the son of Menoetius.[88] Hera is indignant: if Zeus sets such an example, all the gods are going to proceed to do the same for their own offspring, and chaos will ensue, for many are the sons of gods that are fighting around the walls of Troy (16.440–57).[89] But more to the point, she adds, how can Zeus consider saving "a man who is mortal, who has been doomed to die long since?" (ἄνδρα θνητὸν ἐόντα πάλαι πεπρωμένον αἴσῃ, 16.441).[90] Nonetheless, Zeus's wife measures his grief[91] and suggests that he send Sleep and Death to carry Sarpedon's dead body back to Lycia after Patroclus kills him. Zeus complies, but his grief is severe: he sheds droplets of blood from the sky, an allegory of sorrow that portrays him in a profoundly anthropomorphic light, while his sorrow takes on cosmic proportions.[92] The most powerful of all the gods obligingly surrenders to the course of fate (πάλαι πεπρωμένον αἴσῃ): his response emphasizes his helplessness to meddle with the unavoidable nature of human mortality. Even he cannot change the course that every mortal life must follow.

As Patroclus stands above him after dealing him a fatal blow, Sarpedon calls out to a *philos*, the Trojan Glaucus, who is not far. Like the divine Zeus, Glaucus has been looking on as his dear friend undergoes the deadly attack from the son

---

86 This is the point at which Achilles has instructed Patroclus to cease from battle and return to him: 16.86–100. The son of Menoetius does not follow Achilles' instructions, and will never return alive to the Greek ships.
87 On this pattern, see above, p. 26.
88 Zeus has long known that Sarpedon was to die at the hands of Patroclus, as he clearly states in the micronarrative that he offers up in anger to Hera in book 15: 15.56–77.
89 Concerning decision-making in the *Iliad*, and collective decision-making in particular (including among the community of the gods), see Elmer 2013.
90 On the death of Sarpedon as necessary for his immortal glory (*kleos*), see Nagy 1983 and 1990, ch. 5.
91 Pity and care are explicitly connected by the phraseology used here (16.450); see Kim 2000, 107.
92 On Zeus's drops of blood as tears, see Lateiner 2002.

of Menoetius. Like the father of gods and men, however, he too remains helpless to intervene, for he was badly wounded by one of Teucer's arrows. Knowing that Glaucus can do nothing for him to save his life, Sarpedon makes a final demand of his companion before breathing his last: that Glaucus should fetch Lycian leaders to help protect his body[93] and prevent the Greeks from taking his armor (16.492–501). All Glaucus can do in response is feel great pain, because Sarpedon's need and request for help make him feel all the more acutely his inability to provide any, and his utter helplessness to protect his friend and fellow warrior. He is in no position to wage the sort of fierce battle that protecting an important hero like Sarpedon's body is going to require:

> Γλαύκῳ δ' αἰνὸν ἄχος γένετο φθογγῆς ἀΐοντι·
> ὠρίνθη δέ οἱ ἦτορ ὅ τ' οὐ δύνατο προσαμῦναι.
> (16.508–9)
>
> Glaucus could hardly bear to hear Sarpedon's voice,
> He was so grieved that he could not save him.[94]

Glaucus is too far away and too weakened by his own wound to intervene. He never even is able to answer Sarpedon. Instead, in desperation, he appeals to Apollo. The triangularity of the scene, with Sarpedon speaking to Glaucus, who speaks to Apollo, suggests that no interpersonal exchange actually occurs. This failure to initiate an exchange as Sarpedon breathes his last breath helps to underline the isolation of the dying Sarpedon from the rest of the living as well as his *philos*'s helplessness to come to his aid, which Glaucus's desperate prayer to Apollo further underlines. Even when Apollo grants Glaucus renewed strength in response to his prayer (16.514–26), the latter remains unable to fulfill his friend's wish and prevent the son of Zeus's body from being despoiled. The Greeks win the fight for Sarpedon's armor, and Patroclus triumphantly hands it to his fellow Greeks so they can carry it back to their ships (16.663–5).[95]

---

[93] The violation of Sarpedon's bodily integrity and his vulnerability in what follows are stressed by the poet, with the inclusion of such details as Patroclus's pulling his lungs out of from his chest along with the spear (16.505). Regarding ancient Greek conceptions of the physical body (and particularly the violated and suffering body) in ancient Greek literature and culture, see Holmes 2010.
[94] Translation here is from Lombardo 1997.
[95] Apollo only intervenes to cleanse Sarpedon's body after it has been completely stripped of its armor in the aftermath of a savage battle for his corpse that has left him mangled and sullied, and after the Lycians themselves have fled before Patroclus's continued attacks. Then, Sleep and Death carry him off to Lycia (16.667–75). On intimations of hero cult and immortality in the Homeric account of the death of Sarpedon, see Nagy 1990, ch. 5.

The fight over Sarpedon's body and armor is so fierce that his body becomes unrecognizable:

οὐδ' ἂν ἔτι φράδμων περ ἀνὴρ Σαρπηδόνα δῖον
ἔγνω, ἐπεὶ βελέεσσι καὶ αἵματι καὶ κονίῃσιν
ἐκ κεφαλῆς εἴλυτο διαμπερὲς ἐς πόδας ἄκρους.
(16.638–40)

"Even an observant man would not have been able to recognize divine Sarpedon anymore, because he was completely covered, from head to foot, with spears, blood, and dust."[96]

The introduction of an imaginary spectator here ("an observant man") is not unique, as we have seen, but such "anonymous human observers" are rare and significant.[97] However, this imaginary internal audience does more than simply provide "an eyewitness ... invoked by the [narrator] ... to see what in fact is very difficult to see."[98] This witness is one who is "observant" in that he is "knowing" (the particular meaning of φράδμων): we can assume that the knowledge being referred to by the epithet is knowledge of Sarpedon's physiognomy, which is why he would have the ability to recognize him (ἔγνω), were he not so utterly disfigured by the struggle under way for his body. Who might this knowing observer be? No doubt the one most apt to recognize Sarpedon (most φράδμων) would be Glaucus himself. The mention of an anonymous man here both suggests Glaucus's reaction *if he were present* and, at the same time, underscores his absence; he is too far removed from his friend to rescue him or even witness his disfigurement firsthand. That a fictitious spectator should fulfill that role in his stead further emphasizes Sarpedon's isolation from his fellow warriors and allies at the time of his death. Not one of the Lycians has stayed behind to protect Sarpedon's corpse, over which a sinister accumulation of dead bodies has piled up (κείμενον ἐν νεκύων ἀγύρει, 16.661). Even Hector turns back toward the city in the face of such a dire series of events as those caused by Patroclus over the course of his *aristeia*, including the killing and despoiling of Sarpedon. He recognizes that the hand of Zeus is at work behind it all (γνῶ γὰρ Διὸς ἱρὰ τάλαντα, 16.558).

Throughout the fight over his son's corpse, around which the throng of Greeks and Trojans gather "like flies clustering around brimming milk pails" (16.641–3), Zeus looks on; in fact, the poet tells us, he never once averts his

---

96 On the brutal and dehumanizing effects of force within the *Iliad*, see Weil 1941.
97 The quote is from De Jong 1987, 59.
98 Such is De Jong's explanation for it here and in similar passages (1987, 58).

gaze from the horrific sight of Sarpedon being buried under splintered weapons, dirt, and gore:

> ὣς ἄρα τοὶ περὶ νεκρὸν ὁμίλεον, οὐδέ ποτε Ζεὺς
> τρέψεν ἀπὸ κρατερῆς ὑσμίνης ὄσσε φαεινώ,
> ἀλλὰ κατ' αὐτοὺς αἰὲν ὅρα καὶ φράζετο θυμῷ,
> (16.644–6)
>
> Such was the throng around Sarpedon's corpse; and not once did Zeus avert his luminous eyes from the combatants, but all this time he was looking down at them and pondering.

What Zeus is pondering, we are told, is whether he should have Hector kill Patroclus right then and there and bring his *aristeia* to an end. Despite his love for his son and the temptation to do away with the one about to kill him, "it seems preferable" (κέρδιον εἶναι, 16.652) that "Achilles' noble surrogate" (ἠὺς θεράπων Πηληϊάδεω Ἀχιλῆος, 16.653) should continue to press the Trojans back toward their city.[99] The intent gaze of the father of gods and men follows Sarpedon till the very end of the scene. The combination of his deep concern and his inability to intervene in the face of fate focuses the audience's attention on the gravity of the occasion and confers great dramatic intensity and pathos on the scene.

As we will see, something comparable happens when the time comes for Sarpedon's killer to meet his fate, when Patroclus is, in turn, called to his doom. Sarpedon is an important hero, not because he plays a significant role within the plot of the *Iliad* (which he does not), but because of the interpersonal relationships that connect him with friends and foes (he is Zeus's son and Patroclus's victim) and because of the specific poetics of his death.[100] His death is significant largely because it establishes patterns of theme and diction and a template for the two other great heroes' deaths to come: the death of Patroclus (his killer) and then that of Patroclus's killer, Hector.

I turn now to the death of the greatest Trojan warrior, Hector. Though it occurs later than Patroclus's (who dies in the very same book 16 as his Lycian victim Sarpedon), a rapid overview of the features common to the scenes of Sarpe-

---

[99] The impersonal formulation used here leaves the reasons for Zeus's decision to allow Patroclus to continue on his *aristeia* open and somewhat mysterious. In allowing Patroclus to continue on his rampage far beyond the clear boundaries set by Achilles, Zeus is not favoring Patroclus, however; rather, he is allowing him to pursue the path that leads to certain death. Apollo later warns Patroclus of the fatal consequences of his persistence, just as Achilles had earlier. Patroclus does not heed either warning.
[100] On the poetics of Sarpedon's death, see Nagy 1990, ch. 5. On the specific function (and adaptation) of his character within the Homeric *Iliad*, see Aceti 2008, 3–154.

don's and Hector's deaths will be useful here, in order to tease out the similarities and distinctive details of the portrayal of the death of Patroclus in book 16.

Looking on from the walls of Troy: The death of Hector

The death of Hector, like that of Sarpedon, is framed by the spectators who look on while it unfolds. Hector's father Priam is the first to see Achilles (τὸν δ' ὃ γέρων Πρίαμος πρῶτος ἴδεν ὀφθαλμοῖσι, 22.25) in the Trojan plain, advancing straight toward the city. His vision of the hero's outstanding stature and menacing demeanor is elaborated through a number of similes as Achilles, angry at Apollo for pushing him away from the walls of Troy, heads back toward the enemy city with the implacable determination and speed of a thoroughbred sprinting home (22.21–4). The mere sight of his son's foe, conspicuous in the plain as a shining star of ill omen (22.26–30), prompts the king of Troy to cry out in grief at the death of his son, which he knows to be certain if Hector steps outside to face the son of Peleus on his own. Priam desperately seeks to delay or avert the death with a final supplication to Hector that he not face his foe one-on-one, pulling his white hair out in a premonitory and proleptic gesture of mourning (22.37–76). All in vain: Hector is not persuaded. The unshakable nature of his resolve is conveyed by the terse hemistich that follows his father's lengthy speech: οὐδ' Ἕκτορι θυμὸν ἔπειθε ("but he did not persuade Hector," 22.78). Even the graphic image that Priam gives his son of his own decrepit old body, which will be thrown to the dogs if Hector is no longer there to protect it, does not achieve any concrete results; neither does his mother Hecuba's baring her breast to him[101] nor her prediction that neither she nor Andromache will be able to mourn his body if he faces Achilles, because the foe will abandon his corpse to dogs (22.79–89).[102]

The desperate pleas of Hector's father and mother have no effect, for Hector's duty calls,[103] and he prepares to face Achilles, coiled like a serpent

---

[101] On the pathos of the figure of the *mater dolorosa* baring her breast in Homer and the lyric poetry of Stesichorus, see Xanthou's "Stesichorus' women: genealogy, beauty, and heroic motherhood," presented at "The Art of Stesichorus," a two day conference on Stesichorus for the fiftieth anniversary of the publication of D. L. Page's *Poetae Melici Graeci*, St. John's College, University of Oxford, U.K., 29–30 June 2012 (printed publication Xanthou 2015).

[102] On both of these parental supplications, see Kim 2000, 39; regarding supplication in the *Iliad*, see Alden 2001, 186 ff.

[103] On his duty to fight on behalf of all Trojans and the *aidôs* that would stem from not doing so, see his speech to Andromache at 6.441–3.

(22.93) until he catches sight of the son of Peleus, looking like Ares himself (ἶσος Ἐνυαλίῳ κορυθάϊκι πτολεμιστῇ, 22.132). The focalization then shifts from Hector's vision of Achilles, which causes Hector to seize up with fear (Ἕκτορα δ', ὡς ἐνόησεν, ἕλε τρόμος, 22.136), to the gods' view. The momentousness of the confrontation to come is brought out by the fact that *all* of the Olympians are watching closely from above (θεοὶ δ' ἐς πάντες ὁρῶντο, 22.166). Zeus in particular voices his grief on seeing a mortal who is dear to him go to his doom: for Hector never failed to honor him with sacrifices. In his speech, the father of gods and men draws particular attention to his status as witness looking on: ὢ πόποι ἦ φίλον ἄνδρα διωκόμενον περὶ τεῖχος ὀφθαλμοῖσιν ὁρῶμαι ("Ah me, this is a man beloved whom now my eyes watch being chased around the wall," 22.168–9).[104] As he did when Sarpedon faced death, Zeus even asks the other gods to consider whether they might save Hector from death at the hands of Achilles (ἐκ θανάτοιο σαώσομεν), just as he had asked Hera whether they might do so for Sarpedon. This time it is Athena who reminds him of the inescapability of death, which applies even in the case of the best and most beloved of mortals – in fact, as we have seen, it applies *especially* in the case of the greatest heroes, whose *kleos* requires that they die young. She uses the very same formula – an entire hexameter – that Hera had used in the case of Sarpedon: "this mortal man's destiny has already been fixed long since" (ἄνδρα θνητὸν ἐόντα πάλαι πεπρωμένον αἴσῃ).[105]

That Hector is fated to die does not prevent Athena from playing a significant role leading up to his death – albeit not a protective one, on the contrary. While fate cannot be countered, it can, it seems, be helped along, as we are about to see.[106] The only thing that has kept Hector running as far from Achilles as he can until now – how else could he escape Achilles for so long? – is the god Apollo, who stands near Hector now for the very last time, putting strength in the hero's knees:

πῶς δέ κεν Ἕκτωρ κῆρας ὑπεξέφυγεν θανάτοιο,
εἰ μή οἱ πύματόν τε καὶ ὕστατον ἤντετ' Ἀπόλλων
ἐγγύθεν, ὅς οἱ ἐπῶρσε μένος λαιψηρά τε γοῦνα;
(22.202–4)

---

[104] For Zeus' sorrow at the sight of Achilles' pursuit of Hector and the latter's certain death, see 22.167–76.
[105] 22.179; cf. 16.441.
[106] Nagy 1979, 144, discusses the role Athena plays as ritual antagonist to Hector; see 22.270–1, 445–6. In the goddess's own admission, "Achilles *and* she are to be the ones responsible for his death" (22.216–8).

> How then could Hector have escaped the death spirits,
> had not Apollo, for this last and uttermost time, stood by him
> close, and driven strength into him, and made his knees light?

The contrafactual here plays up the fact that Hector's life is holding on by a string.[107] Apollo stands by as an aid, but only for so long; he is quickly relegated to the status of a mere spectator along with Hector's other *philoi*, whose gaze heightens the audience's emotional response as Hector gets closer to the time of his doom.[108]

In the chase scene that ensues, Achilles runs in hot pursuit of Hector, while the latter desperately attempts to get closer to the Western Gate of Troy, where Trojan archers might provide him with some cover. He repeatedly fails to do so: Achilles always cuts him off. The heroes are at a draw: "the one cannot escape his pursuer; the other cannot catch his prey" (οὔτ' ἄρ' ὃ τὸν δύναται ὑποφεύγειν οὔθ' ὃ διώκειν, 22.200). After Apollo briefly appears at Hector's side, Zeus weighs Hector's fate against Achilles' on his scales. Hector's sinks: his time has come.

There is considerable pathos in Athena's deceit of Hector in the scene that follows, in which the goddess takes on the guise of a protective *philos*, his brother Deiphobus, and leads Hector to face Achilles head on, giving him the mistaken impression that he is not alone in taking on the daunting task of confronting the best of the Achaeans, and that aid is close at hand. Hector, in his relief at the thought that he no longer must battle Achilles alone, addresses the disguised Athena, thinking she is Deiphobus. The poet has the great Trojan prince address and describe Athena, whom he has been led to believe is his brother, with words that portray the sort of caring witness who sees, pities (implicitly), and intervenes – the seeing-and-pitying sequence that we have repeatedly noted:

> ὃς ἔτλης ἐμεῦ εἵνεκ', ἐπεὶ ἴδες ὀφθαλμοῖσι
> τείχεος ἐξελθεῖν, ἄλλοι δ' ἔντοσθε μένουσι.
> (22.236–7)
>
> You dared to come outside the wall for me,
> when your eyes caught sight of me, while the others stay inside.

Before Achilles, the best of the Achaeans and Hector, the bulwark of Troy engage in a final struggle, Hector asks Achilles to agree to take the gods as "witnesses

---

107 Regarding how pivotal contrafactuals play up the destructive potential of specific events, see Louden 1993.
108 This was also the understanding of the scholia, according to whom this passage "produces greater emotion(s) now, as in theater" (ὥσπερ ἐν θεάτρῳ νῦν μείζονα κινήσῃ πάθη).

and overseers" (μάρτυροι ἔσσονται καὶ ἐπίσκοποι ἁρμονιάων, 22.255) of an oath that they will both swear: namely, that the victor should return the corpse of the vanquished to his *philoi* (and not despoil it). Achilles rejects the mere idea of such an oath with categorical and superior vehemence. As for the gods, they are indeed watching the scene from above, but they will not be guarantors of the integrity of Hector's corpse, at least not for some time. Soon, it will be dragged in the dust and defiled by Achilles. The duel begins. Achilles throws his spear at Hector and misses. With renewed confidence, Hector throws his javelin at Achilles, and it bounces off Achilles' shield. Hector calls out to his brother Deiphobus, believing him to be close by, to ask him for another spear; but no one is there (22. 295–6). In an instant, Hector understands. Athena tricked him, and his time has come: ὢ πόποι ἦ μάλα δή με θεοὶ θάνατον δὲ κάλεσσαν, "Alas! There is no mistaking it; I hear the gods calling me to my death" (22. 297).

From this point on, Hector becomes an object of spectacle for *echthroi* and *philoi* alike. To the Greeks, he is a passive object of both conquest and admiration. Before killing him, Achilles looks at his "beautiful skin," searching for the most vulnerable spot in the armor that Hector has donned – Achilles' armor, which the latter had given to Patroclus, and which serves as a visual reminder to all, Trojans and Greeks alike, that Hector is the one who killed and despoiled Patroclus (εἰσορόων χρόα καλόν, ὅπῃ εἴξειε μάλιστα, 22.321). That armor is a visual reminder of Patroclus's death at Hector's hand and his subsequent despoiling of his armor, and it is the reason why Achilles, in his thirst for revenge, is now mercilessly bent on killing Hector and rejecting any pleas on his part. When Achilles drives his spear into Hector's exposed neck, the Trojan prince's life breath looks down at him, bemoaning his lost youth (ὃν πότμον γοόωσα λιποῦσ' ἀνδροτῆτα καὶ ἥβην, 22.363),[109] while the Greeks gather round to contemplate (θηήσαντο) his beauty, even as they desecrate his lifeless body, poking at it and wounding it repeatedly with their spears:

ἄλλοι δὲ περίδραμον υἷες Ἀχαιῶν,
οἳ καὶ θηήσαντο φυὴν καὶ εἶδος ἀγητὸν
Ἕκτορος· οὐδ' ἄρα οἵ τις ἀνουτητί γε παρέστη.
        (22.369–71)

And the sons of the Achaeans came running about him,
And gazed upon the stature and on the imposing beauty
Of Hector; and none stood beside him who did not stab him.

---

109 The very same hexameter occurs when Hector kills Patroclus, thereby further establishing a causal and dictional connection between the two scenes: see 16.857.

Then the defilement of Hector's corpse continues, at Achilles' hands this time. From the ramparts of Troy, Priam and Hecuba, Hector's father and mother, are watching. It is unclear how much of the deadly confrontation between Hector and Achilles they have seen; now, at any rate, they see all too clearly a sight excruciating for parents to behold; and they have no power to do anything but lament in response. Achilles shames and defiles Hector's body as they look on: he pierces the Trojan prince's ankles with leather thongs, attaches the corpse to the back of his chariot, and trails and sullies his once beautiful hair in the dust (22.401–4). The king and queen in their old age are utterly helpless to do anything but watch in horror. In the harrowing spectacle of their son's destruction and defilement, they see that they are doomed, along with the city over which they rule, now that the best of the Achaeans is hauling away from their walls the bulwark of Troy, their dead son, Hector, who has been reduced to nothing more than a lifeless corpse, dragged in the mud by Troy's greatest enemy.[110] From Hector's head, towed in the dust of the land he can no longer defend, the poetics move seamlessly to Hecuba's head, from which she tears her shining veil while Priam groans:[111]

> Ὣς τοῦ μὲν κεκόνιτο κάρη ἄπαν· ἡ δέ νυ μήτηρ
> τίλλε κόμην, ἀπὸ δὲ λιπαρὴν ἔρριψε καλύπτρην
> τηλόσε, κώκυσεν δὲ μάλα μέγα παῖδ' ἐσιδοῦσα·
> ᾤμωξεν δ' ἐλεεινὰ πατὴρ φίλος, ἀμφὶ δὲ λαοὶ
> κωκυτῷ τ' εἴχοντο καὶ οἰμωγῇ κατὰ ἄστυ.
> (22.405–9)
>
> So all his head was dragged in the dust; and now his mother
> Tore out her hair, and threw the shining veil from her
> And raised a great wail as she looked upon her son; and his father
> Beloved groaned pitifully, and all his people about him
> Were taken with wailing and lamentation throughout the city.

The Trojan king and queen's extreme pain turns physical and vociferous; it ripples through the city, which erupts with cries of mourning (κατὰ ἄστυ). The narrative and the sounds of grief travel further, into Priam's palace, progressing along an ascending scale of affection from Hector's parents to his most beloved wife.[112]

---

110 On Hector's name and role as the protector of Troy, see Nagy 1979, 145–7.
111 On the symbolism of the torn veil in connection with the fall of Troy, see Dué 2002, ch. 4.
112 On Kakridis's "ascending scale of affection," see Kakridis 1949, ch.1; Nagy 1979, 104–9; Crotty 1994, 51 n. 9.

The poem has been preparing for Andromache's response to the death of Hector since book 6. When Hector returns to see Andromache and his son for the last time, he does not find them, as he expected to, in the halls of his father's palace; Andromache has gone out to the walls because she has heard that the Greeks have the upper hand and that the Trojans are suffering, and she wishes to witness firsthand the situation and its possible outcome, dire though they may be. Her fretful presence on the walls contributes to the buildup toward the climactic moment when she catches sight of Hector's dead body in book 22. Already in book 6, the extreme emotion involved in the act of watching and waiting to see Hector's fate is clear from the phraseology. As Andromache desperately seeks to find out whether Hector is still alive, she rushes up to the walls "like a madwoman" (μαινομένῃ ἐϊκυῖα, 6.389) and stands there "lamenting and weeping" (πύργῳ ἐφεστήκει γοόωσά τε μυρομένη τε, 6.373). In book 22, when she hears the people's wails spread through the city (ἀμφὶ δὲ λαοὶ κωκυτῷ τ' εἴχοντο καὶ οἰμωγῇ κατὰ ἄστυ), Hector's wife once again rushes from her chamber to the walls "like a madwoman" (μαινάδι ἴσῃ, 22.460), asking two of her attendants to come along. She must see for herself what deeds have been done (δεῦτε δύω μοι ἕπεσθον, ἴδωμ' ὅτιν' ἔργα τέτυκται, 16.450). The pathos of Andromache's response to Hector's demise builds up as her words lead the audience to anticipate the impact that the spectacle of her husband, dragged in dust and grimed with blood, will have on her. Seeing her husband's body disfigured with such ruthless brutality proves so unbearable that, in that very moment, Andromache loses consciousness. The phraseology used to describe her reaction suggests that, poetically and emotionally speaking, she too has died; that is, that Hector's death amounts to her own:

αὐτὰρ ἐπεὶ πύργον τε καὶ ἀνδρῶν ἷξεν ὅμιλον
ἔστη παπτήνασ' ἐπὶ τείχεϊ, τὸν δὲ νόησεν
ἑλκόμενον πρόσθεν πόλιος· ταχέες δέ μιν ἵπποι
ἕλκον ἀκηδέστως κοίλας ἐπὶ νῆας Ἀχαιῶν.
τὴν δὲ κατ' ὀφθαλμῶν ἐρεβεννὴ νὺξ ἐκάλυψεν,
ἤριπε δ' ἐξοπίσω, ἀπὸ δὲ ψυχὴν ἐκάπυσσε.
(22.462–7)

But when she came to the bastion, where the men were gathered,
She stopped on the wall and stared; and she saw him
Being dragged in front of the city; the running horses
Dragged him at random toward the hollow ships of the Achaeans.
The darkness of night misted over her eyes.
She fell backward, and gasped the life breath from her.

The audience sees Andromache display the sort of grief and vulnerability that Hector had earlier said he would find unbearable to watch (6.440–65). In their last encounter, he tells Andromache that he prefers to die than live to hear her cry out while being dragged into slavery and taken to Argos or Sparta against her will — for he recognizes that Troy is fated to fall.[113] The visual image of Andromache's misery to come is so concrete in his mind that he even pictures a fictitious witness to Andromache's sorrow, a Greek observer, and his reaction. The imaginary observer conjured up by Hector is pictured seeing her weeping and knowing from the intensity of her grief just how great a Trojan warrior she was wedded to, whose protection she has now lost:[114]

> καί ποτέ τις εἴπῃσιν ἰδὼν κατὰ δάκρυ χέουσαν·
> "Ἕκτορος ἥδε γυνὴ ὃς ἀριστεύεσκε μάχεσθαι
> Τρώων ἱπποδάμων ὅτε Ἴλιον ἀμφεμάχοντο.
> ὥς ποτέ τις ἐρέει· σοὶ δ' αὖ νέον ἔσσεται ἄλγος
> χήτεϊ τοιοῦδ' ἀνδρὸς ἀμύνειν δούλιον ἦμαρ.
> (6.459–63)

And some day seeing you shedding tears, a man will say of you:
'This is the wife of Hector, who was ever the bravest fighter
of the Trojans, breakers of horses, in the days when they fought about Ilion.'
So will one speak of you; and for you it will be yet a fresh grief,
To be widowed of such a man who could fight off the day of your slavery.

The anonymous spectator that Hector imagines witnessing his Trojan wife's mourning is a good illustration of one of the roles played by the emotional lens of *philoi* in the depiction of heroic deaths. In Hector's mind, the mourning widow's pain will serve not merely as a display of her grief but also as a concrete sign of the greatness of the man she mourns (even in the eyes of *echthroi*). In a similar fashion, the depth of Andromache's despair as it is displayed in book 22, along with his parents' demonstrations of extreme grief, are a poetic means of heightening the hero's importance, as the mourners' pain is commensurate with the worth of the man they have lost.[115]

---

113 6.447–9.
114 I assume the onlooker is a Greek based on the fact that the scene Hector envisions takes place in Argos.
115 And yet, as Slatkin 2007, 30–1 emphasizes, Hector's vision of the spectacle of his wife's grief as witnessed by an imaginary onlooker is ambivalent at best; in fact, it dramatizes how little compensation the glorious renown (which Andromache's grief and the onlooker's comments reflect) actually provides in the face of the "bitter desolation" that he envisions. On the challenges to heroic values within epic poetry, especially through lament, see Murnaghan

While Achilles spends his nights tossing and turning in restlessness and unresolved pain at Patroclus's death, he spends the first part of every day dragging Hector's corpse around Patroclus's tomb three times, leaving the body face down in the dust (ἐν κόνι ἐκτανύσας προπρηνέα) when he is finished (24.1–18). All the while, the gods are watching. Eventually they take pity (following the seeing-and-pitying pattern) and urge Hermes to steal the Trojan hero's body. The hero in question is already dead, and the most that can be done is rescue his corpse from further defilement:

> τὸν δ' ἐλεαίρεσκον μάκαρες θεοὶ εἰσορόωντες,
> κλέψαι δ' ὀτρύνεσκον ἐΰσκοπον Ἀργειφόντην.
> (24.23–4)
>
> The blessed gods as they looked upon him were filled with compassion
> And kept urging clear-sighted Argeïphontes to steal the body.

In the end, Hermes does not steal the body; it is Priam himself, king of the Trojans and father of Achilles' supreme enemy Hector, who will fetch his son's corpse from within the tent of the most powerful and deadly of the Achaeans – Achilles. The presence of the gods looking on has no direct bearing on the plot; they see the victim and pity him, but no action is actually taken as a result (at this point at any rate). The function of the divine spectators here seems to be solely to emphasize their pity as a way of underlining by contrast the savagery with which the pitiless Achilles treats his dead enemy's lifeless body.

When Priam brings Hector's body back into Troy from Achilles' tent at the end of book 24, the poet stresses the momentousness of the occasion and the acute grief that the sight of the body provokes by portraying the ripples of sadness that spread from one *philos* to another. The first to catch sight of Priam returning with Hector's body is Hector's sister, Cassandra: the bT scholia comment that "she is watching because she is deeply anxious about her brother and father."[116] Cassandra's fretful searching of the horizon leads her to be the first to see her father, standing in his chariot with his herald at his side. Then she sees Hector laid down beside him: τὸν δ' ἄρ' ἐφ' ἡμιόνων ἴδε κείμενον ἐν λεχέεσσι (24.702). When she sees her brother lying dead on a stretcher pulled by mules, she calls out to the rest of the Trojans to "come and see" Hector: ὄψεσθε Τρῶες καὶ Τρῳάδες Ἕκτορ' ἰόντες (24.704), and the lamenting begins. Lamenting is all that there is left to do before, during, and after Troy is finally taken. With Hector's

---

1999. On the ambivalence of female lament in archaic Greek epic and the role of its themes in shaping the laments of Greek tragedy, see Dué 2006.
116 Noted by Richardson 1993 *ad* 24.699–702.

death, the Trojans have lost the city's main protector; there is no longer any hope of saving it, only a hero to be buried now that his body finally is theirs to honor. Soon Astyanax will be thrown from the walls, Andromache enslaved, and Helen returned to the victorious Greeks.[117]

The Death of Patroclus

No witness, no pity?

We have just examined two of the most important deaths in the *Iliad:* Sarpedon's and Hector's. Patroclus's comes between the death of Sarpedon (Patroclus's victim) and the death of Hector (Patroclus's slayer).[118] As we have seen, the more important the hero, the greater the impact of his death on others and the more prominently featured their reactions at the time of his death. It hardly bears emphasizing that Patroclus is a central hero of the *Iliad*, not least because of his role in and relationship to the community of the Achaeans: he is dearest and closest of all men to the greatest fighter among them, Achilles; he also enjoys the unique status of one who is known by all (Greeks) for his soft temperament, kindness, and compassionate disposition.[119] Moreover, from the time he dons Achilles' armor, Patroclus proves to be an outstanding warrior, mowing down many Trojans, including the valiant Sarpedon himself. His death, then, is hardly a negligible one; its expanse – the sheer amount of verse devoted to it – is one indication of how crucial a turning point it marks in the *Iliad* not only for the poem's plot but also in terms of how it changes Achilles' relationship to the Greeks, the heroic code that he has rejected, and even the human community itself. It is his best friend's death that causes the main hero of the *Iliad* to rejoin the ranks of the Greeks and let go of his rancor toward Agamemnon as his devastating grief and rabid anger at Hector take over his entire being,

---

[117] Andromache: 24.731–2; Astyanax: 24.732–8; Helen: 24.774–5.
[118] Lowenstam 1981 examines the death of Patroclus with an eye to parallel scenes in the *Iliad*.
[119] On Patroclus as "the sweetest and most compassionate of the Homeric warriors" (Parry 1972, 10), see below, nX. The Trojans might beg to differ, as per his "berserker" state in his *aristeia*; perhaps donning Achilles' armor is part of a transformation of Patroclus's character into Achilles' (see for instance Whitman 1958). On Patroclus as a healer, see Austin 1999, 32 ff. On Patroclus's murderous rage in book 16, see Collins 1998.

setting in motion the process that will lead to the fall of Troy, a process to which the last third of the *Iliad* is devoted.[120]

In light of the importance of Patroclus's death (not least when it comes to its function within the *Iliad*'s overarching plot) and in light of what we have observed regarding other major heroes, we might well expect an internal audience of mortals and gods looking on at the time of his death, wishing to protect him, pitying him when he is wounded, and perhaps attempting to intervene or at least expressing the wish to do so, as both Glaucus and Zeus do in Sarpedon's death scene and as Zeus does once more in the case of Hector. The absence of any actual or desired intervention, or attempt at one, is all the more striking as Patroclus dies unusually "slowly," as it were: he is first unarmed by Apollo, then stabbed multiple times, each wound an added occasion in which we might expect another Greek warrior or god to react to his ongoing demise, as the opportunities for pity (and intervention) are multiplied. But no one looks on as the best of the Achaeans' most valued friend goes down. Or rather, there is *no mention* made of any witness, divine or mortal, to Patroclus's death at any point in the elaborately detailed scene of his wounding and death. No one is mentioned explicitly – and that, I believe, is precisely the point, for reasons that I will now seek to elucidate. There is meaning and significance to the absence of spectators and to the silence (on the part of the poet, gods, and characters, including the victim) surrounding the downfall of Menoetius's son. The absence of an actual witness and the silence of Patroclus and the other Greeks leaves room for another set of eyes, another emotional lens, and another voice to insert themselves into the scene.

At the time of his death, Patroclus is hopelessly, desperately alone. There is an anonymous group of Achaeans toward whom he stumbles after he has been violently struck by the god Apollo and stabbed by two mortals, the second of which is the greatest of all the Trojan warriors, but we find no mention of any *philos* looking on as he receives blow after blow right up until the time of his death. Not only is there no fellow warrior standing by, watching and reacting to a scene so tremendously important to the plot of the *Iliad* and so devastating for its central warrior Achilles; there is also a noteworthy absence of any sympathetic divinity looking on, much less intervening to protect him. The only divinity present is the god Apollo, who plays a central role in bringing down the son of Menoetius, and whose assault on a mortal has no equivalent in the entire *Iliad*: nowhere else in the poem do we see a divinity assault a mortal thus directly and

---

120 On the connections between pity, anger, and action in the *Iliad*, particularly in the case of Achilles, see Most 2003.

furtively, approaching him from behind and knocking his helmet off with a deliberate blow from the back of his hand.[121]

The audience does hear *a* voice throughout the horrifying scene of Patroclus's downfall, however. The introduction of this particular voice makes the audience view the entire scene of Patroclus's demise from a particular angle, and a particular emotional lens. Whose? To answer this question, I turn my attention to the central and highly distinctive poetic device through which we hear this voice time and again all through the scene: the apostrophes to Patroclus. I examine those instances in which the poet's voice shifts and thus comes to encompass multiple voices within itself, as the speaker addresses Patroclus directly, in the second person.

You, Patroclus

The abundance of apostrophes is one of the most prominent, unusual, and intriguing aspects of the poetics of book 16, and especially of the *Patrocleia*.[122] The frequency with which the narrator addresses apostrophes to the hero as he carries out his feats on the battlefield is unique. Interestingly, there is a noteworthy increase in the frequency of these apostrophes as the hero's death draws nearer; its highest concentration is found during the protracted, detailed account of his downfall.

Each apostrophe marks a sudden break within the poet's voice.[123] With just one word (in the vocative), the narrator enters into the world of his narrative, breaking through the barrier between the world of diegesis and that of his characters by means of metalepsis, suddenly and abruptly.[124] Throughout book 16,

---

[121] Even Athena's betrayal of Hector in book 22 is merely an indirect means of leading him to his death: see above, p. 38.
[122] For an earlier version of my analysis concerning apostrophes in the *Patrocleia*, see Allen-Hornblower 2012.
[123] For the disruptive "effet de rupture" introduced by the narratorial apostrophe to a character, see Franchet d'Esperey 2006 (esp. 179).
[124] Genette defines metalepsis as "any intrusion by the extradiegetic narrator or narratee into the diegetic universe [...] or the inverse" (Genette 1980, 234–7). See his definition of metalepsis at Genette 1983, 88:

> "a deliberate transgression of the threshold of embedding [...]: when an author (or his reader) introduces himself into the fictive account of the narrative or when a character in that fiction intrudes into the extradiegetic existence of the author or reader, such intrusions disturb, to say the least, the distinction between levels.

the traditional boundary between the world of the Homeric poet and the separate world of his characters is briefly and repeatedly eliminated as he steps into his own narrative and takes on the role of a speaking, feeling character for a series of repeated and significant moments. Bringing to light the role of metalepsis in book 16 will help us better understand the place and role of Patroclus's death in developing the central motif that underlies the scene of his demise and the *Iliad* as a whole: the ineluctability of death for mortals, as well as human helplessness and vulnerability in the face of this ineluctable death.

Apostrophes to characters — those instances where the poet "speaks" to a character directly in the vocative – are always "embarrassing" for the reader and critic.[125] They disrupt the flow of the third-person narrative by bringing the poet, performer, and audience in direct contact with the addressee of the apostrophes – in this instance, one of the characters. In the *Iliad*, the overwhelming majority of apostrophes are addressed to Patroclus (eight of them, all in book 16) and Menelaus (seven of them).[126] Much like a historical present involves a grammatical eruption of the present tense into the tale of a past event, and thus draws the listener into the here and now of that past event, these apostrophes create a sense of greater proximity (spatial and temporal) to the character being thus addressed, as they merge different temporalities and spaces: the mythical past of the story being told, and the here and now of the performance.[127] In the case of Homeric poetry, the *now* of the narrative and the "no-time and no-place" (Budick) that the apostrophe creates are one with the *here and now* of real-time performance before a live audience. No doubt the vividness

---

De Jong devotes a chapter to metalepsis in ancient Greek literature in the volume edited by Grethlein and Rengakos (2009). On the figure of metalepsis, see also e.g., Fludernik 1993, Genette 2004.

125 Culler 1977, 59; Culler identifies apostrophe with lyric itself.
126 For a complete list of all the apostrophes in the *Iliad* and an attempt to categorize them by context, see Henry 1905. One of the categories that Henry distinguishes bears the title, "at an important crisis for the hero apostrophized," which is relevant to my analysis below; however, he omits several examples that belong in that category. On narratorial apostrophes in Homer and Virgil, see Block 1982, 1986. For a consideration of the effect of apostrophes in Homer that goes beyond merely producing pathos, see Di Benedetto 1994, 42–3.
127 "Apostrophe is different from other forms of direct address or from narrative digressions, because in apostrophe all preceding time and place are for an instant totally interrupted. Instead a no-time and no-place is momentarily inserted into the speaker's, and our, quondam world" (Budick 1989, 314). On the tension between the narrative's temporal sequence and the resistance of the apostrophe, whose *now* is the *now* of discourse, see Culler 1977, 68. On the apostrophes' contribution to the characteristic *enargeia* of Homeric poetry, see De Jong in Grethlein and Rengakos, 2009, 93–9; on Homeric *enargeia*, see Bakker, n. 52 and below, p. 72.

of the voice calling out in the second person (in this case, to a character) would be all the more powerfully felt as a result.¹²⁸

Scholars since Antiquity have interpreted these apostrophes as expressions of particular concern on the part of the poet for the characters thus addressed.¹²⁹ Many note that the majority of apostrophes are directed at Patroclus and Menelaus, and see this as a reflection of the fact that these are the two heroes that the poem represents as "unusually sensitive and worthy of the audience's sympathy."¹³⁰ No doubt the large number of apostrophes directed at Patroclus, all con-

---

128 The performing bard would face an interesting choice of whom to look at and appear to address when voicing these apostrophes to characters; he could turn away from his audience, or appear to address them as though they were the character in question, and thus lead them to identify with the addressee. Bakker notes another important effect of apostrophes that is linked to the transgression of boundaries inherent in the metalepsis: they are, he writes, one of the moments in which "the dividing line between private imagination and public experience is at its weakest… the apostrophe marks the point where… the participatory involvement of the poet, and thereby of its audience, is greatest" (Bakker 1993, 23).

129 The scholia on 16.787 describe how the poet condoles with his characters (συναχθόμενος) by way of the apostrophe. For a complete list of all relevant scholia that interpret apostrophes as expressions of compassion on the part of the poet for the character being thus addressed, see De Jong 1987, 13 and 225 n. 40. Pseudo-Longinus's *On the Sublime* 16.2 includes a discussion of the powerful psychological effect of the apostrophe on the listener, due to its sublimity and emotional quality (see Zyroff 1971, 13–4). The compassionate tone of the apostrophe is recognizable across genres; see Culler 1977, 59: the apostrophe "indicate[s] intense involvement," a "powerful outburst of concern." This is not to say that when the poet sticks to the third person, there is no emotional tinge or subjective dimension to speak of within the narration; it is mistaken to speak of "cold objectivity" when the narration remains in the third person; see De Jong 1987.

130 Parry 1972, 9. Patroclus is "the sweetest and most compassionate of the Homeric warriors" (Parry 1972, 10), "der Lieblingsheld des Iliasdichters" (Baltes 1983, 47, including n. 59). On Patroclus as a "loyal, sensible, altruistic character," see also Janko 1992a, 317–8, with bibliography. Parry 1972 offers a definitive and convincing argument against the explanation of apostrophes on strictly metrical grounds (*pace* Matthews 1980). Yamagata 1989, 91, gives a summary of those who align themselves with Parry and those who maintain the metrical explanation, with bibliography. On the emotional effect of apostrophes and their role in eliciting the audience's sympathy, see Zyroff 1971; Block 1986; and Martin 1989, 235 n. 17, with bibliography. In his study of the Homeric narrator, Richardson includes a brief discussion of metalepsis, in which he argues that apostrophes evoke a sense of sympathy in the audience, not because they express any particular emotion on the part of the narrator-poet, but because they create a sense of greater intimacy with the character in question, effected by the metalepsis (Richardson 1990, 170–4). De Jong in Rengakos and Grethlein (2009, 94–5) provides a summary of past scholarly attempts at explaining the presence of apostrophes to characters in Homeric epic. Frontisi-Ducroux (1986, 21–5) proposes a different explanation for apostrophes: she connects the apostrophes to Patroclus in book 16 with his status as the ideal audience to Achilles elsewhere in the poem. Bouvier 2002 raises the interesting point that nowhere in the Homeric epic — an oral performance delivered before an audience — are there any apostrophes to that audience (Bouvier

fined to book 16, contributes to heightening the pathos and overall emotional effect of his excruciatingly slow and horrible death at the hands of Apollo at the end of the book.[131] There is no question that the apostrophe is a powerful "emotional device;"[132] but there is more to them. In order to elucidate and do justice to the significance of the apostrophes that accompany Patroclus before and throughout his *aristeia*, and particularly the two that are addressed to him as he is being killed (16.787 and 16.812), a close examination of the contexts in which these and other apostrophes to him and to Menelaus occur throughout the *Iliad* is in order. We will see that these contexts all share certain formulaic and thematic elements, as well as structural patterns, which take on meaning from their relationship to each other and especially from the variations between them. This, in turn, will enable us to distinguish the particular significance of the apostrophes that recur over the course of Patroclus's death scene, in which I argue that the poet blends different diegetic levels in order to give voice to and make us hear an absent character's voice.

Calling out to the threatened warrior: The *Patrocleia* and Patroclus's doom[133]

There are apostrophes addressed to Patroclus when he reaches new heights in his destructive *aristeia* that seem at first glance to be incongruous, even at odds with the blatantly pathetic contexts in which the other apostrophes occur, such as when he is scattering the Trojans from Epeigeus's body or leaping onto Cebriones' body to despoil him.[134] Why insert an expression of sympathy for the hero in his most glorious moments on the battlefield? The key to understanding the apostrophe's place in such contexts lies in the relationship of the *Patrocleia* to Patroclus's demise: the apostrophe, I submit, marks a juncture at which Patroclus takes a significant step away from the boundaries set by Achilles and

---

2002, 20, with bibliography at n. 23). De Martino (1977) points out that when the poet apostrophizes a character, he is also treating that character, to a certain extent, with the particular sort of reverence with which he addresses the Muse herself.
131 Apollo is only the first of three agents involved. For a fresh take on the surprising presence and role of the Trojan Euphorbus in the killing of Patroclus, when he has already been struck by Apollo and is about to receive a final, lethal blow from Hector (16.806–15), see Allan 2005b.
132 I am borrowing the expression from Griffin 1976, 162; he touches briefly on apostrophes, but his article focuses on the creation of pathos in Homeric poetry through the short "obituaries" given by the poet to heroes at the time of their death.
133 On the relationship of the *Patrocleia* to the rest of the *Iliad*, see Reinhardt 1961, 17–37. On Patroclus's name and function with the *Iliad*, see Bouvier 2002. ch. 5.
134 16.584–5 and 16.754 respectively.

closer to his doom. Each new apostrophe helps to generate a sense of apprehension in the audience and to gradually build up the tension underlying the entire episode of Patroclus's glory on the battlefield that will culminate in his death.[135]

One subset of apostrophes – those that occur within speech formulas – offers a good illustration of this point. Three apostrophes to Patroclus accompany three different speech formulas in book 16: at 16.20, τὸν δὲ βαρὺ στενάχων προσέφης Πατρόκλεες ἱππεῦ ("and with a deep groan, horseman Patroclus, you said to him"); at 16.744, τὸν δ' ἐπικερτομέων προσέφης Πατρόκλεες ἱππεῦ ("and you spoke in bitter mockery over him, horseman Patroclus"); and at 16.843, τὸν δ' ὀλιγοδρανέων προσέφης Πατρόκλεες ἱππεῦ ("And you responded to him, horseman Patroclus, barely able to shake the words out").[136] In response to Milman Parry's statement that apostrophes to characters within the Homeric poems were used strictly for metrical purposes, Adam Parry has argued that this is only true when they occur within speech formulas.[137] The younger Parry goes on to point out, however, that even *these* apostrophes are "emotionally qualified" by a "special, though still formulary, participle in the first half of the line," adding, "only by entirely disregarding the context can these apostrophes be regarded as full equivalents, technically determined, of third-person formulas." Parry does not develop the point any further. I propose that we examine the speech formulas that include an apostrophe in their respective contexts, in order to pinpoint the nature of the emotional qualification that (as Parry suggests) these formulas (and especially the apostrophes that occur within them) introduce into the narrative.

For the first of the three speech formulas, we must turn to the beginning of book 16, before Patroclus even heads into battle. The formula introduces Patroclus's desperate plea to Achilles that he be allowed to wear his armor and enter the fray in his stead: τὸν δὲ βαρὺ στενάχων προσέφης Πατρόκλεες ἱππεῦ (16.20). Patroclus "groans" (βαρὺ στενάχων) here because of the destruction that

---

135 On the various stages that lead up to Patroclus's death in book 16 and the missed "chances" he is given to escape it, see Taplin 1992, ch. 7. See also Di Benedetto 1994, ch. 4.
136 Translations here are Lombardo's (with very minor variations). Each of these speech formulas includes the same form of Patroclus's name in the vocative, accompanied by the epithet ἱππεῦ (horseman). On the parallels between Nestor and Patroclus created by the attribution of the epithet "horseman" to both and their significance, see Frame 2009, ch. 4, §2.16, and §2.17. Yamagata 1989, 102–3, suggests this particular epithet is a "definitive epithet reserved for [Patroclus]" because it is laden with meaning (in a manner not unsimilar to the apostrophe itself, one might add): it is the act of driving Achilles' horses, she notes, that both glorifies Patroclus and leads to his death.
137 Parry 1972, 12–4.

Achilles' absence from the Achaean ranks has wrought upon them, but the participle is also "special," to use Parry's designation.¹³⁸ Its wider significance becomes clear if we turn to its subsequent occurrences in the poem. Each time βαρὺ στενάχων occurs thereafter, it introduces Achilles' laments for his dead friend. The very next occurrence of the participle is following Patroclus's death, when Thetis rushes to Achilles' side in response to his cries of grief, which she has heard from the depths of the sea. She stands by her son "as he groans": τῷ δὲ βαρὺ στενάχοντι παρίστατο πότνια μήτηρ (18.70). The same formula introduces Achilles' words of grief in response to his mother's query, when she asks why he is crying: τὴν δὲ βαρὺ στενάχων προσέφη πόδας ὠκὺς Ἀχιλλεύς (18.78). In his answer, he blames himself for "killing" Patroclus: τὸν ἀπώλεσα ("I destroyed him," 18.82). In that speech, Achilles expresses the fact that, for him, his friend's death amounts to his own, since he no longer has the will to live: he is, in his own words, but "a dead weight on the earth"¹³⁹ (18.90–1 and 104 respectively).¹⁴⁰ The same speech formula, βαρὺ στενάχων, introduces Achilles' laments for Patroclus two more times: when he voices his immeasurable grief at the loss of his dearest friend to the rest of the Myrmidons at 18.323 (ὣς ὃ βαρὺ στενάχων μετεφώνεε Μυρμιδόνεσσιν), and again at 23.59–60 (Πηλεΐδης δ' ἐπὶ θινὶ πολυφλοίσβοιο θαλάσσης | κεῖτο βαρὺ στενάχων πολέσιν μετὰ Μυρμιδόνεσσιν, "But the son of Peleus lay groaning heavily among his Myrmidons on the open beach").

In sum, every time the speech formula βαρὺ στενάχων resurfaces after Patroclus dies, it introduces speeches spoken by Achilles that express pain at this death: Achilles' laments for Patroclus. This makes the ironically tragic nature of the speech formula's presence at the beginning of book 16, where it introduces a speech *spoken by Patroclus*, patently clear. The formula strikes a note of dramatic irony that is all the stronger as it introduces the very speech through which Patroclus (unwittingly) begs Achilles for his own demise, by asking to wear his armor and enter the fray looking like Peleus's son, in order to fight in his stead.¹⁴¹ The audience knows Patroclus is fated to die, and soon: the ineluctability of Patroclus's impending doom is made clear to them in words spo-

---

138 On the connections between Achilles' name, *akhos*, and the pain he causes to the Achaeans, see Nagy 1979, 69–93.
139 This is Lombardo's evocative translation.
140 Regarding tragic figures who endure unbearable suffering but go on living, see Wilson 2004.
141 There is another association of this speech formula with death and lament earlier on, when it introduces Agamemnon's proleptic lament for Menelaus on seeing his brother bleed abundantly in a scene from book 4 (4.153 ff.), which I discuss below.

ken by the gods as well as by the poet himself, in the voice of the narrator.[142] In this instance, the lines immediately following Patroclus's plea to Achilles make the connection between his plea and his death explicit. The poet states that Patroclus was νήπιος ("foolish") to voice such a request because, in doing so, he was unknowingly pleading for his own death:[143]

> Ὣς φάτο λισσόμενος μέγα νήπιος· ἦ γὰρ ἔμελλεν
> οἷ αὐτῷ θάνατόν τε κακὸν καὶ κῆρα λιτέσθαι.
> (16.46–7)
>
> So he spoke supplicating in his great innocence;[144] this was
> His own death and evil destruction he was entreating.

Patroclus's words, spoken with a groan (βαρὺ στενάχων), will in fact prove to be the cause of his death, and his groan is an aural foreshadowing of those to come,

---

142 The poet announces the inevitability of Patroclus's death at several points; see e.g., 11.604 and book 15, where Zeus provides an account of all of the tragic events to come in the last third of the *Iliad* (and beyond). The father of gods and men's summary of all the deaths and destruction to come is so pithy and seemingly unfeeling that it almost appears peremptory (15.56–77). On Zeus's utterance, see Schadewaldt 1965, 111 ff; for a summary of the issues the utterance has posed to scholars since Antiquity, see Janko 1992a *ad loc*. Zeus's summary can be roughly outlined as follows: Apollo will rouse Hector to fight; Hector will drive the Achaeans back to the ships; at this point, Achilles will send out Patroclus to fight in his stead. Patroclus will kill Sarpedon, and then Hector will kill him, with the result that Achilles will kill Hector, and thus enable the Greeks to take Troy.

143 The English word "foolish" hardly conveys the loaded semantic richness of the Greek term νήπιος. The poet uses the same νήπιος in reference to Patroclus when he causes his own death by blatantly disregarding Achilles' advice (16.686–7):

> νήπιος· εἰ δὲ ἔπος Πηληϊάδαο φύλαξεν
> ἦ τ' ἂν ὑπέκφυγε κῆρα κακὴν μέλανος θανάτοιο,
>
> Fool: had he only kept the command of the son of Peleus
> He might have escaped the evil spirit of black death.

(Translation here based on Lattimore 1951, with some minor changes.) νήπιος is used again by Hector in the vocative, right after he has dealt Patroclus the final, deadly blow (16.833). On the mental and social disconnection of those who are called νήπιος in the Homeric poems and the often fatal consequences of their lack of foresight, see Edmunds 1990, 60 ff. On νήπιος and other evaluative and affective words explicitly formulating the poet's judgment of a character's actions, see De Jong 1987, 136–145. Zyroff 1971 discusses the use of terms foreshadowing misfortune in conjunction with apostrophes in the section of her dissertation on "apostrophes to characters" (Zyroff 1971, 125 ff.).

144 This is Lattimore's translation of μέγα νήπιος.

which will echo his, though he will no longer be the speaker moaning, but the one bemoaned.

Therein lies a significant difference between Patroclus's death and those of both Sarpedon and Hector. The Lycian and the Trojan heroes' deaths are anticipated, foreshadowed, and dreaded by those to whom they are most dear. Their *philoi* witness the dangers that they face and make desperate attempts to delay their deaths. Zeus, as we have seen, contemplates carrying Sarpedon off to safety rather than letting Patroclus drive his spear into his son's chest, until Hera dryly reminds him that fate must run its course. Andromache in book 6 and Hecuba and Priam in book 22 beg Hector not to leave the walls of Troy and face Achilles on the plain where he is vulnerable, seeking to delay a death that means their own downfall. Their cries and prayers are nothing short of proleptic laments.[145]

Far from singing a proleptic lament for Patroclus, Achilles readily sends his friend into the fray in his stead, prompted by Patroclus's request.[146] He even does so with words of encouragement in light of the dire situation faced by the Achaeans:

ὄρσεο διογενὲς Πατρόκλεες ἱπποκέλευθε·
λεύσσω δὴ παρὰ νηυσὶ πυρὸς δηΐοιο ἰωήν
(16.126–7)

"Hurry, Zeus-born, horseman Patroclus!
I see fire by the ships!"[147]

Achilles' lack of apprehension regarding Patroclus's fate is the beginning of a long stretch of ignorance on the hero's part, which the poet extends for as long as possible as a source of great dramatic tension and pathos.[148] His crucial blindness starts with the exchange between the two friends at the beginning of book 16 discussed above, when, in response to his friend's tearful plea, he grants that Patroclus should lead the Myrmidons into battle in his place. His ignorance lasts until the beginning of book 18 – long enough not only for Patroclus to be killed, but for Hector to despoil Patroclus of his (Achilles') armor after a savage fight over his corpse causes many deaths on both the Greek and Trojan sides.

---

145 On these laments and their poetic function, see Dué 2006.
146 I agree that Achilles' consent to allow Patroclus to fight in his stead is motivated by *philôtês* (friendship) rather than anger (*mênis*); see Muellner 1996, ch. 5.
147 Note that Achilles is watching (λεύσσω) the Greek ships from afar from a spectator's vantage point. I discuss Achilles' status as spectator of the Achaeans' martial distress more at length below, p. 81ff.
148 Patroclus remains equally unaware that death is upon him until the end, in contrast to Sarpedon and Hector, who know when their deaths are imminent; see below, p. 64ff.

Just as βαρὺ στενάχων does in the examples above, the two other apostrophes to Patroclus that we find within speech formulas also introduce an emotional quality in the line where they occur (and in the speech that the formula introduces). This becomes apparent if we pay attention to the broader context and to the participles that form the core of the speech formulas themselves. The first of the two other formulas occurs when Patroclus, in an attempt to kill Hector, shatters the skull of Hector's driver instead: Priam's bastard son Cebriones. The son of Menoetius speaks tauntingly over the dead man's body, mocking the way he fell from his chariot "like a diver" (16.744–50). The derisive tone of Patroclus's jeer is clear from the introductory formula: τὸν δ' ἐπικερτομέων προσέφης Πατρόκλεες ἱππεῦ ("And you spoke in bitter mockery over him, horseman Patroclus," 16.744).

The second speech formula that includes an apostrophe occurs in a situation that is the reverse of the one above: Patroclus is now the dying warrior, over whom an enemy victoriously takes his stand and prepares to despoil him of his armor. That redoubtable enemy is none other than Hector, the greatest of all Trojan warriors, who has just fatally wounded Achilles' dearest friend. Despite the circumstances, Patroclus taunts the Trojan prince by diminishing the role he has just played in causing his death (Hector, he says, simply "finished him off"[149]) and by predicting Hector's own imminent end at the hands of Achilles.[150] This speech formula, τὸν δ' ὀλιγοδρανέων προσέφης Πατρόκλεες ἱππεῦ ("And now, dying, you answered him, O horseman Patroclus," 16.843), signals Patroclus's physical feebleness (ὀλιγοδρανέω means, literally, "to be able to do little") as he utters a final jibe. But the jibe itself reveals the degree to which Patroclus, in his own eyes, has been equivalent to and a substitute for Achilles ever since he donned his armor, including in his perception of his own might: had not Zeus and Apollo intervened, he boasts, he could have killed twenty Hectors.[151]

The taunts in both of the above scenes, in which speech formulas occur with apostrophes within them, spotlight the growing degree to which Patroclus sees himself as another Achilles. The presence of the sympathetic apostrophe within

---

149 16.850: σὺ δέ με τρίτος ἐξεναρίζεις. For more on the derogatory nature of this comment, see e.g., Lowenstam 1981, 122–3 and Allan 2005b.
150 After Patroclus breathes his last, Hector in turn utters defiant words (16.859–61) over his dead body, which show him to be as fatally dismissive of Patroclus's warning as Patroclus was of Achilles' indirect warnings. Achilles, in turn, will be equally dismissive (albeit knowingly and deliberately) in his own ultimate confrontation with Apollo, in an encounter that is told outside of the *Iliad*.
151 16.843–50.

the introductory words to these taunts, meanwhile, provides a haunting reminder to the audience of Patroclus's actual vulnerability and of his ultimate helplessness to come in the face of death. The apostrophes function like an ominous musical leitmotiv, a regular irruption of the poet's voice into the universe of his character, through which he points up the paradox inherent to Patroclus's every feat on the battlefield: that each new Trojan death he inflicts brings him closer to his own. It is no coincidence that the very last apostrophe that the poet addresses to the hero (the one that accompanies the last of the three speech formulas I have just examined) occurs just as Patroclus is about to utter his final words to Hector before dying (16.843, quoted above). His minutes are counted; immediately after his speech, his *psychê* departs from his body and bemoans his lost youth (16.855–7). When Hector responds to Patroclus with equal defiance, retorting to Patroclus's threat that Achilles will kill him that he (Hector) might well be able to face Achilles down, Patroclus is already dead. The next time Patroclus is called out by name, the speaker is Achilles; the context is one of mourning and lament.

Apostrophes and turning points: danger or death

The poet's apostrophes to Patroclus as he gloriously slays scores of Trojans clearly point to the paradoxical connection between his present glory and his forthcoming doom. This is perhaps most obvious at the height of his *aristeia*, when he kills Sarpedon. After Zeus sends Sleep and Death to retrieve his son's body and carry it to Lycia,[152] Patroclus goes chasing after the Trojans and Lycians in a mad killing frenzy, which culminates in his attempt to scale the walls of Troy[153] – an egregious violation of the instructions and warning Achilles has given him in their last exchange, before sending him into battle.[154] In an emotional comment directed at the audience, the poet calls Patroclus a "fool" for his transgression and wistfully contemplates what could have been:[155]

> Πάτροκλος δ' ἵπποισι καὶ Αὐτομέδοντι κελεύσας
> Τρῶας καὶ Λυκίους μετεκίαθε, καὶ μέγ' ἀάσθη
> νήπιος· εἰ δὲ ἔπος Πηληϊάδαο φύλαξεν

---

152 16.666–83.
153 16.684ff.
154 See 16.86–90 in particular.
155 On the poet's judgment of a character's actions and his use of the term νήπιος, see above, n. 143.

ἥ τ' ἂν ὑπέκφυγε κῆρα κακὴν μέλανος θανάτοιο.
(16.684–7)

But Patroclus, with a shout to Automedon and his horses,
Went after Trojans and Lycians in a huge blind fury,
Fool: had he only kept the command of the son of Peleus
He might have escaped the evil spirit of black death.

The use of a contrafactual clause injects a certain poignancy into the poet's expression of regret, as he evokes a far happier scenario in which Patroclus might have lived (ἥ τ' ἂν ὑπέκφυγε κῆρα κακὴν μέλανος θανάτοιο) had he only respected Achilles' orders (εἰ δὲ ἔπος Πηληϊάδαο φύλαξεν).[156] Soon thereafter, the poet intensifies the emotional tenor of the passage by shifting to the second person and addressing Patroclus directly, with an apostrophe. In this address, the poet poses a rhetorical question to Patroclus that points up the vanity of his killing spree: he asks him to draw up an account of every Trojan he killed in the same breath as he announces to him that the time of his death has now come, as decreed by the gods – a warning utterance all the more harrowing because only the audience, but not the addressee, can hear it:

Ἔνθα τίνα πρῶτον τίνα δ' ὕστατον ἐξενάριξας
Πατρόκλεις, ὅτε δή σε θεοὶ θάνατον δὲ κάλεσσαν;
(16.692–3)

Then who was it you slaughtered first, and who last,
Patroclus, as the gods called you to your death?

The apostrophe to Patroclus here is particularly noteworthy because it is an "emotive adaptation" of the more typical address to the Muses with which other slaying catalogues open;[157] even as he asks Patroclus (rhetorically) to provide the names of his victims, the poet is calling out by name the one who will

---

[156] The injection of such a note of regret gives the audience a sense of Patroclus's tragic involvement in bringing about his own death (although Zeus's role is also mentioned at 16.688). In a direct echo of the narrator's words, Achilles voices the same regret that Patroclus did not follow his instructions when he has a premonition that his dear friend has died, just before he hears the ghastly news of Patroclus's death from the mouth of Antilochus: σχέτλιος· ἥ τ' ἐκέλευον ἀπωσάμενον δήϊον πῦρ | ἂψ ἐπὶ νῆας ἵμεν, μηδ' Ἕκτορι ἶφι μάχεσθαι ("Unhappy! And yet I told him, once he had beaten the fierce fire off, to come back to the ships, not fight in strength against Hector,"18.13–4).
[157] Noted by Janko 1992a, ad loc.

prove to be the ultimate victim of his own killing spree when the episode comes to a close.[158]

The majority of apostrophes addressed to Patroclus in the *Iliad* occur in scenes in which the hero is explicitly threatened by death. If we compare these apostrophes-when-death-approaches with those addressed to Menelaus at other points in the poem, we can better understand their presence, function, and increasing frequency at the time of Patroclus's death at the end of book 16.

In book 4, Menelaus is wounded by Pandarus's arrow (4.134–40). The narrative plays up the dramatic potential of the situation to its fullest. The spectacular image of the red blood covering Menelaus's white thighs is conveyed in vivid terms through an extended simile comparing the blood to the scarlet that women use to stain horses' cheek pieces (4.141–7). The simile concludes with an apostrophe:

τοῖοί τοι Μενέλαε μιάνθην αἵματι μηροὶ
εὐφυέες κνῆμαί τε ἰδὲ σφυρὰ κάλ' ὑπένερθε.
(4.146–7)

So, Menelaus, your shapely thighs were stained with the color
Of blood, and your legs also and the ankles beneath them.

The presence of an apostrophe makes clear that the situation (and the vulnerability of the character in that situation) is urgent and arouses the poet's sympathy to such a degree that he crosses over from his extradiegetic position into the world of his character, thus abolishing the boundary that normally separates them. This intrusion heightens the audience's sense that there is a potential threat to the Atreid's life. The frightful nature of the circumstances is also strongly conveyed through the concurrent use of an internal audience: Agamemnon, who responds to the sight with great alarm. He panics and launches into a proleptic lament, believing his brother's death to be imminent.[159] Menelaus himself is also initially frightened, not by the wound itself so much as by the sight of his brother's reaction to it, though he soon realizes that the arrow did not hit a fatal spot.[160]

---

[158] Frontisi-Ducroux 1986, 21 stresses narratorial apostrophes' formal similarity to invocations to the Muses; see also De Martino 1977, cited above, n. XX.
[159] For Agamemnon's frightened reaction, see 4.148–82.
[160] At 4.150 and 4.183–7 respectively.

The two brothers' distress marks the scene as one of acute crisis.[161] The poet, however, counterbalances this impression with the information strategically inserted between the time Pandarus's arrow leaves his bow and the point at which it reaches Menelaus's flesh:

> Οὐδὲ σέθεν Μενέλαε θεοὶ μάκαρες λελάθοντο
> ἀθάνατοι, πρώτη δὲ Διὸς θυγάτηρ ἀγελείη,
> ἥ τοι πρόσθε στᾶσα βέλος ἐχεπευκὲς ἄμυνεν.
> (4.127–9)
>
> Still the blessed gods immortal did not forget you, Menelaus,
> And first among them Zeus's daughter, the spoiler,
> Who standing in front of you fended aside the tearing arrow.

While the apostrophe within this line (οὐδὲ σέθεν Μενέλαε) signals the poet's concern and points up the fact that the plot is at a crucial juncture, the tension is immediately alleviated by the mention of the gods' shared concern for the hero and the account of Athena's intervention.[162] As we have seen earlier, what we have here is a familiar pattern: seeing the threat facing a beloved mortal, a caring divinity intervenes and saves the day. Zeus's daughter steps in and redirects the arrow, which then hits Menelaus in a less exposed part of his body, where he is protected from a fatal wound by his belt.

If apostrophes are a mark of special concern on the part of the poet, and mark a moment of heightened danger for important heroes, then what are we to make of an apostrophe addressed to an entirely secondary hero, such as Melanippus? This particular apostrophe has left commentators quite perplexed: why is such a distinction granted to an otherwise unimportant hero? The case is deserving of attention, because it makes for an enlightening comparison to keep in mind when we turn to the apostrophes addressed to Patroclus at the time of his death. The apostrophe to Melanippus occurs when he is already dead, killed by Antilochus, but another menace still looms over the hero: that of being despoiled of his armor.[163] The diction strengthens our sense of the threat as the poet describes Antilochus leaping onto Melanippus's corpse "like a dog after a wounded fawn" (Ἀντίλοχος δ' ἐπόρουσε κύων ὥς, ὅς τ' ἐπὶ νεβρῷ | βλημένῳ ἀΐξῃ, 15.579–

---

161 The tradition, of course, precludes the crisis from fully playing out: the death of Menelaus would entail (as Agamemnon repeatedly emphasizes when he begins his proleptic lament [4.148–82]) the *nostos* of all the Greek warriors and hence bring an end to the narrative of the *Iliad*.
162 On the poet's reasons for focusing our attention on both Menelaus and Athena at this decisive point, see Parry 1972, 15.
163 See 15.579–84.

80). This simile plays up Melanippus's vulnerability, as does the apostrophe which immediately follows it:[164]

ὣς ἐπὶ σοὶ Μελάνιππε θόρ' Ἀντίλοχος μενεχάρμης
τεύχεα συλήσων· ἀλλ' οὐ λάθεν Ἕκτορα δῖον,
ὅς ῥά οἱ ἀντίος ἦλθε θέων ἀνὰ δηϊοτῆτα.
(15.582–4)

So Antilochus stubborn in battle sprang, Melanippus,
At you, to strip your armor, but did not escape brilliant Hector's
Notice, who came on the run through the fighting against him.

Just as we observed in the scenes involving a wounded Menelaus, the apostrophe here marks the poet's sympathy for Melanippus, and is prompted by a crisis, a moment of vulnerability for the hero thus addressed by name.[165] It is as though the poet were uttering a warning that remains unheard by its intended addressee. The poet thus introduces a formal signal to the audience (the only ones to actually be able to perceive the signal) that the narrative finds itself at a turning point, whose crucial nature he highlights by breaking down the barriers between his universe and the universe of his characters for a moment and calling out the threatened character's name. A dire event may follow for whichever hero the poet thus addresses. Here, as in the case of Menelaus's wounding, the situation is resolved and the tension released, this time through the intervention not of a god but of a *philos*, one who is like a brother to Melanippus:[166] the bulwark of Troy, Hector. Just as Athena did not forget to protect her beloved Menelaus (οὐδὲ λελάθοντο, 4.127), Melanippus does not escape Hector's notice (ἀλλ' οὐ λάθεν Ἕκτορα δῖον). Just as Athena did when Pandarus's arrow was headed for Menelaus, Hector steps in *in extremis* and prevents the dark scenario foreshadowed by the simile and suggested by the apostrophe from playing out. Therein, I believe, lies the explanation for the presence of this apostrophe to an otherwise unimportant hero: its point, in underlining the threat at hand, is

---

164 The role of similes in foreshadowing the outcome of a battle scene has been thoroughly examined; see e.g., Moulton 1977, esp. 24–6 and 74–5, and Lonsdale 1990. Létoublon 2005, 4 n. 14, provides additional bibliography; also Scott 2009. On Homeric similes in general as a *locus* for poetic competition, see Ready 2011.
165 Zyroff 1971, 37–9, discusses other scholars' assessments of the different but comparable use of the poet's apostrophes to the Muses as a way of heralding a new development or signaling a major change in the plot. Cf. Armstrong 1958, 345, who notes how the poet "signals the crisis" that leads Patroclus to don Achilles' armor with an invocation to the Muses (16.112–3).
166 See 15.551 regarding Melanippus's being treated "like a son" by Priam.

to highlight the role of savior played by Hector at the close of the scene, as he rescues his *philos*'s corpse from being despoiled by the Greeks.

It can be said, then, that apostrophes, by expressing the narrator's sympathy, mark a potential watershed moment in the narrative. This is perhaps never so clear as when Menelaus volunteers to fight Hector one-on-one. Within the space of just one line, the poet calls out Menelaus's name directly in the vocative and then states that such a confrontation would mean certain death for him. Both the apostrophe and the accompanying statement contribute to foregrounding the threat at hand:[167]

> ἔνθά κέ τοι Μενέλαε φάνη βιότοιο τελευτὴ
> Ἕκτορος ἐν παλάμῃσιν, ἐπεὶ πολὺ φέρτερος ἦεν
> (7.104–5)
>
> And there, O Menelaus, would have shown forth the end of your life
> Under the hands of Hector, since he was far stronger than you were.

It remains, however, merely a hypothetical threat; the whole address to Menelaus is part of a "pivotal contrafactual:" "And there, O Menelaus, *would have* shown forth the end of your life."[168] This "would have" *apodosis*, because it precedes the "if ... not" *protasis* in which the ruinous outcome is prevented by Menelaus's brother, Agamemnon (7.106–8), stresses the dire nature of the *possible* outcome of the duel (Menelaus's death), encouraging us to "momentarily ... expect or fear the death of [this] major figure."[169] Agamemnon's role is thus magnified:

> εἰ μὴ ἀναΐξαντες ἕλον βασιλῆες Ἀχαιῶν,
> αὐτός τ' Ἀτρεΐδης εὐρὺ κρείων Ἀγαμέμνων
> δεξιτερῆς ἕλε χειρὸς ἔπος τ' ἔφατ' ἔκ τ' ὀνόμαζεν·
> (7.106–9)
>
> ...had not the kings of the Achaeans leapt up and caught you,
> and the son of Atreus himself, powerful Agamemnon,
> caught you by the right hand, and called you by name, and spoke to you.

---

[167] The link between apostrophes and death has been made by e.g., Henry 1905, 9, who formulates the interesting hypothesis that there is a connection between apostrophes to the dying in poetry and the ritual practice of apostrophizing the dead. See below, n. 237.

[168] By contrast, when he voiced the apostrophe to Patroclus discussed above, the poet also included a mention of the hero's imminent death at 16.692–3 – and no contrafactual. On "if ... not" clauses in the *Iliad*, see De Jong 1987, 68–81, and Lang 1989; on their role in leading the audience down a path that encourages them to envisage the death of a major heroic figure forbidden by the tradition, see Louden 1993, with bibliography (nn. 1–3 especially).

[169] Louden 1993, 184.

As in the previous case we have observed (where Hector intercedes to protect Melanippus's body from despoilment), the dramatic potential of the threat is pointed up by the apostrophe (and, in this instance, the contrafactual it is a part of, which evokes a dire potential outcome) before a protective figure steps in to protect his *philos*. That protective figure's role is aggrandized by the same token. The intervention that prevents Menelaus's death is primarily a verbal one (7.106–19): Agamemnon issues a sharp warning to his brother, in which he marvels at his *aphrosunê* for thinking he might be a match for one whom even Achilles shudders to face, and then leads Menelaus away from certain death (7.113–4).[170] Like Agamemnon's words to Menelaus, the apostrophe is also a warning, but it is one that its addressee cannot hear: it creates a sense of foreboding for the only ones who can hear it — the audience. Menelaus's certain death (were he to actually try to confront Hector) is averted by an intradiegetic character (in this case, Agamemnon), who calls out his name and voices a warning. Because it is voiced within the narrative proper, it can be heard and heeded by the one who is threatened.

The voice of the speaker of narratorial apostrophes, on the other hand, crosses the boundaries between the world of diegesis and that of the characters through metalepsis, but only does so for the audience's benefit; that is, the poet does not actually reach his character's ears; he remains confined to the extradiegetic world of the storyteller. It takes Agamemnon's speech, which echoes the warning that was present but unrealized in the narratorial apostrophe to Menelaus, to actualize that warning, by voicing it within the narrative. In this respect, it bears noting that, when he addresses Menelaus in the vocative, Agamemnon does so at the very same place in the hexameter as the poet did when he apostrophized Menelaus:

> ἀφραίνεις Μενέλαε διοτρεφές, οὐδέ τί σε χρὴ
> ταύτης ἀφροσύνης· ἀνὰ δὲ σχέο κηδόμενός περ,
> μηδ' ἔθελ' ἐξ ἔριδος σεῦ ἀμείνονι φωτὶ μάχεσθαι.[171]
> (7.109–11)

> Menelaus, beloved of God, you are mad; you have no need
> to take leave of your senses thus. Hold fast, though it hurts you,
> nor long in your pride to fight with a man who is better than you are.

---

[170] This is an inverse variation on type-scenes in which gods intervene to encourage one or the other camp *not* to flee; see Fenik 1968, 212.
[171] Compare 7.104: ἔνθά κέ τοι Μενέλαε and 7.109: ἀφραίνεις Μενέλαε.

There are two other scenes that follow a sequence nearly identical to the one in which Agamemnon intervenes just in time to save his brother Menelaus from harm by issuing a sharp warning. In both of the scenes in question, specific formulas serve as verbal markers that death threatens a hero. They appear shortly before a character – a divine one, this time — intercedes and enables the threatened hero to avoid death, by voicing a warning, just as Agamemnon does. These verbal markers are not forms of metalepsis, as apostrophes are, but they function in a similar manner. The scenes in which these formulas occur are of interest to me, therefore, because they provide another pattern which the scene of Patroclus's death follows, but from which it also diverges, in a noteworthy and significant manner. The two scenes occur in books 5 and 16 respectively; the first involves Diomedes, and the second Patroclus.

When Diomedes (in book 5) and Patroclus (in book 16) reach the decisive points at which each has carried his *aristeia* to its limits, that watershed moment is, in both cases, marked by the presence of a traditional "three + one crescendo," a confrontation in four parts which by its very presence points up the seriousness of the threat at hand: it occurs at the moment when heroes reach the pinnacle of their heroic achievements, and come close to death.[172] Death is a distinctly possible outcome of such three + one crescendo confrontations. That the juncture at which both heroes reach the height of their respective *aristeiai* is a critical one in this respect is made clear from the presence of the epithet δαίμονι ἶσος. This particular epithet, by likening them to a god, marks the fact that they have reached the climax of their antagonistic relationship to the god Apollo.[173] After successfully wounding Aphrodite and Ares, the god of war himself, Diomedes confronts the god Apollo:

τρὶς μὲν ἔπειτ' ἐπόρουσε κατακτάμεναι μενεαίνων,
τρὶς δέ οἱ ἐστυφέλιξε φαεινὴν ἀσπίδ' Ἀπόλλων·
ἀλλ' ὅτε δὴ τὸ τέταρτον ἐπέσσυτο δαίμονι ἶσος,
δεινὰ δ' ὁμοκλήσας προσέφη ἑκάεργος Ἀπόλλων·
(5.436–9)

Three times, furious to cut him down, he drove forward,
And three times Apollo battered aside the bright shield,

---

172 I am borrowing the "three + one" designation from Parry 1972, 14. Janko 1992b, 399, provides other examples of what I will call the "triple attempt scenes," in which the fourth attempt, if it is made, results in death for the hero.
173 See Nagy 1979, 142–4: "The deployment of this epithet <δαίμονι ἶσος> coincides with the climax of ritual antagonism between the god and the hero." Only Diomedes, Patroclus, and Achilles receive this epithet, each at a crucial point.

But when on the fourth attempt, like a god, he charged,
Apollo who strikes from afar cried out to him in the voice of terror.

When the triple attempt scene occurs in the case of Patroclus, the latter has already gone far beyond the limits Achilles made clear he should not cross in his instructions, and is reaching the highest point of glory he will ever reach in battle:[174]

τρὶς μὲν ἐπ' ἀγκῶνος βῆ τείχεος ὑψηλοῖο
Πάτροκλος, τρὶς δ' αὐτὸν ἀπεστυφέλιξεν Ἀπόλλων
χείρεσσ' ἀθανάτῃσι φαεινὴν ἀσπίδα νύσσων.
ἀλλ' ὅτε δὴ τὸ τέταρτον ἐπέσσυτο δαίμονι ἶσος,
δεινὰ δ' ὁμοκλήσας ἔπεα πτερόεντα προσηύδα·
(16.702–6)

Three times Patroclus tried to mount the angle of the towering
Wall, and three times Phoebus Apollo battered him backward
With the immortal hands beating back the bright shield.
But when on the fourth attempt, like a god, he charged,
[Apollo] called out to him, aloud, speaking winged words in the face of danger.

Just as Menelaus was by Agamemnon, Diomedes and Patroclus are deterred from pursuing a deadly confrontation with a far greater opponent than they, and their deaths are averted. In an interesting variation on the scenario that applied to Menelaus, the warning that preserves them from death is issued not by a *philos*, but by the lethal opponent himself: Apollo. His stern warnings to both Diomedes and Patroclus present the same elements as Agamemnon's speech to Menelaus, and fulfill the same function: they are an address to the hero in the vocative (Τυδεΐδη, διογενὲς Πατρόκλεες), followed by a reminder of how inferior they are to their stronger opponent and hence inept to the feat that they are attempting.[175] Both Diomedes and Patroclus take heed of Apollo's warning and retreat.[176] They live — in Patroclus's case, however, only for a short while longer.

---

[174] Patroclus has already accomplished practically all of Achilles' objectives from the time he kills his very first man in battle, Pyraichmes (16.287); from that point on, he has been defying Achilles' instructions by going beyond the limits Peleus's son had clearly told him not to cross.
[175] Di Benedetto 1994, 278 underlines the parallels and divergences between the two triple attempt scenes here, and the subsequent one in which Patroclus meets his doom. Di B. takes notice of the pathetic effect created by the foreshadowing of Patroclus's death already in the first triple attempt scene, an effect created by the presence of the apostrophe and the unheard warning that accompanies it.
[176] Compare 5.440-2 (both translations below are Lombardo 1997):

The downfall of Patroclus

Shortly after his first confrontation with Apollo in book 16, Patroclus faces the god again. This second confrontation also follows the triple attempt scene structure. On Patroclus's fourth attempt, we again find the epithet comparing him to a god, δαίμονι ἶσος:

> τρὶς μὲν ἔπειτ' ἐπόρουσε θοῷ ἀτάλαντος Ἄρηϊ
> σμερδαλέα ἰάχων, τρὶς δ' ἐννέα φῶτας ἔπεφνεν.
> ἀλλ' ὅτε δὴ τὸ τέταρτον ἐπέσσυτο δαίμονι ἶσος,
> ἔνθ' ἄρα τοι Πάτροκλε φάνη βιότοιο τελευτή·
> (16.784–6)
>
> Three times he charged in with the force of the running war god,
> Screaming with a terrible cry, and three times he cut down nine men.
> But when on the fourth attempt, like a god, he charged,
> There, Patroclus, the end of your life was shown forth.

This four-part sequence has a different outcome from the preceding one. As Achilles predicted, Patroclus's continued attacks on the Trojans following Apollo's warning have roused the god's anger, and he must pay the price for his stubborn persistence.[177] The audience is led to suspect as much from the beginning of the triple attempt scene, where another epithet, θοῷ ἀτάλαντος Ἄρηϊ (16.784), is

---

> φράζεο Τυδεΐδη καὶ χάζεο, μηδὲ θεοῖσιν
> ἶσ' ἔθελε φρονέειν, ἐπεὶ οὔ ποτε φῦλον ὁμοῖον
> ἀθανάτων τε θεῶν χαμαὶ ἐρχομένων τ' ἀνθρώπων
>
> "Think it over, son of Tydeus, and get back.
> Don't set your sights on the gods. Gods are
> To humans what humans are to crawling bugs."

and 16.707–9:

> χάζεο διογενὲς Πατρόκλεες· οὔ νύ τοι αἶσα
> σῷ ὑπὸ δουρὶ πόλιν πέρθαι Τρώων ἀγερώχων,
> οὐδ' ὑπ' Ἀχιλλῆος, ὅς περ σέο πολλὸν ἀμείνων.
>
> Get back, Patroclus, back where you belong.
> Troy is fated to fall, but not to you,
> Nor even to Achilles, a better man by far."

[177] See Achilles' warning at 16.87–96. According to the tradition (beyond the confines of the *Iliad* proper), Achilles will do the same: he will not back down when faced with Apollo in his attempt to take Troy single-handedly, ignoring the very advice he gives Patroclus at 16.86–100. See Whitman 1958, 201, and Lowenstam 1981, 115–8.

introduced, marking Patroclus for death by likening him to Ares.[178] In this three + one sequence, the fourth attempt is not followed by a warning; we do not hear a word from Apollo, nor from any of Patroclus's fellow Achaeans.[179] Instead, Patroclus is killed. Apollo initiates his slow and implacable demise by striking him from behind and bewildering him, and the Trojans do not fail to seize their opportunity.

I turn now to the moment of Patroclus's downfall, and to the concentration of apostrophes to Patroclus voiced by the poet throughout that crucial scene. In my analysis of the hero's downfall, I seek to shed light on the question of why these apostrophes occur within that scene, and with such frequency. These apostrophes introduce a particular voice and presence into the scene; that voice, unheard and unheeded, contributes to articulating several crucial themes underlying the epic poem as a whole. This voice plays a critical role within a significant scene that gives the audience a "shadow play" of the most important death of all, that of the most formidable of Iliadic heroes, which the audience is never given to see directly within the poem as we have it.[180]

Negativity and absence

Thus far, I have examined the deaths of Hector and Sarpedon, and particularly the important role played by the witnesses looking on at the time of their deaths (whether these observers have the ability to intervene or not). There are significant parallels and variations between these major heroic woundings and deaths, and that of Patroclus. The parallels, but above all the divergences, reveal what demarcates the portrayal of the death of Achilles' *alter ego* (and the role of apostrophes within it) as unique within the poem, thematically, poetically, and structurally speaking.

Two immediate observations bear mentioning from the start. First, it is striking to note that, in contrast to other scenes of major heroes' deaths, there is no

---

[178] On Patroclus as the *therapôn* of Ares himself at this particular point, see Nagy 1979, 292–5; see also Collins 1998, ch. 1.
[179] At 20.447 ff we find another triple attempt scene that is a remarkable variation on the two examined above. Achilles is also called δαίμονι ἶσος as he faces Hector and simultaneously challenges Apollo, but on his fourth attempt, instead of being the *addressee* of words of warning issued by the god, it is *Achilles* who warns Hector that his death is imminent. As the audience knows and as Thetis herself reminds Achilles, Hector's death means his own is to come (18.95–6).
[180] The expression is Whitman's; see below, pp. 88–92.

(obvious) immediate witness to Patroclus's demise. Second, despite or perhaps *because* of the fact that there is no immediate observer looking on, speaking to, or interceding for Patroclus as he wages his final battle, we (as the audience) are all the more prone to notice the *presence* of a particular voice, addressing the hero and calling him by his name, all throughout his downfall. In the ambivalence of that voice lies the key to the entire scene. Bringing to the fore its expressive power is, in turn, crucial to our understanding of the scene's essential relevance to the poem in its entirety.

We have seen how each of the apostrophes examined above occurs at a critical point, and fulfills a similar function: to point up the watershed moment when a given hero faces a potentially deadly threat. The poet, by breaking down the boundaries between his world (that of the narrator) and the world of the events he is narrating, creates a sense of emotional and physical proximity to a given hero, and the transgressive nature of his voice in such moments calls attention to the seriousness of the threat posed to the hero, exalting the audience's sense of danger and momentarily heightening the dramatic effect of the scene. I noted how these marked instances of narratorial metalepsis are often followed by an intervention (or an attempt at one) in word or deed on the part of a god or hero who may or may not be in a position to prevent the grim event under way, but who (at the very least) wishes or attempts to. The recurrence of the pattern (apostrophe signaling danger, followed by another character's intercession) leads to a double set of related expectations within the audience. On hearing the poet apostrophize a hero and violate the hierarchy of narrative levels, we sense that danger looms for the hero in question, and assume that an intervention (even merely an attempted one) is likely to follow.

Such is the case with Patroclus as he continues to charge into the Trojan ranks and confronts Apollo a second time (despite the harsh warning issued by the god in their first encounter). The poet has called out to him earlier in the book, and he calls out to him once more. We might well expect that, as with other heroes, *someone* is going to intervene — but the expected intervention does not take place. Instead, the poet continues to break into the world of his character repeatedly, as one apostrophe follows shortly after another, the last two separated by only a few lines as the situation gets direr (16.786 and 16.812). The frequency with which these apostrophes recur is unparalleled elsewhere in the poem. It is as though the increasing urgency of the situation prompted the poet to persistently enter into the world of his character and call out to the hero who is unwittingly facing his doom. After all, no one else is doing so.

Before I look closely at the final two apostrophes to Patroclus which occur at the time of his death proper (the aforementioned, which occur at 16.786 and

16.812), I want to consider closely two elements within the scene that create a particular sort of spatial, sonic, and social void around the dying hero. These elements of negativity and absence are poetically necessary: they make room for the presence of a particular voice and gaze within the scene, which we might not otherwise perceive.

Patroclus is killed slowly and inexorably. His death is narrated at a pace that makes it seem as though we were watching it happen in slow motion.[181] One of the most conspicuous negative elements of the scene is one that I briefly mentioned above: the exclusion from the narrative of any fellow Greek warrior or sympathetic god watching while Patroclus wages his last battle. Despite the length of the scene and the many opportunities it provides for the poet to introduce the figure of a caring witness within the narrative, we find absolutely no mention of anyone looking on while Patroclus is violently taken down by a god and two Trojans. No potentially sympathetic presence, human or divine, is mentioned on the Greek side; there are only Trojan antagonists: Apollo, Euphorbus, and Hector. The absence of any of the seeing-and-pitying figures that might be in a position to intervene is blatant. Instead of an individual *philos* seeing-and-pitying, there is only an anonymous group of Achaeans, a "group of companions" who are introduced in the narrative only once Patroclus has been violently struck by Apollo and stabbed with Euphorbus's spear: "He tried to shun death and shrink back into the swarm of his own companions" (ἂψ ἑτάρων εἰς ἔθνος ἐχάζετο κῆρ' ἀλεείνων, 16.817). This formulaic hexameter line is noteworthy: sometimes, the warrior who turns back toward his companions does so just in time;[182] sometimes, it is too late.[183] In the case of Patroclus, the occurrence of the formula maintains the suspense for the audience: he is retiring, trying to avoid death. He may still be saved, but death is also not to be excluded.[184]

Not a single one of the companions toward whom Patroclus turns in desperation does anything to aid him; the narrative makes no mention of anyone at-

---

181 On the "slow-motion technique" used by the poet in this scene, see Janko 1992a, 411.
182 For instance, Paris "turns back" when Menelaus comes at him (3.32), as does Helenus when he is wounded by Menelaus (13.596), or Hector when he is struck and nearly killed by the massive slab of stone that Ajax rams into his chest (14.408ff.).
183 Such is the case for Adamas and later Harpalion, struck by Meriones' spear at 13.566ff. and 13.648ff. respectively.
184 Janko notes the "agonizing suspense" of Patroclus's death scene, throughout which "we hold our breath" (Janko 1992a, *ad* 698–711). Di Benedetto 1994 ch. 4 also stresses the ways in which the Homeric poet maintains a sense of ever increasing suspense in his portrayal of Patroclus's death, despite the fact that the audience has known all along that the hero was doomed.

tempting (or even contemplating) to do so. Nor is there any reference made to their emotional response at this point. There is no time. The scene progresses slowly yet with an unstoppable implacability. It seems that all the Achaeans can do is look on while Patroclus, dazed and gravely wounded, begins to stagger back toward them. Meanwhile, Hector is looking on as well. The Trojan hero's name is emphatically positioned at the very start of the line immediately following the mention of Patroclus's stunned, grieving companions (16.818). The bulwark of Troy seizes his chance immediately, making his way through the ranks and ramming his spearhead into the pit of Patroclus's stomach (16.818–21). Only then does the poet revert back to the nameless horde of Greeks. There is still no mention of any action on their part, just a brief evocation of their pained reaction: they are deeply "aggrieved in their hearts" when Patroclus's body hits the ground with a thud (δούπησεν δὲ πεσών, μέγα δ' ἤκαχε λαὸν Ἀχαιῶν, 16.822).

The omission of any mention of another Greek hero from the account of Patroclus's death heightens our impression of his utter isolation from the rest of the Achaeans throughout his demise. No one appears to be able to come to his immediate aid. At any rate, no mention is made of any such attempt. It is only once he is already dead that the poet mentions Menelaus, pushing through several ranks of warriors to reach Patroclus's lifeless body (17.3), and only then that Ajax joins Menelaus as the two of them begin a desperate fight to protect Patroclus's corpse and try to prevent Achilles' armor from becoming Trojan trophies – in vain. Presumably, the sense of isolation created by the narrative is somewhat artificial: that there should not be a single fellow Greek warrior standing by, watching and reacting to the scene – a scene of such tremendous import to the rest of the *Iliad* and to its main hero, Achilles — seems unlikely. It is a deliberate (and therefore significant) exclusion at this crucial juncture. Surely Patroclus is within eyesight or earshot of several major Greek warriors (Menelaus being one of them).[185] It is certain that the gods can see him; and yet there is not a single mention of a god looking on, much less taking pity on or intervening to protect Patroclus.[186] The only god that is mentioned is Apollo, but his presence

---

[185] I earlier noted how Sarpedon calls out to Glaucus for aid in protecting his corpse after his death, to no avail.

[186] The gods' constant gaze and protection are such a given that they are actually expected by the heroes themselves — to such a degree, in fact, that their absence is a cause of indignation for some characters. At 21.231, the river Scamander reproaches Apollo for not following Zeus's commandments and "standing by and protecting" the Trojans. Later, Achilles addresses a reproach to Zeus when he asks how it is that not a single god is protecting him, pitiful though he is, as the river Scamander chases him and attempts to drown him in its swirling waters (21.273–83).

is veiled and goes unnoticed by Patroclus; and Apollo's presence is everything but protective.

Another negative element of the scene is the absence of references to any emotion, perception, or thought on the part of its central character (though we can imagine his terror). The focalization remains consistently external to the scene's victim. At no point during Patroclus's death is there any sort of embedded focalization that would enable the audience to hear Patroclus's thoughts, to feel his fear directly, or to catch some glimpse of his interior world in any way.[187] He is never the focalizer of the scene, and his inner world remains opaque to us.[188] The only explicit mention of any emotion is the emotion of an unexpected spectator to Patroclus's death when he is no more: his life breath flutters out of his body and briefly hovers over it, wailing in grief.[189]

The contrast with Hector's death scene in this regard is striking. When the Trojan hero faces Achilles in the final showdown of book 22, Hector is repeatedly the focalizer of the scene. The audience often sees what he sees and hears his internal thoughts, as they are delivered out loud, in direct speech, when the bulwark of Troy voices his hesitations and fears at what he knows deep down is going to be his last fight, as death looms.[190] The contrast between the two scenes is particularly pointed up by the fact that they share common phraseology. At the pivotal moment when Hector realizes that his brother Deiphobus is not with him

---

187 While Patroclus does remain courageously and remarkably defiant in his dying words to Hector, in which he claims victory because of Achilles' impending murder of his Trojan foe (16.843–54), the bT scholia are somewhat bold in stating that "he is not terrified by death, the severity of his pain, or the lack of anyone to help him" (*ad* 843–54, quoted by Janko 1992a). These emotions may not be mentioned, but we have no grounds for assuming that they are not felt.
188 The only information that the narrator gives is that, when Apollo looses Patroclus's breastplate after striking his helmet off his head, his limbs give way, and "utter confusion reigns in his heart" (16.805, τὸν δ' ἄτη φρένας εἷλε).
189 Patroclus's ψυχή bewails (γοόωσα) the death of the warrior, both at the time of his death at the hands of Hector (16.855-7) and later on when it visits Achilles in his dreams (23.105 ff.). On the particular function and relevance of dreams in Homeric poetry (as well as in Greek culture more broadly), see Guidorizzi 2013. The exact same phraseology that is used to describe Patroclus's grieving ψυχή (three full hexameters, including the key participle, γοόωσα) occurs once more after the death of Hector. The Trojan's death is thus formally tied to Patroclus's, an apt reflection of the extent to which it is also causally tied to it (22.361-3). On this point see Leuzzi 2008.
190 Take for instance his lengthy speech at 22.99–130, when Hector considers various alternatives to facing Achilles head on, such as retreating inside the walls of Troy or coming to an agreement with Achilles and handing Helen back to the Greeks without their having to destroy Troy — all impossible wishful thinking, he realizes.

to aid him in confronting Achilles as he had thought, he knows that he has been tricked by Athena and that he faces certain death (νῦν αὖτέ με μοῖρα κιχάνει, "But now my death is upon me," 22.303). The realization that he is alone is a poignant moment of searing clarity for the hero: he speaks aloud as he recognizes that all is lost but the glory to be gained in facing his certain death bravely (22.297–305). To articulate this horrible lucidity regarding his own imminent death, he uses the phrase ὦ πόποι ἦ μάλα δή με θεοὶ θάνατον δὲ κάλεσσαν, "Alas! There is no mistaking it; I hear the gods calling me to my death" (22.297). Nearly identical phraseology occurs again only one other time in the poem, with minor variants: when the narrator provides the catalogue of the Trojans slain by Patroclus as the Greek hero reaches the height of his *aristeia*. I mentioned the passage earlier, in reference to the fact that it marks the causal and temporal connection between Patroclus's *aristeia* and his impending death:

> Ἔνθα τίνα πρῶτον τίνα δ' ὕστατον ἐξενάριξας
> Πατρόκλεις, ὅτε δή σε θεοὶ θάνατον δὲ κάλεσσαν;
> (16.692–3)

> Then who was it you slaughtered first, who was the last one,
> Patroclus, as the gods called you to your death?

When the gods call him to his death, Hector "hears" them doing so, he says (in his own words); he is aware of the fate to come, and hears it coming, as it were. Patroclus, on the other hand, hears nothing, nor does he say anything about it when his time comes. The only ones who know that the gods are calling him to his death are the audience members, for they hear a knowing voice addressing Patroclus and telling him his fateful time has come, while the hero himself remains oblivious to his imminent doom.[191]

Thus, though the poet allows the audience to watch as though from a close-up vantage point every fatal blow being dealt to Patroclus, he keeps his listeners on the outside of Patroclus's mind and perceptions, never entering into Patroclus's mental world or showing the events from the focalized point of view of the hero. We do not see or hear what Patroclus sees or hears; he is, as it were, blind and deaf for the duration of the scene, unable to perceive that death is close at hand, until the very end. When Apollo strikes him, he does not comprehend the divine aggression to which he is being subjected:

---

[191] Di Benedetto pinpoints the ways in which the Homeric poet marks Patroclus for death and creates in him "un personaggio tutto organizzato nella direzione del patetico" (Di Benedetto 1994, 276 ff.).

> ἤντετο γάρ τοι Φοῖβος ἐνὶ κρατερῇ ὑσμίνῃ
> δεινός· ὃ μὲν τὸν ἰόντα κατὰ κλόνον οὐκ ἐνόησεν,
> ἠέρι γὰρ πολλῇ κεκαλυμμένος ἀντεβόλησε·
> στῆ δ' ὄπιθεν, πλῆξεν δὲ μετάφρενον εὐρέε τ' ὤμω
> χειρὶ καταπρηνεῖ, στρεφεδίνηθεν δέ οἱ ὄσσε.
> (16.788–92)
>
> For Phoebus came against you there in the strong encounter,
> Dangerously, nor did Patroclus see him as he moved through
> The battle, and shrouded in a deep mist came in against him
> And stood behind him, and struck his back and his broad shoulders
> With a flat stroke of the hand so that his eyes spun.

Patroclus does not notice (οὐκ ἐνόησεν) that Apollo is approaching; he cannot see the god who brings him death, for the latter is as imperceptible as he is implacable. He advances toward the hero hidden in a mist (ἠέρι γὰρ πολλῇ κεκαλυμμένος ἀντεβόλησε) and strikes him from behind (στῆ δ' ὄπιθεν) with such overwhelming force that Patroclus's eyes spin (πλῆξεν δὲ μετάφρενον εὐρέε τ' ὤμω | χειρὶ καταπρηνεῖ, στρεφεδίνηθεν δέ οἱ ὄσσε). His blindness and confusion contrast with the poet and audience's shared knowledge that death is near: they can see his doom standing right behind him, in the form of the god Apollo.[192]

The emotional center of the scene and the lens through which it is viewed lie outside of Patroclus. He is being watched and spoken to, but he does not appear to see or hear what is happening to him. The poet creates a void around Patroclus, the better to draw our attention to a voice that calls out to him, uttering his name with some insistence. That voice suggests the virtual presence of an onlooker; it is a crucial poetic tool in conveying presence and absence simultaneously, as we are about to see.

Apostrophes and the poetics of helplessness

Achilles' presence is felt in a very concrete way from the moment Apollo deals the first blow to Patroclus. The poet makes reference to the divine weapons and armor that Achilles gave Patroclus as he sent him into the fray. These weapons were meant to protect his friend, as was the warning Achilles spoke to Patroclus before sending him off (16. 83–100). But the very instruments that were intended to protect the son of Menoetius do no such thing. It is Achilles' armor's

---

[192] Di Benedetto 1994, 276 ff. examines how the Homeric poet creates a pathetic aura that surrounds Patroclus at all times.

inability to protect Patroclus (16.793–804) that the narrator underscores when Apollo strikes the hero on his back: the pieces of armor fall to the ground one after the other, soon to be sullied with grime and gore. The poet specifically stresses how differently the armor had fared in the past and would have now if worn by its proper owner: when Achilles himself was bearing the divinely wrought armor (16.796–9), the gods protected both the weapons and the hero for whom they had been fashioned. Patroclus, by contrast, is increasingly vulnerable and debilitated despite the armor: he is made powerless to retaliate as the invisible force of Apollo knocks off his helmet, shield, baldric, and breastplate, leaving him completely naked and exposed for Euphorbus and the greatest of all Trojan heroes to take his life with the repeated thrusts of their spears. With his growing helplessness, the audience feels the need for an intervention from a fellow warrior or caring god all the more acutely.[193]

That urgent need is further accentuated when, at the time of his death, a voice calls out Patroclus's name – twice, in close succession (16.787 and 16.812). It is not the voice of any human or god within the world of the poem. It is the voice of the poet, who directly apostrophizes Patroclus, with all the vividness and *enargeia* of direct speech.[194] Apollo is making his way toward the hero when the first of the two apostrophes in the scene is voiced, announcing to an unwitting Patroclus that the time of his death has come (ἔνθ' ἄρα τοι Πάτροκλε φάνη βιότοιο τελευτή, "there, Patroclus, the end of your life was shown forth," 16.787). The second apostrophe occurs as the narrator describes Euphorbus's spear wounding Patroclus (ὅς τοι πρῶτος ἐφῆκε βέλος Πατρόκλεες ἱππεῦ, 16.812), just moments before Hector deals him the final, fatal blow (16.805–29). The presence of apostrophes leads the audience to expect an intervention (or at least an attempt at intervention) on the part of a *philos* or god. There is no such thing. The poet calls out to his character with sympathetic apostrophes, but no action or attempt at one follows. The narrator's voice may be abruptly intruding into the diegetic universe of his character, but he cannot take action within that universe, and his character cannot hear him. The calls to Patroclus are voiced to no avail.

---

193 At 16.796, Achilles' bloodied helmet also foreshadows Achilles' own ultimate fate at the hands of Apollo. I return to this below in the final section of this chapter.

194 The *enargeia* of narratorial apostrophes to characters is powerful; it is this very *enargeia* that De Jong believes is the reason for these apostrophes' presence: see De Jong in Grethlein and Rengakos 2009, 94–5. On the vividness (*enargeia*) achieved in Homeric poetry through embedded focalization, which makes the audience "view" the action as though they were spectators rather than mere listeners, see Bakker 2005, chps. 5–9 also cited above, nn. 52 and 127.

The deviation from the pattern of protective interventions following apostrophes is all the more patent as the formula used to address Patroclus when death comes at him (ἔνθ' ἄρα τοι Πάτροκλε φάνη βιότοιο τελευτή, 16.787) is the very same one that occurs when Menelaus is threatened by death at the hands of Hector in book 7 just before he is rescued by Agamemnon — the very same one, that is, except for a small but all-important particle: ἔνθά κέ τοι Μενέλαε φάνη βιότοιο τελευτή, "there, Menelaus, the end of your life *would have* shown forth," 7.104. The only difference between the two hexameters lies in the crucial shift from the particle κέ (7.104) to ἄρα (16.787). The part of the hexameter pertaining to Patroclus (ἔνθ' ἄρα τοι Πάτροκλε) does not have the grammatical marker that makes the *apodosis* referring to Menelaus a contrafactual: κέ (7.104). The poet's statement in Patroclus's case is in the indicative (ἄρα), for death actually does "appear for you, Patroclus," though it merely *would have* for Menelaus, had not Agamemnon launched into the tirade that saves his brother (7.109–19). Agamemnon's presence at his brother's side and the warning speech that he utters deter Menelaus and save him from going to his doom. The parallelism in diction between the two scenes brings out the contrast between Patroclus's and Menelaus's respective fates, making the audience feel the stinging absence of any intervention in word or action from within the world of the characters that might save (or attempt to save) Patroclus from his fate at this stage.[195]

The conspicuously absent figure that might be expected to provide protection here is, of course, Achilles. If he were at his friend's side, we might well imagine him speaking the very same words Agamemnon speaks to Menelaus (*mutatis mutandis*) in book 4, ἀφραίνεις Μενέλαε διοτρεφές, οὐδέ τί σε χρὴ | ταύτης ἀφροσύνης· ἀνὰ δὲ σχέο κηδόμενός περ ("Menelaus, beloved of the gods, you are mad; you have no need to take leave of your senses thus. Hold fast, though it hurts you," 7.109–10). But unlike Agamemnon, the son of Peleus is tragically missing at the time his *philos* faces the greatest danger. His absence is deliberate: in his continued anger at Agamemnon, he has refused to rejoin the Achaean ranks, and sent Patroclus to fight in his stead (though it was never his intention

---

195 Block 1986, 160, notes how the use of the apostrophe in books 7 and 16 underlines the similarity between Menelaus's and Patroclus's situations; she also brings out the contrast between the "arrogant and insensitive protector Agamemnon," who nonetheless successfully rescues his younger brother, and Achilles, whose "sense of honor leads him to sacrifice his friend and protégé." As I noted earlier, it is remarkable that no god intervenes on Patroclus's behalf either, as Athena did, for instance, when Pandarus shot his arrow at Menelaus.

that Patroclus should fall into harm's way).[196] Though Patroclus is his nearest and dearest *philos*,[197] Achilles remains absent and unable to avert the dangerous threat from his friend, and it proves deadly. Patroclus dies alone.[198]

Absence and presence: The Voice of the Helpless Spectator

I previously noted that apostrophes are an instantiation of metalepsis, a boundary crossing that occurs when different diegetic levels are violated. When voicing repeated apostrophes to Patroclus at the time of his death, the Homeric poet is temporarily dissolving the limits between his extradiegetic world and the universe of the events that he is relating, by addressing one of his characters. Genette distinguishes two possible directions, as it were, for the transgression operated by metalepsis: "When an author (or his reader) introduces himself into the fictive account of the narrative or when a character in that fiction intrudes into the extradiegetic existence of the author or reader."[199]

The apostrophes to Patroclus at the time of his death operate in both directions. By speaking to a character within his narrative, the poet virtually enters into the world of his characters. At the same time, the metalepseis that occur within the scene of Patroclus's death enact a transgression in the other direction as well: they allow the voice of a character, Achilles, to intrude into the extradiegetic world of the narrator and poet, who knows and sees what he, as a character, cannot. The narrator speaks the warning that Agamemnon spoke to his brother, and that Achilles is not present to utter to his friend when it matters the most.

When examining the poetics of Greek epic and especially the question of the poetic voice, one need bear in mind what Bakker calls "the pragmatics of fiction:" the specific communicative conditions of Homeric storytelling, which in-

---

[196] Achilles is not present on the battlefield at his side because the Achaeans took away Achilles' *geras* and brought him *akhos* (16.48–79); they robbed him of his honor and caused him pain.

[197] On the *philia* relationship between Patroclus and Achilles, see Sinos 1975. Achilles himself says Patroclus is dearer to him than father and son (19.321–4). I return to this below.

[198] Mueller 1984, 58, contrasts the death of Sarpedon earlier on in book 16 (at the hands of Patroclus) with that of Patroclus himself, who dies "alone and unexpectedly," while Glaucus remains at Sarpedon's side until death overcomes him.

[199] Genette (1983) 1988, 88 (translation from 1988).

volved a live performer before a live audience.²⁰⁰ Bakker's suggestion that, with Homer, we consider all aspects of storytelling in terms of what he calls a "narratology of performance" is essential. For our present purposes, it is important to take into account the fact that the Homeric poet-narrator's voice and those of the characters are, in live performance, all sung by one and the same bard. As he performs, the bard is the voice of the poet and of the characters; his narratees are the audience members listening to his tale.²⁰¹ In the context of oral performance, then, it is one and the same performer who speaks Achilles' and the poet-narrator's lines. Presumably, the virtuosity with which the performer could adopt different voices and inflections to reflect the different utterances and characters for whom he spoke would be one measure of his talent and an arena for competition. It is tempting to imagine that the bard would be able to inflect his voice just so to suggest one voice or another — and perhaps that he could suggest an overlap or combination of different intonations, and hence voices, within a single utterance.

This is directly relevant to our appreciation of the power of apostrophes as an instantiation of metalepsis. Since it is one, unique performer who speaks the multiple voices of the Homeric poem in performance, then the very context and medium of performance – the bard taking on the poet's voice and performing before an audience of listeners – facilitates a seamless shift from one voice to another, including any boundary crossing from the extradiegetic to the intradiegetic level. The power of that poetic voice spoken in performance is that it can even allow for some ambiguous overlap between several voices, including voices that belong to two normally distinct levels of enunciation. The same utterance might seem to be spoken by the poet and also intimate the voice, style, and, hence, the viewpoint (and concern) of a given character.

That, I suggest, is what occurs in the scene of Patroclus's demise. The permeability of the boundaries between the voice of the poet and the voice of his protagonist is essential to our understanding of the place and significance of apostrophes in the scene of Patroclus's death. These apostrophes play an important role in making Achilles' voice and desire to protect Patroclus heard by the audience. By introducing Achilles' voice into the scene and thus making his presence felt, they underscore his absence and actual inability to intervene at the

---

200 See Bakker's chapter on "the narratology of performance" in Grethlein and Rengakos 2009, 117–36. On the rich comparanda provided by South Slavic bards and their performances of epic song, see Elmer and Bonifazi 2011. See also Lord 1960.
201 On the place and role of the bard as a reenactor of Homer's voice, see Lord 1960 and Nagy 1996. On the Homeric poet's claim to a special kind of singing as "a claim to a special kind of voice," see Ford 1992, 172–97.

crucial moment when death comes to his best friend, a death that Achilles will consider to be his own fault.

When the poet makes Achilles' voice heard at the climax of Patroclus's final, fatal encounter, the metalepseis do not only create an overlap of different voices (the poet's with Achilles'), but also contribute to introduce an embedded focalization (Achilles' viewpoint) into a scene that otherwise is told from a third-person narrator's viewpoint. That is, the transgressive use of the poetic voice that addresses the character directly is one of several elements that serve to make the audience watch the scene through the caring lens of the one most directly concerned by the death we are witnessing. The poetics here, then, do not just lead the audience to hear Achilles' voice; they also lead the audience members to watch the scene with Achilles' eyes, in his stead, as though they were he.

I am building here on an argument put forth by others. Mueller (1985) has convincingly argued that the poet makes us view Patroclus's terrifying death through the eyes of Achilles. Referring to the lines describing the last time Achilles sees Patroclus as he walks off to meet his fate, στῆ δὲ πάροιθ' ἐλθὼν κλισίης, ἔτι δ' ἤθελε θυμῷ| εἰσιδέειν Τρώων καὶ Ἀχαιῶν φύλοπιν αἰνήν ("and he stood in front of the door, with the desire in his heart still to watch the grim encounter of Achaians and Trojans," 16.255–6), he states that they

> are a discreet reminder of Achilles' anxiety; they also guide the perspective of the reader, who follows Patroklos where Achilles leaves off. The peculiar horror and pathos of Patroklos' death are in good measure a result *of the manipulation of the reader's response so that he stands in for Achilles and becomes the witness of the friend's death.* From the pursuing glances to the moment of foreboding, Patroklos is never out of the eyes of the audience/Achilles.[202]

The apostrophes contribute to make the audience perceive the scene of Patroclus's death through the emotional lens of Achilles. The emotional impact of the scene is heightened as a result: the apostrophes make the audience view this pivotal scene as though it were being perceived and focalized by the hero to whom Patroclus is dearest, and whom the event of his death will impact the most.

The stance of caring, watchful spectator of the Achaeans' plight is one that Achilles has, in fact, embraced since book 11.[203] By that point, the Achaeans have

---

[202] Mueller 1985, 55–6; italics mine for emphasis.
[203] For Achilles as spectator and arbiter in a different capacity later in the poem, during the funeral games for Patroclus in book 23, see Minchin 2011.

already begun to encounter significant reversals.[204] Achilles, watching from his ship with increasing concern, decides to find out more about the dire situation afflicting his fellow Greeks:[205]

ἑστήκει γὰρ ἐπὶ πρυμνῇ μεγακήτεϊ νηΐ
εἰσορόων πόνον αἰπὺν ἰῶκά τε δακρυόεσσαν.
(11.600–1)

For he was standing on the prow of the great-hulled ship,
Watching the arduous toil and the tearful rout.

The sequence of events leading to Patroclus's death begins. Achilles sees wounded Greeks being carried back to their tents and cannot bear it any longer:[206] he sends for Patroclus, wishing him to find out from Nestor the identity of the wounded Greeks that he has seen. This, the narrator tells us, is the beginning of doom for Patroclus: "He came out like the war god, and this was the beginning of his evil" (ἔκμολεν ἶσος Ἄρηϊ, κακοῦ δ' ἄρα οἱ πέλεν ἀρχή, 11.604).

There is great tragic irony to the fact that the moment in which Achilles begins to take action *because he cares* is the moment in which he sets in motion a series of events that will destroy the one who is dearest to his heart. We might connect this irony to the jarring tension between Achilles' desire and mission to protect his *philoi*, which is the defining heroic *ethos* of every warrior on the battlefield,[207] and the fact that it is Achilles' firm commitment to uphold that same heroic *ethos* that leads him to withdraw from battle (in order to demonstrate the importance of honoring those who espouse the heroic *ethos*, himself included) and hence to be absent at the crucial time of Patroclus's wounding.[208] When protective concern begins to prevail once more as he witnesses the grave reversals endured by the Achaeans, Achilles sends his *alter ego*, first to inquire

---

204 On the pivotal nature of book 11 within the *Iliad*'s plot and structure, see Schadewaldt 1943.
205 On Achilles' concern for the Achaeans as he looks on at the theater of war from his ship, see Whitman 1958, 195, and Kim 2000, 103–20. I agree with Whitman (1958) *pace* Thornton 1984, 133, that Achilles is not watching the Achaeans' losses with a hint of Schadenfreude, despite the fact that the Achaeans' hardships are a part of his plan for revenge against Agamemnon. Rather, as Kim (2000, 103) compellingly argues, Achilles sends Patroclus off to consult with Nestor because of his "rekindled concern" – not because he gloats on seeing "greater humiliation" for the Achaeans (Bowra 1930, 20 n. 55). On the encounter between Nestor and Patroclus, see Minchin 1991.
206 Most recently, he has seen even the healer Machaon in need of healing (11.602–15).
207 See Lynn-George 1996; Kim 2000, ch. 1.
208 On Achilles' uncompromising adherence to the heroic *ethos* that Agamemnon has jeopardized and betrayed by denying him rightful honor, see Whitman 1958, esp. ch. 9.

about the Greeks' situation, and then to fight in his stead; and in doing so, he sends him to his death.[209] The disjunction between Achilles' emotional disposition – his protective care for his *philoi* and, above all, for Patroclus – and his embrace of a passive stance in the war is what leads to a tragic outcome for Patroclus, as it will for Achilles himself. That disjunction is brought out in the poetic voice that calls out Patroclus's name throughout the scene of the latter's death: the voice reminds us of his concern, while underscoring his absence. In his seminal work on the language of heroes, Martin[210] demonstrates how much Achilles' language is akin to the Homeric poet's and concludes that the language of Achilles "is none other than that of the monumental composer; and … the poetic rhetoric of the narrator, in turn, is that of a heroic performer in the role of Achilles."[211]

Martin establishes that Achilles' language foregrounds Homer's own aesthetic.[212] He takes Mueller's important observation that Achilles is the focalizer of the scene of Patroclus's death a step further, noting that Achilles' voice merges with the poet's in this scene, as is manifest in the use of the apostrophe. At the time of Patroclus's undoing, Martin writes, "Homer himself sees the death through the eyes of Achilles, his *alter ego*. In this regard, apostrophe is natural: Achilles, after all, is the one hero who most often addresses Patroclus in the course of the poem. If Homer puts on the role of his hero, this speech habit comes with it."[213]

In addition to addressing Patroclus more often than anyone else in the *Iliad*, Achilles also utters every single address to Patroclus in the vocative within book 16 outside of the poet's apostrophes, with only one exception.[214] Thus, when death comes to Patroclus in the form of an invisible Apollo, the audience hears the poet's voice and viewpoint, but these seem to merge with the absent Achilles' as the narrator shifts from "the otherwise rigidly third-person narrator

---

209 The contradiction between Achilles' concern and his continued absence from the battlefield is pointed up by Nestor when Patroclus pays the old man a visit. Achilles has sent Patroclus to ask about the identity of the wounded warrior whom the best of Achaeans has just seen being carried back to the Greek tents (11.655 ff.). For more on this contradiction, see Kim 2000, 106–9.
210 Martin 1989.
211 Martin 1989, 222.
212 Martin 1989.
213 Martin 1989; see 235–6 on apostrophes in particular.
214 The exception is Apollo, when he utters his warning (16.707–9) that Patroclus is not fated to take Troy. It is worth noting that, ironically, Apollo's and Achilles' warnings have much in common: compare Achilles at 16.89–94.

of the *Iliad*"²¹⁵ to a more direct, second-person address directed at Patroclus. The shift occurs at a crucial moment, just before Apollo strikes the son of Menoetius with a down-turned hand and disarms him, in lines that bear quoting once more:²¹⁶

> ἔνθ' ἄρα τοι Πάτροκλε φάνη βιότοιο τελευτή·
> ἤντετο γάρ τοι Φοῖβος ἐνὶ κρατερῇ ὑσμίνῃ
> δεινός· ὃ μὲν τὸν ἰόντα κατὰ κλόνον οὐκ ἐνόησεν.
> (16.787–9)

> Then, Patroclus, the end of your life was shown forth,
> For Phoebus came against you there in the strong encounter,
> Dangerously, nor did Patroclus see him as he moved through the battle.

We hear the same shift in the poet's voice once again when the young Trojan Euphorbus steps forward, seizing the opportunity to stab Patroclus now that he is naked (deprived of his armor) before hastening back into the Trojan ranks in fear:

> ὅς τοι πρῶτος ἐφῆκε βέλος Πατρόκλεες ἱππεῦ
> οὐδὲ δάμασσ'· ὃ μὲν αὖτις ἀνέδραμε, μίκτο δ' ὁμίλῳ.
> (16.812–3)

> He first hit you with a thrown spear, O rider Patroclus,
> But he did not break you; no, he ran away again, and lost himself in the crowd.

This second apostrophe expresses deep sympathy for Patroclus at a moment when he is made yet more vulnerable and helpless. The audience's heightened sense of apprehension is reinforced by the combination of πρῶτος ("first") and the ensuing negation οὐδὲ δάμασσ' ("he did not break you"), both of which imply that there is more to come. Both of the above apostrophes, spoken in the narrator's voice, call to mind the earlier, intradiegetic utterances addressed to Patroclus by characters within the narrative: most of all Achilles', but also Apollo's, both of whom called out Patroclus's name and warned him against surpassing his limits. Like those earlier warnings, the apostrophes remain without effect, this time with fatal consequences.²¹⁷

---

215 Muellner 1996, 160.
216 On the significance of the down-turned hand, see Lowenstam 1981, chp. 2.
217 The apostrophes to Patroclus can be heard by the audience, but not by Patroclus, for obvious reasons: the speaker of these apostrophes is a poetic voice, a virtual presence that remains outside of the time and place of the narrative. On the inability of the characters to hear the Homeric narrator, see Richardson 1990, 174–5. During Patroclus's *aristeia*, however, characters

The particular pathos of the apostrophes is underscored by the audience's strong sense of Achilles' desire to protect Patroclus, which has been repeatedly emphasized throughout the epic leading up to this scene, most notably in the prayer Achilles addresses to Zeus as he watches Patroclus head into battle (16. 241–5).[218] Since the time he set out with him for Troy, Achilles has been concerned with keeping Patroclus safe and returning him home to his father in Opoeis. After Patroclus's death, Achilles painfully recalls his promise to Menoetius that he would bring his son home to him once more after sacking Troy (18.323–7).[219] Before allowing Patroclus to don the divine armor that was given to him by his mother and letting him enter the fray in his stead, Achilles attempts to protect his beloved friend by urging him not go beyond his limits and what is required to aid the Achaeans at this time: he must push the Trojans away from the Greek ships, and then cease from fighting the Trojans, lest he anger the gods (16.87–96).[220]

This protective care is an essential dimension of the entire scene of Patroclus's death. As Patroclus faces his doom, the apostrophes make the audience hear a caring voice calling out Patroclus's name; we feel the gaze and hear the voice of Achilles, the caring onlooker we would expect to be present. Briefly (but only notionally), Achilles' voice enters into the narrator's diegetic level, and it is as though he were allowed to share in the narrator's omniscience, and virtually and poetically able to see Patroclus's doom play out and to address him. In reality, he can do neither. The point is precisely that this "interplay of situations, characters ... occupying levels that are *prima facie* distinct"[221] is only pos-

---

also address Patroclus, calling him by name, apostrophizing him from within the realm of the narrative; to these addresses, Patroclus remains completely deaf, though they contain crucial warnings. He does not heed Achilles' orders that he cease to chase the Trojans on the battlefield as soon as they are successfully driven away from the Achaean ships; more gravely still, he lends a deaf ear to the very god against whose blows Achilles had specifically warned him, as the divinity who loves the Trojans most: μάλα τούς γε φιλεῖ ἑκάεργος Ἀπόλλων ("Apollo who works from afar loves these people dearly," 16.94).

[218] Zeus only grants Achilles half of his wish: Patroclus will receive glory but no safe return to the ships (16.249–52).

[219] Conversely, Menoetius had advised his son to guide Achilles using his maturity and wisdom, as the older one of the pair (11.780–90). The motif of returning a dear one safely to his home is also found in Agamemnon's lament over Menelaus in the scene where the latter is wounded by Pandarus in book 4 discussed above.

[220] As we have seen, Apollo subsequently utters another warning (16. 707–9). For other examples of Achilles' desire to protect Patroclus, see also 17. 411, 655, 18. 80–1, and Nagy 1979, 102–6.

[221] Fludernik 2003, 383.

sible on a poetic level: Achilles cannot actually see what the poet and audience watch in his stead, nor can he speak to Patroclus; he is, in fact, absent.

As a result of his choice to remain out of the battle, Achilles is confined to the tragic stance of a virtual spectator, with as little power to intervene as the audience members themselves. The apostrophes to the dying hero introduce Achilles' voice and gaze into the scene, making his presence felt in a notional sense, the better to underscore his tragic absence and ignorance, and above all his utter powerlessness at the moment in which his best friend is at his most helpless and vulnerable, with fatal consequences for them both. Similarly, Patroclus cannot hear the voice that is speaking to him. Therein lies the pathetic effect inherent to the use of metalepsis: the boundaries that the poet can cross with his voice cannot actually be crossed by the characters, who remain irreparably and fatally apart within the time and space of the narrative.[222]

Metalepsis thus serves as a poetic means of expressing helplessness.[223] It creates a virtual, poetic presence that draws attention to a glaring absence. Through the repeated apostrophes of the scene, the poet espouses the anxious, caring voice and gaze of one who is absent. The one whom we might have expected to call out thus cannot speak to his friend, and his addressee cannot hear him. This is a highly effective way of expressing both the speaker and the addressee's vulnerability and helplessness in the face of death. The apostrophes create a sense of proximity on a poetic level that stresses the actual, fatal distance between the two characters.

Achilles' delayed vision

Achilles has deliberately adopted the role of spectator for the first two thirds of the *Iliad*. He sits on the sidelines, watching and waiting for his honor to be reestablished as the Achaeans face gradual defeat against the Trojans because they are bereft of their greatest warrior. Looking on with him are Thetis and Zeus, who have promised that his wish (that the Achaeans should suffer because of his withdrawal) will be granted, while Hera and Athena do what they can to protect their beloved Greeks, and Poseidon and Apollo do what they can for their Trojans. Yet up until the death of Patroclus in book 16, Achilles is not a typical case of agent-turned-spectator as defined in the introduction: firstly, he actually

---

[222] On the character thus addressed (in this case, Patroclus) as both "'near,' in the performance, and 'distant,'" as in a movie, see Bakker 1997, 24–6.
[223] For an illuminating discussion of heroic *amêchania* in archaic Greek poetry, see Martin 1983.

chooses to withdraw from the action and merely watch; and second, even when he is in the stance of an observer, he is not passive.

From the time he withdraws to his tent at the start of the poem, Achilles has been in the position of a spectator to the plight of the Greeks and the successes of the Trojans, both of which are the desired outcome of his retreat and a response to Agamemnon's slight to his honor in book 1. The particularity of Achilles' status as spectator leading up to book 16 is that he continues to have an impact on the war, even when he is looking on from the sidelines, as it were: his lack of action (staying out of battle) has as potent an effect on his fellow Greeks' fate as his direct participation. Such is his worth in the theater of war that, even when he chooses to step out of the fray and be no more than a witness to the events around him, he continues to exercise power. This is precisely what makes his plan for revenge against Agamemnon effective: he can influence the action on the battlefield even after he embraces the role of spectator. The only thing that changes is the type of impact that he has on the battleground, which becomes the exact opposite of what it had been when he was involved in the fight. His absence from the front causes destruction for the Achaeans, while his presence on the battlefield caused destruction for the Trojans.[224] What Achilles does not realize until it is too late is that the source of his power over Agamemnon (allowing the Achaeans to incur harm on the battlefield) will prove to be his best friend's doom, and his own.[225]

When death comes to Patroclus in the form of Apollo (followed by Euphorbus and Hector), the poet no longer puts Achilles in the paradoxical position of a spectator who retains power as a passive onlooker. The hero has no power over the spectacle that is unfolding at all, not even the ability to see it – only the responsibility for having set it in motion. Far from being a spectator looking on at the destruction that he has *deliberately* wrought, he is merely a virtual spectator afforded a virtual insight into the event while he remains, in fact, absent and powerless to prevent the harm that he has caused. When the poet makes Achilles' voice and desire heard — the desire to fend off death from one who is, for all intents and purposes, equivalent to himself[226] – he highlights the utter vanity of that desire in the face of fate and ineluctable mortality. Patroclus cannot hear Achilles, nor is Achilles actually present to speak or act. Meanwhile,

---

[224] For an illuminating discussion of Achilles' and Patroclus's names and the connections they establish with the interdependent themes of grief and glory, see Nagy 1979, 94–117.
[225] See Mueller 1985, 35–57 regarding the blindness of the *Iliad*'s protagonists, especially p. 49: "The plot of the *Iliad* is made possible by the blindness of the protagonists."
[226] I return to this below in the section entitled "Mortal Achilles."

death surrounds Patroclus in multiple and unstoppable forms, mortal and divine.

Achilles' agency in causing Patroclus's death is disputable: he withdraws from the battlefield after his argument with Agamemnon in book 1, and then, at the start of book 16, when things take a turn for the worse for the Achaeans (as he had prayed to Thetis that they might), he agrees to give Patroclus his armor so he can join the fray in his stead.[227] Whether or not Achilles can be deemed directly responsible for Patroclus's death, what matters is his own understanding of his role in causing Patroclus's death, which is clearly stated by Achilles himself: τὸν ἀπώλεσα, "I destroyed him" (18.82), he tells his mother Thetis, when she comes rushing to his side on hearing his wails from the depths of the sea.[228] In Achilles' mind, Patroclus's death is his fault.[229]

The gaping disparity between Achilles' protective intent (manifest in his warning speech to Patroclus at the beginning of book 16) and his actual blindness regarding the disastrous future to come after he sends Patroclus into battle is accentuated by the harsh tenor of Hector's speech when he stands over Patroclus's dying body and impersonates Achilles (16.830–41). Hector gloats, taunting the son of Menoetius as he prepares to despoil him and watches the hero breathe his last. Hector imagines the last exchange between the two friends in extremely vivid terms, even performing parts of the fictitious dialogue, quoting what he believes to be an approximation of what Achilles' final words to Patroclus must have been. In doing so, he underscores and mocks Achilles' present helplessness (16.830–40): "Wretch! Achilleus, great as he was, could do nothing to help you" (ἆ δείλ', οὐδέ τοι ἐσθλὸς ἐὼν χραίσμησεν Ἀχιλλεύς, 16.837). Hector's cruel mockery fulfills two related functions. First, by underlining the fact that Patroclus does not receive any protection from his friend here, it helps to call attention

---

[227] As we have seen, Achilles also issues a stern warning to Patroclus to cease from battle immediately after driving the Trojans away from the Greek ships (16.86–100), an injunction that Patroclus disobeys entirely. His recklessness costs him his life, when he might have lived, as the narrator points out (16.684–7). The gods, fate, and Patroclus himself all play a role in his death. Regarding Patroclus's own tragic involvement in bringing about his own death by disregarding Achilles' warning, see above, p. 56.

[228] *Pace* Redfield 1975, 105–109, who denies Achilles the status of tragic hero by claiming that the greatest errors committed in his story are those of others. Compare Hector's self-blame in book 22.99–110, where he acknowledges his responsibility in having caused many Trojan deaths through his brashness. On Hector's last stance and monologue outside the walls of Troy before fighting his last battle, see Taplin 1992, 230–9.

[229] Muellner 1996, 160–1, argues that what Achilles feels is regret rather than guilt. See Finan 1979, 79: "Achilles 'recognises' the loss of Patroclus as the *consequence* of his own anger and the *cause* of his now imposed choice and sealed personal doom."

to Achilles' absence at this crucial moment. Hector's mockery also brings to mind Achilles' loving care for Patroclus, through the disparity between the words that Hector imagines Achilles to have voiced, and the words that Achilles actually spoke to Patroclus earlier in book 16. In his reenactment of an exchange that did actually take place between the two friends, and in which he impersonates Achilles, Hector wrongly supposes that Achilles ordered Patroclus *not* to return to the Achaean ships before killing him (Hector). The audience knows full well that Achilles uttered no such command, on the contrary. Far from instructing his friend not to bother returning to the Achaean ships "before having run his spear through Hector's tunic and bloodied it" (16.840–1), Achilles' directives to Patroclus at the beginning of book 16 expressly voiced his concern to protect Patroclus from the wrath of Apollo. This is the reason he gives Patroclus strict orders to return to him (Achilles) immediately after driving the Trojans away from the ships (16.95–6), and not to attempt any further martial exploits against Troy without him being present.

By the time Patroclus dies, the audience has known for a while that his death would come. The poet makes reference to it both within the narrative and in words spoken by the gods.[230] The disparity between the audience's knowledge of Patroclus's impending doom and Achilles' lack thereof is noteworthy. This disparity is maintainted at the time when Patroclus actually meets his doom: while the audience watches his death from up close as it occurs, Achilles is kept unaware of it, and this remains true for as long as possible. It is an important part of what makes the portrayal of Patroclus's death so profoundly pathetic: it plays up Achilles' blindness to the event, as well as his utter helplessness to alter its course. By making the audience members see what Achilles does not (yet) as though they were watching it through his eyes, the poetry allows them to experience firsthand the hero's powerlessness to intervene in the face of mortality.

The poet plays up the disparity between what the poet, audience, and all the other Greeks but Achilles can see on the one hand, and what the best of the Achaeans had imagined for Patroclus, on the other: a glorious role in the battle and a safe return to his father. At the beginning of book 16, when Patroclus asks Achilles the fatal question that will lead to his death, begging Achilles to allow him to go into battle, Achilles' protective disposition is apparent in his demeanor and his language. He affectionately compares his friend to a "foolish" little girl weeping and tugging at her mother's skirt:

---

230 As we have seen, Zeus predicts the death of Patroclus at 15.53–67. The poet also announces its inevitability at several points; see e.g., 11.604.

> τίπτε δεδάκρυσαι Πατρόκλεες, ἠΰτε κούρη
> νηπίη, ἥ θ' ἅμα μητρὶ θέουσ' ἀνελέσθαι ἀνώγει
> εἰανοῦ ἁπτομένη, καί τ' ἐσσυμένην κατερύκει,
> δακρυόεσσα δέ μιν ποτιδέρκεται, ὄφρ' ἀνέληται.[231]
> (16.7–10)
>
> Why then are you crying like some foolish little girl, Patroclus,
> Who runs after her mother and begs her to be picked up and carried,
> And clings to her dress, and holds her back as she tries to press on,
> And gazes tearfully into her face, until she is picked up?

In comparing his beloved companion to a little girl, Achilles puts himself in the (familiar) role of a protective parental figure.[232] With great tragic irony, Achilles uses the epithet νήπιος to describe his beloved companion, affectionately likening him to a foolish little girl (κούρη νηπίη). Both the poet (16.686–7) and Hector (16.833) subsequently employ the same adjective νήπιος ("fool") to describe Patroclus.[233] Hector uses the epithet in his speech to the dying Patroclus, calling him a "fool" (νήπιε, 16.833) in a distinctly more negative sense: he is a fool, he says, for thinking he could sack Troy and take its women as prisoners.[234] The word is particularly significant here because Hector uses it just before he goes on to imagine the words spoken by Achilles to Patroclus, wherein he mistakenly assumes that Achilles was not protective of his friend. Hector calls Patroclus a "fool" just as Achilles had in that earlier scene, albeit in a very different sense. Ironically, in that scene between Achilles and Patroclus, the speaker him-

---

231 On this intriguing first scene of book 16, see Ledbetter 1993. On the significance of the little girl simile, see Ready 2011, 155–83. On this last exchange between Patroclus and Achilles, see also Bouvier 2002, ch. 5.
232 Achilles also explicitly does so in the embassy scene in book 9, when he describes his role in relation to the Achaean army as that of a mother bird. He is constantly putting his life on the line "like a bird who feeds her chicks, whatever she may find, and goes without herself" (9.323–4). Mills 2000 explores the role of similes, both animal and human, in developing the theme of protection and parental care in the *Iliad*, including its central place in the relationship between Achilles and Patroclus. See also Lynn-George 1996.
233 At 16.686–7, the poet uses νήπιος to describe Patroclus in the very same breath as he expresses regret that Patroclus did not heed Achilles' words. Had he done so, "poor fool," he would have escaped black death (see above, p. 52).
234 Here as elsewhere, I agree with Elmer's observation that, "while it obviously cannot be claimed that every repeated word in the poem gives voice to some significant theme, nevertheless, in the case of words … that express the poem's central themes, every occurrence provides important evidence" (Elmer 2013, 15). On the question of the significance of verbal repetitions within the *Iliad*, see also Allen-Hornblower 2014, 39–46.

self (Achilles) deserves the epithet just as much as his friend. The verbal echo of the term in Hector's speech highlights Achilles' fatal lack of foresight.

Achilles' blindness is maintained for a while after the son of Menoetius is killed. He will be the last one to know about Patroclus's death, later than everyone else: later than the poet, the audience, the gods (including his mother), later than the Greeks and Trojans who battle over his best friend's body ferociously and at length while he remains absent from the scene and ignorant of its outcome. His ignorance is maintained throughout the entirety of book 17, which is devoted to the savage battle over Patroclus's body, over the course of which Hector despoils him and dons Achilles' armor (17.210). Even as the battle over Patroclus's body rages so fiercely that "not even Athena and Ares in their most belligerent moods could have watched it with disdain" (17.399–400), the poet dwells at length on Achilles' ignorance of it all (17.400–11): the divine Thetis herself does not inform her son of his friend's death.[235] Achilles' lack of awareness of what has come to pass ends only when Antilochus comes to him and delivers the unendurable news, as he desperately seeks Achilles' help in protecting his friend's threatened corpse (18.18–21). This knowledge brings about the end of Achilles' anger toward Agamemnon, and the beginning of a new form of wrath, that leads to the death of Hector, and then to Achilles' own.[236]

Achilles' "poetic" knowledge precedes his veritable discovery of Patroclus's death. When the news is finally broken to him at the beginning of book 18, the audience has been led to anticipate his emotional reaction to Patroclus's death from the time when it was occurring. It has been suggested that the apostrophes to the dying in Homeric poetry may be connected with the ritual practice of apostrophizing the dead.[237] Whether or not the connection with ritual is there, it remains true that every address to Patroclus in the vocative following book 16 is uttered by Achilles in lament for his *philos*; the last occurrence is an address to Patroclus's ghost.[238] The apostrophes punctuating the scene of Patroclus's death thus not only echo earlier, protective warnings; they also are a vocal foreshadowing of Achilles' later mournful invocations to Patroclus. Achilles may kept unaware of Patroclus's death from the time it occurs through book 17, but the poetry already anticipates and gives voice to Achilles' excruciating grief[239]

---

[235] The poet highlights the fact that Thetis specifically withholds this information from Achilles; see Beck 2012, 176 ff. on the unusual nature of 17.408–11, wherein the narrator "presents speech that was not actually spoken" by Thetis to Achilles.
[236] On the anger of Achilles, see Muellner 1996.
[237] Henry 1905; see n. 167.
[238] See 18.333, 19.287, and 23.19.
[239] See his reaction at 18.22 ff.

by initiating his transition from ignorance to painful knowledge on a poetic level, before the hero has actually been informed of Patroclus's fate.[240]

Bassett describes the tragic core of Homeric epic as follows:

> Both Attic tragedy and the Homeric poems show clearly that action is only, as it were, the skeleton of the organism, whose life is most deeply revealed *by the effect of the incidents upon the persons.*[241] In Attic tragedy we witness only the psychological "reaction" to off-scene occurrences. In Homer, "father of tragedy," it is less the actions than their dramatized effect upon the persons which makes the deepest impression of the finality of great lives.[242]

He goes on to cite the laments for Patroclus and Hector as examples. I would add that the apostrophes to Patroclus and the Achillean focalization they introduce in the scene of his death are crucial tools in the poet's arsenal that convey the "dramatized effect" of Patroclus's death on his nearest and dearest *philos* – an effect that, in turn, guides the audience's response as well.[243] By expressing the sympathy of the poet and merging the poet's voice with that of a grieving Achilles, the apostrophes play an essential role in foregrounding the tension that lies at the heart of the scene of Patroclus's death: between the necessity that Patroclus (and, subsequently, Achilles) die in order for them to receive *kleos*,[244] and the cost at which this *kleos* comes.

Mortal Achilles

We have seen how the particularities of Patroclus's death, both formal and thematic, help to distinguish it from all the other deaths in the *Iliad*. Its distinctive poetic and thematic characteristics fulfill two essential and related functions. The first is to make Achilles *virtually* present, through multiple elements of form and content that keep him (and his reactions) on the audience's mind, and lead the audience to view the scene as though through his eyes. These re-

---

240 On the depiction of Achilles grieving in vase paintings, see Muellner 2012.
241 Italics mine for emphasis.
242 Bassett (1938) 1966, 175.
243 In her discussion of narrative judgment and audience response in Homer, Block 1986, 160–1, demonstrates that the use of the apostrophe "directs the audience to the necessary response" to Patroclus's death by exposing the cost at which Achilles' adherence to the heroic code comes.
244 On the relationship and tension between *kleos* (glory) and *penthos* (grief) in the Homeric poems, see Nagy 1979, 94–117, including 102 ff., regarding the name of Patroclus. On Patroclus's death as a necessity, because it requires Achilles to reenter battle as his *philos* and acquire *kleos*, see Sinos 1975, 70–9.

peated and marked instances of metalepsis confer a distinctive note of pathos on the episode, by playing up the tension between the presence of a voice evoking Achilles' desire to protect Patroclus, on the one hand, and his inability to do so because he is absent, on the other. The tension inherent in the apostrophes, between Achilles' virtual presence and his actual absence, brings out the helplessness of even the greatest of all Achaeans heroes to protect a beloved fellow warrior from suffering and destruction. The struggle to fend off death from oneself and one's *philoi* and the inability to do so underlies every major Homeric hero's life. To that extent, the apostrophes in the Patroclus death scene play a primordial part in expressing the themes of power and vulnerability, heroism and mortality, which lie at the core of the *Iliad*.

The formal and thematic particularities of the scene of Patroclus's death also fulfill another, equally important function within the Homeric *Iliad*. As we have seen, the poet's utterance of apostrophes, in combination with other poetic means, portrays *Patroclus's* vulnerability in the face of death, and Achilles' powerlessness to prevent it. What is exceptional about the scene of Patroclus's downfall is that it does not merely depict its ostensible victim's helplnessness and vulnerability, but its virtual observer's as well. It is not only Patroclus's death that the audience watches through Achilles' eyes: it is a foreshadowing of Achilles' own. I would like to devote the closing portion of this chapter to examining how the poet suggests that, as we watch Patroclus's death through Achilles' eyes, we are looking on as Achilles (virtually) watches a shadow play of his own death to come. This is the second, related function of the scene of Patroclus's death: that of giving poetic expression to Achilles' helplessness in the face of mortality as well.

Achilles' death is not portrayed within the confines of the *Iliad*, though it was portrayed in other epic traditions.[245] Both Achilles' death and his direct role in the taking of Troy are beyond the scope of the poem (at least in terms of its narrative content). Poetically speaking, however, Achilles is virtually dead from the time that Patroclus falls at the hands of Hector in book 16. In many respects, Patroclus *is* Achilles in book 16: visually and emotionally, as well as thematically and poetically, his death is equivalent to Achilles'.[246] As

---

245 On the death (and afterlife) of Achilles in Homeric epic and beyond, see Burgess 2009.
246 On Patroclus as the *therapôn* of Achilles here, and the *Patrocleia* as a ritual substitution, see Nagy 1979, 292–5, who builds on the study by Van Brock 1959; see also Seaford 1994, 159–80, and below, nn. 251 and 261. Wilson 2002, 203–4 (n. 10) provides an overview of the Patroclus-as-*therapôn* argument, with bibliography. Regarding warrior deaths in battle as a sacrifice for the community, whose pollution the dying warrior takes on, see Redfield 1975, ch. 5.

the audience witnesses the death of Patroclus, it is also watching Achilles': Whitman calls Patroclus's death a "shadow play"[247] of Achilles'. To use another visual metaphor, we might say it is a negative, in the photographic sense, of Achilles' impending doom. The scene of his *alter ego*'s demise exposes the audience to a vision of human helplessness that will apply to him as well.

Both the extent to which Patroclus espouses Achilles' identity at the time of his death and the role of Patroclus's death in providing a poetic equivalent to Achilles' have received ample attention. The identification of Patroclus with Achilles is part of what gives the scene so much of its power; at the same time, the poetics of the scene maintain a distance and a distinction between the two characters, even as their identities mingle and overlap: one character is the actual, dying victim; the other is the caring *philos* of that victim, who is physically absent but poetically present.[248] The apostrophes serve as a reminder that Patroclus, in his death scene, both is and is not Achilles – the distinction between their identities made clear from the mere fact that "Achilles" (through the voice of the poet) here addresses Patroclus in the second person. Muellner calls attention to this point:

> The otherwise rigidly third-person narrator of the *Iliad* actually addresses [Patroklos] in the second-person singular, as a "you," right before the moment of his death. That is a grammatical symptom of the special sympathy and *philotês* his character evokes and expresses. One could characterize Patroklos' substitution for Achilles as the combination of a character that embodies solidarity (a "you") with one who embodies remoteness (a "he") because each is the other's "I."[249]

From the time he dons Achilles' armor, Patroclus enters a phase in which he becomes more than Achilles' best friend: he becomes Achilles' *alter ego*.[250]

---

247 Whitman 1958, 198 ff.
248 Apollo's injunction to Patroclus (16.707–9) in their first confrontation underlines the ambivalent nature of Patroclus's identity in relation to Achilles' in a manner that bears noting for our present purposes. He enjoins Patroclus to be mindful of the fact that he (Patroclus) *is not Achilles*, and is inferior to his friend, and thereby reinforces the audience's sense of the two heroes' distinct identities. But his warning also underscores what the two heroes share, and what Patroclus's fate illustrates when he faces Apollo a second time: that *both* he and Achilles are subjected to fate, and must face certain death.
249 Muellner 1996, 160.
250 Sinos 1975 connects Patroclus's loss of identity with the concept of *philotês*; for a different conception of the relationship between identification and *philotês*, see Kim 2000.

Throughout his *aristeia*, Patroclus seems to have subsumed Achilles' identity.[251] Whitman points out that, in the *Patrocleia*, Patroclus's behavior is ever more at odds with his own nature, and more and more a reflection of Achilles'. He describes the superimposition of the two heroes' identities onto each other as "a kind of double image, as in surrealistic painting ... Patroclus is playing the role of Achilles ... and acts much more like the great hero than himself."[252] On a visual level, the hero is wearing Achilles' armor and is long mistaken by the Trojans for the best of the Achaeans.[253]

Patroclus has "become" Achilles not just superficially and externally, in his physical appearance, but also in terms of his behavior and martial virtuosity: the one who is distinguished by the narrator as compassionate and kind in each of the (relatively rare) appearances that he has made in the narrative beforehand, is now a brutally effective warrior.[254] Patroclus turns into a merciless and highly effective killing machine, as is fitting for a hero in the midst of his *aristeia* albeit unexpected, if not out of character, for the compassionate healer of *philoi* and faithful attendant, the "honey-tempered" Patroclus. Patroclus's words, along with his deeds, point up his martial valor. He reenters the battle for the same reason that Achilles withdrew from it: the desire to prove Agamemnon wrong and rehabilitate Achilles' honor. He is, as it were, the reverse side of the same medal, Achilles' substitute.[255] His (very brief) speeches might as well be Achilles', both in content and tone:[256] they reveal a certain ruthlessness, as when he appeals to the two Ajaxes to join forces to mistreat Sarpedon's body (ἀεικισσαίμεθ' ἑλόντες, "If only we could win and dishonour his body," 16.559), despoil his armor, and massacre with cold bronze each of the *philoi* who try to protect him (16.558–61). His injunction to Meriones that he be a

---

251 Sinos 1975, 30–52 demonstrates how Patroclus only qualifies as the *therapôn* of Achilles so long as he stays within limits that define him as Achilles' "recessive equivalent:" "The *therapôn* becomes vulnerable when he goes off on his own" (Sinos 1975, 33).
252 Whitman 1958, 199 ff.
253 The exact point at which the Trojans discover that the powerful warrior wearing Achilles' armor is not actually the son of Peleus is hard to pin down.
254 Patroclus's martial prowess is not mutually exclusive with his kind disposition; the former is directed at the enemy, while the latter was reserved for when he is among friends: he is, then, upholding the heroic code of "helping friends and harming enemies."
255 Patroclus enjoins the Myrmidons to fight by reminding them that they are to enter the fray in the name of Achilles' honor, urging them to fight so hard (that is, kill so many Trojans) that Agamemnon will be led to see his folly in not recognizing the best of the Achaeans for his excellence (16.269–74).
256 On Patroclus's speeches as akin to Achilles' at this stage, see Whitman 1958, esp. 199–220.

man of deeds rather than one of mere words (ἐν γὰρ χερσὶ τέλος πολέμου, ἐπέων δ' ἐνὶ βουλῇ, "Warfare's finality lies in the work of hands, that of words in counsel," 16.630) also sounds typically Achillean. The harsh, combative tenor of his words is reflected in his deeds, and his rabid efficiency is conveyed by the catalogues of Trojans killed, all of whom are thrown together in an uninterrupted series (16.415–7), and by his last, merciless bout, over the course of which he kills twenty-seven men, charging three times and killing nine with each charge (16.784–5).

Earlier, I noted how the fact that Patroclus is wearing Achilles' armor makes the latter hero's presence felt in the scene, while his divine weapons' inefficacy brings out his inability to protect Patroclus. Achilles' helmet rolling in the dust covered in blood does not only bring out Patroclus's vulnerability and mortality; the striking visual image also foreshadows Achilles' own ultimate death, which will also come at the hands of Apollo. The same is true after Patroclus dies, and Achilles mourns for him: the description of Achilles in his grief, with his head in his mother's lap, is a precise visual foreshadowing of what is to come: it could just as well describe a dead Achilles being lamented by his mother (18.70–2 and beyond). Then, too, his mother will weep and hold his corpse in her arms, cradling his head.

Patroclus's death is so intricately tied with Achilles' own that Thetis immediately begins to lament for Achilles when, roused from the depths of the sea by the sounds of his groans at the loss of his friend, she hears her son describe his grief (18.50–64).[257] As her lament overlaps with Achilles' lamenting for his friend, her response underlines the connection between Patroclus's death and Achilles' own.[258] In Thetis's display of unconsolable grief at the news of Patroclus's disappearance, we are given a measure of the ineluctability of Achilles' death; for though Thetis foresees and repeatedly predicts her son Achilles' death, she, like Achilles in the case of Patroclus, remains nonetheless unable to prevent it, in spite of her divine nature and her foresight.[259] Once Patroclus is dead, Achilles is as good as dead, and there is nothing he or his divine mother

---

[257] Kim 2000, 121–9, examines the many instances in which the language describing Achilles' grief is barely distinguishable from language associated with death.
[258] For a different interpretation of Thetis's mourning as *not* primarily alluding to the death of Achilles, see Kelly 2012.
[259] On the power – and helplessness – of Thetis and her impotent grief in the *Iliad* and beyond, see Slatkin 1991; on Thetis's different role in other epic traditions, see Burgess 2009, ch. 1. Thetis's concern is not Patroclus, but Patroclus's demise as a certain trigger of Achilles' forthcoming death; see Heiden 2008, 224–5. On the poet's ability to make Achilles' early death appear to be the hero's free choice, even though it is fated, see Hirschberger in Montanari, Rengakos, and Tsagalis 2012, 185–96.

can do to change that.²⁶⁰ Patroclus's death is a visual, ritual, and poetic substitute for Achilles', which is never told within the narrative of the *Iliad* as we have it.

It can be said, therefore, that it is not just Achilles' friend's death that the audience watches as Patroclus dies: it is a foreshadowing of Achilles' own. In addition to being the voice and the focalizing gaze of the scene of Patroclus's death, then, Achilles is, notionally, the dying hero himself. He is a behind-the-scenes agent of the scene (he sent Patroclus into battle), a (virtual) spectator of the scene, and an object of spectacle. He is both agent and victim, spectator and object of spectacle. The whole scene does not merely show us Patroclus's death, it shows us the hero's death *as though* it were being seen *through Achilles' eyes*. It is a "rehearsal" of Achilles' death, *as seen by Achilles*. As we watch Patroclus's death through Achilles' eyes, we are looking on as Achilles (virtually) watches a "shadow play" of his own death to come.²⁶¹ Mueller describes the unique process at hand:

> Homer uses the convention of the death speech for Sarpedon, Patroklos and Hektor. But for his protagonist he resorted to a fiction that provided him with richer opportunities to express the consciousness of death. Achilles witnesses and reflects on the death of Patroklos-as-Achilles. He experiences his own death as if it were that of another.²⁶²

The tragic nature of Achilles' doom, which will occur beyond the confines of the *Iliad* proper, is that he will go to his death not simply with the knowledge that he must die but after he has been forced to accept something perhaps more painful: the helplessness, which he shares with all other mortals, and even the gods, to provide his *philoi* — and himself — with absolute protection from death. We watch the death of Patroclus, knowing that Achilles would wish to prevent it, that he will blame himself for it, and that this death is also equivalent to Achilles' own. Budick writes that "by accepting the inevitability of the death of self, fallen and blood-stained, the self acknowledges the other who reveals the self's mortal-

---

260 Redfield's words concerning Hector when he realizes Deiphobus was merely a deceitful god in disguise apply just as aptly to Achilles when he realizes that Patroclus has died: "At the end he can do nothing with his fate except know it. Hector dies because there is nothing left for him to do, because for him there no longer exists a world in which he can act" (Redfield 1994, 159).
261 On Patroclus's death as a "shadow play" of the death of Achilles, Whitman 1958, 198 ff., noted above, n. 247.
262 Mueller 1984, 60.

ity and imperfection."²⁶³ By "watching" Patroclus die through this lens, the audience is given a window onto the hero's response to his own vulnerability and mortality. Achilles at first violently rejects this mortality, before coming to recognize and accept his place among mortals, when he lets go of his pain and anger in the final book of the *Iliad* and allows the aged Priam, king of Troy, father of his arch enemy Hector, to take his son's body back to his city to be properly mourned.²⁶⁴

---

263 Budick 1989, 331. See also Mueller (1984, 57): "The death of Patroclus turns the blind into a seeing Achilles. For the rest of his brief life he will be in a state of clairvoyance that is given to other characters only at the point of death."
264 Regarding book 24 and the scene between Priam and Achilles, see MacLeod 1982; Crotty 1994; Muellner 1996; Wilson 2002. On Achilles' (and other Iliadic heroes') acceptance of his vulnerability as crucial to his reestablishing bonds with the human community, see 2013, ch. 1.

Chapter Two: Spectatorship, Agency, and Alienation in Sophocles' *Trachiniae*

> "Life's but a walking shadow, a poor player
> That struts and frets his hour upon the stage
> And then is heard no more: it is a tale
> Told by an idiot, full of sound and fury,
> Signifying nothing."
> — Shakespeare, *Macbeth*, Act V, scene 5

In this chapter, I examine how and why Sophocles casts the character of Deianeira in the role of spectator in his *Trachiniae*. From the start of the play, the audience is led to embrace the queen's viewpoint. There is not so much action as *reaction* in the play: Sophocles devotes the greater part of the first half of the play to characterizing the figure of Deianeira, by focusing on her reactions to events past, present, and future. Her outlook on the world is specifically defined by her acknowledgment, from the very opening lines of the tragedy, of all mortals' epistemic limitations. In light of the unpredictability of fate and the lack of control that lie at the core of the human condition, the queen questions the reliability of all that she sees, as well as her own and others' ability to interpret or affect what occurs around and to them. She is, in many respects, the ideal spectator: she deciphers the blurry spectacle of life unfolding around her with caution and care, always mindful of the hidden forces that guide her own and other's actions and perceptions, and of the limited ability of mortals to detect these forces' presence and power.

When Deianeira learns that she has lost the love her husband, the hero Heracles, her despair leads her to temporarily and abruptly abandon her customary, passive and cautious stance of careful and compassionate observer. In desperation, she takes the only initiative she ever takes in the entire play, and shifts from the status of spectator to that of agent: she sends Heracles a robe lined with a potion that she believes possesses the magical power to resuscitate the hero's exclusive love for her. Through a prop (a tuft of wool, an inventive dramatic device), the queen then witnesses *in absentia* the full extent of the disastrous consequences of her action. The catastrophic outcome of her gift is also subsequently confirmed through the vivid visual account of Heracles' agony that her son Hyllus relates to her. In the discrepancy between the scene that she had envisioned and the way in which it actually plays out, Deianeira and the audience can measure the vanity of human endeavor, and intuit the unseen yet ever-present hand of the gods, who, it is revealed, are pulling the strings behind the scenes. As the choral passages and Hyllus's enlightened closing words later make clear, the gods (and Aphrodite in particular) have been looking on at the spectacle of human suffering all along; they are its true and deliberate agents, and they witness its aftermath with indifferent detachment, if not satisfaction. The spectacle of her own unwitting fallibility nonetheless proves unbearable to Deianeira, and the queen takes her own life.

The first two thirds of Sophocles' *Trachiniae* offer a surprising point of focus: they are devoted in their near entirety to the female character Deianeira, wife of the hero Heracles and, more specifically, to her perception of and reactions to events past, present, and future.²⁶⁵ This has intrigued scholars: here is a female character who is granted primary importance in a play based on epic material, in which we would expect the main subject to be Heracles.²⁶⁶ She never even finds herself in the glorious hero's presence – at no point do they actually overlap on stage.²⁶⁷ Not only is a woman the center of attention and principal focalizer in a play that we expect to be about Heracles; more striking yet is the fact that this particular woman does not act so much as she *reacts* throughout the play, watching the people and events around her. The audience watches her as she carefully monitors her own responses to these with a combination of prudence and apprehension. The unexpected focus on Deianeira is all the more surprising as it makes the play fall into two parts: one (the larger) focused on Deianeira, the other (roughly the last third) revolving around Heracles' onstage suffering. This dichotomy drew criticism for a time because (to some at least) it seemed that, as a result, the drama lacked in unity. Such a view has been convincingly refuted.²⁶⁸

To help us better comprehend the play's unity, I suggest that we can reconcile the tragedy's two seemingly disconnected parts if we recognize that it hinges on an ironic reversal. The play's protagonist, Deianeira, is defined by her ability to be aware of her own limitations and of the unpredictability of fate: she is haunted by the lessons she has learned from the past, and her gaze is always turned toward the future, in constant anticipation and apprehension of what might occur as a result of the sudden shifts that sooner or later mark every man's fortune. Through an inventive twist, Sophocles puts Deianeira in the position of actually seeing the future — of witnessing the outcome of her only initiative in the entire play – at a point when she is fully able to fathom the disas-

---

265 Throughout this chapter, I use Easterling's edition of the text (1982). Translations are mine (largely based on Lloyd-Jones 1994) unless otherwise specified. According to my (rough) calculations, Sophocles devotes 730 out of a total of 1,278 lines to the portrayal of Deianeira through her own words and especially through her careful consideration of the plight that afflicts her and others. Perrotta 1935, ch. 8 highlights the dramatic and thematic importance of the focus on Deianeira's internal frame of mind and disposition (her "stati d'animo") for our understanding of the play as a whole.
266 On the material and tradition on which Sophocles bases his *Trachiniae*, see Reinhardt (introduction) and Kamerbeek 1963 (also discussed in his introduction).
267 On the intriguing aspects of the *Trachiniae*'s structure and its relevance to the play's themes, see Kitzinger 2012, with bibliography.
268 Easterling 1982 contributed to rectifying such readings of the play by drawing attention to the many elements that confer both formal and thematic unity on the drama; see esp. her introduction. Conacher 1997 examines the interweaving of plot and theme in the play and its use to create different forms of irony.

trous consequences of her action but unable to reverse the course of events that she has set in motion. In the preceding chapter, we saw how the Homeric poet puts Achilles in the virtual position of spectator to the destruction of the one whom he loves most, and blames himself for it; in his *Trachiniae*, Sophocles actually puts Deianeira in the position of watching Heracles die – twice.[269]

In his reading of the play, Falkner emphasizes the important role given to the process of spectating within Sophoclean tragedy generally and the *Trachiniae* in particular. He notes how "the idea of spectacle is itself literally 'theorized' and characters are represented in the act of beholding"[270] and suggests that,

> in Sophocles, the theatrical situation is consistently described in terms that suggest the potential power, privilege, and security of the spectator (*theatês*) over and against the suffering, vulnerability, and even humiliation of the object of sight.... These texts implicitly recognize the power the *theatês* enjoys by virtue of his position as spectator.

Falkner calls this "theatrical superiority." I propose that the act of spectating within the play is, in fact, defined by a powerlessness which the audience shares, and that Sophocles uses the figure of Deianeira, especially Deianeira *qua* spectator of the events and people around her, to articulate the central unifying tragic motifs that underlie the entire play and define the human condition: human fallibility and powerlessness in the face of fate and divine power.[271] It is this same powerlessness which the play's other protagonist, Heracles, also is forced to recognize by the play's end.

Perrotta rightly observes that the play is not so much about the myth of Heracles as it is about how the events that punctuate his life story affect and resonate with one particular character, through whose eyes we watch them all, past, present, and future:

> E così, nelle *Trachinie*, per quasi tutta la tragedia, noi non assistiamo al mito di Eracle drammatizzato, ma alle risonanze che i fatti del mito di Eracle hanno nell'animo di un solo personaggio: di Deianira... tanto è rivissuto attraverso un personaggio.[272]

---

[269] As we will see, Deianeira envisions the death of Heracles not once, but twice: first, when the tuft of wool is consumed to nought before her very eyes; and then once more when her son Hyllus comes to report in graphic detail the slow death that has begun to sap the great Heracles' life as a result of her gift to him.

[270] Falkner in Sternberg 2005, 166.

[271] While Deianeira is the principal character that perceives and reacts in the play, other characters' roles and responses will also be a consideration, especially their reactions to Deianeira's sole initiative and its outcome.

[272] Perrotta 1931, 146. In his chapter devoted to the play (Perrotta 1935, ch. 8), P. lays too much stress on Deianeira's fragility and weakness, and thereby fails to give due attention to

Chapter Two: Spectatorship, Agency, and Alienation in Sophocles' *Trachiniae* — 97

By inviting the audience to completely merge their gaze and responses with Deianeira's, Sophocles equates the vulnerability and helplessness of the human condition with a spectatorship of sorts. Deianeira's trajectory involves embracing, successively, the roles of prudent and compassionate spectator; that of brash agent; and then again that of spectator to the outcome of her own deed. This trajectory exemplifies the arc of human existence, wherein every human effort is ultimately thwarted by forces beyond mortal comprehension.[273]

As she bears witness to destructive events that occur because of her, to her, and in spite of her, Deianeira can do nought but endure in recognition of the harsh truth with which Hyllus, her son, closes the play: that human agency stops where the divine begins and that the line between the two is never quite perceptible to mere mortals. But endure Deianeira cannot: when the spectacle of her own unwitting agency plays out before her eyes, the experience proves so alienating and excruciating that she takes her own life. This is a dark play indeed, one that Whitman ascribes to Sophocles' middle period (the mid-430's), in which he produced what Whitman calls "plays of tragic knowledge," that are "bitter and destructive," their atmosphere "poisoned by a kind of universal despair," with the experience of "learning too late" at their core. That experience of late learning is perfectly encapsulated in the words Deianeira speaks in the moment of searing realization that the gift she has sent to Heracles will destroy him: "And this I learn too late, when it no longer can help" (ὧν ἐγὼ μεθύστερον | ὅτ' οὐκέτ' ἀρκεῖ, τὴν μάθησιν ἄρνυμαι, 710–1).[274]

---

her prudence and consciousness of her own (and all mortals') limits. He also overlooks some of the traits that Deianeira shares with other Sophoclean heroes (which I discuss below).

273 Falkner 2005 makes the compelling suggestion that Deianeira presents the audience with an ideal model of the compassionate spectator because of her gender. It is equally noteworthy, and perhaps more surprising, that it is a female hero who serves to epitomize the human condition in this play. This may be in part because she is especially vulnerable as a result of her gender; that vulnerability, in turn, makes her predisposed to display pity toward others. See below, p. 109.

274 Whitman 1951, 104; the theme of "late learning" is developed throughout his chapter devoted to the *Trachiniae* (ch. 6 *passim*). Dodds 1951, 49 describes Sophocles as "the last great exponent of the archaic world-view." One sees how aptly such a description applies to the *Trachiniae*. Winnington-Ingram 1965 pays homage to Dodds' view, while further exploring some of the insightful, nuanced comparisons between Sophocles with Aeschylus that are evoked by Dodds.

Watching through Deianeira's eyes

Sophocles' prominent use of Deianeira's reactions as she witnesses the events unfolding around her in the first portion of the *Trachiniae* is essential to the depiction of her character. Two central and related traits rapidly emerge from the position she is cast in of spectator to the consequences of her existence. The first is her increasingly acute awareness of all mortals' limitations and, hence, of their vulnerability to powerful divine forces. The second is her exceptional predisposition to compassion, which stems from her recognition that these forces can lead to unexpected results and turns of fortune that remain largely beyond human control.[275] These principal character traits in turn serve to articulate the dark, bitter theme at the heart of the drama as a whole: that even the guiltless must fall victim to "meaningless forces," despite their best attempts to achieve good ends, as a consequence of the "inescapable malignity" of an irrational world.[276] The world of the *Trachiniae* is one in which it is impossible for mortals either to judge the present or know the future, and this despite noble attempts to acquire as much knowledge and wisdom as is humanly possible – including (in Deianeira's case) knowledge of their own limits.

It is with Deianeira's vision of the world — a cautious, pessimistic vision – that the play begins. In this respect, the prologue is highly unusual. Its opening lines do more than provide the habitual expository background information: the fact that they are spoken by the main character, not a divinity or secondary figure, immediately creates a special relationship between that speaker (Deianeira) and the audience. Her lengthy opening monologue is not addressed to anyone in particular; it is mostly a soliloquy (though her nurse is present), heard by the audience and spoken, it seems, for the benefit of the audience only. As Seale notes, from the very start, the spectators are led to embrace her viewpoint:

> Her initial relationship is with the spectators. Her sad reflections are for their benefit and they who have entered into her innermost thoughts become conditioned to watch events through her eyes and through her mental pictures. The action grows out of her consciousness, out of her private grief.[277]

---

[275] On the crucial role played by the recognition of one's own vulnerability in the ability to experience pity, see Arist., *Rh.* 2.8.1385b13–16. Cf. Falkner 1993 on Odysseus in Sophocles' *Ajax* and Johnson and Clapp 2005, 127: "Compassion ... is premised on an understanding of the common inheritance of suffering shared by all human beings." I return to this in more detail in the chapter on the *Philoctetes*. On the role of oracles in the play, in connection with the theme of fate's implacable and unpredictable turns, see Segal 2000.
[276] The quotes are from Whitman 1951, 105–6.
[277] Seale 1982, 183.

Nothing happens in the way of action in the first portion of the *Trachiniae*. From the moment she begins to speak at the opening of the play, Sophocles puts Deianeira in the position of a passive viewer who does not act so much as she perceives and *reacts* to all that occurs around her: she recalls events from the past, witnesses those occurring before her in the present, and apprehends those that might occur in the future.[278] This stance has led many critics to consider her a passive or weak character, with an unnecessarily pessimistic outlook. In fact, Deianeira's alleged passivity is a form of (highly) cautious observation.[279] She starts off the play with an ancient maxim, articulating the unshakable law governing human existence, which is the reason underlying her extreme prudence:

> Λόγος μὲν ἔστ' ἀρχαῖος ἀνθρώπων φανεὶς
> ὡς οὐκ ἂν αἰῶν' ἐκμάθοις βροτῶν, πρὶν ἂν
> θάνῃ τις, οὔτ' εἰ χρηστὸς οὔτ' εἴ τῳ κακός·
> (1–3)
>
> There is a saying among men, which came to light long ago, that you may not completely learn of the lot of mortals, whether it is good or bad, until a man dies.[280]

From this opening maxim on, the queen constantly reminds herself and others of what they do *not* know: nothing is certain, she says, except for what one has experienced directly.[281] Deianeira appears to be excessively pessimistic; but her apprehension actually stems from an unusually acute awareness of the fickleness

---

278 On the central role of the portrayal of Deianeira's character and its relevance to the play's entire plot, see Fuqua 1980.
279 The queen's passivity and her distinctive pessimism are often mentioned by critics as revealing of an overall weakness, deemed to be the distinguishing feature of her character: see McCall 1972, 143 n. 6. I agree on the contrary with Jebb and Whitman 1951, Kirkwood 1941, Kamerbeek 1963, Easterling 1977, Fuqua 1980, *et al.*, who consider the heroine to be both resolute and composed, for reasons that become clearer in what follows. On the noble ideals of Sophoclean protagonists, see also Kirkwood 1958. For now, suffice it to point out that the traits of pessimism and passivity are not so much intrinsic to Deianeira as they are forced on her by circumstance.
280 Translation Seale 1982, 181.
281 See her statement to the Chorus, 141–52, in which she voices the notion that the actual perception and understanding of another's pain requires a form of prior knowledge, which can only be reached through one's own experience:

> You are here, it seems, in the knowledge that I suffer, but may you never learn to know through suffering such agony of heart as mine, of which you now have no experience ... till the time when one is called a woman rather than a maiden, and gets during the night one's share of worries, fearing for one's husband or one's children. Then one could see, looking at his own condition, what evils I am burdened with.

of fate. It is all the more justified in the here and now of the play: an oracle, she tells us, has pronounced the time at which the play's action begins as one that will bring about one of two things – Heracles' salvation or his annihilation.[282]

Unlike other tragic heroes, who are otherwise comparable to her in their dogged pursuit of a truth that is revealed to them only too late,[283] Deianeira is distinguished from the start by her prudence, her altruistic concern for others, and an awareness of her own and others' limitations *qua* mortals.[284] There is no other tragedy in which a character's focus and words revert with such consistency to a conscious and careful assessment of the limits of man's knowledge, even as she struggles to unveil the truth, especially when it pertains to the principal object of her care: Heracles. While this dogged pursuit of truth calls to mind another Sophoclean hero, Oedipus, it bears noting that Oedipus ends up committing the very actions that he had sought to avoid because of an overbearing confidence in his own ability to uncover the truth. Deianeira does not show such arrogant trust in her own abilities.[285] On the contrary, she mitigates each of her statements in a manner that reveals her understanding that every perception, along with any judgments that are formed based on these perceptions, runs the risk of being misguided. Even when she does perceive something clearly, as an eyewitness ("I see ... nor does the sight of this procession escape my watchful eye," ὁρῶ, φίλαι γυναῖκες, οὐδέ μ' ὄμματος | φρουρὰν παρῆλθε, 225–6), she still bears in mind that appearances may or may not be revealing of underlying truths (οἰκτραὶ γάρ, εἰ μὴ ξυμφοραὶ κλέπτουσί με, "they deserve pity, *if their calamity does not deceive me*," 243).[286]

---

[282] Heracles left with Deianeira some prophecies, according to which the time in which they now find themselves is precisely the time at which he will either die or, thenceforth, live happily ever after (79–81; again at 155–77). In the prologue, the audience learns this crucial piece of information along with Hyllus, Deianeira and Heracles' son, from the mouth of Deianeira herself.

[283] The many parallels between Deianeira and Oedipus are underlined by Seale 1982, 181–214.

[284] Whitman 1951, 103–21, sees the theme of "late learning" as central to the *Trachiniae* and especially pathetic in the case of Deianeira because the entire plot is made of up of her "long and painful search for truth" (Whitman ibid. at 110). Winnington-Ingram 1980, 75–6 notes that "the rhythm of the first half of the play is the rhythm of Deianira's fears," summing up the two main traits of her character as one that is "a prey to fear and capable of pity."

[285] Whitman 1951, 106 sees both Oedipus and Deianeira as "examples of high-minded humanity" because they seek to achieve good ends and pursue "the most moral action possible." He does not make the important distinction between Oedipus' confidence and Deianeira's distinctive awareness of her own and others' epistemological limitations.

[286] Italics mine.

Deianeira is preoccupied with the importance of responding to all events in a manner that is just and appropriate by being "always mindful of human weakness and vulnerability."[287] Her character is deeply compassionate, reasonable, and moderate: she sees and judges others' actions and reactions with an eye to equanimity at all times, for she is, in her own words, neither "evil nor ignorant of the ways of men" (οὐ γὰρ γυναικὶ τοὺς λόγους ἐρεῖς κακῇ, | οὐδ᾽ ἥτις οὐ κάτοιδε τἀνθρώπων, 438–9). She wants to be one "who considers things with care" (τοῖσιν εὖ σκοπουμένοις, 296) and wishes to know as much as possible about her situation at any given time, as when she enjoins Lichas to tell her "the whole truth" about Heracles' passion for his captive, Iole (453), "because not learning – that is what would cause [her] pain" (ἐπεὶ τὸ μὴ πυθέσθαι, τοῦτό μ᾽ ἀλγύνειεν ἄν, 457–8). Even if it means facing a painful truth, she strives "not to be mistaken in [her] judgment" (εἴ τι μὴ ψευσθήσομαι | γνώμης, 712–3) and to act always in a manner that is "honorable" and worthy of a "woman of sense" (οὐ γάρ, ὥσπερ εἶπον, ὀργαίνειν καλὸν...γυναῖκα νοῦν ἔχουσαν, 552–3). The statements that other characters make regarding Deianeira reinforce the audience's sense of her laudable character traits: Lichas declares that she thinks "like a mortal, not unreasonably" (θνητὴν φρονοῦσαν θνητὰ κοὺκ ἀγνώμονα, 473).

The prudence and humanity intrinsic to the queen's way of thinking are reflected in her speeches. Their generalizing nature facilitates and encourages the audience's espousal of her viewpoint, as she repeatedly puts forward her (perceived) understanding of every man's limited power in the face of fate. Her very first words, quoted above, are a universally applicable maxim, which sums up an accepted form of popular wisdom of the time, famously put into words by Solon and reiterated in various forms in Greek tragedy and other genres (1–3).[288] The generalizing lens with which she views the human condition leads her to formulate what the audience would view as commendable and profoundly humane judgments, distinctive for their temperance and wisdom. The nobility of the queen's ideals and the model nature of her every response further contribute to making her a character with whom the audience is not only likely but morally encouraged to identify.[289] The audience can readily embrace her careful stance:

---

[287] Easterling 1982, 8.
[288] For instance, Herodotus' *Histories*, book I, in the famous episode between Solon and Croesus. I return to the importance of this statement and its immediate relevance to the play as a whole, and especially its ending, later on.
[289] See Falkner 2005, 167: "In these embedded scenes of spectacle, *Trachiniae* directs our own response as spectators, attempting to create the kind of disposition and sensibility the playwright asks for his own work." Regarding the self-conscious and reflexive nature of Greek trag-

the play makes them identify with her (and not with the hero Heracles, who is but the absent object of her every attention and concern) not only as a result of viewing the action from her vantage point from the very start of the play but also because of the laudability of her point of view and her exemplary moderation.²⁹⁰

And yet, as early as Deianeira's very first speech, she reveals the limits of her knowledge even as she is expressing her mindfulness of them. In the prudent maxim with which she opens the play, she points up her recognition of the shifting nature of fate and the impossibility for "you" to know "whether a man has a good or a bad [life] until one dies" (ὡς οὐκ ἂν αἰῶν' ἐκμάθοις βροτῶν, πρὶν ἂν θάνῃ τις). There is some irony to having Deianeira claim knowledge of the dire nature of her situation at this early point in the play when she in fact remains ignorant of the horrific degree to which the saying applies to herself, given the tragedy that the present day (and drama) has in store for her. She misses the mark entirely regarding the applicability of the old saying to her own life in a painfully ironic way, not only because her plight is going to be far greater than she ever could anticipate, but also because the very words that she uses to describe her fate contain an essential kernel of truth that completely eludes her (on which more in a moment). Of the nature of her misery to come, she remains tragically unaware, even though the notions of unwitting wrongdoing and the unpredictability of tragic turns of fate are at the heart of the opening maxim she utters.

Let us examine her wording more closely: Deianeira states that, "you may not completely learn of the lot of mortals, whether it is good (χρηστός) or bad (κακός), until a man dies." From the very beginning, Deianeira (and we) understand this maxim to mean that one cannot know whether a given individual's life is fortunate or not until his death, because, until that life comes to an end, unpredictable changes and revelations can change its course entirely. One can also take χρηστός in a moral sense, which it often carries, particularly when it is paired with κακός, as it is here, and will be again later on in the play, at a key point.²⁹¹ If χρηστός, paired as it is with κακός, is taken in its ethical sense, then the maxim concerns men's inability to know until they die not just

---

edy, see Dobrov 2001. On the metatheatrical aspects of Sophoclean drama, see Falkner 1993 and Ringer 1998; on metatheater in ancient and modern fiction, see Thumiger 2009.
290 See e.g., Vickers 1979 on suffering and sympathy in Greek tragedy in general, where he states, "the presence or absence of sympathy in a character creating or regarding suffering is throughout <Greek tragedy> agreed to be a mark of the existence or denial of humanity" (Vickers 1979, 70ff.).
291 See *LSJ*, χρηστός, 2.

the twists and turns that the course of their lives may take and how it will affect *them*, but what sort of *impact* they will have on others — a χρηστός life being one that is defined by the positive impact that it has on others, and a κακός life as one that has an adverse effect on them.[292] It is a deliberate choice on Sophocles' part to have the maxim (and the prologue) spoken by Deianeira, a character who is "other-directed" and defines her good or bad fortune entirely in terms of another's (Heracles') wellbeing (or lack thereof).[293] The question that in fact will only be answerable at her death (especially in her case) is that of whether or not she has been useful and beneficial to those toward whom the ties and duties of *philia* require her to be. With typical Sophoclean irony, the poet has Deianeira herself use χρηστός and κακός in opposition to one another, in reference to another character (Lichas), when she coaxes him into telling the truth about Heracles. Her words will apply all too well to her own case:

εἰ δ' αὐτὸς αὑτὸν ὧδε παιδεύεις, ὅταν
θέλῃς λέγεσθαι χρηστός, ὀφθήσῃ κακός.
(451–2)

And if you have schooled yourself in this fashion, when you wish to be called good, you will be seen as evil.

Deianeira does not only wish to "be called" χρηστός; she genuinely pursues that as a worthy ethical goal onto itself. Once she proves κακός in deed while seeking to be χρηστός, "being seen as evil" (ὀφθήσῃ κακός) — particularly in the eyes of Heracles – will be enough of a reason for her to take her own life.

χρηστός is precisely what Deianeira strives to be throughout the play. Hers is a noble and caring mind; Heracles is the object of her every care and concern,

---

292 By Greek standards, those onto whom one should seek to do good are *philoi* (Blundell's 1989 monograph on Sophocles and Greek ethics is evocative of this principle in its very title, *Helping friends and harming enemies*), but Deianeira's standards are even higher. She seeks *not* to harm those who cause her harm and are not *philoi* strictly speaking, such as Iole, who threatens her marriage (but does so inadvertently). Deianeira's profound humanity enables her to shift from natural jealousy to compassion toward Iole; regarding her "umanità profonda," see Perrotta 1931, *passim*; on the noble way in which she responds to this jealousy, see 158–9 in particular. I return to her interactions with Iole below.
293 I am borrowing the expression "other-directed" from Schein 1984, 178, which he uses in reference to Hector in the *Iliad*. On Deianeira's "other-directed" disposition, see below, pp. 115 and 136–9. Gasti 1993 discusses the "social or externalized aspect of Deianeira's morality," a morality that is defined as "outward" and therefore "valid only in relation to society and other human beings."

unto whom she wishes to do good.²⁹⁴ The underlying irony of the play that the maxim encapsulates is that her apprehensive pessimism, voiced from the start, still falls short of the reality that she is about to bear: she will not just *endure* harm but *inflict* it inadvertently, and experience unbearable suffering when she is given the painful opportunity to watch this glaring disparity between intent and actual outcome play itself out. Her lot will be κακός, not just in the sense of sorrowful, as she understands it, but in the sense of "detrimental to others." Causing harm to others is precisely what her kind and noble character seeks to avoid at all costs and in every circumstance, including with regard to complete strangers, even though they may cause her pain and threaten her marriage, as Iole does.²⁹⁵ It is this sort of sorrow – which stems from causing harm to others, whom one ought to love – that ultimately will drive Deianeira to her death.

For the audience members, who knew from the tradition the role that Deianeira was to play in causing her husband to die a horrible death, her statement regarding her knowledge of the unpredictable nature of human life, including her own, delivered with such pessimistic conviction, sounds a woefully ironic note, because she still falls short of intuiting the inconceivable tragedy to follow, even as she expresses certainty that hers (and every man's) knowledge is necessarily limited. Her utterance is, as Seale puts it, "on the verge of truth,"²⁹⁶ as all of Deianeira's attempts to grasp truth are, but just on the verge: she still remains far from suspecting the fatal damage that she is about to cause to her husband and to herself despite being guided by the best of intentions.

That Deianeira should prove harmful (κακή) to Heracles is precisely what drives her fear in the account she gives of a past event that defines her relationship to him: her wedding day.²⁹⁷ This scene is the first of many to dramatize her helplessness by having the spectacle of her own unwitting agency play out before her eyes. Deianeira brings the audience back to the occasion of her marriage

---

294 Deianeira's every exchange, both with the Chorus and with her son Hyllus, is centered on Heracles. Her anxiety and hope for his return build up the audience's expectations of Heracles' appearance on stage, which is delayed until much later on in the play. She cries for Heracles (51), talks about him incessantly (67, 74), and is filled with a longing to see him (105). The Chorus of young women describes her state of permanent fear as indissociable from her central preoccupation: concern with her husband's safe return (εὔμναστον ἀνδρὸς δεῖμα τρέφουσαν ὁδοῦ, 108).
295 I turn to Deianeira's interaction with Iole below.
296 Seale 1982, 181.
297 It was not a happy one; see Ormand (1999: 38 ff.). The past looms large throughout the play, playing a major role in shaping the present and driving its characters' actions and reactions; see Kyriakou 2011, 371–432.

to Heracles, leading them to watch through her eyes the daunting spectacle of two superhuman forces in common pursuit of her great beauty: Heracles and the river-god Achelous, engaged in a violent battle to the death for her hand. She recalls how she meekly waited on the sidelines for her fate to be decided, as a passive, helpless spectator. The scene was so unbearable that she eventually averted her gaze. For an account of it, she says, one should ask someone who was not only present, but actually watched the savage struggle take place (22–5).[298]

No doubt Deianeira's vulnerability and averted gaze offer a pointed contrast to Heracles' powerful, active role in protecting her, a beautiful maiden in distress, when he rescued her from a forced union with a lecherous monster in order to satisfy his own erotic longing.[299] But placing Deianeira in the position of reluctant observer achieves more than merely underscoring her helplessness while she awaits the battle's outcome.[300] What is it exactly about this battle that drives her to turn her face away? Fear, but fear of what? It is worth taking a closer look at the sources of her reluctance to watch her fate play out in the contest. The battle scene and her response to it foreground aspects of her character that shed a significant light on the rest of the play. She was too afraid to witness its outcome, she says, because she felt that she had played a role in provoking it:

ἐγὼ γὰρ ἥμην ἐκπεπληγμένη φόβῳ
μή μοι τὸ κάλλος ἄλγος ἐξεύροι ποτέ.
(24–5)

I sat apart, overwhelmed with terror
lest my beauty should somehow bring me pain.

Some critics have athetized line 25, under the mistaken assumption that Deianeira is expressing some form of narcissism here that would diminish the pathos

---

298 This is precisely the role that the Chorus of Trachinian women will fulfill later. They fill in the details of the fight that led to Deianeira being wedded to the great hero as though they had seen it, though they were not actually present at the scene: see lines 497–530. I return to this account below.
299 On the nature of Heracles' relationship to Deianeira as defined by (and as an expression of) "male homosocial desire," see Ormand 1999.
300 Such a passive role is not surprising in light of the standards and practices of Sophocles' contemporaries; Deianeira is but another marriageable female, confined to the role of a commodity in what amounted to a transaction between two males fighting to obtain her as their bride; see Ormand 1999, 36–59. Wohl also discusses the commodification and passivitiy of the female role here, but offers a different interpretation for why Deianeira refuses to watch (Wohl 1998, Part One).

of the scene.³⁰¹ Such a reading is a misunderstanding of what motivates her fear. The reason she stresses her own beauty in these lines is that her "rank and beauty make her a fitting battle prize."³⁰² Her fear is fear "that Heracles will be defeated on her account, that is, on account of her 'beauty':"³⁰³ it is fear *for her beloved*. Her words convey the intense force of her beauty,³⁰⁴ along with her sense that she has no control over it — an awareness that she has been granted possession of it, that it exerts great power, and that it brings with it the potential for dire consequences. The way she talks about it (μή μοι τὸ κάλλος ἄλγος ἐξεύροι ποτέ, 25) makes it clear that she experiences her beauty as something that is not a part of her: rather, it is an attribute that she did not choose, an alien agent that has grafted itself onto her, which is threatening and might prove destructive to others and to herself. *That* is the source of her fear.

This statement illustrates an important point: Deianeira knows she is powerless when it comes to her own attractiveness and its impact on others; her beauty, by contrast, is both powerful and potentially destructive. Strictly speaking, she would bear no responsibility for the harm caused by her beauty, yet the idea that harm might come of something associated with her still pains her. Though she neither chose her beauty nor controls its power over others, she nonetheless states that if anything should happen to one for whom she cares (Heracles) because of it, this would cause her extreme pain (ἄλγος). The scene of Heracles' combat with Achelous as witnessed by Deianeira shows her reluctance to see Heracles suffer and prepares the audience to experience with particular force the *pathos* of Heracles' actual downfall, not only at the sight of a powerful hero in extreme pain, but above all because they watch the impact of that pain on those who witness his demise and especially on the one who caused it: Deianeira. If Deianeira cannot bear the thought that her beauty — an attribute, a gift from the divine – might cause harm to Heracles, then what will her reaction be when the news arrives that the love-philter that she sent to Heracles proved ruinous to him? Though it will be made clear by the Chorus and other characters

---

301 The anachronism of such a reading is noted by Easterling 1977, 122. The other argument for excising the line is that its proverbial form is deemed inappropriate. The opening maxim of the play is enough to dismiss the latter argument.
302 Easterling 1982 *ad loc.*
303 Reinhardt (1933) 1979 242 n. 6 (originally published in German, 1933; English translation based on the second edition of 1941, published 1979) underscores the altruistic motivation for the queen's concern, which is very much in keeping with her character as we come to know it in the scenes that follow.
304 The Chorus later confirms that it is indeed Deianeira's desirable beauty and the lust that it inspired that led Heracles to engage in the potentially fatal struggle against Achelous (514: ἱέμενοι λεχέων, 523: ἁ δ' εὐῶπις ἁβρά).

that her agency was limited and her intentions pure, and that the decision to use the philter, like her beauty, was the fruit of Aphrodite's will and part of Zeus's divine plan, to Deianeira, the question of intent and agency will not matter when the time comes for assessing her own actions and whether or not her life was κακός.

Pity and Vulnerability

One of the distinctive traits that defines Deianeira's character is directly linked to the queen's understanding of mortal limits: it is her predisposition to pity and compassion for others, even when it threatens her own well-being. This predisposition to pity makes her, in many respects, the ideal spectator, and one with whom, as we have seen, the audience is consequently led to identify.[305]

Every one of Deianeira's interactions with others and each of her reactions to their plight is exemplary for its profound humanity. Early in the play, the herald Lichas brings news of Heracles' victorious sacking of Oechalia, Eurytus's city: the hero is not only alive; he is victorious and on his way home. Lichas joyfully announces the arrival of a group of captive women, the hero's war booty, which precedes the hero's return:

ἴδε ἴδ', ὦ φίλα γύναι·
τάδ' ἀντίπρῳρα δή σοι
βλέπειν πάρεστ' ἐναργῆ.
(222–4)

See, see, dear Lady! You can look on this before your eyes, in all clarity![306]

Lichas assumes that these women will be a welcome sight for Heracles' wife to look upon and relish. After all, the women are tangible evidence of Heracles' vic-

---

[305] Whitman 1951, 106, describes her as "a very exquisite woman." As I mentioned earlier, Falkner argues that Deianeira provides the audience with a model spectator because of her (gendered) perspective, and he connects this perspective with her predisposition to pity (Falkner in Sternberg 2005, 165–92). Contrast Ringer, who argues that Deianeira is "an audience surrogate" but "an imperfect audience" because of her deficient knowledge in contrast with the actual spectators' alleged "omniscience" (Ringer 1998, 54).

[306] See also Lichas: γυναικῶν ὧν ὁρᾷς ἐν ὄμμασιν, 241; τάσδε δ' ἅσπερ εἰσορᾷς, 283. Being an eyewitness to the procession should carry with it a guarantee of the incontestable truth of Heracles' victory and of the queen's own good fortune in connection with his: ἄνασσα, νῦν σοι τέρψις ἐμφανὴς κυρεῖ, 291.

tory, and their presence signals happiness to come, pointing as it does to the hero's imminent homecoming.

From her personal perspective, Deianeira has grounds to rejoice, as the herald and Chorus expect her to. Yet as the procession of female prisoners files before her, she reacts very differently from what others expect. In her response, the audience is given a chance to see her character's compassion and moderation at their peak. She concedes that the women before her are indeed a concrete display of Heracles' glory. She echoes the Chorus and herald's abundant references to the act of seeing as she acknowledges this:

> ὁρῶ, φίλαι γυναῖκες, οὐδέ μ' ὄμματος
> φρουρὰν παρῆλθε, τόνδε μὴ λεύσσειν στόλον·[307]
> (225–6)
>
> I see it, dear maidens, the sight has not escaped my watchful gaze, and I do see that procession.

Yet the queen does not focus on the spectacle's immediate relevance to herself. Instead, she views the scene from a universalizing perspective and sees it as yet another illustration of the human condition in general. Rather than rejoicing in the women's subjection to her powerful husband, she is able to extrapolate and view their misery in broader terms. The mortals that she sees are pitiable (οἰκτραὶ γάρ, εἰ μὴ ξυμφοραὶ κλέπτουσί με, 243), she says, because the plight that they are enduring is the result of an unexpected turn that could just as well befall her or her family at any point — for such is the unpredictable nature of fate:

> ὅμως δ' ἔνεστι τοῖσιν εὖ σκοπουμένοις
> ταρβεῖν τὸν εὖ πράσσοντα, μὴ σφαλῇ ποτε.
> ἐμοὶ γὰρ οἶκτος δεινὸς εἰσέβη, φίλαι,
> ταύτας ὁρώσῃ δυσπότμους ἐπὶ ξένης
> χώρας ἀοίκους ἀπάτοράς τ' ἀλωμένας, (300)
> αἳ πρὶν μὲν ἦσαν ἐξ ἐλευθέρων ἴσως

---

[307] Easterling notes the irony intrinsic to the emphasis on sight and revelation here (even the herald himself is a "revelation" of sorts: cf. φανέντα, 228) in light of what the women's arrival actually means for Deianeira: "The character who is to be deceived [is] asserting the clarity of her vision" (Easterling 1982, 107 *ad* 225–334). Seale 1982, 189, notes the importance of the stress on Deianeira's visual perception here as well and contrasts it with the audience's slightly different visual experience of the scene:

> Deianira not only echoes the words of the Chorus but in a peculiarly redundant way stresses the watchful perceptiveness of her eyes as she observes the train of captives. The audience is bound to react by intensifying its own visual response, to test its own view of the scenic situation against that of Deianeira ... *We are watching Deianeira watch.* (italics mine)

ἀνδρῶν, τανῦν δὲ δοῦλον ἴσχουσιν βίον.
ὦ Ζεῦ τροπαῖε, μή ποτ' εἰσίδοιμί σε
πρὸς τοὐμὸν οὕτω σπέρμα χωρήσαντά ποι
(296–304)

But nonetheless it is the way of those who consider things with care to fear for the man who is fortunate, in case he may one day come to grief. Yes, an awesome pity comes over me, dear women, when I see these unfortunate ones wandering in a foreign land, with no home, and no father; perhaps they were formerly the children of free men. Zeus, god of trophies, may I never see you going against my offspring in that manner.

The queen's "awesome pity" (οἶκτος δεινός, 298) is unexpected and contributes to foregrounding the exceptional degree to which she is able to feel pity for others. Her compassionate disposition is predicated on her recognition of the variable nature of fate and her acute awareness of all mortals' limitations, which have been emphasized from the start of the play. That awareness leads her to recognize every mortal's vulnerability to powerful divine forces and to be predisposed to pity as a result. She can see the concrete signs of Heracles' victory before her clearly but remains conscious that there is no permanence to good fortune. As she watches the women of Oechalia parade their miserable fate before her, Deianeira is reminded of what she shares with them on a universal level as a fellow mortal: that she, too, is vulnerable to unpredictable turns of fortune that remain entirely beyond human control.[308] She notes that the misfortune that has befallen these women came about through no fault of their own: all was a result of Zeus's agency alone, as he "went against" them (πρὸς ... χωρήσαντά). Keeping mortal limitations at the fore of her mind, Deianeira shows great prudence in her emotional reaction to a sight that might appear to benefit her. With the impermanence of fortune in mind, she defines the enlightened onlooker as one who sees a happy man and fears for him: "it is the way of those who consider things with care to fear for the man who is fortunate" (ἔνεστι τοῖσιν εὖ σκοπουμένοις ταρβεῖν τὸν εὖ πράσσοντα, 296). Her apprehension is a form of prudence: it is the recognition of mortal powerlessness in the face of greater forces that feeds her fear of unexpected reversals of fortune. The place of fear in eliciting Deianeira's pity is a textbook example of the mechanics of pity as defined by Aristotle, in which fear occupies a prominent place.[309] That fear is what

---

[308] Regarding the recognition of one's own vulnerability as essential to the experience pity, see above n. 275.
[309] *Rh.* 1378a30–1378b2: "Let pity, then, be a kind of pain in the case of an apparent destructive or painful harm of one not deserving to encounter it, which one might expect oneself, or one of one's own, to suffer, and this when it seems near" (transl. Konstan 2001). It is this fear – the expectation of harm for oneself – that constitutes an essential component of, and condition for,

leads to her extraordinary predisposition to pity. Despite the power and status differential between her and the captives, the queen retains the ability to imagine that these female prisoners, who are now slaves, "homeless and fatherless" (ἀοίκους ἀπάτορας, 300) and, hence, helplessly subjected to another's power, may have been born "of free men," as she was (αἳ πρὶν μὲν ἦσαν ἐξ ἐλευθέρων ἴσως | ἀνδρῶν, 301–2).

Deianeira's constant awareness of the fragility of human existence is a form of enlightened wisdom on a par with Odysseus's in Sophocles' *Ajax*.[310] A comparison between her stance in the scene we are currently considering and that of Odysseus in the opening scene of the *Ajax* is illuminating: the two have much in common, not only in their perception of human vulnerability, but particularly in the way Sophocles casts them both in the role of internal spectators to the plight of others in order to have them acknowledge and vicariously experience human limitations, especially in relation to the divine. In the *Ajax*, as in the *Trachiniae*, the divine and mortal spectators occupy antithetical roles in relation to the spectacle before them.[311] Athena is the agent and willing witness of a spectacle that she stages; Odysseus is the uneasy and reluctant spectator to it. When the goddess Athena invites Odysseus to stand beside her and witness Ajax's humiliating delusion from the secure vantage point of an invisible spectator, the son of Laertes refuses to indulge in mocking his enemy (γέλως ἥδιστος, 79). Instead, he pities him:

Αθ. ὁρᾷς, Ὀδυσσεῦ, τὴν θεῶν ἰσχὺν ὅση;
τούτου τίς ἄν σοι τἀνδρὸς ἢ προνούστερος
ἢ δρᾶν ἀμείνων ηὑρέθη τὰ καίρια;
Οδ. ἐγὼ μὲν οὐδέν' οἶδ'· ἐποικτίρω δέ νιν
δύστηνον ἔμπας, καίπερ ὄντα δυσμενῆ,
ὁθούνεκ' ἄτῃ συγκατέζευκται κακῇ,
οὐδὲν τὸ τούτου μᾶλλον ἢ τοὐμὸν σκοπῶν.
ὁρῶ γὰρ ἡμᾶς οὐδὲν ὄντας ἄλλο πλὴν
εἴδωλ' ὅσοιπερ ζῶμεν ἢ κούφην σκιάν.
(118–26)

---

pity. On the practical aspects of pity in connection with fear, see Belfiore 1992, 181–9, 248–9. On pity, pain, and the narrow relationship between pity and fear, including with regards to the sort of pain that they both involve, see Konstan 2001, 128–36.

[310] The parallel between the two characters is noted by Winnington-Ingram 1980, 76–7. W.-I. also remarks on the tragic irony of the drama, whereby a frame of mind that should lead to the avoidance of disaster does not, in fact, save the character, but precipitates her disaster.

[311] The divine presence is not always as explicit in the *Trachiniae*, as we will see, and with good reason: the elusiveness of the divine is precisely what causes, and indeed constitutes, human powerlessness.

ATH. Do you see, Odysseus, how great is the strength of the gods? Whom could you have found more prudent than this man, or better able to do what the situation demanded? ODY. I know of no one, but in his misery I pity him all the same, even though he hates me, because he is yoked beneath a ruinous delusion – I think of my own lot no less than his. For I see that all of us who live, as many as we are, are nothing but ghosts, or a fleeting shadow.[312]

Taking his place as a mortal beside a gloating god to look on at another mortal, Odysseus is reminded of just how trifling and insignificant human power is in contrast to the gods'. He understands that, in being made to look upon a display of his enemy's abasement, he is, in fact, being given a window onto what he and that enemy share: subjection to divine authority *qua* mortals. Athena reveals that this is, indeed, the point of making Odysseus gaze upon the spectacle Ajax's delusion: to provide her favorite protégé with a vignette of her (divine) dominance (ὁρᾷς, Ὀδυσσεῦ, τὴν θεῶν ἰσχὺν ὅση, 118). Odysseus encapsulates his recognition of human helplessness with a striking set of images: mortals are nothing but ghosts, fleeting through life with no more impact than a shadow (121–6). When Athena shifts to a more openly threatening tone, she proves to the audience that Odysseus's pity, along with the fear from which that pity stems, is entirely justified:

> τοιαῦτα τοίνυν εἰσορῶν ὑπέρκοπον
> μηδέν ποτ' εἴπῃς αὐτὸς ἐς θεοὺς ἔπος,
> μηδ' ὄγκον ἄρῃ μηδέν', εἴ τινος πλέον
> ἢ χειρὶ βρίθεις ἢ μακροῦ πλούτου βάθει.
> (127–30)

Look, then at such things, and never yourself utter an arrogant word against the gods, nor assume any conceit, if you outweigh another in strength, or through the weight of your great wealth.

Odysseus's feeling of pity stems from the temporary voyeuristic stance that the goddess grants him and the resulting realization that he, like Ajax, controls so little of what he knows, sees, and does (85), as his vision may be partial or veiled at any point without his knowledge. Accordingly, what Odysseus sees in Ajax is not a humiliated enemy, who might be a subject for rejoicing, but a fellow mortal, whose blindness, inflicted in the service of a divinity's personal agenda, could just as well be his own. Spectator and object of spectacle alike are only able to see as much as the divine allows them to; their roles are interchangeable and subject to divine whim. Odysseus can easily imagine himself playing the

---

[312] The translation here is based on Jebb 1893.

principal role in an act staged by a god just as Ajax does: to an extent, human existence itself means being unwittingly cast in a miniature play while the gods look on.

Deianeira's circumstances do not particularly invite wariness: she is a queen, in a position of power, and wedded to the mighty Heracles. Yet like Odysseus, she has the ability to see her own vulnerability in the spectacle of others' misfortunes and not to assume that her status as spectator of the plight of others grants her any particular superiority. She recognizes that the individual instantiation of plight and loss of power before her exemplifies the erratic essence of fate, which forms the very fabric of human life and to which she, too, is subjected. Such fickle turns of fortune are to be feared by all, no matter their current power or status.

The supreme irony is that, by feeling pity for the women whose presence will, in fact, soon cause her great harm, Deianeira is illustrating the very limits of mortal knowledge that are the basis for her pity to begin with.[313] The queen is right to be reminded of her own vulnerability as she realizes that the fate of the captives before her might well some day be her own, but she has no sense of the actual direct threat that they pose to her. She is once again "on the verge of truth"[314] when she expresses fear that misfortune might some day befall herself or her loved ones as it has the newly captured women, but she is still far from intuiting that one of these very women will very soon turn out to be a direct source of harm for her. While she feels a commendable pity here based on fear that a similar misfortune might befall her, what she really ought to feel if she possessed full knowledge of the situation is fear and fear alone.

Deianeira gets even closer to the truth and further away from it at the same time when she goes on to single out one of the captives as particularly worthy of her pity because of her demeanor, which reminds her of herself. The woman who stands out from the crowd of female prisoners does so because of her appearance: she seems to be of noble descent. Deianeira imagines that this woman's past status and birth were similar to her own (γενναία δέ τις, 309)[315] and pities her the most (νιν τῶνδε πλεῖστον ᾤκτισα, 312), not only because she sees a similarity between them, but also because of the stark contrast that she imagines there must be between the young woman's past (good) fortune, akin to her own present one, and the misfortune that has now befallen her (312). When De-

---

313 On the limits of Deianeira's knowledge and the ironic degree to which, unbeknownst to her, the women reflect her own misery, see Easterling 1982 and Seale 1982 above, n. 307; also Ringer 1998, 58–61.
314 The expression is from Seale 1982, 181.
315 Those who are most similar to us are most likely to evoke our pity: see Arist., *Rh.* 1386a.

ianeira asks to learn more about the silent beauty before her, the herald, Lichas, pretends not to know her identity and seeks to bring the conversation to an end by stressing the unlikelihood that the maiden will speak: she has, so far, only been given to weeping, he says (322–8).

Kamerbeek believes that the "confrontation" between the two women was a novelty introduced by Sophocles and that the audience would have known the identity of Iole from the first moment Deianeira intuitively singled her out.[316] The only one not to know the identity of Heracles' new mistress, Iole, would be Deianeira herself.[317] If the encounter between the two women is indeed a Sophoclean novelty, the audience would likely have been evaluating it with a comparable scene in mind, in which a queen and a war captive who are going to share the same bed first meet: Clytemnestra's confrontation with a completely silent Cassandra in Aeschylus's *Agamemnon*.[318] Deianeira's every word defines her as the very antithesis of Clytemnestra. Unlike her predecessor, who knows Cassandra's identity and tries to bully her into speaking and coming into the house, Sophocles' Deianeira explicitly voices her desire to let the dazzling young woman be. Deianeira allows her to go into the house "just as she wishes" because she does not want to add any new pain to the girl's plight (329–31).

When she displays such generous concern for the prisoner's well-being, Deianeira does not yet know Iole's true identity, nor the threat that the young woman poses to her marriage bed. But even when she does discover these, the queen's reaction holds further surprises for the audience. A messenger comes onstage and informs Deianeira that Lichas has deceived her by concealing Iole's identity: the beautiful youth that we have been watching the aging Deia-

---

316 Kamerbeek 1963, 6.
317 The herald, Lichas, withholds from Deianeira the identity of Iole and Heracles' newfound passion for her for as long as possible, until he is exposed as a liar by the messenger in the following scene; I turn to this below.
318 The intertextual and intraperformative reference would be all the more obvious as, in other mythic traditions, Deianeira deliberately destroys Heracles using deceit just as Clytemnestra murders Agamemnon by ensnaring him. The tradition of an ill-intentioned Deianeira was so predominant that, by the fifth century, Deianeira would have been associated in the audience's mind with Clytemnestra and Medea both. On Deianeira and Medea, see Davies 1991 (introduction); on Deianeira and Clytemnestra, see Pozzi 1994 (n. 18 with bibliography). For a discussion of the legal use of the distinction between the Deianeira and Clytemnestra in a fifth-century Athenian law court case, with a thorough and nuanced discussion of the thorny question of intention and responsibility in the case of Sophocles' Deianeira, see Wohl 2010. Carawan adopts the viewpoint that Deianeira's character in Sophocles is far closer to that of Clytemnestra than critics allow; the reasons for which I disagree are, I think, apparent throughout this chapter. Carawan also offers a good overview of the different poetic traditions regarding Deianeira before Sophocles (Carawan 2000, 219).

neira contemplate with admiration and pity is the newest object of Heracles' lust.[319] She is the true reason for his having sacked Oechalia and for his delay in returning home to his wife. On hearing the messenger's revelation, the queen confronts Lichas. He sheepishly admits to having concealed the truth because he wished not to wound his mistress's heart (481–2). In Deianeira's response to his revelation, the audience discovers further the nobility and generosity of the queen's character.[320]

Armed with Lichas's avowal, Deianeira realizes the personal and immediate threat posed to her, and to her marriage, by the young woman whose stunning beauty and demeanor she had been admiring and pitying (376–7). Yet even when faced with this revelation, Deianeira, surprisingly enough, reiterates her feelings of pity for Iole. Her words articulate the mental process underlying her emotional response clearly and provide the audience with further insights into the basis for her compassion. Her pity, she says, stems from her lucid assessment of the nature of love.[321] If she were to attempt to fight Heracles' *nosos* (his desire for Iole), she would be fighting the gods (θεοῖσι δυσμαχοῦντες, 492).[322] It would be as vain to battle Heracles' desire for Iole as it would be to enter into a boxing match with the divine (πύκτης ὅπως ἐς χεῖρας, 442) – and all the more vain as the power of *erôs* is such that it holds sway even over the gods themselves (οὗτος γὰρ

---

[319] I believe Seale 1982 is right to stress Deianeira's age and experience as important elements that would be made visually obvious to the audience through her mask, in stark contrast to Iole's youthfulness.

[320] Some scholars, including Kamerbeek, read Deianeira's words as a deception speech on a par with the one uttered by Ajax just before he exits the stage to throw himself onto his sword in Sophocles' *Ajax*. But there is no reason or need for us to interpret her reassuring words to Lichas as a "calculated deception," *pace* Heiden 1989, 68ff. It is highly unlikely that Sophocles would go to such great lengths from the start of the play to present Deianeira as a model of self-restraint and sincerity, benevolent moderation and compassion, only to have her mind-set shift so abruptly to a duplicitous and scheming disposition. I continue to stress the implausibility of such a shift below. See Whitman 1951, Winnington-Ingram 1980, and many others' assessment of Deianeira as an unquestionably "noble, compassionate, modest" character (Easterling 1982, 6). This is Perrotta's understanding of her character as well; he sees her as deeply good, marked by a profound tenderness and gentleness that no Euripidean female character ever equals (Perrotta 1935, 477 ff.). For a different take on the queen's character, see e.g., Carawan 2000.

[321] On the cognitive dimension of pity, see e.g., Nussbaum 1996 and Konstan 2001.

[322] Heracles lost control of his own actions, becoming bewitched (355) and enflamed (368) with passion; he is altogether vanquished by his fearsome desire (476, 489). The portrayal of *erôs* as an infectious disease is a *topos*; see Mitchell-Boyask in Ormand 2012, 318, regarding *nosos* and *erôs* in Greek tragedy, with bibliography. Compare Heracles' madness as *nosos* in Euripides; cf. e.g., Holmes 2010. On the metaphorical depictions of these *nosoi*, see e.g., Biggs 1966 and Segal 1977.

ἄρχει καὶ θεῶν ὅπως θέλει, 443) and rules over her (Deianeira), too (κἀμοῦ γε, 444). The queen's resignation is not simply a trite recognition of the roving eye of man, who does not always take pleasure in the same things (χαίρειν πέφυκεν οὐχὶ τοῖς αὐτοῖς ἀεί, 440); it is an expression of her awareness of how vain it would be to attempt to struggle with a force whose power overcomes even the immortals. Laying blame on her husband, or on the woman for whom he now lusts, would be madness (κάρτα μαίνομαι, 446); for none can fight the divine might of *erôs*.

Perhaps no other Sophoclean hero displays such "other-directed,"[323] benevolent sentiments and such "a quality of purity" as Deianeira when it comes to Iole and her beauty.[324] That beauty – the very reason for which Iole is a threat to Deianeira and her marriage – is also the reason for which Deianeira pities her the most. Though she sees the maiden as a cause of destruction to her own marriage, she never considers Iole guilty or deserving of punishment. She realizes that the captive's ravaging beauty is no cause for condemning her: though Iole is a destroyer and enslaver (ἔπερσε κἀδούλωσεν, 467) she has wrought destruction *unwittingly* (οὐχ ἑκοῦσα, 466) and is wretched as a result (δύσμορος, 466).[325] Iole, in all her dazzling beauty, is but an embodiment of Aphrodite's power; the girl deserves no blame, for she bears no direct responsibility for the wreckage caused by her beauty. Rather, she too must endure its consequences:

> τὸ δ' εἰδέναι τί δεινόν; οὐχὶ χἀτέρας
> πλείστας ἀνὴρ εἷς Ἡρακλῆς ἔγημε δή;
> κοὔπω τις αὐτῶν ἔκ γ' ἐμοῦ λόγον κακὸν
> ἠνέγκατ' οὐδ' ὄνειδος· ἥδε τ' οὐδ' ἂν εἰ
> κάρτ' ἐντακείη τῷ φιλεῖν, ἐπεί σφ' ἐγὼ
> ᾤκτιρα δὴ μάλιστα προσβλέψασ', ὅτι
> τὸ κάλλος αὐτῆς τὸν βίον διώλεσεν,
> καὶ γῆν πατρῴαν οὐχ ἑκοῦσα δύσμορος
> ἔπερσε κἀδούλωσεν.
>   (459–67)

What is so terrible about knowing? Has not Heracles, one man, slept with many other women already? And never yet has any of them incurred an evil word or a reproach from *me*; and this one never would, even if he should become completely absorbed in his love for her, since I pitied her most when I laid eyes on her, because her beauty has destroyed her life, and because, ill-fated, she unwittingly destroyed her native land, and reduced it to slavery.

---

[323] The epithet is used by Schein 1984, 178, in reference to Hector in the *Iliad*. Like Hector, Deianeira is a hero(ine) of *aidôs* (Redfield 1975, 119), focused always on her obligations and responsibilities toward others.
[324] Reinhardt (1933) 1979, 2.
[325] See lines 466–7.

In her response to the unveiling of Iole's identity, Deianeira once again demonstrates her ability to see the universal laws governing her own and other mortals' lives and to recognize the existence of greater forces guiding human action and emotion, which are beyond any individual mortal's understanding. Harmful and painful though it is to her personally, she carefully considers the motivations and consequences of the human behavior before her — specifically, how they extend beyond any individual's responsibility, including Heracles' or Iole's. As Lichas notes, Deianeira, "being a mortal, think[s] like a mortal, and not unreasonably" (θνητὴν φρονοῦσαν θνητὰ κοὐκ ἀγνώμονα, 473).[326]

We are in a better position now to understand Deianeira's observations concerning her resentment of her own beauty and her fear of the consequences it might bring in her opening account of Heracles' struggle against Achelous. Then as now, beauty (Deianeira's then, here Iole's) is connected with erotic love (Heracles' love, then for Deianeira, now for Iole). Both those who possess beauty and those who are irresistibly drawn to it illustrate the lack of true mortal agency in human interactions: the former do not choose to be objects of spectacle and desire and play no active role in the impact that they have on those who see and desire them; the latter, in turn, fall victim to the sight of beauty before them. Deianeira's own past experience puts her in a singular position to recognize Iole's own powerlessness as she watches the young woman, who is dazzling and pitiable all at once in her seductiveness. While the battle between Heracles and the river-god Achelous unfolded, Deianeira turned away from a scene that both implicated her – she would be the cause of Heracles' destruction should anything happen to him – and excluded her, for she was unable to take any action to affect its outcome. With Iole's arrival, she is again a spectator to an illustration of mortal helplessness, but this time she is observing another woman in the role in which she had formerly found herself: Iole is playing the inadvertent and even reluctant role of the object of desire in a destructive scenario in which she did not choose to take part. Deianeira perceives this tableau for what it truly is: an example of the limits of mortal agency. What she does not know is that she herself is about to play a starring and equally unwitting role in that same tableau.

---

[326] Lichas's statement is "one of the most fundamental Greek ideas;" see Easterling 1982, *ad loc*. The herald's description would also aptly describe the extraordinary display of pity on the part of Odysseus in the *Ajax*.

From spectator to agent: Playing Aphrodite

When Lichas confirms that Heracles, "who in all other matters excelled in strength, has been completely vanquished by his love for this girl" (ὡς τἄλλ' ἐκεῖνος πάντ' ἀριστεύων χεροῖν | τοῦ τῆσδ' ἔρωτος εἰς ἅπανθ' ἥσσων ἔφυ, 488–9), Deianeira, in her reply, appears to be attempting to distance herself from his "disease" (νόσος, 491):[327] "I shall not take on myself a disease that would bring a burden on myself, in a vain struggle against the gods" (κοὔτοι νόσον γ' ἐπακτὸν ἐξαρούμεθα, | θεοῖσι δυσμαχοῦντες, 491–2).[328] She speaks with conviction, using the future tense, but one senses that underlying her assertive statement is a fearful, hortatory subjunctive, an exhortation to herself exuding more hope than confidence in her ability to keep the νόσος of love at bay.[329] In choosing to fight against all-conquering *erôs*'s power over Heracles, Deianeira would be battling fate itself,[330] and she is aware that in doing so she would be electing to bring harm upon herself in vain. Her earlier statement to that effect sounds an ominous note: Eros (here personified) rules even the gods themselves, just as he wishes (οὗτος γὰρ ἄρχει καὶ θεῶν ὅπως θέλει, 443), but this means that he rules her, too (κἀμοῦ γε, 444). As Deianeira acknowledges the impossibility of

---

327 Compare 445: τῇδε τῇ νόσῳ.
328 ἐξαίρομαι usually occurs in contexts in which someone is "carrying off" a prize, in a positive sense, while the uncompounded form of the verb can be used to refer to burdens, as is clearly the case here.
329 I do not believe that the queen is conniving here: the words that she speaks are fitting to her nature as we have come to know it, and we have no reason to doubt their sincerity. A cynical reading of her words here would sap the complexity from the central issue of the discrepancy between the purity of her intent and the catastrophic consequences of her actions, so hotly debated by Heracles and Hyllus in the final scene (1021–end). A conniving Deianeira would hardly deserve the attention devoted to the question of her innocence in the culminating scene of the play. Whitman 1951, 115, argues convincingly in favor of Deianeira's purity in very strong and compelling terms: "It is heroic to maintain innocence in a situation such as hers, and if her innocence is denied, the play loses the meaning which regularly distinguishes Sophocles, the heroic humanist, from the psychologist Euripides." I would add that we should take Deianeira at her word when she states that her well-being is inextricably dependent on Heracles' (83–5): ἢ σεσώμεθα [ἢ πίπτομεν σοῦ πατρὸς ἐξολωλότος] κείνου βίον σώσαντος, ἢ οἰχόμεσθ' ἅμα, "Either we are saved if he has saved his life, or we are gone with him." This is proof of her good intentions: she wishes Heracles well, at least partly because it is in her own interest to do so. Her tremendous suffering after she harms him confirms the veracity of her claim.
330 "Strife against Eros means strife against the divine powers in general, against nature and Fate itself" (Kamerbeek 1963, 116 *ad loc.*)

fighting or curing the disease of love, she recognizes its potential to infect her as well.³³¹

Infect her it does. Deianeira leaves the stage to fetch "gifts in exchange for gifts"³³² and sets in motion an endeavor that will prove fatal both to herself and to Heracles. Presumably, the queen hatches her desperate plan between the time of her exit and her return to the stage, at which point she reveals it to the maidens of Trachis. During her absence, while the insidious power of *erôs* begins seeping in and guiding her response to the news of Heracles' treason, the Chorus of maidens sings its first stasimon. Fittingly, the subject of the choral song is the power of Aphrodite (Cypris). The song is an onstage reflection of the mental process that is taking place offstage and a mirror of *erôs*'s ascending sway over Deianeira, rife with many touches of Sophoclean irony and deserving of attention for the light it sheds on the steps leading to Deianeira's fatal initiative.

The Chorus states the theme of its song clearly in the opening line: "A mighty power is Cypris! She carries off victories, always" (μέγα τι σθένος ἁ Κύπρις· ἐκφέρεται νίκας | ἀεί, 497–8). The story that the Chorus goes on to tell is a familiar one: they sing of the contest between Heracles and the river-god Achelous to win Deianeira's hand, which Deianeira has already told from her perspective. In doing so, they fill in the blanks left by Deianeira's story. Hers was an incomplete account because she could not bear to watch the battle for fear of its outcome (22–5). The Chorus was not actually present at the scene, but it tells the tale with the authority of a true eyewitness, "as though [it had been] a spectator" (θάτηρ μὲν οἷα, 526).³³³ With no small amount of irony, the Chorus sings of the younger Deianeira's attractiveness and beauty (ἱέμενοι λεχέων, 514; ἁ δ' εὐῶπις ἁβρά, 523) just after the (now aging) queen has learned that Heracles lusts for the fresh beauty of a woman who is far younger than she. In calling attention to Deianeira's past allure, the song establishes a link between the two objects of Heracles' passion and underscores the ephemeral na-

---

331 On *erôs* progressing from a merely metaphorical disease to a literal, embodied ailment in the play, see Segal 1981, 60–108; also Mitchell-Boyask 2012. On the power of *erôs* guiding all of the characters' actions in the play, see Segal 1995. Wohl 1998 analyzes Deianeira's helplessness in terms of the gender dynamics of the play (see e.g., Wohl 1998, 36).
332 On the significance of this exchange, see Wohl 1998.
333 The text here is very corrupt; in line 526, the manuscript's ματήρ makes no sense given the context. Zielinski's emendation θατήρ is attractive, particularly since it is fitting in an agonistic context: crowds of spectators look on as athletes contend; see Easterling 1982, *ad loc.*

ture of the seductiveness granted by Aphrodite, over which neither woman has any control.[334]

Deianeira plays the same role in the Chorus's song as she did in her own account of the battle: that of a spectator who is unable to intervene and waits piteously as hero and river-god fight over her beauty:

ἁ δ' εὐῶπις ἀβρὰ
τηλαυγεῖ παρ' ὄχθῳ
ἧστο τὸν ὃν προσμένουσ' ἀκοίταν.
(523–5)

She, with her delicate, beautiful face,
sat in the far-seeing hill,
awaiting her bridegroom.

As in her own telling, Deianeira is reduced to a passive stance, an anxious gaze, casting occasional glances toward the battle from afar as it rages on (τὸ δ' ἀμφινείκητον ὄμμα νύμφας ἐλεινὸν ἀμμένει <τέλος>, 527–8).[335] This time, however, the audience is made aware of the presence of another witness who is also looking on closely as the battle unfolds: the goddess of love, Aphrodite. Amid the groans and indistinguishable limbs of the two opponents (517–22), the goddess stands, alone, and looks on as the action that she has staged plays out. Her stance is that of an umpire to the contest that she has set in motion: μόνα δ' εὔλεκτρος ἐν μέσῳ Κύπρις | ῥαβδονόμει ξυνοῦσα (515–6), "and alone in the center stands beautiful Cypris, to umpire the contest." Hers is a dispassionate gaze, providing a "sinister contrast"[336] to Deianeira's anxious one. While the maiden cowers in fear for Heracles, there is no preference on the goddess's part for either one of the two contenders, the monstrous river or the heroic son of Zeus. She is indifferent to the outcome. Far from averting her gaze, she watches the savage struggle closely and takes pleasure in the spectacle: she is a spectator who, unlike Deianeira, was also the willing and deliberate agent of the battle that she is watching.

The ode singing the power of *erôs* comes to an end, and Deianeira returns to the stage. Her stance has changed in several significant respects. She — the pas-

---

[334] On past and present and the repeated motif of the cyclical nature of time in the play, see Segal 1995, 69–94.
[335] The "far-seen" hill (τηλαυγεῖ παρ' ὄχθῳ) that she sits on as she awaits her bridegroom evokes her "anxious gaze" (Jebb *ad loc.*, translating *omma*) and distant viewpoint, as she monitors the battle from afar.
[336] Easterling 1982 *ad loc.*

sive viewer *par excellence* – has hatched a plan of action. She cannot bear to stand by and watch as Iole's youthful bloom "creeps forward" and the young woman blossoms into an ever more desirable beauty while her own attractiveness withers with each passing day:

ὁρῶ γὰρ ἥβην τὴν μὲν ἕρπουσαν πρόσω,
τὴν δὲ φθίνουσαν· ὧν <δ'> ἀφαρπάζειν φιλεῖ
ὀφθαλμὸς ἄνθος, τῶνδ' ὑπεκτρέπει πόδα.
(547–9)

For I see her youth advancing, and mine perishing; and the desiring eye turns away from those whose bloom it snatches.

Deianeira's words call attention to several embedded levels of viewing. Within her utterance, in addition to herself, there is another spectator. That viewer's active, aggressive gaze underscores the passivity of Deianeira's. She is watching Iole's beauty, but she is also watching Heracles watch that beauty and seeing its impact on him. As she watches his gaze shift from her to Iole, she witnesses her own demise in his heart. In describing Heracles' burning desire for Iole, the poetics convey the power of the maiden's beauty over the hero by juxtaposing Heracles' eye with the bloom of youth that his ardent gaze lusts after: ὀφθαλμὸς ἄνθος.[337] Deianeira watches Heracles' gaze as it shifts away from her to the next object of his passion while she remains a bystander, as helpless to stop her beauty from withering as she is to stop his eye (ὀφθαλμὸς) from capturing the next object of his sexual longing, snatching (ἀφαρπάζειν) the bloom (ἄνθος) of Iole as he did hers long ago. This is the point at which Deianieira brings up the "remedy" that has occurred to her: she is going to attempt to leave her stance of spectator and to control Heracles' gaze.

The queen announces to the Trachinian women that she has elaborated a plan:

ταῦτ' οὖν φοβοῦμαι μὴ πόσις μὲν Ἡρακλῆς
ἐμὸς καλῆται, τῆς νεωτέρας δ' ἀνήρ.
ἀλλ' οὐ γάρ, ὥσπερ εἶπον, ὀργαίνειν καλὸν
γυναῖκα νοῦν ἔχουσαν· ᾗ δ' ἔχω, φίλαι,
λυτήριον λύπημα, τῇδ' ὑμῖν φράσω.
(550–4)

This is why I am afraid that Heracles may be called my husband, but the younger woman's man. As I said, it is not honorable for a woman of sense to be angry; but the means I have of remedying pain, I will now tell you.

---

[337] The ardent glance of the lover is a *topos* of Greek poetry; see Jebb *ad loc.*

At first, the queen appears to have come out to the women to ask for their sympathy (συγκατοικτιουμένη, 535), a common occurrence in tragedy and a typically passive response to misfortune; but Deianeira's attitude is no longer passive. Her statement reflects the active role that she has determined to take on in view of the circumstances. She has come, she says, to tell the women "what she has been contriving with her hands" (τὰ μὲν φράσουσα χερσὶν ἀτεχνησάμην, 534).[338] What woman could remain beneath the same blanket with another woman for one man to embrace, and thus share her marriage bed with another?[339] Not one with the means to control her husband's concupiscent gaze. Desperate to retain and revive Heracles' attention, Deianeira remembers that, long ago, she was given a potential "remedy to pain" (λυτήριον λύπημα) by the centaur Nessus, at an equally erotically charged time: he was dying from the wound that Heracles had inflicted on him with one of his inescapable arrows in punishment for Nessus's own lustful desire for Deianeira, whom he had tried to rape while he helped her across the river Evenus. If she were to use the charm (κηλητήριον) that the dying centaur gave her, she would have the power to prevent the hero from ever seeing and, hence, loving another woman but herself: she would, the centaur promised, control his gaze (ὥστε μήτιν' εἰσιδὼν | στέρξει γυναῖκα κεῖνος ἀντὶ σοῦ πλέον, 576-7).

We have seen how Deianeira has, up to this point, been defined by her noble attempts to recognize the lack of veritable control that any mortal has over his or her individual actions, emotions, and perceptions. She has pursued knowledge and as much clarity of perspective as a limited mortal might have, seeking to act with appropriate prudence in light of the limitations of that perspective. In her desperation, however, she forgets how much this lack of control applies to her own person. Having recently uttered a speech in which she claimed that it would be madness to "enter into a boxing match" with Eros who rules all, even the gods (441-2), that is now precisely what Deianeira attempts.[340]

The queen is all too willing to believe in the effectiveness of what is her only and last resort. Just before she unveils her plan, she expresses the vanity of feeling anger toward Heracles: he is but the victim of a disease (νόσος), the disease of love (544). It would not be honorable for her, a woman of sense (καλὸν γυναῖκα νοῦν ἔχουσαν, 552-3), to feel anger toward him; rather, it is fear that she experiences (φοβοῦμαι, 550) lest her husband might actually more aptly be called "the younger woman's man" (τῆς νεωτέρας δ' ἀνήρ, 551, with obvious sexual im-

---

338 ἀτεχνησάμην and χερσὶν both suggest active involvement with some insistence.
339 See lines 539-46.
340 Concerning the process, nature, and consequences of Deianeira's unconsidered decision, see Hall in Goldhill and Hall 2009, ch. 4.

plications). Faced with this dilemma, she temporarily leaves the compliant stance of resignation and enters the ring to face the very divinity with whom she claimed it would be madness to fight. In a sudden and total reversal, the abandoned wife of the hero takes on an active role, seeking to guide the very fate whose unpredictable and uncontrollable nature she recognized with such docile acceptance in the opening lines of the play. While Lichas was the one hiding the truth from Deianeira earlier, now she is the one dissimulating her plan from him, coming out to speak to the women in secret (λάθρᾳ, 533). Discretion is necessary not because she believes that there is any evil inherent to her endeavor but because she might suffer disgrace if it were made known that she is attempting to tamper with matters pertaining to *erôs* and resorting to a degrading and desperate final recourse: black magic (596–7). If she were to fail, the disgrace would be even greater, as she would be exposed as one who not only attempted something unseemly, but did so in vain (μάταιον, 587).[341]

Even as she discloses her plan, Deianeira expressly states the wish "not to know or ever learn anything of rash crimes" and goes on to say that she "detest[s] women who perform them" (582–3). The Deianeira that the audience has come to know is one who differentiates carefully between knowledge from hearsay or mere perception, and knowledge from experience (141–52): the only form of knowledge that she deems reliable is the latter. Her trademark has been the great prudence with which she responds to all situations, in light of the unreliability of human perception and understanding. At this point, however, she expresses a desire for blindness rather than insight: she wishes *not* to know or ever learn anything, κακὰς δὲ τόλμας μήτ' ἐπισταίμην ἐγὼ | μήτ' ἐκμάθοιμι, τάς τε τολμώσας στυγῶ (582–3). To be sure, the sort of knowledge that she rejects is the knowledge of brash, evil deeds. Still, the wish *not to know* is uncharacteristic; it reeks of wishful thinking and weak resolution. Equally surprising and out of character is the fact that she is willing to take a leap of faith despite the uncertainty of the outcome of her plan (οὕτως ἔχει γ' ἡ πίστις, ὡς τὸ μὲν δοκεῖν | ἔνεστι, πείρᾳ δ' οὐ προσωμίλησά πω, "My faith extends so far, that I can believe it, but I have never put it to the test," 590–1). It is precisely because Deianeira's

---

[341] I agree with Whitman 1951, 114–5, that the reason Deianeira asks the Chorus to keep her actions secret is so she can avoid shame, not because she considers what she is trying to do to be shameful in and of itself, but, rather, because there is some shame in having recourse to love potions and especially in failure. Whitman rightly underscores what a "sorry recourse" it is for Deianeira to resort to magic, a decision in which we see "the breaking of the last agonizing threads of self-respect in a sensitive and intelligent woman.... The philter is shameful because of what it means to her own worth. In this act she swallows the last of her pride." See also Kamerbeek 1963, *ad loc.*

turn to action is so out of character that it shows the audience the depth of her despair. The sudden and radical nature of this change is a palpable sign of it.[342] The one who was most wary of the forces beyond human control now attempts to harness them.

I earlier mentioned some strands of the mythological tradition in which Deianeira was, for all intents and purposes, another Clytemnestra – that is, one who killed her heroic husband intentionally as he returned in glory from battle. This has led some scholars to suppose that Deianeira is, actually, not as innocent or altruistic as she may seem here.[343] Such a reading seems to me misguided: any evil intentions or calculation on the part of Deianeira reduce the tragic nature, not to mention the consistency, of her character to a considerable degree.[344] If we consider Deianeira to be cynical or motivated by ill intention, it becomes harder to understand why so great a portion of the play is devoted to portraying her caution and moderation from the start. Moreover, the drama would indeed lack unity (a criticism scholars have long leveled at the tragedy, which I mentioned earlier), if the theme of human fallibility did not tie together her fate and Heracles'.[345] If Deianeira deliberately commits evil, then the patent gap between her intent and the result of her action disappears, as does the pathos that stems from so egregious an error being committed with pure intentions.[346]

Deianeira's initiative is the following: she has decided to send a robe to Heracles, lined with a love philter that will revive his love for her, if Nessus's blood mingled with the Hydra's poison holds the power that the centaur claimed

---

[342] Easterling 1982, *ad* 536–8, points out the paradox inherent to the queen's uncharacteristic decision: "Deianeira is being led by passion to act in a way that contradicts her insight into its power." I agree with Winnington-Ingram 1980, 78 that, while the queen acts out of character by taking such an initiative, this does not result in character inconsistency; rather, "the less characteristic the act, then the greater is the evidence of her desperation — and of the power of Kypris."

[343] For scholars who believe Deianeira is actually being deceptive in this scene, see Carawan 2000, with bibliography. He discusses the "innocent Deianeira" paradigm found in Bacchylides' portrayal of the queen and argues that Sophocles' Deianeira is less innocent as one "endowed with innocent intentions but burdened with guilty knowledge" (Carawan 2000, 190).

[344] I agree with Ormand's rejection of Segal 1981, 88. The latter states that, "recourse to this magic fuses her with her monstrous double, the husband-destroying Clytemnestra." (Segal argues along the same lines in Segal 1992, 80.) Ormand rightly counters that, "Deianeira is hardly a Clytemnestra, stepping into a masculine (monstrous) role. Her desire consistently lacks an active stance... . Rather, she wants to fulfill the traditional feminine role, to be desired by her husband" (Ormand 1999, 50). See also n. 329 above.

[345] I discuss Heracles' discovery of his own fallibility through Hyllus's revelation to him of the centaur's deceit below.

[346] This is also Winnington-Ingram's understanding of her character (1980, ch. 12, esp. 77).

it has.³⁴⁷ In sending the garb to her husband, she is (in part) fulfilling an oath that she had sworn to fulfill should Heracles be granted a safe return (610–5): dutifully to adorn him with the robe in question, as a gift of thanks to the gods. He is to don it and, in his new garb, perform a sacrifice to the gods. Now she intends to line the garment in question with that special ointment, the κηλητήριον, given to her by the dying monster who tried to rape her – an initiative that she has asked the Chorus to keep secret, for reasons we have just discussed.

Over the course of her exchange with the Chorus and Lichas after she has devised the plan, Deianeira's rhetoric reflects the new role that she intends to play. Her words include multiple markers pointing to it. Departing from the status of passive spectator to the roving and uncontrollable gaze of Heracles, she maps out a vision in which she embraces a new role: one in which she is no longer passively watching Heracles watch others but actively staging a scene in which Heracles is the main object of spectacle.³⁴⁸ In the fantasy that she elaborates, she exercises complete control (πράσσω, 600) and adopts a multifaceted role not dissimilar from that of the tragic poet himself. The centaur has provided her with the means to control Heracles' gaze, but her ambitions extend beyond that: she envisages the full-on staging of a performance in which Heracles will be on display for others to see. For herself, she retains a combination of roles: mainly those of author and director orchestrating the spectacle from behind the scenes, as she will not be present at the performance she envisions. She provides detailed stage directions for the realization and enactment of the vision that she has carefully thought out, including specifications regarding what the protagonist, Heracles, will wear (στελεῖν χιτῶνι τῷδε, 612), when the planned performance will take place (ἡμέρᾳ ταυροσφάγῳ, 609), and who his audience will be – the gods (φανερὸς ἐμφανῶς σταθεὶς | δείξῃ θεοῖσιν, 608–9). She has planned for props and messengers as well. Lichas is to be an important actor in the scene she is preparing and directing from afar. The messenger will be the concrete link between her present plan and its execution, the one who will bring to fulfillment her vision, by giving the hero the main prop, the robe, a gift from her hand. It is this robe that will impel the action: a sacrificial performance in full costume. In

---

347 For Deianeira's account of her encounter with the centaur, see 555–81.
348 Compare Athena in the *Ajax*, where the goddess embraces a variety of these roles (as noted by Falkner 1993, 36) with a power and mastery that Deianeira lacks.

the end, the sacrifice of Heracles to the gods does occur, but not at all in the sense that Deianeira had imagined: the sacrificer becomes the sacrificed.[349]

The command that Deianeira seeks to have over the situation is stressed by her constant and uncharacteristic use of imperatives and prohibitive injunctions. She even goes so far as to map out the script of her messenger's lines when she dictates to Lichas the contents of his message to Heracles. The abundance of terms pertaining to sight that she uses in her directives drive home how much she seeks to control not just what Heracles sees but, even more importantly, how he sees *her*. To make her goodwill sound most plausible and Heracles most compliant, she enjoins Lichas to make clear to Heracles that he (Lichas) was an eyewitness to the warm welcome that she gave Iole, the girl that her husband now loves, so that the hero might see for himself, through Lichas's account, her benevolent disposition toward both Heracles and his mistress: "Well, you know from having seen it with your own eyes the welcome I gave the foreign girl, how kindly I received her" (οἶσθα μὲν δὴ καὶ τὰ τῆς ξένης ὁρῶν | προσδέγματ' αὐτός, ὥς σφ' ἐδεξάμην φίλως, 627–8).[350] Her closing statement is both revealing of her desire for control over *erôs* and illustrative of her lack thereof. She asks Lichas *not* to reveal her desire for Heracles before knowing whether it is reciprocal:

τί δῆτ' ἂν ἄλλο γ' ἐννέποις; δέδοικα γὰρ
μὴ πρῲ λέγοις ἂν τὸν πόθον τὸν ἐξ ἐμοῦ,
πρὶν εἰδέναι τἀκεῖθεν εἰ ποθούμεθα.
(630–2)

What else could you say to him? For I am afraid you might be premature in saying how I long for him, before knowing if I am longed for there.

Deianeira cautiously maps out what Heracles should see and know, but also what he should not – or not yet. Given the outcome that awaits Heracles, and the tremendous hatred and anger that he will display toward Deianeira as a result, the irony of her statement here is patent. In a play that is so focused on the

---

349 On the corruption of sacrificial ritual and the reversal of Heracles' ritual status at the time of his death, see Segal 1981, esp. 63–74. Regarding ritual conflation in the *Trachiniae*, see the recent dissertation by Brook 2014, 33–42.
350 Inevitably, we are reminded of Clytemnestra's very different "welcome" to Cassandra in Aeschylus's *Agamemnon*. It bears noting, however, that Deianeira is not inventing any of the details to which she asks Lichas to bear witness: she did, in fact, give Iole an extraordinarily kind welcome, and Lichas was indeed present when she did so. Perrotta 1931, 158–9 takes Deianeira's warm welcome as irrefutable evidence of her innocence and lack of ill intent.

limits of human knowledge and the tragic consequences of late learning, the very wording πρὶν εἰδέναι strikes a particularly pathetic note.

In her instructions to Lichas, Deianeira also includes an abundance of forms of the verb φαίνω and related terms. Deianeira's wish to have mastery over what others (including Heracles) see and know includes the ambition to control when, what, and how her intended audience will see the scene that she has conceived in her mind. This is no average performance that Deianeira is staging, and she is quite ambitious to aim to hold sway over the intended audience that she has in mind: she pictures the ritual occasion of the sacrificial offering as a spectacle that will be a "visible revelation" to the gods (φανερὸς ἐμφανῶς σταθεὶς | δείξῃ θεοῖσιν ἡμέρᾳ ταυροσφάγῳ, 608–9). She conceives of herself as the one who, from afar, "reveal[s] to the gods a new sacrificer wearing a new robe" (καὶ φανεῖν θεοῖς | θυτῆρα καινῷ καινὸν ἐν πεπλώματι, 612–3). Her wording reflects her aspiration to exert control over what the gods see and when.[351] She controls not only what Heracles will see (herself only: ὥστε μήτιν' εἰσιδὼν | στέρξει γυναῖκα κεῖνος ἀντὶ σοῦ πλέον, 576–7) but also who will see *him* wearing the special sacrificial garb, and when: until the time for the sacrifice has come (606–7), she instructs, the light of the sun and the blaze of fire should not lay eyes on the garment that she has sent for him to don. There is something almost blasphemous in the idea or, at the very least, a reversal of the expected relationship between god and man here; the mere formula reeks of inadvertent hybris, for φανεῖν in its middle and compound form, φαίνεσθαι, is evocative of divine epiphanies: the gods are the ones who reveal and conceal things, including their own presence and glory, to and from mortals – not the other way around.[352]

As Deianeira attempts to shift from the stance of passive witness to that of stage director, she adopts a role not unlike the one played by Cypris in the choral ode that immediately precedes her present exchange with the Chorus and Lichas. In that ode, as we have seen, Aphrodite acts as umpire of a contest that she has provoked. Here, Deianeira hopes to stage a performance whose results should provide her with a pleasurable outcome: reviving Heracles' love for her. She is, in effect, playing Aphrodite, setting events in motion and watching

---

[351] Interestingly, Deianeira again uses the verb φανεῖν when she realizes the actual outcome of her initiative (666); at that point, however, she uses it in the middle-passive φανοῦμαι, in a manner that reveals her complete lack of control over her action and the reputation that results from that action. Rather than being one who reveals things (φανεῖν) to the gods, she is but a mortal, to whom truths are revealed, only too late.

[352] Regarding the place of seeing and being seen in divine epiphanies, and the poetics of sight in Greek encounters with the divine, see Henrichs 2010, especially 32–4 (with additional bibliography at n. 61).

them play out. (Unbeknownst to her, she is playing a part in a scheme orchestrated by its stage director and spectator: Cypris herself.) As it turns out, the centaur was telling the truth, and Deianeira *will* be able to control Heracles' gaze, but not in the way that she anticipates. She has, it is true, been given the power to prevent the hero from ever seeing or loving another woman but herself (ὥστε μήτιν' εἰσιδὼν | στέρξει γυναῖκα κεῖνος ἀντὶ σοῦ πλέον, 576–7), but Nessus's words were as deceptive as they were truthful: Heracles will, in fact, never set eyes on another woman, because he will never look upon the light of the sun again.

Watching Deianeira watch Heracles burn

Deianeira is dead by the time Heracles comes on stage, offering up the spectacle of his excruciating agony for all to see. She never sees the repercussions of her endeavor firsthand. Yet the queen actually does see the outcome of her initiative on two different occasions: first, through the sight of a tuft of wool burning; then, vicariously, through her son Hyllus's vivid account of what happened once the poisoned robe began to take effect.

I begin with the first of Deianeira's two visions of Heracles' demise. Through the introduction of an object, a piece of the woolen fleece that she had used to smear the special potion inside the garment she sent to Heracles as a gift, Sophocles puts the queen in the position of viewing, with great precision and from close up, the ruinous consequences of her attempt to rekindle the hero's desire for her. The only comparable example in extant tragedy of so tangible an impression of a death to come on the part of one directly involved in that death is the prophetess Cassandra's vision at the end of Aeschylus's *Agamemnon*. Standing before the house of Atreus in terror, she sees the bloodshed – past, present, and future – that pollutes the palace and her own imminent slaughter (as well as Agamemnon's) at the hands of the king's wife, Clytemnestra.[353] In Cassandra's case, the one who has the vision is the future *victim* of the murder she foresees; Deianeira, on the other hand, is both the perpetrator *and* the victim of the murder that she foresees: for the vision of Heracles' death leads her to take her own life. Timewise, Cassandra sees a murder that is going to take place in the future; what Deianeira sees is what she (rightly) suspects is either imminent or may perhaps even taking place offstage as she is speaking. That her vision of Heracles' pain is nearly

---

353 A., *Ag.* 1072 ff.

if not actually simultaneous with its onset offstage becomes clear from the fact that Hyllus's account of it follows immediately thereafter.

Deianeira describes what she has seen in a detailed report to the women of Trachis: she has witnessed, she says, an unspeakable sight (φάτιν ἄφραστον, 693–4). The tuft of wool that she had used to rub the garment she sent to Heracles with the centaur's potion melted away the moment it came into contact with the sun's rays, disintegrating and then leaving behind a strange, clotted foam (693–704). She recounts the horrible vision using multiple verbs that refer to the act of seeing (ὁράω, δέρκομαι, βλέπω), and shifts seamlessly from the preparations she and the internal audience of Trachinian maidens saw (ὥσπερ εἴδετε, 692) to what she caught sight of, moments later. Deianeira makes it seem as though the moment of the wool's crumbling were occurring before the audience's eyes with all the more vividness and immediacy as she begins her account with a present tense (δέρκομαι, 693). She also further draws her audience into the scene, making them picture it along with her, by using the second person (ἂν βλέψειας, 700) and employing a visual comparison that would be familiar to all: that of sawdust falling to the ground during the cutting of wood (μορφῇ μάλιστ' εἰκαστὸν ὥστε πρίονος | ἐκβρώμαθ' ἂν βλέψειας ἐν τομῇ ξύλου, 699–700). The expressions of caution and apprehension characteristic of the queen in the first part of the play resurface here, but with a tragic overtone: Deianeira voices fear, (δέδοικα, 663), an awareness of her lack of knowledge and lack of power to decide what is best (οὐκ οἶδ', 666; οὐκ ἔχω τάλαινα ποῖ γνώμης πέσω, "I do not know, in my distress, what decision to come to," 705), and despair (ἀθυμῶ, 666). At this point, none of her emotions concern an uncertain future (see e.g., φοβοῦμαι μὴ, 550); they regard actions that have already been committed, with an outcome well beyond what she had anticipated. The irreparability of her deed is aptly conveyed by the perfect tense (γυναῖκες, ὡς δέδοικα μὴ περαιτέρω | πεπραγμέν' ᾖ μοι πάνθ' ὅσ' ἀρτίως ἔδρων, "Women, I am afraid that I went too far in all that I lately did," 663–4) and corroborated by the fact that she is (virtually) watching these consequences unfold from a distance, even as they are taking place, or are about to, outside of her scope of vision and grasp.

In his study of Sophocles' *Trachiniae*, Seale shows how the idea of "revelation" informs the whole action of the play – revelation all the more riddled with irony and pathos as there is a "high level of knowledge built into the predisposition of Deianeira," as we have seen.[354] From the start of the play, Deianeira has been turned toward the future, always expecting the worst and assuming that, by recognizing the limits of her own knowledge, she has protected herself

---

354 Seale 1982, 182.

from the errors that stem from *not* recognizing such limits. Yet there is a gap between what Seale calls Deianeira's virtual knowledge and her actual knowledge, and the gap is not bridged until it is too late, at a time when she is unable to intervene in any way. The vision of the tuft of wool being destroyed provides that bridge, giving Deianeira a graphic view of Heracles' destruction to come.

Part of the bridging of that gap is pointed up by Deianeira's speech. Over the course of her description of the burning wool, she is progressively forced to acknowledge just what she has done through the very process of telling the Chorus what she has seen. She proceeds from fearful doubt (οὐκ οἶδ', 666) to the realization that her action was blind (προθυμίαν ἄδηλον ἔργου, 669–70) to recognizing that she now has knowledge of the outcome of her action at a time when it is *too late* for that knowledge to serve her: ὧν ἐγὼ μεθύστερον, | ὅτ' οὐκέτ' ἀρκεῖ, τὴν μάθησιν ἄρνυμαι ("this I learn too late, when the knowledge cannot serve me," 710–1). Despite some interspersed, hopeful hesitations, the queen acknowledges the inevitable. By the end of her speech, there is no longer any doubt in her mind: she knows (οἶδα, 714) that the arrow destroyed every beast it touched and that, through the charm, she will destroy Heracles (μόνη γὰρ αὐτόν, εἴ τι μὴ ψευσθήσομαι | γνώμης, ἐγὼ δύστηνος ἐξαποφθερῶ, "For I alone, if I am not mistaken, will destroy him, wretch that I am" 712–3; πῶς οὐκ ὀλεῖ καὶ τόνδε, "How will it not destroy my husband as well?" 718).

Deianeira thus finds herself in the strange position of visualizing the fate of the hero from afar, through the ingenious dramatic innovation of the tuft of wool consumed before her eyes. The pathos of the scene stems from the tragic combination of the queen's ability to see with utter clarity the unwanted consequences of her actions – Heracles' suffering and death – and her complete powerlessness to prevent them. She is, once again, a passive spectator, a stance with a searing tension at its core. Deianeria's utterance when she realizes what she has done encapsulates this tension perfectly: ὁρῶ δέ μ' ἔργον δεινὸν ἐξειργασμένην ("I see that I have done a terrible thing," 706). The use of an accusative in reference to herself (μ'... ἐξειργασμένην) where we would expect a nominative (ἐξειργασμένη) is unusual: for if the subject of the introductory clause (ὁρῶ), the one viewing, is the same as the one "having done" a terrible thing (ἐξειργασμένην), then the participial form in the indirect statement should reflect the identity of its subject with that of the introductory verb, by a shared nominative case. The nominative ἐξειργασμένη would reflect the identity of the viewer and the doer: the former is seeing in the present what she (the doer, and the same subject) has just done (with consequences continuing in the present, before her very eyes). But the use of the accusative is a deliberate variation on the expected grammatical scheme and that is precisely the point: it aptly conveys Deianeira's feeling of alienation from her deed. Its outcome could not be more removed from what she had intended — so much so, in fact, that she perceives it as though it had been committed by someone else; the accusative (μ'... ἐξειργασμένην) is a terse and pointed grammatical reflection of the queen's sense of utter alienation from her initiative, whose consequences entirely betray her pure intentions. This surprising accusative highlights the dramatic tension between the active role that she knows she has played in Heracles' demise (ἐξειργασμένην) and the role to which she is now confined: that of witness (ὁρῶ) to what has occurred as a result of her agency. As Easterling explains, "She is looking at her situation as it were from the outside."[355] Deianeira witnesses her own situation with the helplessness of a bystander.

After Deianeira describes the combustion of the fleece to the Trachinian women, her worst suspicions are confirmed. She watches Heracles burn for a second time, as it were, through her son Hyllus's account of Heracles' demise. Hyllus's retelling puts the audience and Deianeira in the position of spectators, enabling them to visualize the spectacle of Heracles' agony from the speaker's closeup vantage point. His report is rife with horrid details, providing a picture of the hero at the time of his doom that is of great visual precision. Thus, he describes the poison's relentless progress and the searing pain it causes the hero by making reference to Heracles' sweat pouring over his body (ἱδρὼς ἀνῄει χρωτί, 766) as the robe "clings to his sides" (προσπτύσσεται | πλευραῖσιν ἀρτίκολλος, 767–8) while the poison "feeds upon him like a hateful serpent" (ἐχθρᾶς ἐχίδνης ἰὸς ὥς, 771).

There are multiple levels of witnesses to the scene of Heracles' demise, whose reactions to the sight of Heracles in agony vary, especially when he takes extreme, violent action in response to his pain. One level is made up of those eyewitnesses that were present at the scene, whose responses to the visual spectacle are recounted by Hyllus. These eyewitnesses include Hyllus himself, a homodiegetic narrator who describes his own reactions at the time he saw the event unfold (and who continues to respond with great emotion as he retells it), and a crowd of spectators. Another level of onlookers consists of those to whom the account is being told, whom we might call second-hand eyewitnesses. This group of addressees includes, first and foremost, Deianeira; there is, in addition, the external audience.

These addressees (Deianeira and the audience members) are both watching two different things simultaneously. First, there is the event itself, which they both see through the lens of its principal eyewitness, Hyllus. But they are also watching something else, to which Hyllus's account gives equal importance:

---

[355] Easterling 1982 *ad loc.*

the *reactions* that Heracles' demise elicits. Heracles' reactions when he learns that Deianeira was the instigator of the gift that is now killing him is a particular point of focus for the wretched queen, as the hero and his disposition toward her have always been the only thing that mattered to her, and are the very reason for which she took the initiative of sending the gift to begin with. Before Hyllus begins his account, Deianeira draws attention to the visual power of his report with a question that effectively positions her at the eyewitness's virtual side: "Where did you approach him, and stand by him?" (ποῦ δ' ἐμπελάζεις τἀνδρὶ καὶ παρίστασαι; 748). Deianeira's imagined vision of her orchestrated "revelation" of Heracles' glory to the gods is still vivid in the audience's minds. The discrepancy between the triumphant moment that she had envisioned and the actual scene depicted by Hyllus, in which the great hero is slowly destroyed by an all-consuming fire, translates into visual terms a disparity that amplifies Deianeira's lack of vision (in the recent past) and her present powerlessness. As she listens to Hyllus, Deianeira watches her agency play out, and watches both Heracles (within the account) and Hyllus (standing before her) as they react to it with outrage and dismay. There is no doubt in anyone's mind — not even Deianeira's – that she is the agent of Heracles' excruciating death: she is the one who provoked the destruction being described to her of a great man, a fact that her son dwells on repeatedly. As an addressee listening to the account of what she has done, the queen is now but a helpless spectator to the scene being reported. She hears the details concerning Heracles' tremendous physical violence toward Lichas (a violence ultimately intended for her, as we will see below), and faces Hyllus's verbal abuse. Meanwhile, she herself listens and looks on in complete silence.

The external audience embraces Hyllus's vantage point, but not his accusatory disposition. Its members visualize the scene along with Deianeira and, like her, they see its effects on the various internal audiences (and on the hero himself). But the principal object of the audience's attention is not Heracles, nor even Hyllus, but Deianeira herself; it is not only the account of Heracles' agony, but the *effect* of that account (and of the agony it portrays) on the one who caused it that they would be closely monitoring. All would, no doubt, keep their eyes intently fixed on the principal instigator, addressee, and victim of the account in question: the queen. They are watching her "watch" the spectacle of her beloved husband's undoing and seeing her react to the sight of the destruction that she has unwittingly wrought, a sight made more painful still for her by the fact that it is mediated through Hyllus's (mistakenly) unforgiving gaze. The spectators, then, are not just watching the spectacle of Heracles' agony; mainly, they are watching the principal character concerned, Deianeira, as she receives confirmation of what it is she has done, and they are listening with Deianeira's ears, as it were, as Hyllus's harsh words bear down on her relentlessly.

Hyllus links each of the manifestations of Heracles' pain back to his mother, hurling accusations at her and taking each symptom of Heracles' agony to be an additional, incriminating sign of her culpability.[356] He believes Deianeira's intent to have been evil and curses her. Beyond the noxious potion with which she has lined Heracles' robe, Hyllus sees Deianeira's betrayal itself as a source of pain for Heracles: the latter's suffering increased tenfold, Hyllus says, when the hero learned from Lichas that it was in obedience to *her* orders that the herald brought the robe as a gift for him. Heracles interpreted this news as a sure sign of his wife's treachery, and "when he heard it, an agonizing convulsion laid hold of his lungs" (κἀκεῖνος ὡς ἤκουσε καὶ διώδυνος | σπαραγμὸς αὐτοῦ πλευμόνων ἀνθήψατο, 777–8).

While the audience members' attention is inevitably fixed on Deianeira's reaction throughout this scene, that reaction is never explicitly mentioned, much less described, by Hyllus or any other character present.[357] The queen maintains a complete, ominous silence for the duration of Hyllus's report on Heracles' horrifying condition, never uttering a word of response or a cry of despair, right up to the moment when she exits the stage for the last time. Even so, the audience have come to know Deianeira's disposition and nature well, and have been given all the elements necessary to be able to fathom the unbearable suffering that she undergoes during Hyllus's account, the consequences of which the nurse's report will soon confirm when she comes onstage to announce that her mistress has committed suicide. The audience members are the only ones to know (along with Deianeira) that with each new word of blame that her son hurls at her and each new horrifying detail of Heracles' agony, he provides Deianeira with a confirmation of what she has seen in the consumption of the tuft of wool: that the outcome of her plan is precisely the opposite of what she had sought to achieve. She now knows with absolute certainty that she has destroyed the sole object of her every care and attention, the one man to whom she had dedicated her entire existence. Instead of resuscitating his love for her, she has evoked her cherished husband's dire hatred and loathing, and caused him to meet a horrific end. She has nothing left to live for.

---

[356] See e.g., τὸ σὸν φέρων δώρημα θανάσιμον πέπλον· | ὃν κεῖνος ἐνδύς, ὡς σὺ προὐξεφίεσο "your gift, the robe of death... he put *[it]* on, *as you had instructed*," 758–9); τὸν δυσδαίμονα | Λίχαν, τὸν οὐδὲν αἴτιον τοῦ σοῦ κακοῦ, ("unhappy Lichas, who was in no way guilty of *your crime*," 772–3); italics mine.

[357] We can only guess at Deianeira's (presumably prostrate) posture and any other movements or gestures that occur, as no actual stage directions are embedded within Hyllus's speech; only the Chorus points out that she slowly exits the stage at the end.

The uncompromising and scrupulous rectitude of Deianeira's character have been a focal point since the start of the play, and she earlier voiced the resolution to kill herself should Heracles be harmed by her: ταύτῃ σὺν ὁρμῇ κἀμὲ συνθανεῖν ἅμα ("I too shall die with him," 720). Every new incriminating detail that Hyllus flings at his mother concerning Heracles' horrific condition increases her unexpressed inner turmoil, and brings her closer to her own self-inflicted death. When Hyllus underlines her guilt and seeks to blame and shame his mother, the effect achieved for the audience is precisely the opposite: mindful of Deianeira's innocence, their pity for her undeserved suffering continues to grow accordingly.

Hyllus's account includes a report of what happened when Lichas revealed to Heracles that the robe he had donned was given to him by Deianeira. The hero responds with an exceedingly savage act, a display of daunting power despite his circumstances, reminding all of his formidableness, the better to point up its futility in the face of fate. Even the great hero's extraordinary strength is of no use to him in the face of suffering: it serves no purpose but a meaningless, unjust, and destructive one. Seized with uncontrollable rage at the news that his wife sent him the robe that is now burning him alive, Heracles takes hold of the messenger who has delivered the hateful news, grabbing him by the foot and hurling him onto the rocks below, where Lichas's head smashes to pieces, his white brains pouring out of his cranium and peering out through his hair (κόμης δὲ λευκὸν μυελὸν ἐκραίνει, 781).

Witnessing Heracles' brutal murder of the herald along with Hyllus is the aforementioned crowd of anonymous spectators. The point of their presence is, it seems, to introduce an additional, impartial audience (they are not kin) to the scene of Heracles' undoing and to his savagery. By foregrounding their unanimous reaction to Heracles' suffering and his ghastly action, Sophocles plays up the pitiable horror of the scene. On seeing the hero kill the herald with such merciless violence, the crowd lets out a cry of dismay:

> ἅπας δ' ἀνηυφήμησεν οἰμωγῇ λεώς,
> τοῦ μὲν νοσοῦντος, τοῦ δὲ διαπεπραγμένου·
> κοὐδεὶς ἐτόλμα τἀνδρὸς ἀντίον μολεῖν.
> (783–5)
>
> And the whole people broke the silence with a cry at the sickness of the one, and the undoing of the other; but no one dared to come near the man.

The horrifically violent act of reprisal evokes their pity for Lichas (because he is an innocent victim), but also pity for Heracles, because the very violence of his act provides a measure of his suffering (τοῦ μὲν νοσοῦντος). The internal spectators' pity for Lichas and Heracles is mingled with sheer horror and fear at Heracles' demonstration of unbridled savagery and power: "But no one dared to come near the man" (κοὐδεὶς ἐτόλμα τἀνδρὸς ἀντίον μολεῖν, 785).

Hyllus's narrative of Lichas's death puts Deianeira in a position to see Heracles' hatred for her concretely illustrated in an actual deed. The extreme violence that the hero inflicts on Lichas is a displacement of the emotions that he feels toward his wife: Lichas, though innocent, bears the brunt of Heracles' anger as a stand-in for the absent Deianeira. As we have seen, as Deianeira watches Heracles suffer through Hyllus's eyes, she is not just a spectator but also the indirect victim of the entire scene: learning of the suffering that she has inadvertently caused her beloved causes her to suffer in turn. In a similar way, when she sees the fate Lichas meets at Heracles's hands, she vicariously experiences Lichas's fate as her own, knowing that the hatred taken out on Lichas is in fact directed at her. Watching both of these — Heracles' agony, and Lichas's dreadful end — does not put her in a position of detached superiority at all; she is closely involved in the spectacle(s) that she sees, and it bears direct consequences for her, in the present (by the emotional distress it causes her) and in the future (given the drastic action she determines she must take as a result). The herald's undoing is a concrete illustration of where she stands in Heracles' eyes: an object of hatred and revenge, and this reads as a death sentence for her — not because she fears he might kill her, but because the sole being that gave meaning to her existence is now annihilated, and this through her own fault.

Lichas's undeserved and tragic fate suggests what Deianeira's fate would be *a fortiori* if she should ever come into her beloved husband's presence: for she is behind the plight that causes Heracles such extreme anger.[358] The audience can now fully perceive the searing irony of Deianeira's earlier request, when she asked that Lichas not reveal her desire for Heracles to the hero before knowing whether the hero reciprocated her love.[359] Hyllus specifically draws a distinction between Lichas and Deianeira, exculpating the herald while underlining his mother's guilt: "It was your gift alone" (τὸ σὸν μόνης / δώρημ', 775–6). His point is that the herald is worthy of pity because of his innocence when it comes to Heracles' death, while his mother would not be pitiable should she incur a similar fate to his at Heracles' hands, because her punishment would not be undeserved. There is some pathos to Hyllus's showing pity for Lichas while he withholds it from Deianeira: it foreshadows the pity that he will

---

358 That Heracles would not hesitate to inflict a painful and violent death on his spouse (and in fact wishes he had the power to) is later confirmed by the hero himself, to none other than their son, Hyllus (1066–9, and again at 1107–11).
359 See 630–2, quoted above, p. 125.

come to feel for the queen (along with the Chorus and nurse), once he has been made privy to her innocence, when it is too late and she is already dead.

In the eyes of others: Action vs. intent

Hyllus begins his report by wishing his own mother were dead (ἣ μηκέτ' εἶναι ζῶσαν, 735). His wish is about to come true. Once he finishes his harrowing retelling of Heracles' protracted agony, Deianeira exits the stage in complete silence, never to be heard again – one of the most eloquent and distressing silences in Greek tragedy, to which the Chorus calls attention by warning her that it will be considered a further sign of her guilt.[360] The queen's lack of an attempt to defend her innocence in the eyes of her son is another telling reflection of her character. It is worth pausing here a moment to ask what it is, exactly, that drives Deianeira off stage without a word.

Deianeira has just seen the spectacle of her fallibility and powerlessness play out: Heracles' doom was foreshadowed in the tuft of wool, reduced to nothing when it was hit by the rays of the sun; now the reported scene of Heracles' agony has confirmed her worst fears. In the scene that preceded Hyllus's report, as she increasingly realized the role that she has inadvertently played in causing Heracles' demise, she stated her intention to take her own life should her suspicions prove right:

> καίτοι δέδοκται, κεῖνος εἰ σφαλήσεται,
> ταύτῃ σὺν ὁρμῇ κἀμὲ συνθανεῖν ἅμα.
> ζῆν γὰρ κακῶς κλύουσαν οὐκ ἀνασχετόν,
> ἥτις προτιμᾷ μὴ κακὴ πεφυκέναι.
> (719–22)
>
> Well, I have determined, if he suffers harm, that in the same movement I too shall die with him. For a woman who places the highest value on being good, it is not bearable to live life with the reputation of being evil.[361]

We have seen that the crowd of spectators to Lichas's gruesome death is marked by fear of Heracles ("No one dared to come near ..."). That fear may well model and reflect the fear that the external audience feels for Deianeira on hearing Hyllus's account of the herald's death, but fear is not the reason Deianeira leaves

---

[360] Lines 813–4. Regarding Deianeira's silence, see Perrotta 1931, 40ff. On silence as a herald of death here and elsewhere, see Montiglio 2000, esp. 239–40.

[361] That the noble-born (and noble-minded) should pursue other-directed good and reject the shameful is also central to the *Philoctetes*, as we will see in ch. 4. On the centrality of the latter to the *Philoctetes* prologue, see for instance Adkins 1960, 189.

the stage. The only reason she would experience fear at this point would be if she actually supposed that she might encounter Heracles, in which case she would no doubt meet with precisely the sort of reprisal to which Lichas has been subjected. In fact, there is no fear to be experienced by her, since she has already decided on death. Because of her earlier, solemn utterance ("I too shall die with him"), the audience knows that, as they and the queen see the pain of Heracles (as well as his hatred for Deianeira) play out in the scene recounted by Hyllus, they are watching Deianeira see the conditions that are to lead to her death at her own hands be unequivocally and irrevocably fulfilled.

The image of Heracles in agony and Lichas unjustly punished are not terrifying for Deianeira. For her, it is a painful spectacle, putting before her the evidence that her action has gone against the single defining emotion that has guided her entire existence: her love of Heracles. This spectacle provides her with the opportunity to see just how little power she has to control his love for her, much less her own existence and how her action will be perceived. We can best get a sense of what drives Deianeira to take her own life if we turn back to her reaction on seeing the tuft of wool destroyed to nothing, a sight which makes up the first of the two "scenes" in which she witnesses the ruinous outcome of her initiative. At the time, she voices her despair at the thought of soon "being revealed" to have committed great harm, using the verb φαίνω, in the passive (φαίνομαι). This is the very same verb that she had used in the active when her ambition was to control Heracles' gaze and (to a certain extent) even the gods':[362]

> οὐκ οἶδ'· ἀθυμῶ δ' εἰ φανήσομαι τάχα
> κακὸν μέγ' ἐκπράξασ' ἀπ' ἐλπίδος καλῆς.
> (666–7)
>
> I do not know; but I despair that I will soon be revealed to have committed a great wrong, when my hope was for good.

Deianeira's passivity and helplessness has reached a new level: she is no longer merely a passive onlooker; she is now reduced to the passive object of others' gaze (φανήσομαι), a gaze that she cannot control. As her own words acknowledge, the outcome of her action (not her intention) defines her as culpable in others' eyes.[363]

We have seen how Deianeira's nature is exceptionally predisposed to pity. We might expect her to assess her own deed according to the same (compassion-

---

[362] See 612–3.
[363] Deianeira cannot control what others see of her: her action is manifest, while her good intention is internal and hidden, and there is nothing she can do to change this.

ate) standards and (understanding) rationale that she has applied to others: that is, with a keen eye to just how little knowledge and true agency mortals have, herself included. She would do well to acknowledge that she is worthy of pity by taking into consideration, as she so generously did in the case of Heracles and Iole, how much her own action has been guided by forces beyond her control. She does in fact concede that she acted the way she did (resorting to a love philter when she was not sure of what it would do) because she fell victim to a monster's charms (ἔθελγέ μ', 710): she knows, and states, that she acted under the influence of the centaur and, hence, acknowledges that she does not bear full responsibility for the destruction that she has wrought.[364] By her own standards, and by any ancient Greek standard, she is worthy of pity. Yet Deianeira does not at any point ask for the pity of others. The only time she requests the Trachinian women's pity is when she initially unveils her plan to use the magic love potion to them (συγκατοικτιουμένη, 535). After she realizes the consequences of her initiative, she does not ask for any such pity, and appears to take sole responsibility for the destruction of Heracles:

μόνη γὰρ αὐτόν, εἴ τι μὴ ψευσθήσομαι
γνώμης, ἐγὼ δύστηνος ἐξαποφθερῶ·
(712–3)

For if I am not to prove mistaken in my judgment, I alone, miserable one, shall be his ruin.

Where Deianeira's agency ends and where her limits in the face of greater powers begin are not considerations that the queen will take into account.[365] The audience knows from having been granted abundant access to Deianeira's inner world that her moral integrity was and remains untainted: the life that she has led has been irreproachable in intent. Yet she determines that the sincerity

---

364 The centaur is part of the continuing chain of the power of *erôs*, as the Chorus goes on to emphasize to a considerable degree (more on this below).
365 I should make clear that I do not mean to suggest that any characters (including, of course, Deianeira) believe that she bears no responsibility in bringing about Heracles' fate, or her own misery. If mortals were merely pawns to divine will, then tragedy would hardly be tragic. The role of hidden (and especially) divine forces in causing mortal suffering is a complex one, which never precludes human responsibility; see e.g., Dodds 1951; Winnington-Ingram 1965; and Buxton 2007, especially 182–7, with bibliography. Cairns 2013 also offers a discussion of the prominent role of the gods in human action, and stresses the importance of avoiding the pitfall of assuming that the Homeric and early tragic conceptions of agency and causation are more primitive and merely the beginning of a linear progression toward a more rational approach to these questions (see Cairns' introduction to the recent volume he edited on Greek Tragedy and archaic thought, ix-liv).

of her good intentions is of no use.³⁶⁶ Her life is no longer bearable, not because she perceives her action as evil (she of all people knows that her intention was pure), but because she realizes that every one of her efforts to lead a worthy life has been futile. Every thought, intention, and morally exacting standard to which she held herself – all have been in vain, in light of the fact that an external force and agent has led her to cause irreparable harm and evil. Her existence – its goal, its nature – has been taken out of her hands. She sees no value in continuing a life that does not conform, in deed or reputation, to the principles that she valued the most and sought to apply with unfaltering care. She must die along with Heracles because, though she is a woman defined by the fact that she wills the good (ἥτις προτιμᾷ μὴ κακὴ πεφυκέναι, 722), in the end she will be seen to have committed evil for having unwittingly caused suffering, and that is all that matters.³⁶⁷ In the spectacle of Heracles' agony and in the reactions of Hyllus, she has been given the chance to see the glaring disparity between the noble moderation that she strove to maintain in every aspect of her life and the horrid outcome of her deed, which is all that others can see. It is because of this disparity that she takes her own life, not because of the prospect of corporeal punishment at Heracles' hands.

The many parallels between Sophocles' Deianeira and the character of Ajax in the play that bears the hero's name have been noted;³⁶⁸ yet there are some differences between them that are worth mentioning as well, insofar as they contribute to defining the nobility of Deianeira's character and help us to understand the lofty ideals that motivate her tragic decision to take her own life. Like Ajax when he seeks to slaughter the Atreids (and Odysseus) to avenge his honor, only to be fooled into slaughtering cattle through the temporary madness inflicted on him by Athena, Deianeira acts in a way that produces a result that is not at all what she had set out to do. Ajax determines that he must die because the thought of his enemies mocking him is unbearable: it would cause him further dishonor, in addition to the dishonor of having been passed up as the recipient of Achilles' armor. Deianeira, on the other hand, determines that she must take her own life because she has incriminated herself in the eyes of the one whose judgment matters to her most: Heracles. What makes her circumstances unbearable to Deianeira after she sees the fleece destroyed is not that she has

---

366 The degree to which Deianeira is guilty or not is not Sophocles' point of focus as much as it is to show "what happened, how and why it happened" (Winnington-Ingram 1980, 78) and how Deianeira considers her intent to be irrelevant, in light of her action's devastating consequences.
367 Whitman 1951, 112. The heroic *ethos* expressed by Deianeira here invites parallels with Sophocles' *Ajax*, as I discuss below.
368 See Knox 1964, 41.

been unsuccessful in destroying her enemies, as is the case for Ajax, but that she has inadvertently destroyed the one who was most dear (*philos*) of all to her and whose relationship to her has defined her entire existence. Her motivation for taking her own life is based on the harm she has caused to others, not to herself, in keeping with the "other-directed" nature of her character.[369]

If Ajax is an Achillean figure, refusing to compromise his values when the society to which he belongs leaves him unable to live in accordance with them, then Deianeira's *ethos* is more reminiscent of Hector's. I earlier drew a parallel between the two on other grounds, and I believe it is illuminating to draw a parallel at this point as well. At a crucial point in book 22, Hector is being chased by Achilles and so terrified that he contemplates going back inside the walls of Troy rather than face sure death. As he weighs the option of seeking refuge and fighting from a less vulnerable position, he realizes that, in not following the advice Polydamas gave him to order a Trojan retreat, he has been the cause of many Trojans' deaths, a result that goes against the very reason for his presence on the battlefield to begin with: to save as many Trojan lives as he can. On realizing that he has inadvertently done just the opposite through the mistake of assuming he could continue to rely on his own strength (22.105–10), Hector decides that he must face Achilles and certain death and, thus, die with glory. The alternative, retreating within the walls of his city, would mean experiencing shame: the *aidôs* of standing before Trojan men and women after being a cause of destruction for his and their *philoi*.

The added pathos of Deianeira's situation when compared with Hector's is that she has no Achilles to face, no noble death on behalf of others through which she might reestablish and preserve her honor. When she runs to her bedchamber to stab herself on her marriage bed, it is because she sees with unendurable clarity that she has failed in what mattered the most to a woman with her values: living life righteously and loving and being loved by her husband, Heracles. There is no battle fray into which she can run the way Hector does; there is nothing left for her to do but immolate herself on the marriage bed

---

369 See Kirkwood 1941, 207: "[Deianeira's] last sentence recalls Ajax's similar resolve: as Ajax, so Deianeira has a firm concept of the noble life; but while Ajax's concerned matters of personal glory, Deianeira's is concerned entirely with her love for Heracles." Gasti 1993, 21 mentions the discrepancy that Deianeira observes to be true in Heracles' case, between "having a reputation for being true and noble" (ὁ πιστὸς ἡμῖν κἀγαθὸς καλούμενος, 541) and his faithlessness in reality (bringing home a concubine with whom the faithful Deianeira must share her bed). In Deianeira's case, it will be the opposite contrast between appearance and reality that will apply: inwardly, she is irreproachable, but in the outer realm, she will be perceived as and have a reputation for evil (κακῶς κλύουσαν, 721).

she shared with Heracles by thrusting a sword through her side.³⁷⁰ Deianeira's suicide will elicit great pity from other characters, whose emotional responses to her death provide repeated opportunities to stress the purity of her intentions and, thus, her innocence. But her death will achieve nothing in terms of how she is perceived by the single object of her concern, in whose eyes she has no means of rehabilitating herself. She has no illusion that it will; her only goal in taking her own life is to relieve her pain, as living has become unbearable (οὐκ ἀνασχετόν, 721). As with Ajax's suicide, the significance of Deianeira's death in the eyes of others remains a subject of debate in the closing of the play, throughout which Hyllus attempts to defend his mother's innocence. The main point of that debate, however, is to bring out its own vanity: while Odysseus does obtain permission from the reluctant Atreids for Teucer to be allowed to bury Ajax, Deianeira's innocence is never recognized by Heracles.

The divine agent and spectator: Cypris

In contrast to Heracles' violent reaction to the news that Deianeira is the one who sent the deadly gift to him, the Chorus draws a considerably more complicated picture of agency and guilt when it comes to the hero's death. Their third choral song sets the queen's action within a broader chain of causation, in which her own responsibility is played down and her culpability all but dismissed. Instead, the Chorus foregrounds the queen's powerlessness in the face of fate and, above all, the shattering power of *erôs*.³⁷¹ The ode begins,

> ἴδ' οἷον, ὦ παῖδες, προσέμειξεν ἄφαρ
> τοὔπος τὸ θεοπρόπον ἡμῖν
> τᾶς παλαιφάτου προνοίας
>
> (821–3)

---

370 On the significance of the place of Deianeira's suicide and the unusual (male, heroic) method that she employs to kill herself, see e.g., Loraux 1985, 38–43; Wohl 1998, 35–7; Ormand 1999. Foley 2001, 97, notes that this is "a highly sexual suicide." On the gender-bending at hand, see Mirto 2007.
371 The same will be true of Hyllus, who earlier was so quick to accuse his mother and so unforgiving. The moment he is informed that Deianeira's intentions were pure and that she was beguiled by the centaur (934–5), he recognizes her innocence (ἄκουσα, 935) and rescinds his accusations, even crying out in pity when he sees what his mother has done to herself (ἰδὼν δ' ὁ παῖς ᾤμωξεν, 932). The nurse is unambiguously pained at her mistress's demise: far from incriminating her, she too finds her pitiable, and states that anyone who had been there to see it would have pitied her as well (κάρτ' ἂν ᾤκτισας, 897).

> See, maidens, how quickly the oracular saying of the ancient prophecy has come upon us!

In reminding the audience that Heracles' death is the fulfillment of an oracle, the maidens downplay Deianeira's part in bringing about her husband's demise. They also trace back the cause of Heracles' devastating affliction to the manipulative powers of the monster Nessus: it is "the cunning constraint of the Centaur with its deadly snare [that] stings [Heracles'] sides" (831-3);[372] the hero "suffers every torture from the deadly sting *caused by the cunning words* of the black-haired one as it boils up."[373] The centaur's ruse, or snare, is designated with the term ἀνάγκα (832): the mysterious and powerful pull of necessity underlies the chain of events and drives them toward a fated destiny, following a course that had long been predicted. The Chorus also highlights Deianeira's extenuating circumstances: what she did, she did ἄοκνος, "with no foreboding" of the horror that was to come (841); all that she could see (προσορῶσα, 842) was "the great disaster of the new marriage hurtling toward the house" (a *periphrasis* for Iole).[374] The women of the Chorus do recognize that Deianeira bears *some* responsibility ("part of the deed she supplied herself," τὰ μὲν αὐτὰ | προσέβαλεν, 843-4), but that is precisely the point: that what came about did so only *partly* because of her; it was also "by the agency of alien counsel, at a fatal meeting" (τὰ δ' ἀπ' ἀλλόθρου | γνώμας, 844-5).[375] That Deianeira's desperation should have led her to take an action with such devastating consequences is a perfect illustration of an archaic motif that Sophocles explores here in almost Aeschylean fashion, by giving subtle consideration to human agency and its relation-

---

[372] εἰ γάρ σφε Κενταύρου φονίᾳ νεφέλᾳ
χρίει δολοποιὸς ἀνάγκα
πλευρά, προστακέντος ἰοῦ,
ὃν τέκετο θάνατος, ἔτεκε δ' αἰόλος δράκων
(831-4)

[373] μελαγχαίτα τ'
ἄμμιγά νιν αἰκίζει
ὑπόφονα δολόμυ-
θα κέντρ' ἐπιζέσαντα.
(837-40)

[374] ὧν ἅδ' ἁ τλάμων ἄοκνος
μεγάλαν προσορῶσα δόμοισι
βλάβαν νέων ἀΐσσου-
σαν γάμων...
(841-4)

[375] The "agency of alien counsel" is Easterling's translation of the careful choice of words here which, she notes, is intended to point up "the agency of *another* (Nessus) by contrast with that of D. herself (*auta*)" (Easterling 1982, *ad loc.*).

ship to the divine: "Sophocles shares with Aeschylus the belief that human destiny is influenced by divine powers in a way which involves the very psychological processes of the human-beings themselves."[376] The Trachinian women pay tribute to Deianeira's innocence, underlining her affliction (her lament, ὀλοὰ στένει, 846, the "pale dew of her close-packed tears," ἀδινῶν χλωρὰν | τέγγει δακρύων, 847–8) and the ruinous consequences that her deed will have for her.

Deianeira's fate (suicide), a "great disaster" (μεγάλαν ἄταν, 850), is steadily creeping forward (ἁ δ' ἐρχομένα μοῖρα, 849). As the ode seamlessly transitions from Deianeira's weeping to the general flood of tears that has been set in motion (ἔρρωγεν παγὰ δακρύων, 851),[377] the image of the flood connects the queen's distress and death to their source: the illness that "streams over" Heracles (κέχυται νόσος, 852), which she has caused, and which will also bring about her own death. The metaphor of the flood of tears followed by the disease washing over Heracles point up the causal connection between Heracles' doom and her imminent demise.

The Trachinian women include Heracles himself in the chain of causation leading up to his downfall, for he is the one who fell in love with Iole. They make clear his role in setting off the chain of events leading up to his death when they lament the "black point of the defending spear, which then brought the swiftly running bride from lofty Oechalia by its might:"

> ἰὼ κελαινὰ λόγχα προμάχου δορός,
> ἃ τότε θοὰν νύμφαν
> ἄγαγες ἀπ' αἰπεινᾶς
> τάνδ' Οἰχαλίας αἰχμᾷ·
>
> (856–9)

The maidens are not only alluding to the role played by Iole in prompting Deianeira to resort to her desperate, ultimate recourse: they are making reference to

---

[376] Winnington-Ingram 1965, 124. Schein makes the interesting comment that in contrast to what we find in Aeschylus and Euripides, "at the moments of decisive choice and action in Sophocles' plays, the gods are nowhere to be found — at least not the Olympian gods" (Schein 1997, 123). The gods do influence human beings in the moments in which they make significant choices or take significant action, but they are acting behind the scenes, as it were, and their conspicuous absence at crucial turning points is essential to conveying the detached and distant, yet influential exercise of power, which we see Cypris wield in this play. I return to this point below.

[377] The flood of tears is not the Chorus's; it is one that sweeps over all in response to both Deianeira's and Heracles' fates. Cf. the hot streams of tears that burst from Deianeira's eyes as she runs desperately around the palace before committing suicide, according to the nurse's eyewitness account (καὶ δακρύων ῥήξασα θερμὰ νάματα | ἔλεξεν, "ὦ λέχη τε καὶ νυμφεῖ' ἐμά, 919–20).

Heracles' role, as the wielder of the black spear who introduced Iole into his and Deianeira's household, betraying his wife's devoted love and their marriage.[378] Yet as they do Deianeira, the maidens also deem Heracles worthy of pity (πάθος οἰκτίσαι, 855), because the responsibility he holds for causing Deianeira's and his own pain is only partial. The main cause of all the harm that has come to pass is kept for the end of their song.

The choral ode closes with an essential and chilling vision: the revelation of an eerie witness who has been looking on in silence as all of these disasters have unfolded, from the centaur Nessus's attempted rape of Deianeira, to the monster's punishment at Heracles' hands, to Heracles' lust for Iole, to Deianeira's use of Nessus's deadly potion in an attempt to counter that lust. The main thrust of this third choral *stasimon* is the revelation of Cypris's undetected presence at all of the painful, tragic events that have afflicted Heracles and Deianeira. The goddess Aphrodite is another spectator, one who is the true agent of it all, the orchestrator who has set all of the tragedy's events in motion and woven together the entire web of causation. She has been watching the human misery that she has caused all along in silent, delighted contemplation:

ἁ δ' ἀμφίπολος Κύπρις ἄναυδος φανερὰ
τῶνδ' ἐφάνη πράκτωρ.
(860–1)

Cypris, silent in attendance, is revealed
as the doer of these things.[379]

This disturbing epiphanic revelation of the goddess Aphrodite depicts her as a voiceless *voyeur*, enjoying the display of her own power as it plays out before her, while the mortal victim of that power, Deianeira, also watches the consequences of her actions and, because of them, suffers tremendous pain and dies. These lines are strongly reminiscent of the presentation of Cypris in the first stasimon, where she was shown standing in the midst of the fight between Heracles and Achelous for Deianeira, looking upon the battle that she had set in motion with a combination of relish and detachment (μόνα δ' εὔλεκτρος ἐν μέσῳ Κύπρις | ῥαβδονόμει ξυνοῦσα, 515–6). At the time, she was already contrasted

---

[378] In a similar vein, when the Chorus members hear from the nurse that Deianeira has taken her own life, they point to the captive's arrival as a cause for the queen's suicide in no uncertain terms: Deianeira's death was "engendered" by Iole and Heracles; their offspring is "a mighty Erinys" (ἔτεκ' ἔτεκε μεγάλαν | ἀνέορτος ἅδε νύμφα | δόμοισι τοῖσδ' Ἐρινύν, 893–5).
[379] This translation is from Easterling 1982, *ad loc.*

with Deianeira, the other witness, whose extreme fear that "*[her]* beauty might bring *[her]* pain" (25) made her avert her gaze.

The choral song brings out the contrast between divine and mortal spectator, both of whom look on as the disastrous chain of events plays itself out before their eyes, but from diametrically opposite stances. Cypris provides a foil for Deianeira, who has twice witnessed the horror of a spectacle in which she has played the inadvertent and voyeuristic roles of both viewer and actor, and faced concrete visual evidence both of her own destructive power and of her powerlessness to anticipate or control it. In each instance, Deianeira can only look on as a spectator from without as the drama unfolds (Heracles' battle with Achelous first, and then his battle with the disease that burns him to death), her own role within it remaining beyond her grasp. Meanwhile, the main force behind the action of the entire play also embraces the role of spectator, but in a radically antithetical position defined by power and pleasure: Aphrodite, hidden agent of it all, enjoys the spectacle of human strife and suffering because, devastating though its consequences may be, it is an illustration of her power.

The revelation of Aphrodite's role is strategically placed: the choral song unveils the goddess's presence as spectator and agent right after Hyllus wrongfully accuses his mother of having killed his father and just before Deianeira's nurse arrives distraught with the news that the queen has taken her own life. There is great pathos in the fact that, even as the maidens sing an ode that pinpoints Aphrodite as the hidden agent behind the destruction that all have just witnessed – an ode that largely exculpates Deianeira from blame for her deed – offstage the queen is meanwhile running frantically to her room to stab herself to death. Realizing that she has been tricked by the centaur and manipulated by *erôs*, the queen kills herself just as the Chorus exposes the goddess's responsibility and troubling delight in all that has come to pass.[380]

---

[380] Schein 1997 offers an illuminating examination and discussion of how, in Sophocles, divinity usually reveals itself toward the end of a tragedy, in a manner that "refocuses what has been done, and suffered, forcing characters in the play as well as audiences and readers to *adopt a different viewpoint* and challenging them to make sense of what has happened from this new angle of vision" in a manner that contributes to an atmosphere "that is already oppressive with the sense of human beings caught in the necessities of their own passions" (Schein 1997, 125–7).

Watching Deianeira die

Having seen incontrovertible evidence of the destruction she has wrought, Deianeira departs from the stage and takes action for the second (and last) time in the play, by taking her own life. In the final moments leading up to Deianeira's death, the audience is given access to her interior world and a full measure of her despair from the outside looking in, as it were. The entire scene is related by her nurse, who watches it unfold from where she is hiding, paralyzed with horror while her mistress rushes about in extreme distress and finally stabs herself to death. The audience thus sees and fathoms Deianeira's extreme desperation through the eyes of an internal witness, who watches her from up close. The nurse reports each of the queen's pained gestures and desperate words while she prepares for her self-inflicted death without ever intervening, for the simple reason that she, too, realizes only too late what it is her mistress intends to do, thereby also illustrating the play's tragic theme of learning too late.

Deianeira's suicide occurs offstage, of course; but her nurse, who saw it all, gives the Chorus of maidens a step-by-step account of the queen's final, desperate wanderings about the house. She is a caring witness, a *philê* who provides emotional and physical proximity to the scene. Her closeup vantage point, from which the Chorus and audience can "see" the scene unfold, heightens the pitiableness of the whole account of Deianeira's death. The nurse generates a vicarious feeling of proximity to the events in her listeners, which increases the emotional effect of it on all who are thus able to "see" it through her lens, Trachinian women and audience alike.[381] When the Chorus asks, "Did you see this violent deed, helpless one?" (ἐπεῖδες – ὦ μάταια – τάνδε <τὰν> ὕβριν, 888),[382]

---

[381] The nurse's eyewitness status and proximity are also a guarantee of facticity : her closeness to the events makes them appear not just vivid but factual. That facticity is such that the Chorus can lay claim to it as well, bearing witness to the veracity of what the nurse saw, though they were not present: "You shall learn it, so that you can bear me witness" (πεύσῃ δ', ὥστε μαρτυρεῖν ἐμοί, 899). It is important also to note that the nurse remains unnoticed as she follows her mistress into her bedchamber: she "hides her face" (κἀγὼ λαθραῖον ὄμμ' ἐπεσκιασμένη | φρούρουν· ὁρῶ δὲ τὴν γυναῖκα δεμνίοις | τοῖς Ἡρακλείοις στρωτὰ βάλλουσαν φάρη: "And I watch her, hiding my face, and I see her throwing blankets on the bed of Heracles," 914–6). She also specifies that the queen "hid herself where nobody could see her" (κρύψασ' ἑαυτὴν ἔνθα μή τις εἰσίδοι, 903), which provides proof of the authenticity of Deianeira's distress: since the queen assumes that she is alone and unseen by others, there is no reason for us not to take her every word and deed as anything other than completely genuine.

[382] Some scholars take ὦ μάταια to be reproachful – "pauvre sotte" (Mazon in his Belles Lettres edition) – while Easterling 1982 *ad loc.*, following Radermacher 1914 *ad loc.*, believes the Cho-

the nurse replies "I saw it, as one standing by!" (ἐπεῖδον, ὡς δὴ πλησία παραστάτις, 889)[383] and harps on the greater emotional impact that such physical proximity can generate: "If you had been close at hand to see the nature of her action, you would have pitied her more still" (μᾶλλον δ' εἰ παροῦσα πλησία | ἔλευσσες οἷ' ἔδρασε, κάρτ' ἂν ᾤκτισας, 896–7). Closeup vision and pity are explicitly connected, the one increasing the other.[384] We look on with her as she experiences pain at the undeserved suffering of the noble Deianeira, without being able to do anything to stop that suffering, nor prevent her drastic action to follow. The audience members watch and pity Deianeira through the nurse's attentive but ultimately helpless lens; meanwhile, the queen shows no such pity for herself.

The nurse's passivity in the face of what she witnesses has frustrated many critics and even led some to suppose that she does not care for Deianeira and is somewhat indifferent to the queen's doom.[385] Yet there is no reason to suppose that the nurse does not care for her mistress; the Trachinian maidens emphasize her distress when they see her approaching with the news of Deianeira's death, and this already should be enough to dispel any suspicions of indifference on her part.[386] There is, perhaps, some artificiality to having a caring witness stand by in a room (though she does eventually run off to get help) while the object of her care, her beloved mistress, prepares to commit suicide; but dwelling on the implausibility of such a scenario misses the point. Moreover, it is not implausible to assume that the nurse does not intervene because she does not realize the gravity of her mistress's intentions and that, if and when she does, she is frozen in disbelief and can only look on in horror. At any rate, the emphasis in this scene is on the nurse's tragic incapacity to prevent the horrible march of fate

---

rus is expressing "a horrified desire to reject the news unless the nurse actually says it." Kyriakou 2006, 118–9 and 169–70 discusses the semantic range of μάταιος.

383 Compare Deianeira's question to Hyllus at the start of his account of Heracles' demise, which also resulted in positioning her at the eyewitness's virtual side: "Where did you approach him, and stand by him?" (ποῦ δ' ἐμπελάζεις τἀνδρὶ καὶ παρίστασαι; 748).

384 I discuss the role of the senses (including sight) in evoking pity more extensively in ch. 4; see nn. 692 and 696 of that chapter, in which I deal with sight and pity in particular.

385 Serghidou 2010, 143–4 on the contrary rightly stresses the nurse's care and helplessness to intervene as she witnesses her mistress's distress.

386 The Trachinian women specifically make a note of the nurse's emotional attachment to her mistress when they describe her sad demeanor before she begins the account and the "cloud upon her eyes" (συνωφρυωμένη) as she approaches them (866–70). In her report, the nurse does not describe any emotion in response to her mistress's demise; the horror of the events and Deianeira's profound distress speak for themselves.

from following its course — not, as some would have it, on an idiotic passivity on the servant's part, which would hardly strike as tragic a note.

When the nurse hears Deianeira bid her bridal bed "farewell forever" (τὸ λοιπὸν ἤδη χαίρεθ', 921), she realizes what the queen intends to do, and the dramatic tension of her account reaches its peak. She describes frantically running to fetch Hyllus in an attempt to prevent the worst, to no avail: when the two of them return to the bedchamber, they find that Deianeira has stabbed herself to death by thrusting a sword into her side. By asking why the nurse does not intervene directly instead of running to get help, as some scholars do, one misses the main effect of her return onto the stage shortly thereafter. The nurse's exit introduces a time lag between the point at which she realizes Deianeira is going to commit suicide and when she finds the queen dead. After the irreparable has been done, the poet has the nurse return, accompanied by Hyllus. The focus of her account is not on the suicide itself, which she does not see and hence does not report, but on its aftermath and particularly on its effect on the one who witnesses that aftermath along with her, but with the added torment of responsibility: Deianeira's son with Heracles, Hyllus.

The nurse as powerless spectator is another instantiation of human helplessness within the play: she watches the one for whom she cares suffer tremendously, without being able to come to her aid. She is not, however, responsible for her mistress's plight. In the wake of Deianeira's death, it is Hyllus who is put in the position of helpless onlooker, as was his mother; his character is subjected to the same pattern of late learning: he views the outcome of his words as she did the outcome of her deeds – after the fact, when nothing can be done.

When Hyllus and the nurse arrive in Deianeira's bedchamber, they see (in a vivid present tense, ὁρῶμεν, 930) that she has driven a two-edged sword into her side and lies dead on top of the conjugal bed that she shared with Heracles. From this point on, the nurse's account zeroes in on Hyllus's reaction to what he sees. He cries out in anguish, for he has acquired, in the meantime, essential knowledge from "those in the house" (τῶν κατ' οἶκον οὕνεκα, 934, presumably servants) that Deianeira's gift to Heracles can be traced back to the manipulative power of the centaur. By the time he sees his mother dead by her own hand, he knows that her intentions were pure, and that his curses and imprecations were unjust:

> ἰδὼν δ' ὁ παῖς ᾤμωξεν· ἔγνω γὰρ τάλας
> τοὔργον κατ' ὀργὴν ὡς ἐφάψειεν τόδε,
> ὄψ' ἐκδιδαχθεὶς τῶν κατ' οἶκον οὕνεκα
> ἄκουσα πρὸς τοῦ θηρὸς ἔρξειεν τάδε.
> (932–5)

> When he saw [her], her son cried out; for he realized, the wretch, that in his anger he had driven her to that deed,[387] having learned too late from those in the house that it was in innocence, and because of the monster, that she had done it.[388]

Hyllus's devastated response to his mother's death points up her innocence and his own crushing feeling of responsibility as he comes to understand that he unfairly burdened her with a crime that she committed unwittingly. His relationship to the spectacle before him is very much the same as Deianeira's to the spectacle of Heracles' agony, which she "saw" indirectly through Hyllus's report. Just as Deianeira blamed herself for the death of Heracles ("For if I am not to prove mistaken in my judgment, I alone, miserable one, shall be his ruin," 712–3),[389] Hyllus blames himself for his mother's death and assumes that his curses are what led her to take her own life (938–40, quoted below). Like Deianeira when she looked on at Heracles' agonizing death through her son's accusatory lens, Hyllus, in the nurse's eyewitness account, is a spectator looking on at a death that (he has good reason to believe) is a direct consequence of the wrongful accusations that he leveled at his mother in their last encounter.[390] He realizes the consequences of his words, as Deianeira did the consequences of her deeds, only when it is "too late": ὄψ' ἐκδιδαχθεὶς (934).

The nurse concludes her account with a gnomic utterance, a general reflection on mortal limitations:

> ὥστ' εἴ τις δύο
> ἢ κἀπὶ πλείους ἡμέρας λογίζεται,
> μάταιός ἐστιν· οὐ γὰρ ἔσθ' ἥ γ' αὔριον
> πρὶν εὖ πάθῃ τις τὴν παροῦσαν ἡμέραν.
> (943–6)

> ... so that if anyone reckons on two days or more, he is doing so in vain; for there is no tomorrow until one has made it through the present day in happiness.

---

387 The translation here is Jebb's and reflects the meaning of ἐφάπτω, "to tie on." Jebb does not see any ambiguity in Hyllus's statement: he (Hyllus) actually led her to do what she did.
388 Hyllus does not explicitly connect the monster's influence to the power of *erôs*, as the Chorus does, but his reaction does not exclude it. The main point remains: he sees the queen's deed as part of a chain of causation in which she has been a pawn to forces beyond her power.
389 As we have seen, Deianeira blames herself despite realizing that the centaur played a key role in her deed.
390 Hyllus's accusations do contribute to driving Deianeira to her suicide, but only because his curses illustrate what she feared — that she is now seen (φανεῖσθαι) as one who is evil, κακῶς κλύουσα; hence, by her standards, she must die along with Heracles (720–2).

She speaks thus after describing how Hyllus lay down beside his mother, covering her with kisses and groaning:

> κἀνταῦθ' ὁ παῖς δύστηνος οὔτ' ὀδυρμάτων
> ἐλείπετ' οὐδέν, ἀμφί νιν γοώμενος,
> οὔτ' ἀμφιπίπτων στόμασιν, ἀλλὰ πλευρόθεν
> πλευρὰν παρεὶς ἔκειτο πόλλ' ἀναστένων,
> ὥς νιν ματαίως αἰτίᾳ βάλοι κακῇ,
> (936–40)

And then her unhappy son never ceased to lament, weeping over her, nor to cover her with kisses, but lying side by side with her he uttered many a groan, saying that he had charged her falsely with the crime.

The gnomic utterance with which the nurse concludes ("if anyone reckons on two days or more, he is doing so in vain," 943–5) applies to Hyllus, but it also brings the audience back to the maxim with which Deianeira opened the play, whose truth (regarding the blindness of mortals as to the nature of their own fate) she only partly grasped then. The queen's fate has just illustrated the maxim she herself had voiced; by echoing the maxim once more after the queen's horrible torment and death, the nurse reminds the audience of just how short Deianeira fell of realizing the degree to which it applied to her own life.

Watching Heracles die

The ending of the *Trachiniae* poses many interpretive problems; critics still widely disagree in their understanding of the significance of Heracles' suffering.[391] For the first two thirds of the play, the famed hero does not appear onstage: instead, he is an object of talk and admiration on the part of all the characters (Deianeira above all) and the Chorus.[392] The buildup preceding what all anticipate to be Heracles' glorious return home is shattered in an instant by his actual, much-awaited entrance in the final third of the play – not, as the other characters (and the audience) have been anticipating, as a hero in all his blazing (!) glory, but as a pathetic object of spectacle in the throes of great pain, burning alive in the gar-

---

[391] Easterling's introduction (1982, 6–12) offers a good overview of some of the central issues and various possible readings of this problematic ending.
[392] McCall 1972, 143, dubbed this part of the play "waiting for Heracles." On the built-up anticipation of Heracles' return and his glorification through the onstage characters' and Chorus's expressions of admiration for the hero, see e.g., Nooter 2012, 63–5.

ment sent to him by his own wife.³⁹³ He is carried onto the stage, silent and looking as though he were dead (ὕπνον ὄντα, 970).

I started this chapter by making mention of those scholars who do not see how the sudden focus on Heracles in the final section of the tragedy, which features the hero's agony prominently and at length, fits with the rest of the play. These critics, as we have seen, have determined that the drama falls into two disjointed parts, with two protagonists, and no unifying thread between them. In fact, the unity of the play becomes most apparent in this final section, as the powerlessness that these two protagonists share and that defines both of their fates comes to the fore. The spectacle of Heracles' excruciating pain is not to be understood as independent from the focus on Deianeira in the first two thirds of the play; the two are, in fact, closely linked. Just as "the audience's thoughts of the expected but absent Heracles heighten their reaction to the initial presentation of Deianeira,"³⁹⁴ the audience's thoughts of Deianeira heighten its reaction to the presentation of Heracles. From the very start of the play, the audience has been watching events through Deianeira's eyes; the tragedy has not been about Heracles so much as about the effects of Heracles' life story on Deianeira.³⁹⁵ After she exits the stage one final time to commit suicide, the audience members and Hyllus remain as witnesses — to Heracles' pain, of course, but also to something more.

From the moment Heracles appears, his pain is the ostensible focal point of the scene, but the conspicuous display of his suffering is not gratuitous visual ostentation of the sort that Aristotle criticized.³⁹⁶ The emphasis is not only, or even mainly, on the spectacle of Heracles' pain for its own sake but on his suffering as a measure of human fallibility: his own fallibility, but also that of Deianeira, who inadvertently caused the demise of the very one whom she so passionately desired to keep at her side. The moment Hyllus sees Heracles, it is Deianeira's fallibility and pitiableness that are at the fore of his and everyone's mind. His very first words to Heracles are telling in this regard. As his father bel-

---

393 Erôs as nosos is a topos of Greek literature, but in the Trachiniae the destructive power of love is enacted on stage in a literal manner (see above, n. 322). As Heracles is devoured by the burning ointment, the metaphorical and the physical become one: the poison from the centaur, captured by Deianeira after the monster lusted after her, destroys the hero because of his love for Iole and Deianeira's love for him – each step in this chain of causation the work of erôs. Mitchell-Boyask (2008, ch. 6) connects the Trachiniae's plot with the plague, and argues that such a composition date is essential to our understanding of the play's portrayal of Heracles' death.
394 McCall 1972, 144.
395 I stress this point at the start of this chapter.
396 Po. 1450b, 1453b.

lows with pain and anger at the one who caused it (Deianeira), Hyllus seeks to defend and rehabilitate his mother, in his father's mind and in the face of justice:

> ἐπεὶ παρέσχες ἀντιφωνῆσαι, πάτερ,
> σιγὴν παρασχὼν κλῦθί μου νοσῶν ὅμως.
> αἰτήσομαι γάρ σ' ὧν δίκαια τυγχάνειν.
> δός μοι σεαυτόν, μὴ τοιοῦτον ὡς δάκνῃ
> θυμῷ δύσοργος. οὐ γὰρ ἂν γνοίης ἐν οἷς
> χαίρειν προθυμῇ κἀν ὅτοις ἀλγεῖς μάτην.
> (1114–9)

> Since you have given me leave to respond to you, father, be silent and hear me, sick though you are; for I shall request of you something which in justice should be granted. Lend yourself to me, not in such a mood that you are out of temper, and stung with anger; for then you would not be able to know how mistaken you are in pursuing satisfaction as you do, and how mistaken you are in your resentment.

Hyllus is the "*trait d'union*" between the two parts of the play:[397] he connects the part that precedes Deianeira's death and the one that follows it. Both his words and his reactions to the torments of his mother and father, which he witnesses in close succession, play a significant role in bringing out the interconnected nature of Heracles' and Deianeira's respective fates. From the time Deianeira dies, his character stands in for his mother and represents her on stage. His viewpoint provides a lens through which the audience watches Heracles' demise as though they were viewing it through the eyes of Deianeira herself. As he stands by and witnesses his father's tremendous pain and as he listens to him inveigh against his mother's disastrous action, Hyllus, unlike Heracles, knows his mother's true intention and her error, and embraces her compassionate and pessimistic outlook. He too comes to realize and articulate what Deianeira had come short of grasping until it was too late: the unforeseeable gap between mortals' aims and their actions, and how every mortal falls victim to some form of divinely inspired deception. For such was the case for his mother, for himself, and, as Heracles is soon to discover in his exchange with Hyllus, such is the case for the great hero as well.

Heracles is, in the closing scene, the main point of focus in a spectacle towards which the play has been building up. First, there was the vision that Deianeira had of his glorious revelation of his garment to the gods, when she was preparing to send it to him. Now, there is the execution of her plan and vision, a

---

[397] This is the expression used by Perrotta when he describes Hyllus's role as one that provides a continuum between the two protagonists (his parents) and the two parts of the play (Perrotta 1931, 139; Perrotta 1935, 473 ff. also points up the aesthetic unity of the play).

vision that has gone horrifically awry, spiraling out of her control and rapidly shifting to a scene of hideous destruction. Between her aim and its outcome, there are two virtual sightings that build up the audience's expectations until Heracles' arrival onto the stage, howling in agony: the audience (and the now dead Deianeira) have already been given access to his spectacular torment, first, with the tuft of wool and then, with Hyllus's eyewitness account. Heracles' return to Trachis is spectacular indeed, but it could not be further from what the queen had envisioned in her mind's eye: the protagonist of the imagined victory drama has turned pathetic victim, and Deianeira, the stage director of the spectacle, has taken her own life in despair. The blatant discrepancy between the anticipated sight and its realization underscores her lack of agency and control over her own and her husband's fates in the face of forces beyond her understanding; it is, as the Chorus has told us, Aphrodite who runs the show. If Deianeira experiences her mortal limitations from the standpoint of a virtual spectator to Heracles' agony, Heracles experiences his limitations by becoming a powerless object of spectacle. Both experiences illustrate the power of *erôs* and the powerlessness of mortals to control their own lives in the face of divine powers greater than themselves.

The hero who was an object of desire, admiration, and awe before he appeared is now an object of spectacle and pity. For the entire closing scene (*exodos*), the slayer of monsters and conqueror of cities is reduced to nought but an "unspeakable sight" (ἄσπετον θέαμα, 961) to be gazed upon in wonder. The spectacle of his body being subjected to the torture of Nessus's bitter poison translates into visual terms the hero's failure to overcome his monstrous adversary despite having killed him. It puts on display the limits of Heracles' power; it also reminds us of Deianeira's. With every new cry of pain[398] and every new accusation against his wife, Heracles provides the audience with a double measure of human powerlessness and fallibility. Each emphasizes simultaneously the disparity between Deianeira's intent and the consequences of her action and the disparity between the victory that the hero believed he had won over the centaur and his present, dreadful defeat at that centaur's hands (so to speak). The limits of human knowledge and the deceptive power of the divine shine through in both of their fates.

Though pierced with searing pain as the poison begins to take effect, Heracles is acutely aware that there are witnesses to his suffering and that he has become an object of others' gaze. Hyllus describes how, when the hero first caught

---

[398] For an overview of the anthropological and cultural significance of the cry that takes into account considerations of gender, see Sébillote-Cuchet 2003.

sight of his son weeping as he watched his father suffer, he expressed the wish that no one should see his downfall and that his son should take him "where no man can look upon *[him]*":

ἀλλ' ἆρον ἔξω, καὶ μάλιστα μέν με θὲς
ἐνταῦθ' ὅπου με μή τις ὄψεται βροτῶν·
(799–800)

Lift me and take me out of this, and, if you can, place me where no man can look upon me!

Though he never explicitly says as much, Heracles' desire to be hidden from sight is likely based on a feeling of shame at his sudden vulnerability. The sight of Hyllus weeping in response to his plight is not welcome: it provides him with proof that he has become so helpless in the eyes of others that he is now an object of pity and grief. For the great hero, such tangible external confirmation of his physically degraded state and powerlessness is hardly bearable. He is used to wielding power in his relationships to others, mortals and monsters alike.

Soon thereafter, the hero loses consciousness. He awakens after Hyllus has had him transported to Trachis. By then, he has abandoned the thought of attempting to hide his stabbing pain from the gaze of others. Instead, he seeks to have some form of control over the spectacle he has to offer, even in the midst of his increasing weakness and stinging pain. Rather than seeking to hide it, he willfully puts his agonized body on display and encourages all to gaze upon it. In an effort to influence others' perceptions of his suffering, he reappropriates the abominable spectacle that Deianeira has created (despite the best of intentions), making it his own:[399]

καὶ νῦν προσελθὼν στῆθι πλησίον πατρός,
σκέψαι δ' ὁποίας ταῦτα συμφορᾶς ὕπο

---

[399] Heracles' self-conscious assessment of his degraded status because of his suffering involves his seeing himself as effeminized. He is, in his own words, "weeping like a girl" and feeling abased to the status of a "womanish creature" (1071–5) by his pain. On the gender reversal (and misogyny) inherent to these self-deprecating remarks, see e.g., Winnington-Ingram 1980, 85; Loraux 1995, 121; Wohl 1998, 9; Ormand 1999, 56; Cawthorn 2008, ch. 4; Lyons 2012, 85–6. As Heracles describes his "effeminate" response to his pain (1070–5), one cannot help but think of Deianeira, who remained completely silent when she heard Hyllus's account of Heracles' agony, despite suffering such unbearable torments as to choose to take her own life. Heracles utters the cries that Deianeira never did. Pickard-Cambridge (1968, 141) and Jouan 1983 argue that the roles of Deianeira and Heracles would have been played by one and the same actor. On role distribution and the ability to create meaning by assigning several roles to the same character in ancient Greek plays, see e.g., Damen 1989.

πέπονθα· δείξω γὰρ τάδ' ἐκ καλυμμάτων.
ἰδού, θεᾶσθε πάντες ἄθλιον δέμας,
ὁρᾶτε τὸν δύστηνον, ὡς οἰκτρῶς ἔχω.
(1076–80)

And now draw near and stand close by your father, and see what a calamity has done this to me; for I will show it to you without a veil. Look, gaze, all of you, on my miserable body, see the unhappy one, his pitiable state!

These lines are directed principally at Heracles' son, Hyllus, and at his attendants, but his insistent plea that he be seen, with its three verbs denoting sight (σκέπτω, ὁράω repeated twice, and θεάομαι), would no doubt be perceived as a direct injunction to the external audience itself: he wants "all" to be his spectators and to bear witness to his suffering (ἰδού, θεᾶσθε πάντες). Why?

Heracles' self-display is not, or at least not only, a form of narcissistic exhibitionism.[400] The way in which he directs others' gaze toward himself and stages the spectacle of his own agony is directly linked to his desire for revenge. He holds Deianeira responsible for his pain. The more he draws attention to its intensity and to his own pitiable condition, the more he believes he is providing grounds for incriminating her in others' eyes as well: by making his audience recognize the extremity of his suffering, he aims to make them measure the depth of the injustice his wife has committed against him.[401] In fact, however, Heracles achieves the opposite effect: the spectacle of his suffering does convey its severity to all, but it does not incriminate Deianeira as he believes it does, much less justify his desire for revenge in the audience's eyes. Instead, it heightens the pity that his audience feels *for the queen*. The more he incriminates and seeks to destroy her, the more deserving of pity she appears to the audience and her son Hyllus, the nurse, and the audience members, all of whom know that the queen's noble nature carried with it good intentions; the recent news of her suicide has provided further proof of her innocence.[402]

---

400 This is not to say, however, that the hero does not exhibit a degree of self-centeredness that is less acceptable by modern standards; see Easterling's 1982 introduction.

401 In evoking a high degree of pity from his spectators, especially Hyllus, Heracles also has the concrete goal in mind of convincing his son of the necessity of putting an end to his misery (1033–5). It is later decided that it would not be appropriate for the wretched Hyllus to light his own father's body on fire, as Heracles requests of him. In addition to the pain that slaying his own father would cause him, Hyllus would be shedding the blood of kin and incurring pollution (1206–7).

402 Perrotta 1935, 474 underlines the role played by Heracles' maledictions in bringing Deianeira's kindness and devotion to the fore of the audience's mind; he also notes that Sophocles prompts the audience members to feel pity toward *both* protagonists as a result.

In the belief that his wife is guilty of having caused him great and fatal pain and that she did so deliberately, Heracles wishes to inflict commensurate pain on her in retribution. He begins by voicing the wish to see Deianeira die in similarly excruciating circumstances to his own:

τὸν φύτορ' οἰκτίρας, ἀνεπίφθονον εἴρυσον ἔγχος,
παῖσον ἐμᾶς ὑπὸ κληδός· ἀκοῦ δ' ἄχος, ᾧ μ' ἐχόλωσεν
σὰ μάτηρ ἄθεος, τὰν ὧδ' ἐπίδοιμι πεσοῦσαν
αὕτως, ὧδ' αὕτως, ὥς μ' ὤλεσεν. ὦ γλυκὺς Ἅιδας
(1034–7)

Take pity on your father, draw a sword that none would blame and strike beneath my collarbone! Heal the agony with which your godless mother has enraged me! May I see her fall in the same way, the very same, in which she has destroyed me! O delightful Hades!

Heracles, who has become a helpless object of others' gaze because of Deianeira's misguided attempt at staging a victorious return, wishes to reclaim a sense of power.[403] He proposes to dramatize the injustice that he has suffered before our very eyes, by conjuring up a hypothetical tableau of extreme brutality, in which Deianeira would be made into an object of spectacle on a par with himself: he requests that Hyllus bring the queen into his presence so that he might inflict violence on her to the point of killing her. His plan is to then be in a position to display her mangled corpse next to his agonized self. He has a specific spectator in mind for the tableau: their son, whom he wants to put in the position of a judge of pitiableness, as it were. In the scene imagined by Heracles, Hyllus would look upon and compare the two bodies, and the two experiences of pain: his mother's lifeless corpse, bludgeoned to death, and his father's burning body:

ὦ παῖ, γενοῦ μοι παῖς ἐτήτυμος γεγώς,
καὶ μὴ τὸ μητρὸς ὄνομα πρεσβεύσῃς πλέον.
δός μοι χεροῖν σαῖν αὐτὸς ἐξ οἴκου λαβὼν
ἐς χεῖρα τὴν τεκοῦσαν, ὡς εἰδῶ σάφα
εἰ τοὐμὸν ἀλγεῖς μᾶλλον ἢ κείνης ὁρῶν
λωβητὸν εἶδος ἐν δίκῃ κακούμενον.
(1064–9)

My son, become my true-born son, do not honor the name of your mother more! Take the one who bore you from the house into your own hands and hand her over to mine, so that I may know for certain whether you suffer more on seeing my body tortured than on seeing hers justly maltreated!

---

403 On Heracles' building an altered heroic persona for himself in these lines, see Nooter 2012, ch. 2.

The response that Heracles expects to elicit from his audience (Hyllus) is based on the assumption that he (Heracles) will be deemed more pitiable, because Deianeira, for all the pain to which she will be subjected, will nonetheless be receiving a punishment that is deserved, while his own agony is not. He has not yet been made aware of his wife's death, much less of the fact that it was self-inflicted. Deianeira is guilty in his mind; therefore, he can expect Hyllus to respond with some degree of satisfaction (as he says he will) to the violence he intends to inflict on her, because it will be inflicted, he believes, as just retribution.

Chilling and cruel though the image may be, the premise for the brutal act that Heracles envisions is the belief that his wife has willfully caused his death through calculated guile. The hero's impulse to obtain revenge and the hatred that he feels toward her are, by ancient Greek standards, justified in this scenario (though it seems likely the extremity of the revenge that he proposes to exact here would not be condoned):[404] he believes that she betrayed the *philia* between them and proved herself to be an *echthra*.[405] For the audience, the pathos that stems from Heracles' fantasized revenge comes not from the fact that he wishes his wife to experience severe pain commensurate with his own but from the fact that the suffering he wishes on her would be *undeserved*, because, as only Heracles' audience knows, she is innocent. That, and only that, is the reason she would be worthy of pity, in the eyes of the Ancients.[406]

The fictitious scenario is a source of great pathos because two of its fundamental premises – Deianeira's guilt and evil intent, which would make her punishment justified, and her being alive – are misguided. Hyllus has not yet revealed to his father that the hero's destruction is not, in fact, the result of his wife's calculated betrayal. The disparity between Heracles' perception of Deia-

---

[404] See for comparison my discussion of the brutal death of Aegisthus at Orestes' hands in Euripides' *Electra* in the next chapter.

[405] See Konstan in Roisman 2014, under the entry "Hatred": "Hatred in Greek is thus a legitimate emotion, elicited by vice, unlike the modern idea that hatred is inevitably a negative sentiment (as in 'hate crimes')." Revenge, when justly inflicted, is condoned by the Greeks. For as long as Hyllus thought his mother was guilty, he wished her dead (735).

[406] The definition of pity provided by Aristotle in his *Rhetoric* that I quoted earlier bears repeating here, with an emphasis on the fact that pity is evoked when the harm being witnessed by the pitier is harm "of one *not deserving* to encounter it": "Let pity, then, be a kind of pain in the case of an apparent destructive or painful harm of one not deserving to encounter it, which one might expect oneself, or one of one's own, to suffer, and this when it seems near" (*Rh.* 1378a30–1378b2, transl. Konstan 2001). Konstan 2006 stresses the importance of this specific condition (that the object of pity must not be deserving of their pain in order to be pitied) throughout the chapter in which he deals with that particular emotion.

neira and the carefully portrayed female protagonist of unshakable nobility, generosity, and prudence that the audience has come to know reaches a climax here, as the spectacle of Deianeira's wrenching suicide, related by her nurse, forms a pathetic backdrop to Heracles' fantasies of revenge.[407]

That the external audience's main object of pity on seeing the spectacle of Heracles' pain is Deianeira rather than the hero himself is corroborated by the internal audience's response to the tremendous pain that he must endure. For despite that pain, he does not evoke as much pity from the internal audience (mainly Hyllus) as we might expect. This is due at least in part to the fact that Heracles is not humanized by his suffering.[408] Rather, his extreme pain seems to initiate his transition to the realm of the dead and perhaps to the realm of the immortals, distancing him from his fellow mortals.[409] Though his suffering and helplessness are quintessentially human, his reactions largely alienate him from those around him and from the audience. Heracles rejects any human response to his demise, condemning his own tears as womanish (καὶ τόδ' οὐδ' ἂν εἶς ποτε | τόνδ' ἄνδρα φαίη πρόσθ' ἰδεῖν δεδρακότα, "No one can say he saw this man do such a thing before," 1072–3; "Now such a thing has shown me as a womanish creature," νῦν δ' ἐκ τοιούτου θῆλυς ηὕρημαι τάλας, 1075) and forbidding his son from manifesting any grief of his own, even though he charges him with orders that are cruel: to light the pyre that will lead to his own father's death and to marry Iole, the very woman who is responsible for both his mother's and his father's dooms:[410]

---

407 At 1049–50, he calls his robe a "woven covering of the Erinyes" (ὁ στυγνὸς Εὐρυσθεὺς ἐμοὶ οἷον τόδ') and Deianeira, who had it sent to him, "the daughter of Oeneus with beguiling face" (ἡ δολῶπις Οἰνέως κόρη).

408 Contrast Philoctetes in Sophocles' play that bears his name, as discussed in ch. 4. Winnington-Ingram 1980 82 ff. compares Heracles to Ajax in his harshness and violence, and notes that the very characteristics that lead him to be so repellent to the audience's eyes are also what made him so great in the eyes of Deianeira and his son, as well as the Chorus.

409 The tradition of Heracles' divinization is not referred to within the play, but the audience would be familiar with it from the tradition; see Kamerbeek's introduction. At the same time, the omission of any allusion to his subsequent divinization contributes to point up Heracles' powerlessness, and the suffering intrinsic to the human condition that he epitomizes in this play (along with Deianeira). That he should suffer thus despite being the son of Zeus is another means of stressing the gaping distance between suffering mortals and the distant and detached gods, which featured prominently in the choral ode that I discussed earlier, in which Cypris looks on coldly at the pain she causes, and which is harped on again by Hyllus in the play's final lines, as we are about to see.

410 Hyllus expresses his bafflement at Heracles' expectation that he wed one who was "the sole cause of [his] mother's death, and of [Heracles'] being in the state [he is in]" (ἥ μοι μητρὶ μὲν θανεῖν μόνη μεταίτιος, σοὶ δ' αὖθις ὡς ἔχεις ἔχειν, 1233–4). Painful though the exe-

> ... γόου δὲ μηδὲν εἰσίδω δάκρυ,
> ἀλλ' ἀστένακτος κἀδάκρυτος, εἴπερ εἶ
> τοῦδ' ἀνδρός, ἔρξον· εἰ δὲ μή, μενῶ σ' ἐγὼ
> καὶ νέρθεν ὢν ἀραῖος εἰσαεὶ βαρύς.
> (1199–1202)
>
> And let me see no tear of lamentation, but do the work without mourning and without weeping if you are this man's son! If you fail to do so, even from down below, I will wait for you, cursing you and causing you grief.

Heracles' focus is on what *must* be done: he pronounces edicts, speaking with the authority of a *deus ex machina* or a seer, dictating the terms of his own death and the conditions of the continuation of his line.[411] Accordingly, Hyllus never actually voices his pity for Heracles in his father's presence; he obeys his will under constraint.[412] In fact, despite Heracles' horrendous circumstances, Hyllus's focus from the beginning of their exchange is on rehabilitating his mother's image in his father's eyes. The Chorus does not express pity for Heracles either; instead, before exiting the stage, they voice fear at the outcome of his destruction – fear for themselves and fear for the future of Greece, which will lose so great a hero (1112–3). These words of fear, which glorify the hero rather than pity him, are the maidens' last.

The silence of Heracles

Deianeira takes her own life because, in her words,[413] "for a woman who places the highest value on being good, it is not bearable to live life with the reputation

---

cution of Heracles' orders will be, Hyllus is willing to obey them: he will do the necessary by lighting Heracles' funeral pyre (or having it lit), hastening his father's death, and he will marry his father's mistress, despite the cruel irony there is in his having offspring with Iole, who caused both of his parents' deaths. He feels compelled to do these things (ἐπεὶ κελεύεις κἀξαναγκάζεις, 1258) because Heracles has called on the gods to witness them (τούτων μάρτυρας καλῶ θεούς, 1248). His acceptance is a form of submission to the paternal will, which he associates and even equates with the divine (τοιγὰρ ποήσω, κοὐκ ἀπώσομαι, τὸ σὸν | θεοῖσι δεικνὺς ἔργον, 1249–50).

411 Though his insistence that Hyllus marry Iole may stem from possessive, erotic reasons, the marriage is also required by the mythological tradition, according to which the Heraclidae were to descend from Hyllus and Iole.

412 When Hyllus does express pity, he does not voice it directly to the sufferer, and this is despite Heracles' repeated requests for Hyllus to pity him.

413 These lines provide the principal motive for Deineira's suicide, and bear quoting once more for this reason.

of being evil" (ζῆν γὰρ κακῶς κλύουσαν οὐκ ἀνασχετόν,| ἥτις προτιμᾷ μὴ κακὴ πεφυκέναι, 721–2). Was Deianeira right to assume that she would have a reputation for evil (κακῶς κλύουσαν)? Who, if anyone, would perceive Deianeira as evil because of the harm she caused? In deed, Deianeira is no different from Clytemnestra: she has caused the death of her husband; in her intentions, character, and nature, however, she is Clytemnestra's polar opposite. The entire first half of the play is devoted to driving that point home, laying stress on her prudence, moderation, noble aspirations, and caring concern for her husband. Sophocles' Deianeira *does* turn out to be κακή, the opposite of beneficial, in her *actions*, proving destructive both to the object of her love and to herself. Yet whether she is to be considered κακή or whether her innocent intentions should be taken into account in the assessment of her life is precisely what Hyllus and Heracles debate at the end of the play. The closing exchange between Hyllus and his father, in which Deianeira's husband and her son argue over her innocence, pits her noble goals (represented by Hyllus) against the heinous consequences of her actions (highlighted by Heracles, both through the horrendous state that he is in and through his recriminations). In the tension between intent and deed, and between Deianeira's nature as we have come to know it and Heracles' perception of that nature, lies one of the principal tragic effects of the play as it comes to an end.

Hyllus's and Heracles' divergent views of Deianeira's culpability in the closing scene suggest once more (and in yet another way from the one noted earlier) that her opening maxim, despite its pessimism, still falls short of the truth: for it is apparent from the debate following the queen's death that "you may not completely learn of the lot of mortals, whether it is good (χρηστός) or bad (κακός)" not until a man dies, but even *after* that mortal's death. If we take the maxim (as I have suggested that we should) in a moral sense, then the question of whether a man has had a good or bad life remains open even after death, since it depends on external perception, and thus can remain a subject of debate. Reputation is determined by others' perceptions of and reactions to one's life, including (and perhaps especially) after one's death, when it is too late to influence these perceptions and reactions; and these vary from one individual to the next. A similar dispute takes place over Ajax's corpse in Sophocles' play that bears the hero's name: whether or not he deserves burial hinges on the question of how others are going to define his life *after his death*. The Atreids consider him to have been an enemy (ἐχθρός, πολέμιος, and hence κακός), while Odysseus argues that the many achievements that he accomplished before turning on his fellow Greeks have made him φιλός (that is, one who was beneficial to the community of his *philoi:* χρηστός).⁴¹⁴ The characters in question — Ajax and Deianeira — are completely powerless to act and, hence, to influence their reputations after their deaths.

The expectation of Deianeira's reputation being set aright in Heracles' eyes builds from the very beginning of the exchange between Hyllus and his father, during which the audience eagerly awaits the moment when Hyllus will reveal the tragic truth about his mother's innocence and her death. Hyllus's indignation (τὸ νεμεσᾶν),⁴¹⁵ as well as the audience's, no doubt, grows on hearing Heracles unjustly besmirch the wife he does not know is now dead. It reaches a culminating point when Heracles voices the wish to inflict tremendous pain on her. Along with Hyllus's indignation, his wish to see the misguided perception, on which Heracles' anger hinges, set aright – namely, the mistaken assumption that Deianeira committed harm deliberately – also grows. Hyllus's (reasonable) expectation is that, on discovering the truth, Heracles will rescind his desire for revenge and recognize her innocence.

When Heracles learns of Deianeira's death, however, he does neither of the above. Instead, he expresses satisfaction that she is dead, along with regret that he was not able to brutalize her himself. To be sure, at this point, he still believes that Deianeira willfully betrayed him, for Hyllus has not yet had the chance to destroy the premise on which Heracles' desire for revenge is based. And yet, even when Hyllus *does* make clear to Heracles Deianeira's good intentions and presents her suicide as evidence of the purity of these intentions, the hero dismisses her intent as irrelevant, claiming that only her action counts, and nothing else. The full exchange is worth quoting:

Υλ. τῆς μητρὸς ἥκω τῆς ἐμῆς φράσων ἐν οἷς
νῦν ἔστ' ἐν οἷς θ' ἥμαρτεν οὐχ ἑκουσία.
Ηρ. ὦ παγκάκιστε, καὶ παρεμνήσω γὰρ αὖ
τῆς πατροφόντου μητρός, ὡς κλύειν ἐμέ; (1125)
Υλ. ἔχει γὰρ οὕτως ὥστε μὴ σιγᾶν πρέπειν.
Ηρ. οὐ δῆτα τοῖς γε πρόσθεν ἡμαρτημένοις.
Υλ. ἀλλ' οὐδὲ μὲν δὴ τοῖς γ' ἐφ' ἡμέραν ἐρεῖς.
Ηρ. λέγ', εὐλαβοῦ δὲ μὴ φανῇς κακὸς γεγώς.

---

414 S., *Aj.* 974 ff. φίλος and ἐχθρός are used rather than χρηστός and κακός in the debate over Ajax's worth to society, but the two pairs pit similar camps against one another: those who contribute to others within their community in a positive way and those who are detrimental to them.

415 I am using "indignation" here in reference to Aristotle's definition and use of τὸ νεμεσᾶν, one subcategory of which includes pain at the undeserved misfortune of the good. On the different aspects of Aristotle's τὸ νεμεσᾶν, see *Rh.* 2.9.1387a2; *EN* 2.7.1108a35–b6; *EE* 3.7. 1233b23–27; Moles 1984, 325 ff.; also Konstan 2006, ch. 5.

```
Υλ. λέγω. τέθνηκεν ἀρτίως νεοσφαγής.                                    (1130)
Ηρ. πρὸς τοῦ; τέρας τοι διὰ κακῶν ἐθέσπισας.
Υλ. αὐτὴ πρὸς αὑτῆς, οὐδενὸς πρὸς ἐκτόπου.
Ηρ. οἴμοι· πρὶν ὡς χρῆν σφ' ἐξ ἐμῆς θανεῖν χερός;
Υλ. κἂν σοῦ στραφείη θυμός, εἰ τὸ πᾶν μάθοις.
Ηρ. δεινοῦ λόγου κατῆρξας· εἰπὲ δ' ᾖ νοεῖς.                             (1135)
Υλ. ἅπαν τὸ χρῆμ' ἥμαρτε χρηστὰ μωμένη.
Ηρ. χρήστ', ὦ κάκιστε, πατέρα σὸν κτείνασα δρᾷ;
Υλ. στέργημα γὰρ δοκοῦσα προσβαλεῖν σέθεν
ἀπήμπλαχ', ὡς προσεῖδε τοὺς ἔνδον γάμους.
Ηρ. καὶ τίς τοσοῦτος φαρμακεὺς Τραχινίων;                               (1140)
Υλ. Νέσσος πάλαι Κένταυρος ἐξέπεισέ νιν
τοιῷδε φίλτρῳ τὸν σὸν ἐκμῆναι πόθον.
                (1122–42)
```

HY. I have come to tell you about my mother, how it now stands with her and how she did wrong by accident.
HE. You utter villain, have you again made mention of the mother who has killed your father, in my hearing?
HY. Yes, for things stand so with her that silence would be wrong.
HE. Indeed no, when you think of the wrong she did before!
HY. Not when you consider what she has done this day as well!
HE. Speak, but take care that you are not revealed to be a traitor!
HY. I will speak; she is dead, newly slain!
HE. At whose hand? A miracle, told by a prophet who speaks evil!
HY. By her own hand, not that of any other.
HE. Ah me! Before she could die at my hand, as she should have done?
HY. Even your mind would be altered, if you were to learn all.
HE. What you have begun to say is dire; but tell me what you have a mind to tell!
HY. She did altogether wrong, but her intent was good.
HE. Was it a good action, villain, to kill your father?
HY. Why, she went wrong thinking that she was applying a philter, having seen the bride who is in the house!
HE. And who among the men of Trachis is so great a sorcerer?
HY. Nessus the Centaur long ago persuaded her to inflame your passion with such a love charm.

Hyllus attempts to rehabilitate Deianeira in Heracles' eyes; his continued efforts make Heracles' lack of recognition of her innocent intentions all the more noteworthy. When Heracles dismisses Hyllus's defense of Deianeira's pure intent, indicating that only the outcome of her initiative (his death) matters (χρήστ', ὦ κάκιστε, πατέρα σὸν κτείνασα δρᾷ, 1137), Hyllus has not yet unveiled the fact that her action was not only laced with good intentions but also guided by the influence and trickery of another: the centaur Nessus. What is most striking is that, when his son *does* go on to mention that the cunning of the centaur is what "persuaded her to inflame <his> passion with such a love charm" (1141–

2), Heracles does not reconsider his judgment of Deianeira. Hyllus delivers the news of Deianeira's suicide to Heracles and reveals the crucial fact that she had resorted to Nessus's blood because she sought to be loved by the hero, thus providing proof not only of her good intentions, but also of the actively destructive role the centaur played in his downfall. Still, Heracles does not express any pity for the queen, nor does he acknowledge her innocence, as Hyllus had hoped he would. Even after the essential revelation of Nessus's role, which diminishes Deianeira's responsibility considerably, the dramatist keeps Heracles noticeably silent regarding Deianeira and the question of her guilt.[416] The hero simply ignores the proof of her innocence. He does not express mitigated hatred or any emotion whatsoever in response: he says nothing at all.

To grasp the particular pathos that comes with Heracles' silence on the matter of Deianeira's innocence, we might turn, for comparison's sake, to a Euripidean play, the *Hippolytus*, in which the destructive power of Aphrodite also looms large, and a character (Theseus) is also directly responsible for another's death, because of his misguided trust in an incriminating suicide letter left behind by his wife Phaedra. Theseus believes Phaedra's account, according to which his son Hippolytus dishonored her with sexual advances, and curses him. Poseidon fulfills Theseus's curse by having Hippolytus dragged to his death by his horses in a horrendous chariot accident. Theseus is then informed of Phaedra's scheme and of Hippolytus's innocence. Father and son are reunited when the latter is brought back onstage on a litter, close to death. Over the course of their final encounter, despite the horrid circumstances and painful nature of his gruesome demise, which he knows to be a result of his father's curse, Hippolytus bemoans Theseus's lot, going so far as to declare it more worthy of sorrow than his own: "*In light of your mistake*, I feel greater sorrow for you than for me" (στένω σε μᾶλλον ἢ 'μὲ τῆς ἁμαρτίας, 1409). Though he is dying an excruciating death, Hippolytus still deems himself less worthy of sorrow than his father, Theseus, who caused that painful death by mistake (τῆς ἁμαρτίας). One could readily apply Hippolytus's rationale to Heracles' and Deianeira's respective roles, as well – if the two met, Heracles, despite dying a slow and painful death, should bemoan Deianeira's lot more than his own and consider her more worthy of sorrow than himself because of her mistake. No such encounter ever occurs; Deianeira dies first. All that is left are the appalling, imaginary encounters in which Heracles pictures himself wreaking dreadful violence on his wife before he is made aware of her innocence, and his complete lack of acknowledgment of Hyllus's arguments for her innocence after he hears them.

---

[416] This important point is also noted by other scholars, including Sorum 1978 and Ormand.

As Euripides' drama closes, Theseus recognizes Hippolytus's innocence, and Hippolytus recognizes Theseus's error. Sophocles, on the other hand, never provides his audience (or the dead Deianeira) with the satisfaction of having Heracles recognize her innocence or her suffering, as Hippolytus does Theseus's.

The two plays do share a significant element in their endings: the similar role played by the gods, whose power over mortals and cold detachment from the suffering they cause to them are brought out in the way they look on at human suffering, from the stance of a distant spectator. In Euripides' play, Artemis leaves Hippolytus, her devoted protégé, to die alone, because she must not look upon a corpse.[417] The audience is reminded in the play's closing that the destruction that has been wrought is all due to the power of *erôs:* Hippolytus's neglect of Aphrodite in favor of Artemis made him and Phaedra the victims of the goddess of love.

I will turn to the comparable role of the gods in the ending of the *Trachiniae* shortly. For now, I want to dwell a moment longer on the absence of any similar encounter between Heracles and Deianeira to the one that occurs between Theseus and Hippolytus. Sophocles deliberately excludes any such encounter between Heracles and Deianeira for the same reason that he keeps Heracles entirely silent on a matter so crucial that it led Deianeira to kill herself – how she would be perceived by others and by Heracles especially. It is clear that the construction of the play in such a way that husband and wife never meet is not a dramatic flaw, as some have thought, but a dramatic necessity: it deprives Deianeira of the opportunity to provide an explanation of her intent and clarification regarding her manipulation by the centaur, and it deprives her of a chance to obtain Heracles' pity, which would be a recognition of her innocence. Such an encounter would be a chance for Heracles to recognize, while she still lived (as Hippolytus does with Theseus), that his wife's destructive act was inadvertent and that she does not deserve to have her reputation shattered. But husband and wife are never united onstage or by any form of virtual address from one to the other, dead or alive; she never has the chance to ask for pity, and he never voices any.

Whatever Heracles' reasons for remaining silent when it comes to his wife's innocence, the profoundly pitiable and involuntary nature of Deianeira's mistake remains unacknowledged by him till the very end. The last word the audience hears from Heracles regarding Deianeira is that her action was not χρηστός (1137) — a term whose moral and social connotations hark back to the maxim

---

[417] The gods cannot look upon the dead, and so Aphrodite "leaves behind a long friendship," in Hippolytus's words (1441).

with which Deianeira opened the play.⁴¹⁸ Though he later explicitly states that the centaur is the one who killed him (1163), he does not, at any point, satisfy Hyllus's (and the audience's) desire that Deianeira's pure intentions be granted the just acknowledgment that her noble character deserves in Hyllus's eyes. We never hear Heracles exculpate his wife or retract his earlier wishes for revenge, and it is never suggested that he thinks of Deianeira as innocent, much less that he pities her; he simply no longer utters a single word about her.

Though the Chorus and Hyllus recognize Deianeira's innocence and appear to disprove her assumption that, no matter how innocent her intentions and no matter how inadvertent the ruinous outcome of her action, she would still be called evil (κακῶς κλύουσαν, 721), her dark prediction regarding her reputation proves to be all too true as far as Heracles is concerned. Even after Hyllus explicitly points to Nessus's role in the hero's demise, she is never rehabilitated in the eyes of the one who was the center of her world, who has described her as an object of his hatred and never goes back on this evaluation of her.

Heracles' silence is yet another dramatic instantiation of Deianeira's powerlessness, which we continue to see even after her death. To the extent that Heracles never speaks a single word that might point to her rehabilitation in his eyes, we can say that Deianeira is tragically correct in her assessment that she will have a reputation for doing harm (κακῶς κλύουσα). If Heracles' silence is anything to go by, then she has failed, irreparably so, at what mattered to her most: living a life that will be considered commendable and having Heracles reciprocate her love. His silence proves to the audience that Deianeira's status in his eyes was indeed irretrievably damaged. It does not matter that others – the nurse, the Chorus, Hyllus, and most certainly the audience – recognize her innocence, because the one whose perception of her guided her every action and deed does not. When she decides to take her own life, it is out of a concern for her status in the eyes of others, particularly Heracles: the queen's desire not to be seen (903) is a sign of her great shame and despair at the thought that the hero might see her.⁴¹⁹ Heracles' silence reinforces our sense of Deianeira's powerlessness to control not only her deed and its outcome but also the reputation that stems from that deed. Her son, who has represented her onstage since her death, presents the hero with several opportunities to recognize the purity of his wife's intent — all to no avail. Hyllus fails to redeem her and her honor in the eyes of the only one whose opinion mattered.

---

418 See my remarks regarding χρηστός at the beginning of this chapter.
419 Kamerbeek notes this shame, *ad loc.* I agree with Jebb, *pace* Kamerbeek: "[Hyllus's] occupation reminded her that Heracles would soon arrive, and decided her to act at once."

Does the silence that Heracles maintains regarding Deianeira indicate that he considers her guilty and an object of hatred till the very end? We cannot know for sure. Even if it does not, the mere fact that he remains silent reveals just how marginal she is to the hero's existence and concerns. Deianeira's every decision, including the one to take her own life, stems from the central role that Heracles and his perception of her play in defining the worth of her existence in her own eyes. Her importance to Heracles' existence, on the other hand, is inversely proportional to the hero's importance to hers: since the initial "snatching" of her youth by his possessive, objectifying gaze, she has remained as peripheral to his vision as he has been central to hers.[420] In a reflection of the marginality of Deianeira to Heracles' concerns, when Hyllus reveals to him that the centaur is the one who provided her with the poison and tricked her into thinking it was a love potion, the hero's attention turns instantly away from her to what the centaur's role reveals with regards to his own heroic past: Heracles lost a battle that he had until then thought he had won. The only information that Heracles retains from Hyllus's revelation about the centaur's poison is what pertains directly to him and his fate. He is finally able to understand the meaning of the divine oracle of which his own father, Zeus, had made him aware long since. He realizes that he is now fulfilling his destiny to die "not ever at the hands of any of the living, but of one who is dead, an inhabitant of Hades" (πρὸς τῶν πνεόντων μηδενὸς θανεῖν ποτε, | ἀλλ' ὅστις Ἅιδου φθίμενος οἰκήτωρ πέλοι, 1160–1). He, the victorious monster slayer, was only so in appearance; his battle against the monster was a defeat, not a victory. In the end, he is the victim of the very one over whom he thought he had exerted power.[421] The revelation regarding the centaur's role in causing Heracles' demise leads the hero to recognize his powerlessness in the face of fate, the oracle, and *erôs*.[422]

---

[420] Deianeira's marginal status in Heracles' eyes is examined in detail by Ormand 1999, ch. 2; at p.59, Ormand notes that this is a reflection of the "painfully marginal" status of women in a "society ... that defines itself by homosociality and endogamy."

[421] Two of Heracles' labors involving monsters are recalled in the play: the slaying of the Hydra of Lerna and the killing of the centaur Nessus, which he accomplishes with an arrow poisoned with the Hydra's blood. The philter that Deianeira uses to inflame Heracles with desire is a mixture of the Hydra's poison with the centaur's blood. The ambiguity of Heracles' power is explored by Segal 1981, 60–108, whose analysis brings to the fore how Heracles, the heroic sacker of cities and slayer of monsters *par excellence*, destroys any obstacle in his way with so brutal an efficiency and such savage energy that the line between civilizing power and bestial force is blurred.

[422] Perrotta 1935, 484–5 underlines the two aspects of the hero that Sophocles chooses to stress: on the one hand, the violent, uncompromising man; on the other, the mortal and suffer-

Meanwhile, his silence in response to the realization that he did not truly overcome the centaur (which amounts to saying that the power of *erôs* had the better of him) illustrates Deianeira's powerlessness to redeem herself in his eyes. Neither of them has had any power over *erôs*, which has destroyed them both — a theme that the third choral ode pointedly developed following Deianeira's final exit from the stage. This is a truth that Deianeira, Hyllus, and Heracles all come to see, only when it is too late.

Divine agents and spectators

The gods are nearly absent from the *Trachiniae*; no character role is assigned to one, and they neither appear in a *deus ex machina* at the end nor intervene in any way to aid Heracles, Zeus's own son, in his agony. The traditional motif of divine control of human affairs occurs across poetic genres;[423] the gods' general absence from the *Trachiniae* is conspicuous and deliberate. We never see them or hear them utter a word onstage; they loom large in the play, but in the background, a direct reflection of their complete disengagement from the human suffering that they play such a significant role in causing.[424] Their presence is mentioned at key points, where it becomes apparent that their power is commensurate with the distance that they maintain from the consequences of wielding that power. Like the tragic character of Deianeira, the gods in this tragedy are agents-turned-spectators: they look on as the consequences of their agency play out. But while witnessing the aftermath of her initiative ultimately causes Deianeira to take her own life, even though she realizes how small and powerless a role she has played, the gods are spectators who take pleasure in the outcome of their intervention, from a dispassionate and distant vantage point, precisely *because* of the destruction that they have caused. No matter the outcome, they take pleasure in the exercise of their power in and of itself and in watching whatever effect that power may have.

In the *parodos* of the play, in response to Deianeira's lamentation and anxiety regarding the fate of Heracles, the Chorus offers up what is intended as a consolatory rhetorical question: "For who has seen Zeus so lacking in counsel

---

ing hero. P. argues that it is to foreground the latter that the poet deliberately omits any reference to the tradition according to which Heracles was divinized.

[423] Thus, the entirety of the *Iliad* is none other than the fulfillment of the will of Zeus (*Il.* 1.5): Διὸς δ' ἐτελείετο βουλή.

[424] Regarding the Sophoclean emphasis on the obscurity of divine will for humans, see Parker 1999.

for his children?" (ἐπεὶ τίς ὧδε | τέκνοισι Ζῆν' ἄβουλον εἶδεν, 139–40). The motif of Zeus's (alleged) concern for mortals returns at the close of the play, at a point when the events that have unfolded – Deianeira's erroneous initiative and suicide and Heracles' torturous death – have pointed up the naïveté of the Chorus's earlier utterance. Hyllus, Heracles' son and Zeus's grandson, is the speaker; his are the last words spoken in the entire play.[425] He is preparing to oversee his father's death, as Heracles had requested, and thus to be orphaned of both parents.[426] When his companions are silently brought in for the gloomy purpose of lifting Heracles' already decaying body and carrying him to the funeral pyre where he will be burned alive, Hyllus asks these attendants to show great sympathy to him (Hyllus) because they know (εἰδότες) the great unkindness of the gods in these events:

αἴρετ', ὀπαδοί, μεγάλην μὲν ἐμοὶ
τούτων θέμενοι συγγνωμοσύνην.
μεγάλην δὲ θεῶν ἀγνωμοσύνην,
εἰδότες ἔργων τῶν πρασσομένων .

(1264–7)

Lift him, companions, showing great sympathy for me in what has happened, and knowing of the great unkindness of the gods displayed in these events.

Commentators have noted the unusual term that Hyllus uses for "sympathy" here: συγγνωμοσύνην (1265). It occurs nowhere else in extant Greek literature and seems likely to have been coined by Sophocles for the sole purpose of creating a rhyme with the term ἀγνωμοσύνην, which occurs in the same position in the line immediately following (1266).[427] The rhyme draws attention to the contrast that is central to Hyllus's last words. On the one hand, there is the sympathy that mortals must feel for one another (for which Deianeira offered an exemplary

---

425 Scholars have long debated the attribution of the last of these lines (1275–8). Their gnomic nature and the fact that the codas to Sophoclean plays are typically choral have led some to believe that these were spoken by the Chorus, yet Jebb rightly underlines the fact that the Chorus has been silent since 1113. Dramatically and thematically, moreover, it is effective to have Hyllus left alone to sum up with appropriate solemnity the lesson(s) of his parents' fate and to have him be the one to introduce the additional and essential revelation of Zeus's agency underlying all that has come to pass, with which the play comes to an end.
426 Hyllus has dreaded his looming status of orphan from the time he heard of his mother's death: πατρός τ' ἐκείνης τ', ὠρφανισμένος βίον, 942.
427 The striking nature of the parallel and the uniqueness of the term are noted by Winnington-Ingram 1980, 74 in his discussion of the ending of the play when he underlines the surprising nature of Hyllus's words of bitter complaint in light of Sophocles' reputation for piety.

standard): they all share in the powerlessness of the human condition: all things stem from the gods; all sufferings must be endured, while none can be reliably foreseen. On the other hand, there are the all-powerful gods, who show a complete lack of feeling (ἀγνωμοσύνην) regarding the suffering that they are always behind, in some way or another – for, as Hyllus goes on to explain, "None of these events is not Zeus" (1278).

Hyllus ends the drama with a statement that echoes the one with which his mother began it.[428] The maxim that Deianeira spoke in the very first lines of the play underscored the limited capacity of mortals to have any knowledge regarding fate and what the future holds, a maxim which has proven all too true in its applicability to its speaker, but to a degree that the audience now knows she was still tragically far from beginning to fathom. After his initial remark asking for the Chorus's sympathy and pointing up the gods' indifference, Hyllus goes on to distinguish between mortals and the gods *qua* spectators. Both look on at the human condition, and both have seen the dire events that have unfolded within the time frame of the play. For mortals, however, he equates watching with helplessness, as the future remains obscure and unpredictable for all: "Which events will happen, nobody can foresee" (τὰ μὲν οὖν μέλλοντ' οὐδεὶς ἐφορᾷ, 1270). We are reminded of the coda with which Sophocles has his Chorus conclude the *Ajax:*

ἦ πολλὰ βροτοῖς ἔστιν ἰδοῦσιν
γνῶναι· πρὶν ἰδεῖν δ' οὐδεὶς μάντις
τῶν μελλόντων ὅ τι πράξει.
(1418–20)

Mortals can judge of many things once they have seen them; but before seeing it no man can prophesy what his fortune shall be in the future.

The "contrast between mere sight and vision" in the above coda aptly points up the gap that is stressed in both of these Sophoclean dramas (and others, to be sure, including the *Oedipus Rex)* between mortal attempts to see and know, on the one hand, and the true knowledge and vision that come only when the gods are willing to grant it, only too late, on the other.[429]

In closing, Hyllus turns to the Chorus of maidens to bid them farewell, and underscores the passive role that they have played as onlookers to horrors in

---

[428] He therefore also echoes the nurse's words that I discussed above, which also harked back to the play's initial maxim.

[429] This contrast is noted by Golder and Prevear in the notes to their translation of the *Ajax* (1999, *ad loc.*).

which they had no hand and no say: "You have lately seen terrible deaths, and many sufferings unprecedented" (μεγάλους μὲν ἰδοῦσα νέους θανάτους, | πολλὰ δὲ πήματα <καὶ> καινοπαθῆ, 1276–7). He then goes on to contrast these mortal onlookers with another set of spectators to human misery: the gods, "who beget us and are called our fathers, and yet look on such sufferings as these!" (οἳ φύσαντες καὶ κληζόμενοι | πατέρες τοιαῦτ' ἐφορῶσι πάθη, 1268–9). As "fathers" of humankind, these divine spectators might be expected to be protective and show some concern, yet the gods simply watch as the spectacle of human suffering unfolds.[430] While mortals' plight can and often does evoke pity from fellow mortals, provided they recognize that they share in the helplessness that they see in others and recognize their own vulnerability in it, the suffering that the gods cause mortals brings them nothing but shame: "Things as they stand are pitiful for us, and shameful for them" (τὰ δὲ νῦν ἑστῶτ' οἰκτρὰ μὲν ἡμῖν, αἰσχρὰ δ' ἐκείνοις, 1271–2) – shameful in the eyes of mortals, of course, not to their own indifferent gaze. The gods of Sophocles are pitiless.

Why does the gods' status as spectators bring them shame, we might ask? The explanation comes with Hyllus's very last words: these gods are more than just spectators – they are agents. The momentous statement with which Hyllus ends the play makes clear the gods' role in bringing about suffering, which they go on to simply "look at" (ἐφορῶσι) as it unfolds; it bears quoting once more: "None of these events is not Zeus" (κοὐδὲν τούτων ὅ τι μὴ Ζεύς, 1278). We are reminded of Aphrodite, who was said to rejoice in the status of detached umpire (ῥαβδονόμει ξυνοῦσα, 516) as she watched the battle that she herself had provoked between Heracles and Achelous unfold, while Deianeira (whose beauty, she feared, was the cause of it all) averted her gaze in horror. Hyllus's words are also reminiscent of the end of the third choral song, in which Cypris also features, standing by and looking on in silence, revealing herself as "the doer of it all" (τῶνδ' ἐφάνη πράκτωρ, 861), even as Deianeira takes her own life offstage because of the role she has played inadvertently. The image of the silent divine spectator relishing the spectacle of his or her own power is again evoked here with Zeus, ending the play with a figure who is the polar opposite of the pathetic figure of Deianeira: she too is an agent-turned-spectator, but a human one, whose pain on witnessing the aftermath of her actions is such that she kills herself. The words of Schopenhauer concerning drama come to mind as we are told by Hyllus that, "None of these events is not Zeus." In his essay on the art of literature, he describes the art of drama as "the most perfect reflection of human

---

430 Cf. e.g., E., *Hipp.* 1363, where, in his agony, Hippolytus asks, "Zeus, Zeus, do you see this?" Ζεῦ Ζεῦ, τάδ' ὁρᾶις;

existence" and defines the climactic stage of drama as the one in which it "aims at being tragic." At that point, he says, "we are brought face to face with great suffering and the storm and stress of existence; and the outcome of it is to show the vanity of all human effort."[431] Seeing through the lens of Deianeira has led the audience to realize just that. The *Trachiniae* puts before us (and before Deianeira's eyes) a typically Sophoclean motif: "the overwhelming sense of human helplessness in the face of divine mystery, and of the *atê* [disaster] that waits on all human achievement."[432]

---

[431] Schopenhauer 1891, 75.
[432] Dodds 1951, 49.

Chapter Three: From Murderer to Messenger: Body, Speech, and Justice in Greek Tragedy

{Με.} τί χρῆμα πάσχεις; τίς σ' ἀπόλλυσιν νόσος;
{Ορ.} ἡ σύνεσις, ὅτι σύνοιδα δείν' εἰργασμένος.

Menelaus: What ails you? What is your deadly sickness?
Orestes: My conscience; I know that I am guilty of a dreadful crime.
— Euripides, *Orestes* (395-6)[433]

I turn in this chapter to a specific sub-category of agents-turned-spectators: the killers of Greek tragedy that are made to report their own deeds to the audience. While the figure of Deianeira as an internal spectator in the *Trachiniae* epitomizes the ideal spectator whose gaze the audience readily embraces, the agents-turned spectators that I consider in the present chapter engage the audience in a different manner. That the murderers themselves should deliver the account of the killings that have taken place offstage is a deliberate variation on the messenger speeches of Greek tragedy. I analyze both the language and the content of their speeches, paying particular attention to how the killers' own perspectives touch on the broader, central questions of justice and morality that are raised by the act of killing *philoi* in each of the plays.

The murderers-turned-messengers that I examine present the spectator in the theater with their subjective version and view of the deed that they have committed. They offer an especially interesting and fertile ground for investigation, because all three playwrights have treated the killing that I focus on: namely, that of Clytemnestra at the hands of her children, Orestes and Electra, with an eye to the earlier murder of Agamemnon at her own hands, which provoked her murder in retaliation. The killers' points of focus vary considerably from one playwright to the next. I analyze their verbal and physical relationship to the body, both during the act (as they retell it) and in its aftermath (as they face the corpse onstage). I am particularly interested in a feature that the two principal scenes that I consider (the death of Agamemnon in Aeschylus, and the death of Clytemnestra in Euripides) share: the murderers-turned-messengers are not simply narrators relating and reacting to their own deed, but also reenactors of the killing they have committed — onstage, before the audience. The miming in the present (including the vivid present of performance) of violent deeds from the recent past introduces another visual (and highly subjective) depiction of these murderous acts, by putting them before the perpetrators' and the audience's eyes after the fact. My aim is to elucidate what such an *a posteriori* miming of a past deed achieves, in dramatic and thematic terms, by considering the additional perspectives and versions of the killing that they offer up – to the audience, but above all to the murderers-turned-messengers themselves.

The two murders that I examine are closely related causally speaking; both are instantiations of the internecine strife that results from the curse on the house of Atreus. I begin with Clytemnestra's murder of her husband in Aeschylus's *Oresteia*. Her account of his assassination is exceptionally rich and complex in texture, due in large part to her abundant use of imagery. I

---

[433] Euripides' *Orestes*, translated by E. P. Coleridge (New York, 1938). For an assessment of these lines as the first reference to the phenomenon of conscience in Greek tragedy, see Cairns 1993, 303 (including nn. 136-7) with bibliography.

argue that the imagery Aeschylus makes her employ draws subtle yet critical causal and thematic connections between her deed and the perverse, driving force that led her to commit her act, a force which also underlies all the other destructive acts that occur within the trilogy. The links that the layers of imagery thus establish function as a metanarrative embedded within the character's own, personal narrative: Clytemnestra's words and vision reveal her perverse relationship to Agamemnon's body, and that relationship is set against a broader pattern of destruction and vengeance that rears its head throughout the trilogy, whereby what is traditionally associated with life and birth is conflated with (and even replaced by) death and destruction. In typical Aeschylean fashion, the imagery that Clytemnestra employs (and the literal and figurative vision that this imagery conveys) plays a role in revealing the limits of her agency, as the divine forces at work in her and every mortal endeavor are brought to light.

The second example of murderers-turned-messengers that I analyze in this chapter is the next logical step in the cycle of vengeance afflicting the house of Atreus. After Clytemnestra kills Agamemnon, her children kill their mother to avenge their father. The matricide is depicted by all three tragedians, and the audiences of the fifth century saw Orestes and Electra kill their mother in Aeschylus's *Oresteia* (the *Choephori*), Sophocles' *Electra*, and Euripides' play by the same name.[434] This offers opportunities for enlightening comparisons between the different extant versions. Critics have already paid close attention to the parallels and differences between the dramatists' depictions of the matricide. The innovative approach that I adopt here is to concentrate on the differences between the matricidal children's own accounts of their actions and their reactions once they step back and take stock of what they have done after the fact. The main case I zero in on is Euripides' treatment of the aftermath of Clytemnestra's death; however, I take the other two tragedians' versions of the scene into consideration as well, in order to try and fully grasp the originality and significance of Euripides' choices. As their mother did in Aeschylus's *Agamemnon*, the matricidal siblings in Euripides' play are put in the role of narrators, reenactors, and spectators of their own deed after the fact. When they mime the murder of their mother onstage, they watch it unfold a second time, as though through new eyes, and experience a radical shift in their emotional response to it. In the siblings' reenactment of their mother's death, Euripides revisits the Aeschylean portrayal of the matricide in a new light, and presents the moral and social issues that it raises from a fresh angle.

This chapter looks at a common situation in tragedy — one in which *philoi* have turned violent and, with drastic consequences, committed the murder of their kin.[435] The scenes I focus on are far less common, however: I examine those speeches in which the murderers themselves are the ones who play the role of witnesses to and reporters of their murderous deed. These accounts make for a very different sort of speech from the typical messenger speech reported by a secondary figure who may have been a participant in the action but is never the perpetrator of the deed herself.

---

[434] These are only the extant plays depicting the matricide.
[435] See Belfiore 2000.

Greek tragedy is full of gory scenes of murder and suicide, but these by convention could not be represented onstage.[436] Instead, a messenger or herald who was present at the scene would provide an account of it.[437] Typically, this role is filled by a secondary character or anonymous figure whose purpose in the play is often limited to reporting the death that has occurred out of the audience's sight. These evocative and powerful reports are alone responsible for conveying the horrific nature of the killings that have taken place.

Messenger speeches were long considered to be "objective;" this assumption has now been convincingly questioned.[438] In her study of Euripidean messenger speeches, De Jong refutes the notion that there is a so-called objectivity to *any* "I as witness" messenger accounts of events and highlights the subjectivity that actually shines through in these allegedly factual accounts.[439] Her analysis of the style of presentation of messenger speeches begins with a lengthy quote from Barlow, which I reproduce here because it touches on several points that are relevant to the present investigation:

> Where imagery in monody conveys the irrational and subjective attitudes which characterize the singer of that monody, that of the messenger must seem to convey a rational account of objective fact, the existence of which has nothing to do with him personally, except in the sense that he has happened to observe it. For the messenger is the one character in the play who is not caught up in the complicated entanglements of family dispute. He is an outsider in the sense that he is not of the same family or the same social class as the protagonists, and it is as a detached observer that he reports what he sees, as he comes upon it as it were cold, or by chance. The pictorial language of the messenger speeches, accordingly, is suited to what is demanded of an eye-witness account of a crime, poetically conceived in the narrative mode ... Euripides never allowed a messenger to lie: his description of the catastrophe, coming as it usually does at the highest point of tension in the play, is the definitive one.[440]

Rejecting Barlow's claim that the messenger is a "detached observer," De Jong shows that Euripidean messenger speeches, for all their supposed eyewitness accuracy, are actually charged with considerable emotion and rife with subjective

---

[436] On the far-reaching consequences that such prohibition of onstage bloodshed had for the representation of violence in tragedy, see Henrichs 2000. See also Goldhill 1991. Seidensticker 2006 addresses the question of why the depiction of violence has such a fascinating effect upon the audience, past and present.
[437] Sophocles' hero committing suicide in *Ajax* is a notorious exception. The staging of his death is a subject of much discussion; see e.g., Seale 1982, 164–7. On the staging of Greek drama, Taplin 1978 remains a reference.
[438] See De Jong 1991 and Barrett 2002.
[439] De Jong 1991, 63 ff.
[440] Barlow 1971, 61.

touches. No matter that the messenger is, in most cases, anonymous and is not always otherwise developed or involved in the action, and never in a significant way when he is. Factual though it may be, the narrative mode and the imagery employed in these speeches are by no means objective and detached,[441] regardless of how personally uninvolved the messenger may be and how seemingly dispassionate his account. There are, inevitably, hints of subjectivity that shine through these seemingly purely factual reports – for any vantage point is, by definition, subjective. These reports are first-person narratives, in which the narrator and focalizer is also a participant in the action that he reports; he is, therefore, engaged, even biased, and restricted in his knowledge and scope.

Some of these messenger speeches are especially emotional. There are a number of scenes from Greek tragedy in which benevolent onlookers (usually slaves) see loved ones endure pain and face death and then report what they have seen with grief. Deianeira's nurse, whom I discussed in the previous chapter, is one example. Such internal witnesses heighten the impact of their *philos'* demise, conveying it to the audience with greater immediacy and emotional involvement. The nature of these witnesses' relationships to the dead involves them personally in the scenes they are recounting. The situation gets more complicated, and also more interesting perhaps, when those relating the news are not only *philoi* but also the very ones who have caused the death they are reporting.

First-person accounts by murderers of their own violent acts committed offstage are significantly more biased, subjective, and emotional, at the very least because of the characters' personal stake and direct involvement in the action that they are reporting: they are relating not just an act that they *witnessed*, but an act that they have committed. They are the principal actors, the doers of the deed that they are now reporting, telling the tale of the destructive act after the fact. For shorthand, I will refer to these characters as murderers-turned-messengers in what follows.

I mentioned in the introduction the important narratological distinction between a first-person, "homodiegetic" narrative, and a third-person, heterodiegetic narrative.[442] The speeches I look at in this chapter are atypical messenger speeches: they are all first-person narratives, told by a narrator who is also a character within the narrative that she is recounting. These characters participate

---

441 De Romilly 1958, 118, writes of tragic messenger speeches in general: "Par definition, le récit de la tragédie dénoue une attente anxieuse, il s'adresse à des gens émus; il est fait par quelqu'un qui partage leur emotion, et l'éprouve d'autant plus vivement qu'il vient de participer à l'action ou au moins d'y assister."
442 See the introduction, p. 6ff.

in the events that they represent to the (internal and external) audience. Their story is told by one who fulfills the roles both of narrator and focalizer.[443] As we will see, in the scenes of particular interest to me, they also take on an additional role: that of reenactor and even spectator of their own murderous deed.

My goal in what follows is to try to determine why the respective playwrights each chose, in certain cases, to have the killer himself offer up an account of his act after committing it and what sort of vision, or access to a vision, the audience is thus granted not only of the deed but also of the murderer himself.[444] What impact does that death have on the one who brought it about? How did he (or she) respond to the act of killing during the deed, and does this response differ from how he reacts after the fact, as he recounts the murder from the vantage point of a spectator, while the visible evidence of his bloody deed (a corpse) lies before him for all to see? What is the point of having an assassin recount his act and voice his emotions in response to what he has done? What difference does it make for the audience to hear the perpetrator's perspective on his deed, and what function does presenting the murderer's angle on and reactions to his own actions fulfill for the audience? Clearly, the audience is not expected simply to mirror, condone, or condemn the killer's reaction to his deed. The foregrounding of so subjective and involved a perspective fulfills other functions as well.

The central point of dramatic interest for the audience is not so much the death itself – that it occurred and how – but how the murderer-turned-messenger portrays those deaths. What his account foregrounds, more than the act itself, is *the killer's vision* of, and response to, the deed committed. In the process of narrating what he has done, the murderer is in the unusual and strange position of watching, like a spectator, a scene in which he was actively involved as an agent moments prior. He is, effectively, in the role of *a posteriori* eyewitness to his own deeds. As the killer recounts his deed, he takes a figurative step back and watches, alongside the audience, while the scene of his own crime unfolds before his and our eyes, as he represents it in words, shaped and restricted by his subjective lens (and, perhaps, by his agenda). The murderer-turned-messenger provides a mental picture of the scene for the audience; he virtually watches the murder unfold a second time as he retells it, making abundant references to the act of watching and seeing and thus inviting the audience to take note of what it is he dwells on, visually speaking, in concrete terms. Meanwhile, on-

---

[443] De Jong 1991, ch. 1, offers a helpful typology of first-person narratives in messenger speeches and an overview of their characteristics, including, primarily, restriction and bias.
[444] I refer to "the murderer" here in singular, but one of the main cases that I will consider actually involves a pair of killers.

stage lies visible evidence of the outcome his action, for all to see, including for the killer himself: the corpse of his victim, rolled out on the *eccyclêma*.[445] What the audience members see onstage, and how they perceive it, may or may not be in congruence with the vision that the murderer provides in his account, or with the vision that he had of the deed at the time he committed it. In the scenes in which these murderers-turned-messengers feature, their reactions derive their meaning from the relationship and tension between these different visions and perceptions: the murderers' past vision, their present viewpoint, and the audience's.

In the murderers' points of focus, both onstage after the fact and within their retrospective visions of what they have done, the audience is able to see their differing conceptions of justice come to light. The murderer's account of the act of killing as he perpetrated it constitutes an exceptionally rich opportunity for characterization and psychological insight. Hearing about a murder from the killer herself and seeing the deed and its aftermath from within the confines of that killer's vision can be a forceful means of dramatizing a death and characterizing the murderer in question. It also is especially effective in providing a closeup focus on the central issues and values that the dramatists have the killer zero in on. What he prioritizes in his actual, physical gaze is revealing of the conceptions of justice and morality to which he gives preeminence. His perception of the victim and his physical relationship to him (or her), be it onstage in the here and now (the corpse) or offstage in the immediate past (the body of the victim as he saw it during the killing), are rife with information. What he hides and what he reveals, in speech, deed, or gesture, particularly when it comes to the body of the victim, is a direct reflection of the differing values and conceptions of justice that each killer embraces and presents us with a window onto those to which the dramatists appear to give priority, or which they subversively invite their audience to question.

Seeing the act of killing and the body (or bodies) on which death was inflicted from within the confines of the killer's restricted vision, the audience is given a measure of how much his perception of events is incomplete, biased, perverted, or, simply, changed by the mere fact that he is looking back on them as he recounts them.[446] What the murderer zeroes in on, both literally and figuratively, at the time of the killing and afterward as he retells it, provides the audience

---

[445] In some cases, the assassins deliberately choose to hide the corpse from their sight, a gesture as telling as their words themselves.
[446] In his detailed study of the stagecraft in Aeschylus's plays, Taplin gives systematic attention to what the audience is given to see on stage, and the thematic and dramatic relevance of these visual elements within Aeschylean tragedy (Taplin 1977).

with a point of reference for how warped or limited his vision of the victim(s), or of his own role, is or was at the time that he committed the murder. While the audience members are led to embrace the killer's viewpoint, the temporary adoption of such a focalized gaze also enables them to see its limitations and biases, in light of the complementary knowledge with which they are equipped through other characters' speeches as well as through the intertextual and interperformative comparisons that they are led to make with other tragedians' depictions of the same murder.

I look at two (related) examples of murderers-turned-messengers in this chapter. The first example is that of Clytemnestra reporting the murder of her husband in Aeschylus's *Agamemnon*. The second is that of her children, Orestes and Electra, who kill their mother in order to avenge their father's death at her hands. The killing of the queen by her own children was treated by all three tragedians and presents an interesting opportunity for the critic to compare the different ways in which each of the playwrights choose to have the matricidal siblings portray and react to their deed in first-person narratives in their respective works. Euripides' treatment of the matricide is the main object of my investigation, but we can only grasp the latter's idiosyncrasies if we first turn an attentive eye to both Aeschylus's and Sophocles' treatments of the same deed and, indeed, the same scene.

Part One: The Murder of Agamemnon: Imagery and vision

Clytemnestra's moment of truth

At the end of the *Agamemnon*, the first of the three plays of Aeschylus's *Oresteia*, the eponymous hero, king of Argos and leader of the expedition to Troy, returns victorious to his palace and enters his home for the first time in ten years.[447] While he bathes, his wife, Clytemnestra, ensnares him in a garment that she uses as a net and stabs him to death. All we hear during the actual (offstage) killing of Agamemnon are his cries, overheard by the Chorus and audience.[448] Once the deed is done, the audience sees Clytemnestra herself come into view and listens to her account of the murderous act, offered up by a disturbingly unrepentant killer.

---

[447] Any lines quoted without specification of source from here on in this chapter are from the *Agamemnon*. I follow the edition of the *Agamemnon* text adopted by Denniston-Page 1957, unless otherwise indicated. The translations are based on Fraenkel 1950 and Lloyd-Jones 1970.
[448] Lines 1343–5.

The report of Agamemnon's murder is given an unusual treatment in several respects. Typical messenger reports of deaths that have taken place offstage focus, as might be expected, on the killer's and the victim's respective gestures, words, and actions at the time of the death. These narratives are specific and concrete, though not necessarily unemotional; they may include references to the reporter's (or other internal audiences') reactions to the scene.[449] When messengers do mention (or imply) their emotional responses, they usually do so in simple, direct language, naming the emotion(s), often after mentioning an especially pathetic detail that evoked their tears. Deianeira's nurse in Sophocles' *Trachiniae* clearly displays her horror at witnessing the scene of her mistress's suicide; so does Jason's servant when he describes the deaths of Creusa and Creon in Euripides' *Medea*.[450]

Clytemnestra's report of Agamemnon's death is remarkable in comparison with these typical messenger speeches. First of all, it is Clytemnestra herself who delivers it. Her relationship to the dead man – she is his wife and his killer, and now she is the messenger that reports on his death — makes for a particularly evocative and emotional depiction, whose content and language are deserving of our close attention. Though her own husband's blood is on her hands, the queen does not shy away from admitting her deed to the Chorus of Elders. Why does Aeschylus have *her* be the one to give so detailed an account of the king's slaughter and make her dwell at length on her reaction to the act?[451] In what follows, I propose to tease out what effect is achieved by having the audience view the event through Clytemnestra's eyes, as she herself delivers the news to the audience and Chorus members in a distinctly colored first-person account.

The queen does not immediately launch into her tirade concerning the killing itself. She prefaces her account with an important preamble that marks the description of her act as especially worthy of the audience's attention. This preamble amounts to the dramatist commenting on the importance of his character's forthcoming speech. Clytemnestra makes clear that she has reached a turn-

---

[449] Messengers may make reference to their emotional response even when their relationship to the dying is not one of *philia*: thus, Talthybius, a Greek herald, recounts the Trojan captive Polyxena's sacrifice at the hands of Neoptolemus in Euripides' *Hecuba* with considerable emotion. On messengers' emotions, implied or explicitly mentioned in their reports, see De Jong 1991.

[450] Both are concerned by the fates of those whose deaths they saw because they are the victims' servants. Mastronarde 2010, 118, contrasts the slower emergence of the Chorus members' indignation at the deaths of Creusa and Creon, who are favorably biased toward Medea.

[451] On the importance of considering Clytemnestra's gender in the assessment of her act and particularly how it is judged by others in the play, including the Chorus, see Foley 2001, 201 ff. Regarding the gendered speech of women in Greek tragedy, see McClure 1999.

ing point when it comes to her wielding of words and explicitly invites the Chorus (and audience) to take note of that change. The statement she is about to make is, quite literally, a moment of truth:

> πολλῶν πάροιθεν καιρίως εἰρημένων
> τἀναντί' εἰπεῖν οὐκ ἐπαισχυνθήσομαι·
> πῶς γάρ τις ἐχθροῖς ἐχθρὰ πορσύνων, φίλοις
> δοκοῦσιν εἶναι, πημονῆς ἀρκύστατ' ἂν
> φάρξειεν ὕψος κρεῖσσον ἐκπηδήματος;
> ἐμοὶ δ' ἀγὼν ὅδ' οὐκ ἀφρόντιστος πάλαι
> νείκης παλαιᾶς ἦλθε, σὺν χρόνωι γε μήν·
> ἕστηκα δ' ἔνθ' ἔπαισ' ἐπ' ἐξειργασμένοις.
> (1372–8)

> I have said many things hitherto to suit the needs of the moment, and I shall not be ashamed to contradict them now. How else could anyone, pursuing hostilities against enemies who think they are friends, set up their hunting-nets to a height too great to overleap? This showdown was something that had long been in my thoughts, arising from a long-standing grievance; now it has come – at long last.

Clytemnestra stresses two major points in this preamble that guide the audience's understanding of the description that is to follow. First, she reveals that her agenda, killing Agamemnon, has been shaping every one of her utterances until this point: everything she has said before was contrived for expediency's sake (πολλῶν πάροιθεν καιρίως εἰρημένων). Only now has the time come when she can shamelessly (οὐκ ἐπαισχυνθήσομαι) reveal the blunt truths that she had been hitherto concealing. The extent of her earlier deception was tremendous: so far from the truth were some of her previous statements that, in speaking the truth, she will now directly contradict them (τἀναντί' εἰπεῖν). By insisting on the extensive planning and the sheer amount of time that went into preparing for the murder (πάλαι, παλαιᾶς, σὺν χρόνωι γε μήν), she further builds up the audience's expectations and sense of the momentousness of the present occasion and the statement that she is about to make. It is not suspense about what has occurred that keeps us asking for more: it is the fact that, at long last, we are about to hear the truth from Clytemnestra about how she really feels – about Agamemnon and about what she has done to him. Her preliminary note regarding the newly candid nature of her language marks what will follow as revelatory.

Leading up to the slaughter of Agamemnon, the queen had shaped every one of her statements – whether it was addressed to the Chorus or to the king himself – in a careful, deliberate, and manipulative manner, so as to disguise her intent. Conversely, she now bares herself to all in a manner that is deliberately provocative and forthright. Every one of her previous utterances was either an outright lie or laden with double meaning, each of them designed to elicit trust so she could carry out her murderous plan without incurring suspicion. Scholars have pointed up how masterful and crafty the queen is in her manipulation of language and, hence, her manipulation of others, particularly through her skillful use of ambiguous speech, which enables her to speak in a way that simultaneously reveals and conceals the truth.[452] A case in point is her description of how faithful she has been to Agamemnon. In a statement that is entirely truthful, she says that she knows as little about "pleasure from another man" as she knows about "the dipping of bronze":

γυναῖκα πιστὴν δ' ἐν δόμοις εὕροι μολὼν
οἵανπερ οὖν ἔλειπε, δωμάτων κύνα
ἐσθλὴν ἐκείνωι, πολεμίαν τοῖς δύσφροσιν,
καὶ τἄλλ' ὁμοίαν πάντα, σημαντήριον
οὐδὲν διαφθείρασαν ἐν μήκει χρόνου   (610)
οὐδ' οἶδα τέρψιν οὐδ' ἐπίψογον φάτιν
ἄλλου πρὸς ἀνδρὸς μᾶλλον ἢ χαλκοῦ βαφάς.
τοιόσδ' ὁ κόμπος, τῆς ἀληθείας γέμων,
οὐκ αἰσχρὸς ὡς γυναικὶ γενναίαι λακεῖν.
                        (606–14)

May he find his wife faithful in his house,
Just as he left her, the watchdog of the palace,
Loyal to him, an enemy to his ill-wishers,
One alike in all things; in the length of time
She has destroyed no seal set there by him.
I know no more of delight — nor of censorious rumor —
Coming from another man, than I know how bronze is dipped.
Such is my boast, a boast replete with truth,
Not shameful for a noble lady to utter.

What makes this statement so disturbing is that what Clytemnestra says is perfectly true, but not in the way she knows others will understand it. She does know a lot about pleasure from another man, as she makes clear when she describes how Aegisthus "kindles the fire in [her] hearth" (ἕως ἂν αἴθηι πῦρ ἐφ' ἑστίας ἐμῆς | Αἴγισθος, 1435–6). About "the dipping of bronze," she knows just "as much" – not "very little" as the Chorus is led to believe (by design), but very

---

452 Clytemnestra's character's deft ability to manipulate language to calculated ends, her sexual aggressiveness, and the reversal of gender norms that she epitomizes have all been the subject of careful studies; see e.g., Zeitlin 1978 and Foley 1981; on her ability to manipulate language in particular, see Winnington-Ingram 1983, 211 ff.; Goldhill 1984, 85 ff.; McClure 1999, 73 ff. (who speaks of Clytemnestra's "shifting verbal genres"); and Foley 2001, 207 ff.

much indeed, as she demonstrates by dipping metal into the flesh of Cassandra and Agamemnon when she commits the double murder.

After Clytemnestra commits the deed that she has been plotting, her words no longer are intended to conceal or manipulate, and they no longer have any deliberate double meaning. The successful killing of Agamemnon directly impacts how she uses language and, therefore, how the audience should understand her use of it. From here on out, Clytemnestra is sincere. Of course, one might do well to suspect so cunning a character of having an agenda and of continuing to dissimulate, even now that she claims to be transparent; but we no longer have any reason not to take her words at face value because she, in turn, no longer has any reason to conceal her thoughts.

The actual content of her speech is a further indication of its genuine nature. Until the killing takes place, every word she speaks is consciously framed in a manner that is intended to be neither morally nor socially reprehensible, so as not to rouse suspicion. Conversely, now that she has killed Agamemnon, the egregiously provocative way in which she depicts the murder of her husband, the ruler of Argos and a war hero, as well as the way she dwells on her own glee, lends authenticity to her statement. Clearly, Clytemnestra is not seeking to please here (!), either in relating the deed, or in describing the delight that she took in it. This "inhuman gloating over murder" is unacceptable by her addressees' (the Elders') standards, as she well knows: χαίροιτ' ἄν, εἰ χαίροιτ', ἐγὼ δ' ἐπεύχομαι ("Rejoice in it or not, as you please; I glory in it!" (χαίροιτ' ἄν, εἰ χαίροιτ', ἐγὼ δ' ἐπεύχομαι, 1394). Clytemnestra's defiant statement and attitude are, in and of themselves, a badge of authenticity, and point up her complete lack of dissimulation.

These introductory words to Clytemnestra's depiction of her deed are stage directions of sorts, explicit verbal markers that play up the queen's transparency and invite us to consider her every word with particular care because of the candidness with which she is going to speak. In this way, Aeschylus is indicating that the audience should listen in and take these words seriously: Clytemnestra is about to speak truthfully and openly and offer up her unfiltered inner thoughts and emotions for the first time in the play.

The ensuing tirade is extremely vivid. Each of her words is carefully chosen, and each reveals a singular and candid vision and version of the event, to the Chorus and to the spectators, while it is still very fresh. She accompanies her speech with gestures, making it seem as though the murder is virtually happening before the audience's eyes: she is both the perpetrator and reenactor of the deed, for which she simultaneously provides a commentary. For it is clear that Clytemnestra acts out her speech: she includes references to her movements and gestures, and to the violent blows she dealt, each of which is retold in succession, one by one. Diggle notes:

> "As she speaks she re-enacts the murder. She murders him again in mime ... the scene has been, so to speak, frozen in time.... . She uses the present tense because she strikes again in mime."[453]

The queen's vantage point is complex in light of the fact that she combines these multiple roles: that of agent (in the past, within her narrative) and that of messenger (in the present, relating that narrative), as well as that of reenactor, whereby the past and the present fuse before the audience's eyes, all the more so as the queen describes her husband's slow agony and her reaction to it in the present tense, making it seem as though the event were unfolding in real time.[454] As she speaks and acts out the scene, Aeschylus leads his audience to see the death of Agamemnon through her eyes, making the audience members feel as though they were present at the queen's side, looking on as she watches her husband die by her own hand for the second time, in her mind's eye.[455]

As she utters her triumphant speech, Clytemnestra is standing over the bodies of Agamemnon and his concubine, the Trojan prophetess Cassandra, which lie before her, their corpses rolled out on the *eccyclêma* for all to behold: "I stand where I struck" (ἕστηκα δ' ἔνθ' ἔπαισ', 1379).[456] She does not mention any explicit, direct motives for her deed here, nor does she make any apology

---

[453] Diggle 2005, 216–8.
[454] It has occurred only moments before.
[455] With the use of the present tense, the graphic imagery, and the choice of so involved a speaker, Aeschylus pushes to its limits the restrictions imposed on Greek tragedy, whereby acts involving violence and bloodshed were not to be represented onstage. In his *Electra*, Euripides will do the same with the matricides' account of Clytemnestra's death at their hands.
[456] The Chorus later describes how she towers over the corpses gleefully: "Standing over his body like an evil crow, she exults in singing a tuneless hymn of triumph" (1472–4):

> ἐπὶ δὲ σώματος δίκαν
> κόρακος ἐχθροῦ σταθεῖσ' ἐκνόμως
> ὕμνον ὑμνεῖν ἐπεύχεται.

On the use of the *eccyclêma* in general, Cropp (1988) 2013, 227 *ad* 1172–1232 provides bibliography. On critics' assessment of the visual correspondence between Clytemnestra standing over Agamemnon's and Cassandra's dead bodies, and Orestes standing over Clytemnestra's and Aegisthus's, see Taplin 1977, 458. On the dramatic function of corpses on stage, see Di Benedetto and Medda 1997, ch. 7.

for it.⁴⁵⁷ Instead, as she describes the gestures and actions that were involved in the killing itself, her words play up the most shocking element of her entire account: how she saw the murder while it unfolded as something quite other than a murder.⁴⁵⁸ Far from hiding her exultation, she dwells on her response to the deed as she went about performing it. There is not a shadow of remorse in her strange utterance; it is rife with stunning details that make clear the actual pleasure that she derived from her husband's downfall and slow agony at her hands:

> οὕτω δ' ἔπραξα, καὶ τάδ' οὐκ ἀρνήσομαι·
> ὡς μήτε φεύγειν μήτ' ἀμύνεσθαι μόρον.
> ἄπειρον ἀμφίβληστρον, ὥσπερ ἰχθύων,
> περιστιχίζω, πλοῦτον εἵματος κακόν,
> παίω δέ νιν δίς· κἀν δυοῖν οἰμωγμάτοιν
> μεθῆκεν αὐτοῦ κῶλα· καὶ πεπτωκότι
> τρίτην ἐπενδίδωμι, τοῦ κατὰ χθονός,
> Διὸς, νεκρῶν σωτῆρος, εὐκταίαν χάριν.
> οὕτω τὸν αὑτοῦ θυμὸν ὁρμαίνει πεσών,
> κἀκφυσιῶν ὀξεῖαν αἵματος σφαγὴν
> βάλλει μ' ἐρεμνῇ ψακάδι φοινίας δρόσου,
> χαίρουσαν οὐδὲν ἧσσον ἢ διοσδότῳ
> γάνει σπορητὸς κάλυκος ἐν λοχεύμασιν.
>   (1380–93)
>
> So I accomplished the deed – and I shall not deny it –
> so that he could neither escape nor ward off doom.
> An inextricable sheath, like a net for fish,
> I throw around him, an evil wealth of dress;
> Then I strike him twice; and uttering two cries

---

⁴⁵⁷ Clytemnestra later does speak in her own defense by invoking the death of Iphigeneia (and the presence of Cassandra as well) as a motive and justification for killing Agamemnon. She makes multiple appeals to *dikê* and provides a framework of justice for her actions in response to the Chorus's reproaches. See e.g., lines 1431–4. On Clytemnestra's "apology" (as in, "defense speech"), see Foley 2001, 211 ff. To reflect the importance of the death of Iphigeneia in motivating Clytemnestra's words and actions in the *Oresteia*, Ariane Mnouchkine prefaced her production of *Les Atrides* 1992 at the Théâtre du Soleil with Euripides' *Iphigeneia at Aulis*.

⁴⁵⁸ The murder was a double murder, but Cassandra is clearly peripheral to Clytemnestra's main point of focus; later on, she describes Cassandra as "a side-dish to [her] bed" (1446–7): ἐμοὶ δ' ἐπήγαγεν | εὐνῆς παροψώνημα τῆς ἐμῆς χλιδῇ. The text has been contested (e.g., by Denniston-Page 1957). I agree with Lloyd-Jones 1970, 107, that Clytemnestra's sadistic pleasure is entirely plausible and likely, despite the fact that "some scholars find it unthinkable that Clytemnestra should say that the pleasure of having killed her husband's concubine should heighten her own sexual satisfaction." My analysis of her response to Agamemnon's death in what follows corroborates this point.

he lets go his legs, on the spot; and after he has fallen
I add a third stroke, a welcome prayer-offering
for Zeus below the earth, the savior of corpses.
Thus fallen, belching out his own spirit,
and breathing forth a sharp offering of blood,
he strikes me with a dark sprinkling of gory dew,
while I rejoice no less than does the crop
in the gladness⁴⁵⁹ sent by Zeus, during the birth pangs of the bud."⁴⁶⁰

The queen's disturbing description of her emotional response to her murderous deed – unabashed *Schadenfreude* – heightens the abomination of the killing in the audience's eyes. Her lack of repentance is blatant, and the chilling nature of her self-congratulatory relish further exposes the monstrosity of the act that she has committed.⁴⁶¹

Her reaction is, to put it mildly, not one that would likely have been espoused or condoned by the audience. While caution is always in order regarding what we can assume the audience's reactions to a given scene might have been, it seems safe to assume that a war hero returning to a household of adultery and betrayal is hardly likely to have evoked a divided or uncertain response from the spectators (especially in a fifth-century, predominantly male audience).⁴⁶²

---

459 Γάνος, "gladness," is generally understood as "rain" here.
460 The most significant changes in my translation compared to prior commentators' lie in lines 1389–92. I attempted to render the sacrificial metaphor of σφαγήν by partially adopting Zeitlin's suggestion, "a swift sacrificial offering of blood" (Zeitlin 1965, 474). For the different usages and connotations of the sacrificial terms θύειν vs. σφάζειν, see Henrichs 2000, 180: "Σφάζειν refers more specifically to the act of slaughtering the animal. As the marked term, σφάζειν carries associations of violence and bloodshed that the tragedians exploit." Sidgwick 1890, 68, comments on the "bold stretch of language" in the expression αἵματος σφαγὴν, stating, "We should say his life-blood by an opposite metaphor."
461 Clytemnestra's distinctive and defining traits throughout the trilogy are her transgressive impulses with regard to gender and familial roles, sexuality, and power (for bibliography, see above, n. 452). The challenge she poses to masculinity and male power is stated early on in the play by the watchman who speaks of her male heart (ἀνδρόβουλον κέαρ, 11), in contrast to Aegisthus's effeminacy (he is addressed as γύναι by the Chorus at *Ch.* 1625). In Cassandra's vision of the killing of Agamemnon, Clytemnestra is the "bull" striking Agamemnon, the "cow" (1125–8). Wohl exposes the sadism of Clytemnestra in connection with her transgressive identity in the political, social, and sexual realms (Wohl 1998, 103 ff., with bibliography at 235 n. 6). Bonnafé 1989 sees the queen as a dreadful parody of the Homeric hero. Morrell 1996–7, n. 4, offers helpful bibliography regarding gender dynamics in the so-called red carpet scene.
462 Her response to Agamemnon's death is all the more shocking as it contrasts with Cassandra's horror and pity at the same man's imminent death, though she is his captive, and Clytemnestra is his wife. Cassandra's vivid response immediately precedes hers and Agamemnon's

Yet the queen's report is surely meant to do more than merely incriminate her in our eyes, making her a monstrous creature because she rejoices in a monstrous deed. In the words of Vellacott, "If Aeschylus's lines present in Clytemnestra a creature as repulsive as some eminent scholars describe, then the *Oresteia* is neither profound nor a tragedy."[463] If the point of her words were solely to stress the ghastly nature of her deed and of her character by making apparent the pleasure she experiences in killing her husband, then another character could just as well have fulfilled this function by providing a description of the queen's reaction from an external onlooker's perspective. This might in fact have been more effective at alienating the audience from her if, say, that character's own horrified reaction were made clear, providing a foil to the queen's deranged delight and thus pointing up just how unnatural and disquieting her deed and her response to it are.[464] Clytemnestra's speech is a messenger speech – and part of the point of it is (as with every messenger speech) to report what has unfolded outside of the spectators' range of vision. But what is the point of having *her* be the one to speak the words that she does here? Her prefatory words called attention to the special, revelatory nature of this speech, and I suggest that we follow Aeschylus's implicit instructions that we pay as much, if not more, attention to the *language* she employs to deliver the report as to the content of her account, which any character might have delivered in her stead.

Clytemnestra adopts surprising language to recount her deed. She describes the killing of Agamemnon as though it were a ritualized and celebratory performance and speaks in an unusually poeticized manner, using complex imagery that is highly visual.[465] Her words convey *how she sees* the killing in both a literal and a figurative sense as she reenacts it for the audience, and how she responds to it as a result of that vision. Taking Clytemnestra at her word, as she has invited us to do, we might do well to notice how much her speech reflects not only her actual vision, but also the logic that she embraces and the principles that she defends, and how much these shape her visual perception of the murder, to an extent that eludes the speaker herself and reveals the power of the perverse logic that expresses and perpetuates itself through her agency.

---

deaths, and is still fresh on the audience members' minds when Clytemnestra comes forth, gloating.
463 Vellacott 1984, 9.
464 An example of a contrast between different characters' emotional responses to a single deed that achieves precisely this result can be found in Euripides' *Medea*, where Medea's reaction to the tale of Creon and Creusa's fate – relish — contrasts with the messenger's horror.
465 On the power of visual images in Greek poetry and art and in Aeschylus's *Agamemnon* in particular, see Ferrari 1997. On the use of visual imagery in Greek tragedy, see Ieranò 2011.

The highly poeticized manner in which Clytemnestra relates her deed involves an abundance of complex and layered imagery. Aeschylean imagery is distinctive in its ability to create meaning through repetition and the subtle weaving of visually and thematically interconnected images – a quality that creates meaningful connections between the three plays of the *Oresteia*, the only extant trilogy that we have.[466] This imagery establishes visual, semantic, and thematic connections between individual characters' actions and the central motif that underlies the trilogy as a whole: the cycle of vengeance plaguing the house of Atreus. The imagery that we find within Clytemnestra's utterance is one example of this: we can best understand it by turning to related images that occur at other points in the trilogy, in her own and other characters' speeches, as well as the Chorus's. The visual language that Clytemnestra employs makes the audience peer into the past and future and envisage their connections with the present, the action being performed, and the words being spoken onstage.[467] It connects her individual act to other murderous acts that preceded it and to those that will follow, including her own death at the hands of her children. These connections cast her agency in a light that reaches well beyond the confines of the individual and complicate the audience's perception and assessment of her act considerably more than is often allowed for.[468]

Clytemnestra's words situate her deed outside of a narrow framework of justice within which responsibility can be pinned on a single individual. And so it is that she can state with complete sincerity, in the agonistic exchange in which she engages with the Chorus after her initial description of the act of murder itself:

καὶ τήνδ' ἀκούεις ὁρκίων ἐμῶν θέμιν·
μὰ τὴν τέλειον τῆς ἐμῆς παιδὸς Δίκην,
Ἄτην Ἐρινύν θ', αἷσι τόνδ' ἔσφαξ' ἐγώ,
οὔ μοι Φόβου μέλαθρον ἐλπὶς ἐμπατεῖ
(1431–4)

This you hear as well, the solemn power of my oath!
I swear by the Justice accomplished for my child, and by Ruin and the Erinys, for whom I

---

[466] Lebeck 1971 remains a reference work for its analysis of the many connections established throughout the Aeschylean trilogy through imagery. See also Sommerstein 2010, esp. 171–80, and Rutherford 2012, 119–62. For an overview of Athenian views of motherhood and of the images of maternity and fertility that surround Clytemnestra in the *Oresteia*, see McClure 2012.
[467] Regarding "the past beneath the present" in Aeschylean and Sophoclean tragedy, see Kyriakou 2011.
[468] One of the exceptions to this is Winnington-Ingram 1948.

sacrificed this man,
for me no expectation walks the hall of Fear.

Though the Chorus members repeatedly return to the idea of Clytemnestra's individual guilt,[469] they, too, evoke the Spirit of Strife that haunts the house of Atreus (1460–1), sometimes referring to it as the *daimôn* that controls and afflicts the house (1468–71), a spirit of great wrath (βαρύμηνιν, 1482), insatiable in its appetite for ruinous events (ἀτηρᾶς τύχας ἀκορέστου, 1483–4). They acknowledge the divine prompting behind mortal acts, traceable back to the will of Zeus (1485–8). The degree to which responsibility can be assigned to Clytemnestra is, ultimately, mitigated by the Chorus members' own assessment, hostile though they are to Clytemnestra and her action. Even as they condemn the agency of adulterous women who have been a source of ruin such as Clytemnestra (1470), they also relegate them to the status of tools, acting under the influence of a spirit assailing the house of Atreus and controlling it:[470]

δαῖμον, ὃς ἐμπίτνεις δώμασι καὶ διφυί-
οισι Τανταλίδαισιν,
κράτος <τ'> ἰσόψυχον ἐκ γυναικῶν
καρδιόδηκτον ἐμοὶ κρατύνεις·
ἐπὶ δὲ σώματος δίκαν
κόρακος ἐχθροῦ σταθεῖσ' ἐκνόμως
ὕμνον ὑμνεῖν ἐπεύχεται <   >.
                    (1468–74)

Spirit that assails this house
and the two Tantalids so different in their nature,
and controls it, in a way that rends my heart,
through the agency of women whose souls were alike![471]
Standing over the corpse, like a hateful crow, it glories
In tunelessly singing a song.

The Chorus's words echo Clytemnestra's statement that she acted not as the king's wife but as a semblance of her past self and as an embodiment of "the

---

469 As they lament for Agamemnon 1489–96, they address him and bemoan the fact that he was "laid low in treacherous murder by the hand [of his wife] with a two-edged weapon" (δολίωι μόρωι δαμείς | ἐκ χερὸς ἀμφιτόμωι βελέμνωι, 1495–6).
470 Thus, they acknowledge that "an avenging spirit from a father's crime might be [her] accomplice" (πατρόθεν δὲ συλλήπτωρ γένοιτ' ἂν ἀλάστωρ, 1507–8). Dodds 1960 provides a subtle assessment of the relation between human and divine agency and causation (and hence responsibility) in Aeschylus's *Oresteia*, especially at 25 ff.
471 The reference is to Clytemnestra and her (half-)sister Helen.

ancient savage avenger of Atreus, cruel banqueter": φανταζόμενος δὲ γυναικὶ νεκροῦ | τοῦδ' ὁ παλαιὸς δριμὺς ἀλάστωρ | Ἀτρέως χαλεποῦ θοινατῆρος (1500–3).[472] Just as Agamemnon's blood is turned into a bountiful gift of nature and a sacrificial offering, so too is the Chorus and audience's vision of the one spilling that blood transformed, in keeping with the sinister logic at work in the scene playing out before us: it is not Clytemnestra but some evil spirit who stands over his body, like a crow, singing a tuneless song.

This is a thoroughly Aeschylean depiction of human action: it is always inextricably enmeshed with divine influence (and even deception, in some cases) — a central tenet of archaic thought that comes across both in Clytemnestra's and in the Chorus's words. The place of the gods in guiding human action and perception does not eliminate the notion of human responsibility, however. There is nothing simplistic about this archaic conception of causality, and part of my goal here is to bring out in how complex a manner the concepts of human agency, and hence responsibility, are dealt with here.[473]

In another portion of her speech, Clytemnestra describes the scene of Agamemnon's murder to the Chorus using language that is not imagistic but reflects her understanding of her role as part of a chain of events, impelled by hidden avenging forces. The true agent of the murder of Agamemnon was not her, she declares, but a shadow or phantom (φανταζόμενος) of the king's wife, "the ancient, savage avenger" (ὁ παλαιὸς δριμὺς ἀλάστωρ), the very embodiment of the curse on the house of Atreus, who took murderous action in the guise of Clytemnestra:

μὴ δ' ἐπιλεχθῇς
Ἀγαμεμνονίαν εἶναί μ' ἄλοχον.
φανταζόμενος δὲ γυναικὶ νεκροῦ
τοῦδ' ὁ παλαιὸς δριμὺς ἀλάστωρ
Ἀτρέως χαλεποῦ θοινατῆρος
τόνδ' ἀπέτεισεν,
τέλεον νεαροῖς ἐπιθύσας.

(1498–1504)

But do not consider
that I am Agamemnon's consort!

---

[472] On the Chorus's denial of Clytemnestra's ability to have any true independent agency because of her gender, see Foley 2001, 201 ff.
[473] Cairns's introduction to the recent volume he edited (Cairns 2013, ix-liv) provides an excellent overview of the complexity of these principal tenets of archaic thought; cf. the complex question of Deianeira's responsibility, discussed in ch. 2, and the important discussions of Dodds 1951, *passim*, and Winnington-Ingram 1965 on the subject.

> But in the likeness of this dead man's wife
> the ancient savage avenger
> of Atreus, cruel banqueter,
> slew him in requital,
> sacrificing a grown man after children."

This might seem like a facile defense for the murder of which she is guilty and a rhetorical means of avoiding responsibility. In fact, however, the many parallels in theme and diction between this statement and other passages in the trilogy (including choral songs) stress the truth that Clytemnestra expresses here regarding the cycle of violence that afflicts the house of Atreus, caught in the spiral of a self-perpetuating curse. Her words are not an attempt to manipulate the Chorus into thinking of her deed as one for which she was not responsible. The crime that immediately motivates Clytemnestra – Iphigeneia's sacrifice at the hands of Agamemnon – is not the only basis for her action. Here, she explicitly points to a power that both transcends and guides every individual initiative, her own included: her deed was executed by the power that drives all of the members of the house to their destructive actions. She is an agent within a broader chain of agents, one of many instantiations of the anger and thirst for destruction characteristic of the spirit of revenge ruling over the house, whose existence preceded her deed and will continue after her death, embodied by the avenging deities that are the Erinyes.

Through the imagery in Clytemnestra's language, however, Aeschylus does more than establish thematic and visual connections between different murderous acts and thus point up the common avenging force at work in all of them them. If we consider drama as narrative, then part of our work in examining how that narrative functions is to envisage the ways in which the editorial and narrative knowledge of the dramatist, *qua* omniscient, governing consciousness, is introduced into his plays.[474] It is most often the narrative's temporal manipulations through *analepsis* (flashback) or *prolepsis* (flash-forward) that receive critics' attention: the complex temporal schemes that the playwrights elaborate within their dramas, whereby they only reveal as much as they wish, when they wish, either to the internal narratees (the characters) or the external narratees (the audience) to create effects of foreshadowing, suspense, or irony. I suggest that the layers of imagery within Clytemnestra's speech function as a metanarrative within her account of her deed.[475] Previous scholars' observations regarding

---

[474] On drama as narrative, see my introduction, p. 11.
[475] On the multivalency and over-determinacy of meaning that results from the mixing of voices in Aeschylean poetry, see Griffith 2009.

Aeschylus's deployment of imagery highlight how it serves as a means of pointing up connections between different actions in his trilogy. I suggest that the imagery also allows us to see a perverted logic that actually informs Aeschylus's characters' vision. Through that imagery, the dramatist communicates with his audience a form of knowledge that extends beyond this character's own understanding and awareness. Aeschylus's murderers are not just logical, cold-blooded avengers; they are enforcers of a destructive principle whose driving force and twisted logic lie outside of them, whereby death has replaced life in every way possible: logically, visually, and even in the emotional realm.

We might speak of a metanarrative dimension to this imagery, then, because of the way that it reveals not just how much the past poisons the present (that is, the central theme of the vengeance cycle that drives the action of the trilogy forward) but also the logic that Clytemnestra unwittingly obeys in enforcing the cycle of vengeance. While the queen is well aware of her role as an avenger and states at various points that she is deliberately perpetuating a cycle of violent acts that feed on each other, what is implicit in her words, but remains beyond her conscious grasp, is the perverse logic through which death has, in effect, replaced life in her eyes and mind-set. That distorted logic actually informs her vision and version of the event to an extent that she herself does not begin to fathom, coldly lucid though she may appear to be in the face of the murder she has committed. Clytemnestra may be a conscious avenger, but her act and the way she views it go well beyond expressing the enforcement of justice through the infliction of death. Her words expose how much she, like others, now sees death as a form and source of life.

Only the dramatist and his audience — and, to some extent, the internal audience formed by the Chorus – can perceive the warped nature of the queen's vision: to Clytemnestra, Agamemnon's spouting blood is a legitimate source of joy and renewed life. Her emotions and the vision that she describes are to be taken seriously. The dramatist suggests, through her words, the overarching perversion that not only governs the actions of each and every avenging character in the *Oresteia* but actually informs and warps their vision. By explicating the evocative breadth and function of the images to which she resorts, we can better understand the Aeschylean vision of human agency as limited in the face of the greater forces that inform and shape it. More importantly perhaps, we are able to see how much the destructive cycle of vengeance does not just generate destruction through the logic of blood calling for more blood, but also gives rise to a vision in which destruction has become the only possible source of vitality and life.[476]

In order to kill Agamemnon, Clytemnestra casts a net-like garment over him while he is being bathed. In recounting the murder, she envisions each deadly blow as a life-giving moment of exultation, and we look on with her, through the unperturbed lens of one who sees the death that she is inflicting as part of a ritual sacrifice carried out with systematic precision. It is important not to assume that Clytemnestra's language is merely figurative. She does not describe her action *as though* it were a sacrificial offering; she actually views and experiences the last of the three lethal stabs that she deals to Agamemnon as "a votive offering to Zeus below the earth" (1385–7): her words, like her vision, fuse the polluting act of shedding the blood of kin with the purifying ritual of pouring libations. This amalgamation of murder with sacrifice is hardly unique in Greek tragedy.[477] When Agamemnon sacrificed his daughter Iphigeneia at the altar, he carried out a literal sacrifice;[478] Clytemnestra, in turn, sees her own murderous act as a religious ritual, thus accentuating the extent to which it is not only a direct response to but also a perpetuation of the logic underlying the perverted act committed by Agamemnon against his own flesh and blood.

The queen's vision of Agamemnon's death has a direct bearing on her reaction to it: pure, unadulterated joy. In the closing lines of her description, her narrative moves away from her actions themselves to her reactions to them, and her words further point up how much the killing of Agamemnon forms a continuum with his murder of their daughter Iphigeneia. She amalgamates the spilling of Agamemnon's blood with the very sources of life, through an abundance of images that each deserve our attention, and which I reproduce here:

βάλλει μ' ἐρεμνῇ ψακάδι φοινίας δρόσου,
χαίρουσαν οὐδὲν ἧσσον ἢ διοσδότῳ
γάνει σπορητὸς κάλυκος ἐν λοχεύμασιν.
(1390–2)

---

[476] McClure 2012 discusses the language of childbirth, nurture and agriculture in the *Oresteia* and highlights its subsequent influence on Sophocles' *Electra*.
[477] On the motif of corrupted sacrifice in Greek tragedy, Zeitlin's 1965 article remains a reference. Seidensticker 2006, 111–2, also calls attention to the emotional impact of the perversion at hand.
[478] Zeitlin 1965 analyzes how the murder of Iphigeneia constitutes a prototype for the other murders of the trilogy.

> He strikes me with a dark sprinkling of gory dew,
> while I rejoice no less than does the crop,
> in the gladness sent by Zeus, during the birth-pangs of the bud.

The erotic suggestiveness of the description is obvious, particularly if (as others have suggested) one reads it with literary parallels in mind.[479] Celestial and cosmic births are often expressed in anthropomorphic terms, and the engendering of life in nature is often depicted as a form of sexual encounter. A passage from Aeschylus's *Danaides* offers a typical instantiation of such anthropomorphism: an allegorized male Sky impregnates a female Earth with rain (or another sky-born moisture, such as dew).[480] In earlier depictions of cosmogonic births, rain is also equated with semen: in the *Rig Veda*, the Maruts "lay their strength in (the earth) as a husband the embryo."[481] Other, much later texts also attest to the association of dew with the engendering of new life.

The poetic *topos* of cosmic generation shines through in Clytemnestra's account, but with a twist: rather than representing cosmic and natural elements in terms of human sexuality and reproduction, she represents human murder and death in natural and cosmic terms: Agamemnon's blood, as it strikes her, is a "dark sprinkling of gory dew" (ἐρεμνῇ ψακάδι φοινίας δρόσου), and it is also god-given "gladness" (διοσδότῳ γάνει) – a vitalizing morning dew that nurtures plants, providing welcome moisture to a "crop" (σπορητός).[482] Δρόσος and the related ἐέρση ("dew") were both used in Greek poetry to refer to semen, leav-

---

[479] Concerning the clear sexual undertones of her tirade, see in particular Moles 1979, Herington 1986, and Pulleyn 1997. To my knowledge, only O'Daly (unconvincingly) denies any such *double entendre* (O'Daly 1985, 10).

[480] *Danaides*, frag. 44 Kannicht; source: Athen. 13.600a. For an analysis of cosmological parallels with the sexual act and the significance of dew (δρόσος) in these contexts, see Boedeker 1984. Herington 1986, 28, provides further examples, including from Nonnus's *Dionysiaca* (41.63–4), wherein the equation of dew with semen is explicit.

[481] *Rig Veda* 5.58.7, translation Boedeker 1984, 14. On Greek cosmologies' reflection of Indo-European concepts of the male as *reproducteur* (the term used by Benveniste), see Benveniste 1969, 230–5, where he cites as an example the generative male power of the Maruts (rain gods). For analogies between rain, urine, and semen with reference to the Maruts, see Nagy 1974, 231 ff., especially 233. Herington 1986 offers a useful overview of the literary passages (Greek and Latin, but also Vedic) referring to the mating of Earth and Sky.

[482] Fraenkel 1950, *ad loc.* underlines how the metaphor brings out a strong sense of the queen's hatred by *antiphrasis*, through the "loving detail κάλυκος ἐν λοχεύμασιν," which contrasts "pure blessing ... with wild polluting destruction wrought by Clytemnestra's deed." For the association of the floral motif with erotic pleasure, see Judet de la Combe 2001, 630, who includes parallels such as Zeus and Hera's hierogamy in *Il.* 14 or the *Homeric Hymn to Aphrodite* 87 (κάλυκας τε φαεινάς).

ing no doubt that her words are a dreadful parody of cosmic generation.[483] Not all known accounts of celestial generation are couched in terms of an auspicious sexual union between cosmic elements. In a well-known example found in the *Theogony*, new life stems from a destructive act: Cronos severs Ouranos's genitals, and the blood and semen emanating from his members mingle with the earth and the brine of the sea respectively, giving birth to the Erinyes and the Giants on the one hand and Aphrodite on the other.[484] The sexually suggestive imagery that Clytemnestra employs also associates blood with life – but there is, in the case of Agamemnon, no birth to speak of (be it sexual or cosmic), only a dying king, bleeding to death.[485] As Wohl notes, sexual transgression characterizes both Agamemnon's and Clytemnestra's violent acts: "Just as Iphigeneia's sacrifice was a rape, Agamemnon's murder is intercourse."[486] This is in keeping with the general inversion of human relationships that pervades the *Oresteia:* "In the *Oresteia* normal human relationships are seldom present, and mostly have to be deduced from their inversion."[487]

The folklorist Alan Dundes has noted the different possible associations of liquids with life or death: "Life depends on liquid. From the concept of the 'water of life' to semen, milk, blood, bile, saliva, and the like, the consistent principle is that liquid means life while loss of liquid means death."[488] The shedding of blood and the raining of dew are antithetical by nature: dew conveys life (and was often associated with maidenhood),[489] while blood, when shed, leads to death; when the blood of kin is shed, pollution ensues as well.[490] In Clytemnestra's words, the power of liquid to mean life or death is conflated into one para-

---

483 On the semantic ranges and usages of δρόσος and ἐέρση, see Boedeker 1984, 3–5 and 53 ff.; the first chapter of Boedeker explores images of dew used in reference to generation and birth. Kyriakou 2006, 112, in a note on *Iphigeneia in Tauris* 255, gives a sense of the polysemic range of δρόσος when used in metaphors or as a euphemism for a wide range of liquids, including wine and bodily fluids.
484 Hes., *Th.* 184–5 and 190 ff.
485 On the connection between the corrupted sexual pleasure Clytemnestra derives from inflicting death and the theme of perverted fertility, see e.g., Belfiore 1983. See also Stanford 1972; Vickers 1973, 350–425; Moles 1979, 180–3; and Morgan 1992.
486 Wohl 1998, 107–8.
487 Vickers 1973, 356. See Goheen 1955, 132 ff., regarding the corruption of the mother-son relationship between Orestes and Clytemnestra.
488 Dundes 1981, 266.
489 Regarding maidens, purity, and liquids, see Ferrari 1997. Regarding the association of dew with notions of ethereal purity, see Boedeker 1984, 60–1.
490 Concerning blood pollution, see the referential work by Parker 1983 (esp. 32 ff., 74 ff., and 104 ff); see also Eck 2012. On pollution in Greek tragedy specifically, see Meinel 2015.

doxical verbal and visual whole: the loss of blood becomes a sprinkling of fertilizing dew. The conspicuous incongruity of the terminology calls attention to the perverseness of her vision, as she equates the king's blood showering onto her with the generative powers of Sky providing moisture to Earth.[491]

To pinpoint the particular function fulfilled by the imagery in Clytemnestra's language, let us turn for a moment to another messenger speech that also includes imagery and also reports a death scene. Though this account is also a colored first-person narrative, the messenger in question did *not* play an active role in the scene that he recounts, but remained a mere observer throughout. The speech occurs in the scene preceding Agamemnon's first appearance on stage. It is spoken by a herald, who describes to the Chorus how a dreadful storm has destroyed the entire Greek fleet except for one ship. He goes on to relate how he and other survivors surveyed the aftermath of the storm and saw the sea's surface "blossoming with the corpses of Achaean men and their wrecked ships" (ὁρῶμεν ἀνθοῦν πέλαγος Αἰγαῖον νεκροῖς | ἀνδρῶν Ἀχαιῶν ναυτικοῖς τ' ἐρειπίοις, 659–60). The use of metaphor within the messenger's account of what he saw introduces the trope of the *adynaton*, a poetic process favored by Aeschylus:[492] the proverbially barren sea is said to be "blossoming" with the dead bodies floating on its surface like lilies on a pond, to chilling effect. Just as Clytemnestra's speech combines dew (δρόσος) with bloodshed (φοινίας), the herald uses imagery suggestive of vegetation, youth, and life, and associates it with death – the dead bodies floating on the "watery grave" (Ἅιδην πόντιον, 667). The jarring combination of ἀνθοῦν (blossoming) with νεκροῖς (corpses) results in the creation of a sinister visual image. It functions in a fashion similar to Clytemnestra's vision of Agamemnon's death in that its effectiveness stems from the incongruity at its core.

The parallel ends there, however. The inclusion of paradoxical imagery within the herald's language does not tell us anything about its speaker: he does not take action in a way that enacts the unnatural association of life with death that his imagery comprises. The verbal association that he establishes may point to a certain emotional response on his part – dismay at the abundant deaths around him – but it does not reflect any sort of broader logic that impacts and guides his vision or his actions. The imagery does not function as a metanarrative inserted by the poet into his character's speech that helps shed light on its emotional and

---

[491] Fraenkel 1950, 656: "There are few equally powerful lines in the whole of Greek tragedy. The horror is inescapable when the sweet miracle of the carefully tended sprouting and growth of crops becomes a symbol of inhuman gloating over murder."

[492] An analysis of the *adynaton* in this passage and in Aeschylus more broadly can be found in Stieber 2006. For an extensive treatment of the *adynaton* in Greek poetry, see Dutoit 1936.

thematic underpinnings. The language of Clytemnestra, on the other hand, grants the audience a vision of her own mental image of her deed in a manner that is more than metaphorical. The imagery that she uses establishes paradoxical verbal and mental associations and juxtapositions between life and death that are a reflection of the queen's actual vision and of the distinctly "negative sexuality" that informs it.[493] That vision amalgamates and inverts the sources of death with the sources of life, in keeping with the logic that underlay the acts that preceded hers (killing one's own child) and those that will follow (killing one's own mother).[494]

To understand how the imagery within Clytemnestra's speech functions as a metanarrative in relation to her own principal narrative concerning the death of Agamemnon, it is useful to think of the way a musical leitmotiv complements a given character's words. We can only say very little, and with great prudence, regarding the ways in which music and dance functioned in tragedy as "non-textual narrative threads"[495] because of the scanty evidence that we have concerning them, but we can safely assume that whenever music was played along with sung or chanted words and whenever choral dancing or other rhythmic gestures came into play, these could have functioned as a metanarrative, in that they would have informed and affected the audience's understanding of the logic and interpersonal dynamics of a given scene or speech. Similarly, the imagery employed by the queen reveals the sick perversion that drove her to her deed, through a logic that was born in the past, poisons the present, and prepares to corrupt the future.[496] The crimes perpetrated against their kin by the various

---

[493] In her exploration of the "the dynamics of misogyny" at work in the trilogy, Zeitlin 1978, 157–8, discusses the perversion of family relations in the *Oresteia*. She views the scene in which Clytemnestra bares her breast to her son Orestes in supplication before he murders her as involving a gesture that is both maternal and erotically charged. "Orestes hesitates, but realizes that the destruction of the *negative sexuality of his mother* is the only way to redress the wrong done in destroying his father, and reinstitute positive male sexuality." See also Rose 1992, 230–1, and Rabinowitz 1992, 43. Schein 2011b 73–4 examines how the language of hatred in the *Oresteia* reveals the confusion of *philia* and *echthra* as "a defining feature of the trilogy."
[494] An interesting parallel can be found in Aeschylus's *Persae*, 821–2, discussed by Cairns 2013, xvi (and n. 38). Cairns points up how the notion of "a harvest of *atê*" that we find in the speech of Darius's ghost is part of a "complex of vegetation imagery that accompanies the archaic chain." His words could just as well apply here, though it is not *atê* but the Erinys that is at work in Clytemnestra's murderous action.
[495] Markantonatos 2002, 26.
[496] On the perversion of nature and the destruction of life sources in the *Oresteia*, see Vickers 1973, 360ff; on metaphors of generation in the *Oresteia* in connection with the cycle of vengeance in the *Oresteia*, see also Sewell-Rutter 2007, ch. 3 n. 73. Iphigeneia's death, in addition to constituting a corruption of ritual sacrifice – it is literally performed as a sacrifice, during which

members of the house of Atreus are all characterized by a "distortion of all that is life-giving."⁴⁹⁷ Nourishment and generation are repeatedly sought in the destruction of the very sources of life. The perverted source of Clytemnestra's satisfaction at the death of Agamemnon is not just the curse that has governed the house of Atreus since the feast of Thyestes, one generation before the time in which the *Agamemnon* is set, but also the abominable logic to which this curse has given rise.⁴⁹⁸ Allusions to Atreus's original crime are scattered throughout the three plays at significant points, where connections between the curse born from his deed and new crimes to come are made apparent,⁴⁹⁹ because of the perverted logic whereby life sources have become associated with death. This logic returns as a regular leitmotiv throughout the trilogy, and one of the ways it manifests itself lies in the prominent use of metaphors pertaining to procreation. A brief overview of selected examples shall have to suffice for our present purposes.

In a passage that immediately precedes Agamemnon's arrival onstage, the Chorus uses metaphorical language that mingles birth and life (τίκτει, 759; γέννᾳ, 760) in reference to the cycle of violent murders afflicting the house of Atreus:

τὸ δυσσεβὲς γὰρ ἔργον
μετὰ μὲν πλείονα τίκτει,
σφετέρᾳ δ' εἰκότα γέννᾳ

(758–60)

For the impious deed thereafter begets more such deeds, similar to the stock whence it came from.⁵⁰⁰

Using language pertaining to generation and childbirth, the Chorus of Elders' utterance suggests the perpetuation of destruction to come. Other examples of lan-

---

she is lifted above the altar "like a goat" (*Ag.* 207–11) – is depicted as a corrupted marriage ritual in the *parodos* of the *Agamemnon*. On the association of death with marriage, see Lebeck's discussion of the term *telos* and how it serves to connect sacrifice with marriage (Lebeck 1971, 68–73). The corruption of marriage and ritual is also discussed in Zeitlin 1965, 464 ff. and Rehm 1994, ch. 3 in particular (43–58).
497 Goheen 1955, 134.
498 Atreus sought revenge against his brother Thyestes by slaughtering Thyestes' children and serving them to their father at a banquet. Regarding ancestral fault as a core idea of Greek culture, see Gagné 2013, esp. ch. 7 concerning tragedy, and the Atreidae in particular.
499 In the closing lines of the *Choephori* (1063–76), the crimes of Atreus and Thyestes are emphatically brought to the fore and connected with Agamemnon's death (1073–4).
500 Translation mine, based on Lloyd-Jones 1970, who uses "stock" for γέννα.

guage mingling life with death abound. In the *parodos*, the Chorus uses a simile in which vultures lose their offspring and, as bereaved parents, become ravishers (eagles) in their grief.[501] The moment their offspring is destroyed, they are pushed by some mysterious force to seek revenge for the destruction of the life lost by performing a similar destruction of future offspring: they devour a pregnant hare, her womb teeming with young.[502]

It is in this light that we should understand the simile that Clytemnestra employs when she compares her joy in Agamemnon's blood to the way a crop rejoices in the rain, using a clear sexual *double entendre*. Clytemnestra's ecstatic recounting after she slaughters her husband puts forward the same motif I have been stressing until now as central to our understanding of the trilogy and its characters' unrepentant actions and words: that of death and blood being sought in retaliation for life and fertility lost. In the words of Goheen, "Because Agamemnon has destroyed her child, Clytemnestra's fertility is now in lethal bloodshed."[503] In killing his daughter Iphigeneia, Agamemnon actually destroyed his own flesh and blood. His act took life back from the one to whom he had given it. The Chorus's insistence on his daughter's virginity at the time of her death emphasizes the idea that, in sacrificing her, it is not merely her person but her potential fertility that is destroyed.[504]

The queen's description of her deed highlights how much the murder of Agamemnon both contributes to and reflects the disorder plaguing the house of

---

501 For a discussion of the range of interpretations of this omen, see Peradotto 1969, 239 ff.
502 Line 119. Compare the paradox inherent to Artemis's anger at the destruction of innocent young, which leads to her demanding the destruction of other young in compensation (140–4).
503 Goheen 1955, 133 ff.; see Loraux 1990 on the destructive impulses of mothers in mourning.
504 Repeated allusions to Iphigeneia's virginity (209–10, 215, 245) call attention to the fact that she has not yet borne children and that she never will. She was brought to Aulis in the belief that she was to be wedded, an occasion that would normally have been a celebration of fertility (the *proteleia*), which turns out to be a perverted ritual slaughter and a human sacrifice. Lebeck 1971, 68 ff., offers an interesting analysis of the mingled images in the passage, pinpointing how they refer sometimes to the rite of marriage and sometimes to the rite of sacrifice. "Whereas a marriage normally heralds procreation, fertility, the *proteleia* for Iphigeneia is the death of a virgin, fertility destroyed before it can flourish" (Vickers 1973, 354). Cassandra points out to the Chorus, just before she is slaughtered by Clytemnestra, that she has had no children (*Ag.* 1207–8: Χο. ἦ καὶ τέκνων εἰς ἔργον ἤλθετον νόμῳ; | Κα. ξυναινέσασα Λοξίαν ἐψευσάμην). The pertinence of the omen of the pregnant hare (119 ff.) devoured by the eagle before giving birth comes to mind: see Heath 1999a, 27 ff. The biological phenomena of pregnancy and childbirth and their uses and abuses in ancient culture and literature are discussed in detail by Romani 2004, with bibliography.

Atreus,[505] which renews itself in a perpetual cycle of violence. From the curse on the house stems a form of destruction that feeds on itself continually, ruining life and its very sources.[506] The close examination of Clytemnestra's poetic depiction of the death she has inflicted brings to light how much her vision, which amalgamates birth with death and fertility with murder, points to a generalized disorder that runs through the trilogy, rearing its head with every new destructive deed in response to the previous one and in preparation for the next. Clytemnestra's language indicates that she is partly an agent of that pervasive destruction, the logic of which informs her perceptions and reactions. The imagery that she employs, in associating death with life, reveals her vision to be symptomatic of a broader perversion pervading the entire trilogy.

Clytemnestra's vision is, without question, a disturbing one, which makes starkly apparent to the audience that her avenging gesture is, at the same time, a further trangression of justice, a new crime; yet as her words convey her perversion, they place her warped perception firmly within the general destructive pattern that afflicts the house of Atreus. Clytemnestra is yet another manifestation of the corrupted relationship of each member of the cursed family to the sources of life itself, a pattern which can be traced back to Thyestes' cannibalistic feast on his own children. Aeschylus's portrayal of Clytemnestra's delight is a depiction of horrifying *Schadenfreude* on the part of a disturbingly sadistic wife, but it is also revealing of much more than merely individual sentiment as a motivator for Clytemnestra's action and subsequent reaction.

Such is the Aeschylean world: one in which the gods and other forces greater than man lurk behind every human initiative, influencing and prompting human action in ways at which mortals can often merely guess. Every agent of destruction in Aeschylus's *Oresteia* acts in conformity with an order that lies in perpetuating a certain form of disorder, each one of them moved by their own motives, but also by greater forces. The imagery in Clytemnestra's messenger speech is a poetic instantiation of an immensely disturbing logic: it reveals how much her own vision is warped and follows a pattern of disorder that remains in place

---

[505] For comparison's sake, see Cassandra's words (1072–1330), which repeatedly refer to Thyestes' feast and blood in the house of Atreus and inextricably link past, present, and future; see also the Chorus at 1507–12, where they trace the destruction back to Atreus and Thyestes once more. Vickers 1973, 374, provides an actual chart recapitulating the various bloody episodes that are interconnected in and by the prophetess's "cyclic survey."

[506] In her study of how the webs of Aeschylean imagery are "intricately interwoven" and mutually shed light on one another, Lebeck highlights the image of the spilling of blood and the endless cycle of violence that the image of that blood flowing to the ground enacts (lines 1114–22, Lebeck 1971, 84 ff.).

until Athena makes the Erinyes into Eumenides or "benevolent ones" in the third play. They are the agents through whom the perversion, contamination, and replacement of life by death is finally rectified and the natural order reestablished, as creation and procreation are redeemed from their sinister associations. As chthonic deities, they can withhold fertility, but they can also promote it.[507] They are not merely forces of destruction but agents of *both* fecundity and destruction.[508] Their story is the mirror image of Clytemnestra's evolution from fertile to destructive power, as they go from being forces of gruesome destruction to endorsing the role of fecundative patrons of the city of Athens.

Part Two: Matricide: Speech and the Body[509]

After Clytemnestra murders Agamemnon, her children Orestes and Electra plot against and kill their mother (and her complicit lover, Aegisthus) in order to avenge their dead father. All three tragedians depict the matricide: Aeschylus in his *Oresteia* and Sophocles and Euripides in their respective *Electra* plays.[510] My interest lies especially in Euripides' portrayal of the matricide, but the distinctive features of his depiction are best brought out if we consider it in comparison with the other two tragedians'. The first part of my analysis will thus be devoted to an examination of the aftermath of Clytemnestra's death in Aeschylus and Sophocles.[511] As Kitto stated, "what is interesting in the comparison of the three dramatists is not their moral attitude to a very simple problem, but their dramatic attitude to the situation and to the actors in it."[512] In what fol-

---

507 See Vickers 1973, 421–3.
508 For the Eumenides as forces of destruction in response to the dishonor into which they were cast, see *Eu.* lines 780–5.
509 For an overview of the wide range of semiotic uses of the body in ancient Greek theater, see Griffith 1998.
510 The respective dates of Sophocles' *Electra* and Euripides' *Electra* are still a matter of debate. This does not preclude our comparing the two plays. Euripides mainly engages with his Aeschylean model; as we will see, Sophocles exaggerates certain Aeschylean elements that Euripides departs from quite radically.
511 As Foley 1975, 112, notes, when considering Euripidean plays (especially later ones), it is just as important to consider "the play that it is not as ... the one that it is," with an eye to the plural mythological traditions which the audience would bear in mind. For a recent and detailed comparison between Aeschylus's and Sophocles' treatments of the murder of Clytemnestra, see Kyriakou 2011, 315–70. McClure 2012 brings to light the ways in which the imagery of the *Oresteia* surrounding motherhood influenced Sophocles in his composing the *Electra*.
512 Kitto 1939, 349.

lows, I closely examine, not what we might assume to be the playwrights' moral attitudes toward the problem at hand (matricide), but the visions of the characters themselves.

In Euripides' *Electra*, Clytemnestra's matricidal children present an intriguing example of murderers-turned-messengers. Leading up to their action, Euripides' matricides adopt the same driving principles as Aeschylus's and Sophocles' do: observing the oracle of Apollo and avenging their father's death.[513] Like their mother in Aeschylus' *Agamemnon*, the siblings who commit the murder are put in the role of messengers in Euripides' portrayal, reporting on what they have done. They reenact their deed for the audience, and as they retell it, they watch the scene unfold a second time, becoming spectators to their own deed after the fact. But as the matricides shift to the position of spectators of their deed, the audience observes a radical shift in their response to it. Unlike Aeschylus's Clytemnestra, who takes great pleasure both in the deed itself and in the retelling of it, when they reenact the murder of their mother, they watch it unfold with eyes suddenly opened to the reality before them. When they shift to the stance of spectators, their vision of their deed changes as they watch it *a posteriori*.

In his depiction of the aftermath of his matricides' act, Euripides engages with the other two dramatists' portrayals of the matricides' reactions after the fact. As he revisits the scene, Euripides has Orestes and Electra give prominent place to Clytemnestra's body, in their speeches and in their gaze, in direct and stark contrast to the telling exclusion of the maternal body from the siblings' field of vision and speech in Aeschylus and Sophocles both.[514] The visual omissions in Aeschylus, which are taken to an even greater extreme in Sophocles, involve the siblings' avoidance of any visual contact between themselves and their mother's corpse. In Euripides' *Electra*, on the other hand, the act of looking at their mother's corpse lying before them leads to their recognition not only of the humanity of the victim but also of the inviolable bonds that bind them to that victim as kin, which they have irreparably violated. Euripides' drama thus

---

513 This is not to say that Aeschylus's *Oresteia* does not leave us with a sense of unease and some questions as to the carrying out of the oracle, settled though the matter of justice is (partly thanks to the god himself) in the *Eumenides* by way of a trial. On Aeschylus's dark vision of divinity and its agency in human life as portrayed in the *Oresteia*, see Dodds 1951 and 1960 as well as Winnington-Ingram 1965. On the question of Apollo's oracle in the *Oresteia* and Euripides' foregrounding of issues and tensions that are left latent in Aeschylus, see Roberts 1984.
514 On Euripides' provocative rejection of past traditions in Euripides' *Electra* , see e. g., Arnott 1981.

exposes the blind spots that the espousal of a narrow range of vision in Aeschylus and Sophocles creates and the human cost at which they come.[515]

The Death of Clytemnestra in Aeschylus: The Tyranny and the robe

Aeschylus's account of the murder of Clytemnestra in the second play of the *Oresteia* trilogy, the *Choephori*, involves no *a posteriori* recounting of their mother's death on the part of her murderous children. In the scene that follows the killing, no other character but the doer of the deed (Orestes) is onstage, save, perhaps, a silent Pylades who has, in all likelihood, remained at his side. After killing his mother, Orestes explains his reasons for the murder to the Chorus members, who, though they cry out at the "loathsome death" (στυγερῶι θανάτωι, 1008) that Clytemnestra has endured, nevertheless do not question its legitimacy (ἀλλ' εὖ γ' ἔπραξας, 1044), thereby contributing to the general tone of just vindication ruling over the scene.

Before killing Clytemnestra, Orestes first kills her lover and accomplice in usurping Agamemnon's power, Aegisthus, son of Thyestes. The morally unproblematic nature of this killing is clearly reflected in the swiftness with which it occurs and the limited space it occupies within the dramatic text.[516] The death is dealt with quickly. All the mentions that are made of it appear intended to connect Clytemnestra's own death to come with it and thus play up her culpability. There is no description of Aegisthus's death itself after the fact: no messenger comes onstage to announce it, and no one describes the scene after it occurs. There is no opportunity for any sort of emotion to be elicited from the audience in reaction to the death, save for the Chorus's brief expression of joy at the news that Aegisthus is dead, before it carefully proceeds to distance itself from the scene so as not to seem complicit ("Let us stand away from the action that has been completed," ἀποσταθῶμεν πράγματος τελουμένου, 872), presumably out of wariness of the remaining tyrant in power, Clytemnestra. We simply

---

515 For a thorough investigation of the dramatic role of sight and sound in Euripidean tragedy, see Marseglia 2013.
516 On the related brevity of Aegisthus's appearance onstage (only 17 lines), see Taplin 1978, 346–7. Orestes shows great satisfaction at having inflicted due punishment on the adulterer and tyrant Aegisthus, who deserved the treatment he received (Αἰγίσθου γὰρ οὐ λέγω μόρον, 989), as prescribed by law – a reference to contemporary practices concerning adulterers (see Lysias 1; Cohen 1991). The killing of Aegisthus is morally, socially, and politically unproblematic: he had usurped Orestes' father's throne and taken Orestes' mother as his lover. Orestes ignores his corpse in a manner that is unsurprising and not noteworthy; the case of Clytemnestra is less simple.

hear Aegisthus's cry (ἒ ἒ ὀτοτοτοῖ, 869) and his servant's declaration that his master "is no more," followed by his frantic attempt to wake Clytemnestra and warn her that a similar fate awaits her (875–84). Both the servant's reaction and the queen's ability to rapidly decipher his cryptic statement that "the dead are killing the living" (τὸν ζῶντα καίνειν τοὺς τεθνηκότας λέγω, 886) point to the degree of complicity between her and Aegisthus, making her appear all the more deserving of her impending death. To the servant's statement, Clytemnestra replies, without missing a beat, "Quick! Someone give me an axe to kill a man!" (δοίη τις ἀνδροκμῆτα πέλεκυν ὡς τάχος, 889). She realizes that the stranger in the house is Orestes and that a similar fate to the one inflicted on Aegisthus awaits her at the hands of her own son unless she takes matters (and an axe) into her own hands.

When her plan to meet violence with violence fails, Clytemnestra bares her breast to her son – an attempt to play up the sacred obligations that come with the bond between mother and child by drawing attention to her body and reminding him how she (allegedly) suckled him as a babe (896–8).[517] She accompanies the physical gesture with an appeal to the reverence that her breast should evoke as a tangible reminder of the "corporeal inextricability" that binds a mother to her child.[518] Following so closely on a cry that shows her prepared to slaughter her own son, such an appeal does not carry much credibility in the eyes of the audience. (We can assume that Orestes did not hear her call for a weapon, or her appeal would be laughably vain.) The sacred nature of maternity, symbolized by the bared breast, makes Orestes waver. He asks his companion Pylades, "What should I do? Should respect (*aidôs*) prevent me from killing my mother?" (Πυλάδη, τί δράσω; μητέρ' αἰδεσθῶ κτανεῖν, 899). In response, Pylades speaks his only lines in the entire play, raising the specter of another form of reverence – the reverence owed to oaths sworn to the gods:

ποῦ δαὶ τὸ λοιπὸν Λοξίου μαντεύματα
τὰ πυθόχρηστα, πιστά τ' εὐορκώματα;[519]
(900–1)

---

[517] τόνδε δ' αἴδεσαι, "Reverence this [breast]," 896. That Clytemnestra suckled Orestes is largely contradicted by the nurse's earlier account of how *she* (not Clytemnestra) reared and fed Orestes as an infant.
[518] The quote is from Murnaghan 1988, 32, who pays close attention to the place of the body in the speeches of Greek tragedy and the values that its place within, or exclusion from, a given speech reveals. On *aidôs* in this scene, see Cairns 1993, 200; on the role of *aidôs* in connection with violations of *philia*, see Belfiore 2000.
[519] It is not clear which oaths are being referred to, though we can assume they were sworn by Orestes to Apollo; see Garvie 1986 *ad loc*.

Then what becomes in the future of Loxias' oracles delivered at Pytho, and of faithful, sworn pledges?

Pitting it against the principles of justice put forward by Apollo, Orestes rapidly dismisses the reality of the living, breathing body that gave birth to him. When he declares Pylades the winner (κρίνω σε νικᾶν, 903), he speaks in the voice of an impartial judge, assessing the question of justice with a view to divine commands: human ties have been dismissed and are no longer a consideration. According to Apollo's will, the fatal blow he is about to deal to his mother is just punishment, regardless of the relationship between punisher and victim. Words – divine oracles and sworn oaths and the abstract concepts of justice put forward by Loxias – take precedence over the tangible corporeality of a mother's flesh and the physical blood ties that bind a mother to her child. Pylades coldly articulates the precedence that he believes should be given to the divine over human relationships: "Consider all men to be your enemies, rather than the gods!" (ἅπαντας ἐχθροὺς τῶν θεῶν ἡγοῦ πλέον, 902).

Clytemnestra makes a final, desperate attempt to save her life by threatening Orestes with the looming prospect of her Furies chasing after him – and fails. She quickly comes to the conclusion that her doom is inescapable ("It seems as though I am making a useless living dirge to a tomb," 926).[520] Recalling her dream of the serpent drawing blood at her breast, she recognizes its prophetic nature and exits the stage for the last time.[521] We do not even hear her scream. When she is shown to the audience again, it is as a corpse, lying alongside the body of her murdered lover Aegisthus as the two are rolled out on the *eccyclêma*, in a conspicuous visual echo of the scene in the *Agamemnon* in which she stood over Agamemnon's and Cassandra's dead bodies, gloating.[522] Now it is Orestes who stands over two dead bodies and who, like Clytemnestra, delivers a speech about the double murder he has committed, accounting for his deed. There is, it seems, more ambivalence to his assessment than to Clytemnestra's of the murder she committed, as is evident at the very least from the fact that, unlike the queen, he does not recount the act but steers notably clear of the matricide itself. We are never told how the actual murder unfolded, only what led to it (Agamem-

---

[520] Sommerstein 2008, *ad loc.* notes that she might be referring to Orestes' metaphorical deafness to her entreaties or to the fact that she is uttering her own funeral lament; such ambiguity is most likely deliberate on Aeschylus's part.
[521] For a discussion of the likely absence of Aegisthus's corpse from the stage throughout this scene, and its dramatic and thematic effectiveness, see Taplin 1978, 355–6.
[522] Regarding the *eccyclêma* in this scene and in that following Agamemnon and Cassandra's murder in the *Agamemnon*, see above n. 456.

non's death, which is Orestes' motive) and what it means on a broader civic and political level: Apollo's will has been fulfilled, Agamemnon's death has been avenged, and therefore justice has been done.[523]

Orestes is well aware that there is an audience (in addition to himself) to the aftermath of his deed. He explicitly invites all who "hear of these crimes" (τῶνδ' ἐπήκooι κακῶν, 980) to follow his gaze, taking their viewership and perception into his own hands. When he asks all present — ostensibly the Chorus members – to "behold" (ἴδεσθε δ' αὖτε. 980) the spectacle before them, the external audience is bound to feel included in the addressees. While Orestes appears to be taking responsibility for and endorsing his murderous deed, as Clytemnestra did, he does not make any mention of the corpses *qua* bodies before him.[524] At no point does he look at, much less draw attention to, his mother's bloodied body or her individual identity as mother. Instead, he detracts from both her and her lover's actual, physical presence and corporeality. He defines Clytemnestra solely by the deed that she committed with Aegisthus's aid (usurping Agamemnon's power by killing her husband), not by the ties or duties stemming from the natural and fundamental parental bond that links victim and killer to each other as mother and son. When he asks that the audience bear witness to the rightful nature of his act, he carefully guides its perception of the bodies before it (and him), lumping his mother together with her partner in crime, the man complicit in the killing of his father and the illegitimate usurper of his power over the land. He instructs his audience to consider the two human beings as a single abstraction, "tyranny" (τυραννίδα), an appellation that is in and of itself a justification for the avenging murder that he has committed and that enables him to avoid any terms that would point to Clytemnestra's relationship to him as a mother:[525]

---

[523] Taplin 1978, 357 ff. notes how the visual correspondence between the two double murders — Agamemnon and Cassandra, and now Clytemnestra and Aegisthus — is "too close for comfort" and prompts the Chorus to voice a disquieting response (1007–9, 1018–20). The audience is provided the visual evidence in this mirror scene that "the blood feud has repeated itself," in a manner that makes the selective nature of Orestes' viewing (focusing on the robe rather than the bodies, as we are about to see) stand out all the more starkly. Taplin also notes other visual components of the tableau here that mark the ambivalence of the matricide, including the fact that Orestes would likely be holding a sword in one hand, while holding a suppliant's branch and wreath in the other.

[524] Taplin 1978, 359 notes that "there is an optimistic neglect of the consequences of the murder" during most of the *Choephori*.

[525] On the somatics of disengagement, see Goldhill 2012, 44 n. 18 with bibliography.

> ἴδεσθε χώρας τὴν διπλῆν τυραννίδα
> πατροκτόνους τε δωμάτων πορθήτορας·
> (973–4)
>
> Behold the twin tyranny of this land, the murderers of my father and ravagers of my house![526]

Orestes uses the spectacle before him to emphasize the motives for his action and its result: the dead are not dead bodies so much as embodiments of a tyranny, of power stolen from his father and usurped from its rightful heir (Orestes himself); these deaths have brought an end to the usurpation of the power over Argos that belonged to his father, which now rightfully belongs to him. By contrast, though they dwell on the wrongs committed by Clytemnestra and Aegisthus and recognize the necessity for justice, the Chorus of libation bearers nonetheless laments for Clytemnestra, and even for Aegisthus, when the queen exits the stage to meet certain death: "I lament even the double downfall of these two" (στένω μὲν οὖν καὶ τῶνδε συμφορὰν διπλῆν, 931).

One stage prop in particular aids Orestes in his avoidance of the reality of the maternal body lying before him: the garment that Clytemnestra used to constrain Agamemnon's movements and bind his limbs together in order to make him defenseless and kill him with ease. For the duration of the speech he delivers in the aftermath of his deed, Orestes keeps his and his audience's gaze fixed on the object. By zooming in on this specific visual element of the spectacle, he centers his focus and the spectators' on a tangible reminder of his mother's crime. The ostentatious presentation of the garment amounts to a prominent visual exhibition of his mother's wrongdoing. He is, in effect, using the prop to stage Clytemnestra's guilt, putting it on display for all to see as he directs his attendants to spread it out ("Spread it out ... and display the device," ἐκτείνατ' αὐτὸ καὶ ... στέγαστρον ἀνδρὸς δείξαθ', 983–4),[527] inviting them once again (cf. 973) to take in the spectacle of his mother's guilt for themselves ("stand beside it in a circle," κύκλωι παραστᾰδόν, 983). In doing so, he emphasizes the importance, if not the necessity, of avenging his dead father:

---

[526] Cf. S., *El.*; when the old slave comes to announce the false news of Orestes' death, he describes Clytemnestra in ambiguous terms that make her physical appearance a reflection of the illegitimate rule she exercises alongside Aegisthus: πρέπει γὰρ ὡς τύραννος εἰσορᾶν (664) can be understood as "she certainly has a royal look," but also as "she looks quite the tyrant," as March 2001, *ad loc.* points out.

[527] The order of the lines is problematic: see Sommerstein 2008 *ad loc.*

ἴδεσθε δ' αὖτε, τῶνδ' ἐπήκοοι κακῶν,
τὸ μηχάνημα, δεσμὸν ἀθλίωι πατρί

(980–1)

Behold, you who are hearing of these crimes,
the contrivance that imprisoned my wretched father!

While it effectively (and perhaps literally) hides Clytemnestra's bloody corpse from his and the audience's eyes by deflecting their attention, the garment simultaneously brings another body – Agamemnon's – back to the fore. Orestes recalls how Clytemnestra used the robe as a contrivance (τὸ μηχάνημα) to "fetter [Agamemnon's] arms and bind his feet together" (πέδας τε χειροῖν καὶ ποδοῖν ξυνωρίδος, 982). In looking at the robe, Orestes is led to picture Agamemnon's body "in its coffin, feet and all" (998–9).[528] If the bodies weren't still lying before us, we might forget that Clytemnestra and Aegisthus have been killed; the only death and body that matter in Orestes' speech are Agamemnon's, as Orestes' words, gestures, and point of focus make abundantly clear.[529] Orestes' speech, along with his gestures, hide Clytemnestra's body from his and the audience's sight.

The connection between the visual display of the garment and Orestes' concern with justice is spelled out in what follows. The spectacular exhibition of Clytemnestra's guilt (a justification for his action, in that it has punished the guilty) is intended not only for the immediate audience around him but also for the benefit of Zeus. Orestes asks the father of gods and men to look on as well (στέγαστρον ἀνδρὸς δείξαθ', ὡς ἴδηι πατήρ, 984), knowing that he will be held account-

---

[528] The "coffin" is a reference to the bathtub in which the king was entrapped and stabbed to death (Sommerstein 2008, 339). The specific reference to the king's arms and feet points to the *maschalismos* that we have earlier been told Clytemnestra inflicted on her spouse's body. The Chorus informs Orestes that, after killing Agamemnon, she ritually dismembered his body, cutting off his hands and feet and tying them around his neck and under his armpits (439). This *maschalismos* is also pointedly mentioned in Sophocles' *Electra* (445). For an assessment of the historical and literary sources we have concerning the practice of the *maschalismos*, see Muller 2011.

[529] Complementing this focus on the garment is a process whereby Orestes makes his mother into an abstraction through his words. His search for the right word to define the ensnaring device used by his mother to kill his father ("a net, a snare, a hobbling robe," 999–1000) serves as a jumping off point for defining Clytemnestra herself with increasingly disparaging and distancing terms. This, in turn, gives rise to a number of comparisons ("This is the sort of thing that a footpad might get for himself, a man who led a life of beguiling travellers and robbing them," 1001–4), over the course of which he assimilates Clytemnestra sometimes to a hunter (the robe is "something to catch a hunted beast," ἄγρευμα θηρός, 998), sometimes to a monster, as when he debates whether to call her a "moray-eel or viper" (μύραινά γ' εἴτ' ἔχιδν' ἔφυ, 994).

able for the matricide that he has just committed. In asking the supreme god, enforcer of justice, to look upon the robe (rather than the bodies before him), he stresses what he takes to be conspicuous visual evidence of his mother's guilt, assuming that the sight of the bloody robe should be enough to point up the punishable nature of Clytemnestra's deed and exculpate him of his own ruinous act. He deems the mere sight of the robe sufficient to convince the god to act as witness to the righteousness of the revenge that he has exacted when he stands trial (987–9). Orestes even turns to the garment itself, invoking its power to bear witness to the deed committed by Clytemnestra, stained as it still is with the blood of Agamemnon:

> ἔδρασεν ἢ οὐκ ἔδρασε; μαρτυρεῖ δέ μοι
> φᾶρος τόδ' ὡς ἔβαψεν Αἰγίσθου ξίφος·
> φόνου δὲ κηκὶς ξὺν χρόνωι ξυμβάλλεται
> πολλὰς βαφὰς φθείρουσα τοῦ ποικίλματος.
> νῦν αὐτὸν αἰνῶ, νῦν ἀποιμώζω παρών,
> πατροκτόνον γ' ὕφασμα προσφωνῶν τόδε·
> (1010–5)

Did she do it or did she not? This garment is my witness to how it was dyed by Aegisthus's sword; and the stain of blood ... has contributed to ruining many of the dyes in the embroidery. Now I can praise the man, now I can fully lament him, being present here and addressing this woven garment that killed my father.[530]

One factor contributing to Orestes' ability to ignore his mother's lifeless body lying before him, killed by his own hand, is that he considers her to have played no more than the role of a vessel in the process of giving him life.[531] He describes himself as an offspring of Agamemnon alone (ἐξ οὗ τέκνων ἤνεγκ' ὑπὸ ζώνην βάρος, "She had borne the weight of his children beneath her girdle," 992). In doing so, he follows the Chorus's lead. Before her death, it provided Orestes with preemptive advice by prescribing him what to retort *verbatim* to any attempt on Clytemnestra's part to defend herself with claims to motherhood:

> ἐπαῦσας θροεούσαι
> "τέκνον", "ἔργωι πατρός" αὔδα,
> καὶ πέραιν' ἀνεπίμομφον ἄταν.
> (828–30)

And when she cries to you, "my child!" cap that by shouting "my *father's* child!" and complete an act of destruction that carries no blame.

---

[530] On the difficulty of the translation here, see Garvie *ad* 1016–7.
[531] On *philia* and the obligations of *aidôs* that attend it, see Cairns 1993.

The reduction of the mother's role to that of a mere vessel in the conception of offspring is also at the center of Apollo's argument exculpating Orestes during the trial scene in the *Eumenides*, where the god uses Athena's birth from Zeus and Zeus alone as an example (657–73). Apollo's (questionable) biology lecture suggests that the mother plays no role in the actual conception of a child.[532] Clytemnestra's status as mother, and the sacred place of her body as the one that gave birth to the matricidal killers, is thus dismissed in the *Eumenides*, and Orestes is acquitted.[533]

This is not to say that Aeschylus presents an uncomplicated picture of matricide that ignores the problematic nature of killing one's mother. I am not arguing that he presents a simplistic account of the killing of Clytemnestra as, ultimately, divinely sanctioned and morally justified. The fact that the human jury is tied in the *Eumenides* and that Apollo's and Athena's arguments during the trial are questioned certainly suggests that the picture of justice is far more complex than Orestes would like it to be, and the physical presence of the Erinyes onstage at the end of the *Choephori* shows that even the gods are divided when it comes to condemning or condoning his act. The Chorus voices ambivalence about the murder after it occurs, and Orestes follows suit to a degree, expressing some mixed feelings about his deed.[534] Soon, Clytemnestra's Furies will

---

[532] It is unclear to what extent Apollo's somewhat sophistic lecture is to be taken seriously when it comes to Aeschylus and his contemporaries' conception of what the biological process of human reproduction involved. Podlecki 1989 *ad loc.* prudently states that the theory "would perhaps not have sounded as ludicrous to A.'s audience as it does to us" but proceeds to underscore the "haughty and sophistic" nature of Apollo's lecturing, which does not, in his mind, obscure the blatant truth that "Orestes did violence to one of the most basic and sacrosanct of human relationships, that between a child and a mother." The main point to retain here is that Aeschylus chooses to have the character of Orestes relegate this relationship to the background and bring other ties and obligations to the fore.

[533] Murnaghan 1988, 32–5, discusses the ways in which "the passage from bodily engagement to speech" is notable throughout the *Oresteia* when it comes to Orestes' confrontations with his mother's body. She demonstrates how this passage culminates in "the invention of a new form of spoken engagement, the legal trial," during which "the mother is no longer present in the form of a living human body," as the reenactment of the confrontation between mother and son is mediated through the voice of Apollo.

[534] For the Chorus's ambivalence, see e.g., 1007–9, 1018–20; these lines present a stark contrast to the Chorus members' earlier encouragement of the matricides leading up to their deadly act. Before Orestes kills his mother, the women imagine that the house shares in their emotional response to his return, praying to the "god of the portal" to allow the house to "raise its head in happiness and … with friendly eyes behold in [Orestes] the brilliant light of freedom" (807–11). For Orestes' ambivalence about the deed after the fact, see 1016–7: "I do grieve for her deeds, and for her suffering, and for my whole family, having acquired an unenviable pollution from this victory."

begin pursuing Orestes and will do so for the better part of the *Eumenides*. The justice of their cause — punishing the bloodshed of kin – is recognized by Athena herself.

Even the stagecraft of the death of Clytemnestra points to the ambivalence of Aeschylus's portayal of Orestes' deed. It provides a visual echo of Agamemnon's death and thus defines Orestes' act as a continuation of his mother's earlier deed. The parallel expresses a visual and causal link between the two murders and can be read in two possible ways. On the one hand, by evoking the original murder that Orestes is now avenging, it underscores the justice of his deed: righteous vengeance has been exacted.[535] On the other hand, the parallel also suggests that the present murder is a perpetuation of the perversion and disorder that were inherent to the first. The two interpretations are not mutually exclusive: the revenge is righteous and fulfills the god's command, while it also perpetuates a reversal of the natural order of the type that has been characteristic of each murder stemming from the curse on the house of Atreus.[536]

One may wonder whether the audience would have been allowed to keep the body of Clytemnestra within their sight or whether she would have been completely obscured by the robe held up at Orestes' command. Any staging that left her body in full view of the audience would presumably contribute to sapping Orestes' claim that he has accomplished a righteous deed, given the pathos inherent to the sight of a mother gored to death by her own son. One could even argue that Orestes' averted gaze itself exposes his own awareness of the disquieting nature of his act: the very deliberateness of his denial of the maternal body and his obsessive focus on the robe in its stead might actually suggest the malaise that comes with killing one's mother, rather than indicating that he does not recognize its seriousness.[537] If, in having his servants hold up the garment for all to see, Orestes hides the bodies of Clytemnestra and Aegisthus from view, then he would be using the bloodstained garment to cloak the nature of his deed in the garb of justice; or, to put less negative a spin on it, he would be guiding the audience's and his own gaze away from the matricide and toward

---

[535] This is the case in Sophocles, who establishes a clear verbal echo between the two, as we are about to see, in a manner that suggests that justice has been done.
[536] On the portrayal of justice in the *Oresteia* and its ambivalence, see Lloyd-Jones 1971, 89–95.
[537] Taplin 1977, 357–9 describes this mirror scene as illustrating, through interperformative reference, "first and foremost that the blood feud has repeated itself." He also contrasts an enlightened and rightly fearful Orestes, coerced by Apollo, with what he sees as an unrepentant and power-thirsty Clytemnestra. The latter aspects of her character are essential, but I hope to have brought to light some of the other nuances of her persona and of Aeschylus's portrayal of her actions.

what the trilogy's central (surviving) characters ultimately emphasize as what they deem most important in political and familial terms: obeying Apollo and avenging his father. It is impossible to know whether or not the robe was used in this way. At any rate, there are, at the very least, some tensions and ambivalence already present in Aeschylus, which Euripides seizes on in his *Electra*, bringing to the fore the potential for a character's vision, as well as stagecraft and gestures, to highlight the complex moral issues central to this scene.

Sophocles' *Electra:* Viewing Clytemnestra's body through other eyes

Before I turn to the highly different depiction that Euripides gives of the matricidal children in the same situation in his *Electra*, I want to examine briefly Sophocles' portrayal of Orestes' and Electra's reactions to the murder of their mother in his play by the same name, paying special attention to what these characters focus on and see and what conception of justice and morality their line of vision and their responses to their deed reflect. In Aeschylus's depiction, as we have seen, Orestes keeps his gaze firmly away from his mother's corpse; but the audience also hears notes of ambivalence sounded regarding the morally and humanly problematic nature of matricide, including by Orestes himself.

Sophocles' presentation of the matricidal pairs' reactions after killing their mother is unequivocal: in their eyes, the justice of their deed is never in question.[538] He does away with any trace of the moral qualms and tensions that were present, though rejected, in Aeschylus's play. Clytemnestra's children's sense of just vindication in Sophocles seems unmitigated. A brief overview will bring to light how much more clear-cut the issues of morality and justice are in his play (as seen in the eyes of the matricides), in stark contrast to Euripides' portrayal of the aftermath of Clytemnestra's death and the way in which her children "see" it both literally and figuratively in his *Electra*.[539] To be

---

[538] That justice should be on their side does not preclude the children's recognition of the shameful violation they have committed, as noted by Wheeler, who also points out, however, that there is no *crise de conscience* on Orestes' part after he kills his mother (Wheeler 2003, 380–7).

[539] The act is nonetheless portrayed as shameful, for all the justice that the matricides attribute to it; see MacLeod's careful study of the play's language and the characters' argumentation (MacLeod 2001). Sewell-Rutter 2007, ch. 5, convincingly argues that Sophocles stands apart from Euripides and Aeschylus, both of whom are concerned with "doubly motivated action and its bearing on mortal decisions," (110) while Sophocles is not. Sewell-Rutter's chapter offers a good overview of the widely diverging interpretations of the play, including (especially) when

clear: I am not stating that Sophocles does not offer up any glimpses of ethical complexity nor point up the problematic nature of the act of vengeance; what I am concerned with here are the terms in which *the killers themselves* see (or choose to see) and depict their deed. Whichever one of the two *Electra* plays came first, it is clear that the two playwrights made radically different choices when it comes to the depiction of the matricide as it is seen by those who commit it. The matricidal children's vision of, and relationship to, the physical body of their mother in particular provides an important measure of their values and of the interpersonal ties and obligations to which they give priority.[540] In what they see, we are able to perceive the highly different conceptions of justice that each of the playwrights puts forward in his play.

The mere idea that the infliction of pain might, in some cases, be justly deserved is problematic to a modern mind.[541] Our modern ethical standards reject the idea that any suffering is somehow merited by the sufferer and that such suffering, if "deserved," should not evoke our pity. Not so in antiquity, where "helping friends and harming enemies" was the standard heroic and popular moral code to live by: by these standards, any pain that one inflicted on those who threatened oneself or one's *philoi* was merited, in light of their status *qua* enemy.[542] One illustration of the straightforwardness with which such a principle of conduct was embraced is the way in which Sophocles – and Clytemnestra's children – deal with the murder of the queen in his *Electra*. At no point in this play is it intimated that the children see the vengeful killing of their own mother as problematic (though we cannot ever exclude that their unqualified response might have been deemed problematic by at least some members of the audience). Throughout the play, the siblings' view of their killing of their treacherous mother is categorically positive. Leading up to her death, the queen incriminates herself in her children's and the audience's eyes in every interaction between her and other characters. Electra witnesses each of these interactions,

---

it comes to the matricidal vengeance and how it is portrayed, with bibliography. For the play's subtle handling of ethical questions, see also Winnington-Ingram 1980, 217 ff.

540 The body holds a central place both in characters' language and in its actual, visible presence on stage; see Falkner 2005 and Cawthorn 2008.

541 See Konstan 2001 and 2006 on an important condition to pity in Aristotle's definition of the emotion: the victim of the misfortune being witnessed can only be pitied if she is undeserving of her fate (Arist., *Rh.* 2.8.1385b13–16. Sandridge 2008 uses the convenient notion of "merit-based pity" in reference to this Aristotelian definition. See above, n. 541.

542 On the distinction between deserved and undeserved suffering and how it shapes Greek popular morality, see Dover 1974; on its implications regarding the emotion of pity, see Konstan 2001 passim. On the *ethos* of "helping friends and harming enemies" as it is applied in Sophoclean tragedy, see Blundell 1989.

directly or indirectly, and provides a foil for her mother's active rejection of maternal affection, including in the *agôn* scene that pits the two women against each other in the second episode.[543]

Each of Clytemnestra's interactions forfeits any chance of the audience considering her to be deserving of pity. In what follows, I offer a brief overview of the many ways in which the tragedy displays Clytemnestra's alienation from her children and the proportional intensity with which the tragedy plays up the bonds that bind Orestes and Electra to each other and to their father. This overview enables us to see how this alienation culminates in the scene of Clytemnestra's execution and its immediate aftermath. My analysis of the death scene and of the children's response to it examines how the audience's perception of Clytemnestra is mediated after her death, at a time when the question of the intrinsic immorality and unnaturalness of matricide would pose itself especially if the maternal corpse were in full view. Instead, Sophocles sees to it that the audience and Clytemnestra's children do not see her body directly after she has been killed: they only see her through Aegisthus's eyes, in a way that both enacts her alienation from her children and offsets any of the moral ambivalence that we see in Aeschylus.[544]

There are no redeeming character traits in Sophocles' Clytemnestra. The coldness with which she sees the plight of her own children, for which she is directly responsible – Electra reduced to rags and miserable living conditions; Orestes nearly killed, and exiled — makes her undeserving of pity in turn.[545] In Aeschylus, as we have seen, both Orestes and Apollo question the strength of the maternal bond by undermining its biological basis. In Sophocles, both the Chorus and Clytemnestra's children repeatedly underscore the fact that she does not deserve the very name of mother. The Chorus attributes a maternal role to itself, underlining Clytemnestra's lack of maternal affection and care by contrast:[546]

---

[543] Lines 516–659.
[544] On Orestes', Electra's, and the Chorus's "narrowly selective view of the past" throughout Sophocles' *Electra*, see Kyriakou 2011, especially 347–70.
[545] On those predisposed to pity as deserving of pity in turn and those who lack pity as undeserving of it, see n. 560.
[546] Electra's words also point to an attachment to Orestes that is maternal in nature. She calls him "child" and regrets not having had the chance to administer proper burial rites to him. She bemoans having reared him and suffered through "the labor of love" (1145) for nothing as a mother might (cf. *Ch.* 235–45, where she takes on the role fulfilled by the nurse Cilissa in Aeschylus (734–82). It is Electra who is compared to a nightingale by the Chorus — the figure of eternal, maternal grief, reminiscent of the figure of Procne (see March 2001 on lines 107, 147–9, and 1077). Regarding female speech in Euripides, see Chong-Gossard 2008.

> ἀλλ' οὖν εὐνοίᾳ γ' αὐδῶ,
> μάτηρ ὡσεί τις πιστά,
> μὴ τίκτειν σ' ἄταν ἄταις.

"Well, at least it is out of love, like a true-hearted mother, that I tell you not to add misery to miseries."

(233–5)

On cue, Electra explains the basis for her continued laments: the outrages committed against her by her own mother, "the mother who bore me" and "has become all hatred" (ἣ πρῶτα μὲν τὰ μητρός, ἥ μ' ἐγείνατο, | ἔχθιστα συμβέβηκεν, 261–2).[547]

Clytemnestra's death is preceded by a lengthy debate between Electra and her mother, which is an opportunity for Electra to remind the audience of the multiple grounds that she and Orestes have for considering Clytemnestra an enemy, not a *philê*.[548] In the midst of the *agôn* between the two women, Electra defines her relationship with Clytemnestra (597–8) in terms of the latter's political and social power, unjustly usurped and unjustly wielded over Argos – not by the familial bonds that *de facto* unite them. She makes no reference to those bonds at all.[549] In her response to Clytemnestra's claims regarding the just nature of her revenge against Agamemnon after he took Iphigeneia's life, Electra centers her rebuke on the usurpation of power that her mother has accomplished.[550] In addition to the accusations that Electra levels at her (the killing of Agamemnon, the affair with Aegisthus, the mistreatment of her own daughter, and the exile of

---

[547] There are many examples of such denials of Clytemnestra's motherhood; see e.g., 273–4; 1146, addressing Orestes: "For you were never more dear to your mother than you were to me, and I was your nurse"; 1154, "our mother who is no mother"; 1194: "A mother she is called, but she is nothing like a mother," which closely echoes *Ch.* 190–1: "my mother, who has an impious spirit towards her children that belies the name of mother." Most powerful in driving home Clytemnestra's shortcomings as a mother, perhaps, is the messenger speech falsely announcing Orestes' death, which presents the audience with a test of Clytemnestra's maternal love, which she fails. I return to it below.

[548] On the *agôn*, see Foley 2001, 146 ff. Winnington-Ingram 1980, 246 suggests that some of Electra's extremism may appear to be directly inherited from the very mother whom she so virulently fights. On the similarities between Electra and her mother in Sophocles' play, including in the arguments that they level at each other (a breach of *aidôs* as grounds for retaliation is what motivates both to murder), see Kirkwood 1958, 140 and Winnington-Ingram 1980, 246 as well as Blundell 1989, 169 ff.; on the irony of this similarity in *physis* between the two, see also Cairns 1993, 244–9.

[549] Lines 584–94.

[550] Wheeler 2003, 387 rightly notes that "Sophocles' text does not forge any Aeschylean chain of retaliations."

Orestes), a choral comment emphasizes the incriminating nature of Clytemnestra's response to Electra's legitimate accusations, which reveals the queen's lack of concern for what is righteous or just:

ὁρῶ μένος πνέουσαν· εἰ δὲ σὺν δίκῃ
ξύνεστι, τοῦδε φροντίδ' οὐκέτ' εἰσορῶ.
(610–1)

I see that she is breathing fury. But I no longer see her caring as to whether she has justice on her side.[551]

Clytemnestra's statements contribute to making the audience share in Electra and Orestes' indignation: she stresses the fact that she is thriving, while her legitimate children are cast out of the house because they pose a threat to the power that she and Aegisthus have usurped by killing the children's father.[552] In her prayer to Apollo (648–51 especially), she notes her enjoyment of that power and her fear that the control she wields over the house of Atreus may be lost. She even goes so far as to pray for the death of her own son, expressing the hope that the gods, children of Zeus who can "see everything," might aid her in her wish that Orestes be killed, for only then might she live in peace.[553]

Because the children feel no familial bond to Clytemnestra, it is fitting that they do not look upon their mother's body after Orestes carries out the matricide. Beforehand, however, Electra watches her mother closely, taking note of every instance in which she incriminates herself further in their eyes. Thus, Electra witnesses the queen's brazenness in action: she describes watching (ἐγὼ δ' ὁρῶσα, 282) her mother set up shockingly inappropriate and brazen song and dance celebrations and offering up sheep in sacrifice to the gods who saved her every month on the anniversary date of the day on which she murdered her husband. Meanwhile, Electra displays her own faithful attachment to her father and brother while she is hidden inside the house alone (280–5), lamenting while suppressing her tears because her mother scolds her for her self-pity ("Are you the only

---

[551] March 2001 *ad loc.* notes, "The words have almost the force of a stage direction, and the masked actor playing Clytemnestra would no doubt be making her anger apparent through his gestures." March's commentary gives compelling reasons for considering these words to be relevant to Clytemnestra, not Electra. If they concerned the latter, the Chorus would be expressing doubt as to whether justice remains a primary concern for Electra or not, which is never a matter of debate in the play (see March 2001 for an overview of the discussion). At no point in the tragedy does the Chorus consider Electra to have gone too far.

[552] That the unjust should thrive while the just should suffer is a source of indignation by Aristotelian standards; see above, n. 415.

[553] See line 657.

one whose father is dead?" 289–90) and threatens her with punishment for having smuggled Orestes away when he was still an infant to prevent his killing.[554] Electra points up the necessity of engaging in vengeful and destructive conduct, because of the evils that have been and continue to be committed around her (308–9).[555] Even Chrysothemis, who embodies a reasonable counterpart to her sister's perpetual and excessive mourning, nonetheless describes Electra's course of action as just (τὸ ... δίκαιον, 338, 466).[556]

There is no portion of Sophocles' *Electra* more incriminating of Clytemnestra than the scene in which the false news of Orestes' death is reported by his old and faithful slave (680–763). The news is delivered at a crucial turning point at the center of the play, in an exceptionally long set speech that has no equal (in terms of length) in any of Sophocles' extant plays. In his tale of Orestes' chariot-racing accident, the messenger provides an elaborate narrative, describing the young man's demise in slow motion and including every last detail of the excruciating death in his brilliantly wrought, fabricated account. Thus, he describes how Orestes was dashed to the ground with his legs in the air and dragged by his galloping horses till his body became so mangled that it was unrecognizable, even by his friends (ὥστε μηδένα | γνῶναι φίλων ἰδόντ' ἂν ἄθλιον δέμας, 755–6). The precision of the description pertains not only to Orestes' ordeal but also to the reactions of those who witnessed it: a fictitious embedded audience within the messenger's narrative cries out in pity (750) on hearing the tale of one who "had achieved so much and then met with such disaster" (οἳ' ἔργα δράσας οἷα λαγχάνει κακά, 751). In this invented tale, Orestes cuts a quintessentially tragic figure: the hero cut down in his prime. Hence the fake audience members' sorrow and the messenger's feigned pain at recounting the disaster (ἐν λόγοις | ἀλγεινά, 760–1) – a pain he expresses openly, welcome though he anticipates his report to be to Clytemnestra and Aegisthus alike (λόγους | ἡδεῖς, 666–7).

---

554 The detail is introduced in the opening lines of the play by the old slave (1–10).
555 On Electra as a Sophoclean hero, who is both agent and victim of the Furies, see Winnington-Ingram's chapter on the *Electra* (W.-I. 1980, 217 ff.).
556 It bears mentioning, however, that Sophocles makes clear in the language of his play that the matricides show a shameful lack of respect (*aidôs*) for their mother. Though they sometimes recognize the ambivalence of their initiative, they choose to disregard the complexity of the ethical situation they are in (see Cairns 1993, 241–9). Sophocles thus allows his audience to glimpse the ethical issues at hand in the matricides' action (killing their mother), but chooses not to have the matricides themselves address it as often or conspicuously as their Aeschylean and (especially) their Euripidean counterparts. For a summary of the affirmative as opposed to the ironic reading of the play, see Lloyd 2005, 99–115, with bibliography.

The character of the old slave provides the audience with an emotional foil for Clytemnestra's disturbing reaction to his fabricated tale. The servant concludes with a comment intended to stress his deep affection for Orestes:

> τοιαῦτά σοι ταῦτ' ἐστίν, ὡς μὲν ἐν λόγοις
> ἀλγεινά, τοῖς δ' ἰδοῦσιν, οἵπερ εἴδομεν,
> μέγιστα πάντων ὧν ὄπωπ' ἐγὼ κακῶν.
> (761–3)

Such is my story for you, painful indeed when told, but for those who witnessed it, as we did, the greatest sorrow that my eyes have ever seen.[557]

The messenger thus offers a test, a challenge of sorts for Clytemnestra to follow the example that he sets before her. As Clytemnestra briefly vacillates and wonders whether she should consider the news terrible or beneficial (ἢ δεινὰ μέν, κέρδη δέ, 767), the slave pushes her to define her response clearly by feigning fear that she might consider him the bearer of bad news: μάτην ἄρ' ἡμεῖς, ὡς ἔοικεν, ἥκομεν ("It seems that I have come in vain," 772). The queen reassures him (or so she thinks), stifling a "passing pang" of maternal grief with all too much ease, thereby displaying precisely the sort of incriminating response that the messenger had anticipated.[558] Her lack of maternal attachment is patently obvious from her astonishing lack of grief and is witnessed directly by the spectators: she utters happy words of relief at the news of Orestes' death.[559] By making her character lack pity to such a shocking extent, Sophocles eliminates any claim she has to being deserving of pity, in her children's eyes and in the audience's.[560]

---

[557] Compare the role played by Cilissa, Orestes' nurse, who, in Aeschylus' *Choephori*, takes on the role of maternal figure for Orestes in lieu of Clytemnestra and offers up a speech replete with expressions of grief at the false news of the death of Orestes. In her case, it is news she actually believes, while the messenger in Sophocles fabricates both the event and his reaction to it. Cilissa's grief establishes a contrast with Clytemnestra's cold relief at the news of the death of her own son: the nurse, in her account of Clytemnestra's fake display of grief, describes how the queen masks her joy and "laughter within" (A., *Ch.* 737–40). Taplin 1978, 347 connects what he calls the "Cilissa act" and the "Aegisthus act" — two brief one-character acts – and points out how both "undermine Clytemnestra's position as mother."
[558] Waldock 1951, 183; see lines 770–1 where Clytemnestra briefly points to her lack of hatred for her children ("Giving birth is a strange thing; even when they treat one badly, one does not hate one's children"), an acknowledgment that does not, however, lead to any concrete demonstrations of grief or remorse, on the contrary.
[559] See lines 773–87.
[560] On a predisposition to pity as a criterion for deserving pity, see Stevens 1944, 6 ff.; also Blundell 1989, 29: "Pity is owed to the compassionate, but the pitiless deserve no pity" in reference to D. 21.100 ff., 25.84 and Th. 3.40.3.

Electra serves as a counterpoint to Clytemnestra in her response to the news. Right away, before she even hears the account of the pathetic circumstances surrounding Orestes' death, she cries out in grief, expressing a feeling of annihilation that is to be expected at the news that an immediate family member is dead (674, 677). When she feigns believing in Clytemnestra's fleeting grief, Electra further underlines the contrast between her own response and Clytemnestra's, calling attention to her mother's relief at her son's demise when she states with dripping sarcasm and scorn:

ἆρ' ὑμῖν ὡς ἀλγοῦσα κὠδυνωμένη
δεινῶς δακρῦσαι κἀπικωκῦσαι δοκεῖ
τὸν υἱὸν ἡ δύστηνος ὧδ' ὀλωλότα;
(804–6)

How grieved and distressed the unhappy woman was, don't you think, in all her terrible tears and laments for her son, dead in such a way? No, she went away gloating.

When Orestes and Pylades come onstage with the urn that allegedly contains the dead Orestes' ashes, the scene's function is to foreground the sincere bonds of *philia* and genuine mutual affection that unite brother and sister, in blatant contrast to the absence of any familial bonds or affection between them and their mother.[561] The funeral urn becomes a visual metonymy for the strength of the siblings' ties. In witnessing Electra's physical attachment to the urn that supposedly contains his ashes, Orestes is able to see firsthand his sister's devotion to him and her pain at his (alleged) death.[562]

The bond that Electra feels for her brother is indistinguishable from her attachment to her father, Agamemnon. When Orestes finally reveals his identity (1222–3), she expresses her joy in terms that define her brother as dear to her primarily as Agamemnon's son: "offspring of a body most dear to me" (γοναὶ σωμάτων ἐμοὶ φιλτάτων, 1233). The bold use of the plural here (σωμάτων ἐμοὶ φιλτάτων) evokes not one but two bodies, including Clytemnestra's. That very ambiguity further underscores the deliberate nature of Electra's exclusion of her mother's body and role in Orestes' birth: her words suggest both parents, while clearly she has in mind Agamemnon alone.[563] A similar dynamic can be

---

561 A similar function is fulfilled by another unusual passage – the "recognition duo" (Kamerbeek 1974), the only one we have in the extant plays of Sophocles (but there are many Euripidean equivalents; see March 2001, 212).
562 While still in disguise, he asks her to lay down the urn so he can reveal his identity to her; her resistance serves to convey in physical terms the power of her attachment to her brother (1205–16).
563 The telling use of the plural in this sense is noted by Jebb *ad loc.*

seen in her attachment to the servant who, out of faithful duty to the dead Agamemnon, saved Orestes from death when Clytemnestra tried to have him killed so her reign over Argos would be unthreatened: when the servant's identity is revealed to Electra in a second recognition scene of sorts, her response underscores her bond not so much with the servant but with her father, Agamemnon. The power of that bond is brought out in Electra's focus on specific parts of the servant's body, which played a role in aiding Agamemnon: ὦ φίλταται μὲν χεῖρες, ἥδιστον δ' ἔχων | ποδῶν ὑπηρέτημα ("O dearest hands, O messenger whose feet were kindly servants!" 1357–8). In the servant, she sees her own father: χαῖρ', ὦ πάτερ· πατέρα γὰρ εἰσορᾶν δοκῶ ("Welcome, Father, for it is a father that I seem to behold," 1361). His presence is the closest thing to having Agamemnon himself on stage. Just before Orestes and Electra kill their mother, the servant puts the matricides' motive for the killing before the audience's eyes by making Agamemnon present on stage in as concrete a manner as possible. When the servant states, "Now is the time to act" (νῦν καιρὸς ἔρδειν, 1368), Orestes prepares to head into the house by paying his respects to the images of his father's gods, which are standing by the portal – yet another visual reminder of Agamemnon and of his children's allegiance to him.[564]

Clytemnestra is killed before Aegisthus, one of several significant respects in which Sophocles' portrayal of her death differs from both Aeschylus's and Euripides'. As a result, there is no time for Orestes and Electra to focus on their mother's death: the looming threat that Aegisthus still poses enables Sophocles to shift his characters' – and the audience's – focus away from the slaughter of their mother almost immediately. Clytemnestra is done away with in a mere twenty-seven lines. The very brevity of the act and the speed with which the action – and her children – move on from her murder both play an instrumental role in conveying a simple message: the event is not one to dwell on. It is, however, a subject for rejoicing. While Orestes stabs Clytemnestra to death offstage, all that the audience can perceive of the actual death are the queen's cries; standing before the spectators are Electra and the Chorus, whom we watch as they react with joy to the sounds of the matricide being committed.

The moment in which Clytemnestra is slaughtered is strongly reminiscent of the moment of Agamemnon's death in the *Oresteia*. Near the end of the *Agamemnon*, we hear the king cry out as Clytemnestra strikes him: "Oh, I am struck deep

---

[564] Lines 1372–5. The mention of the gods standing at the portal of the palace is strongly reminiscent of the passage from the *Choephori* in which the Chorus of women suggests that the palace shares in their emotional response to Orestes's return: they pray to the "god of the portal" to allow the house to "raise its head in happiness and … with friendly eyes behold in [Orestes] the brilliant light of freedom" (807–11).

with a mortal blow!" (ὤμοι, πέπληγμαι καιρίαν πληγὴν ἔσω, 1343). In Sophocles, it is Clytemnestra whom we hear crying out as Orestes fatally wounds her in retribution for Agamemnon's death:

ΚΛ. ὤμοι πέπληγμαι. ΗΛ. παῖσον, εἰ σθένεις, διπλῆν.
ΚΛ. ὤμοι μάλ' αὖθις. ΗΛ. εἰ γὰρ Αἰγίσθῳ γ' ὁμοῦ.
(1415–6)

CL. Ah, I am struck!
EL. Strike twice as hard, if you have the strength!
CL. Ah, again!
EL. I wish it were Aegisthus, too!

In Aeschylus, the stagecraft created a visual parallel between Orestes standing over the two dead tyrants in the *Choephori* and Clytemnestra's earlier triumphant stance over Agamemnon and Cassandra in the *Agamemnon*. In Sophocles, it is a verbal, not a visual echo with Aeschylus' *Agamemnon* that draws a connection between Agamemnon's murder and Clytemnestra's and stresses the fact that the one is committed in retaliation for the other. When Clytemnestra desperately pleads for Orestes to take pity on her (ὦ τέκνον τέκνον, | οἴκτιρε τὴν τεκοῦσαν, 1410–1), we do not hear Orestes waver as we do in Aeschylus.[565] Instead, we hear from Electra, and her words are a far cry from voicing a sense of the *aidôs* due to a mother.[566] She points out that the queen deserves no pity, because she showed none to Agamemnon,[567] and delights in her mother's having met the same fate as he did (παῖσον, εἰ σθένεις, διπλῆν, "Strike twice as hard, if you have the strength!" 1415).[568]

The queen's *Schadenfreude* when she murdered her husband is the basis for Electra's. In Aeschylus, the siblings' (and the audience's) perception of Clytemnestra's execution contains some seeds of ambivalence. Here, Electra echoes Clytemnestra's joy as we recall it from the *Agamemnon* and strikes a distinctively satisfied chord. When Orestes comes back out of the house once the deed is

---

565 Both Aeschylus and Euripides show Clytemnestra baring her maternal breast in a gesture of supplication; here, the maternal body remains unmentioned, making the lack of pity or *aidôs* of her children easier to condone.
566 The dying Clytemnestra cannot hear her words, of course; they are intended for the Chorus members and the audience.
567 Lines 1142–3. This echoes a comment she makes earlier in the play regarding the fact that she alone experienced pity for her father when he died his pitiful death (100–2).
568 Taplin 1978, 351–2 also makes a note of how much Sophocles has been influenced by the *Cho.* in his pacing of the scene and the rapid succession of movements and short appearances that create such a pace.

done and Electra eagerly asks, "How goes it?" (πῶς κυρεῖ τάδ', 1424), he tersely replies, "All is well in the house" (ἐν δόμοισι μὲν | καλῶς, 1424–5). Neither regret nor remorse appear to phase either Orestes or Electra:

ΗΛ. τέθνηκεν ἡ τάλαινα;
        Ορ. μηκέτ' ἐκφοβοῦ
μητρῷον ὥς σε λῆμ' ἀτιμάσει ποτέ.[569]
                (1426–7)

El. Is the wretched woman dead?
Or. Have no fear that your mother's arrogance will ever degrade you again.

Both of the siblings employ a vindictive tone that underlines the certainty with which they believe in the justice of their mother's execution.[570] The sounds of Clytemnestra's violent death do cause the women of the Chorus briefly to shudder (her cry is "horrible to hear," 1408), but they express no pity; in their minds, the justice of the queen's slaughter is never in question.[571]

The moment the queen understands that she is doomed, she cries out words that confirm the enmity between her and her children: "The house is empty of friends, and full of murderers!" (αἰαῖ. ἰὼ στέγαι | φίλων ἐρῆμοι, τῶν δ' ἀπολλύντων πλέαι, 1404–5). The matricide is committed shortly thereafter.

As she is dying, Clytemnestra calls on Aegisthus. The mere mention of her lover and fellow tyrant is a reminder of their complicity in killing and usurping the power of Agamemnon and of the fact that they are lovers. After the queen is killed, there is no time to dwell on her death and no room for pity or regret, as there will be in Euripides' *Electra*, where Aegisthus is killed long before Clytem-

---

[569] For a different reading of these lines, see Kamerbeek 1974 *ad loc.*
[570] March 2001 *ad loc.* takes the parallel in a similar way, *pace* Friis Johansen 1964 *ad loc.* according to whom Sophocles' conception of the murder of Clytemnestra is identical to Aeschylus' conception of Agamemnon's. On revenge in Greek tragedy, see Mossman 1995 (esp. 169–77).
[571] The women of the Chorus support the offspring of Agamemnon and their mission (to avenge their father) unconditionally throughout. Just before it is carried out, they describe the killing that Orestes intends to commit in terms that reveal their belief that it is sanctioned by the gods and an act of justice: Orestes and his friend Pylades are ὑπόστεγοι | μετάδρομοι κακῶν πανουργημάτων, "pursuers of villainy" (1386–7) who are going to make their dream a reality (τοὐμὸν φρενῶν ὄνειρον αἰωρούμενον, 1390; for the dream, see 472–503). On dreams in Greek culture, see Guidorizzi 2013. I am in full agreement with Kyriakou 2011, 339–47, who rejects as implausible the reading certain scholars have proposed of the Chorus's pronouncement at 1058–65.

nestra.[572] Aegisthus soon comes onstage, and his sheer presence is yet another reminder of Clytemnestra's treacherous association with him. The looming threat that her lover and fellow tyrant poses to the siblings enables Sophocles to move on quickly from the matricide, while Aegisthus's threatening presence and the power that he wields help to further legitimize the killing of Clytemnestra after the fact.[573]

It is a measure of how successful Sophocles is in building affection and sympathy in his audience for the sibling protagonists, and enmity toward the tyrannical usurpers of their power, that even (some) modern viewers respond to the scene in which Orestes stabs his own mother repeatedly with a sword by echoing Electra's satisfaction and excitement. In Sophocles, with Clytemnestra's death, there is no sentimentality, regret, or pity to speak of on the part of the matricides. They are absent to such a degree that Vickers remarks, "It could be that Sophocles ... like Electra, hates Clytemnestra."[574] Knox notes that, at a performance he attended, when Electra called out to her brother, encouraging him to keep stabbing their mother ("Strike twice as hard, if you have the strength!"), a member of the audience could not contain his enthusiasm and jumped to his feet, shouting "Bravo! Bravo!" – mirroring the siblings' feeling of vindication and the pleasure that attends it.[575] Aegisthus's death tends to elicit a similar response, as do the words with which Orestes concludes the play:

---

[572] After her death in Sophocles' play, the children do not refer to Clytemnestra as a mother; they use only indirect phrases (e.g., ἡ τάλαινα), including a periphrasis that defines her by the arrogance that characterized her, primarily in terms of the harm she inflicted on Electra (μηκέτ' ἐκφοβοῦ | μητρῷον ὥς σε λῆμ' ἀτιμάσει ποτέ, 1426–7, quoted above). Scodel 1984, 84 draws attention to the noteworthy fact that the only Furies in the Sophoclean *Electra* are Furies of a sort unheard of anywhere else: they are associated not with murder, but with the adultery of Aegisthus and Clytemnestra.

[573] Aegisthus, who has just been informed of Orestes' (false) death (1442–4), approaches, as Electra notes, "with delight" (χωρεῖ γεγηθώς, 1432), an observation that serves to remind the audience of the enmity that he bears the children; his (misguided) *Schadenfreude* at the thought that Orestes is dead justifies theirs at the thought of killing him.

[574] Vickers 1979, 571.

[575] Knox's observation is noted by March 2001, *ad loc.* Heath 1987, 11 uses the expression "emotive hedonism" to describe the audience's experience of Greek tragedy. I return in more detail to the tragic pleasure associated with revenge below, concerning the death of Aegisthus in Euripides' *Electra*. While the satisfaction that the audience takes in seeing revenge carried out successfully does not necessarily require them to identify with one particular party (Konstan 1999, 9), in the case of Orestes and Electra *versus* Aegisthus, as we have seen, the identification of the audience with the siblings has been carefully prepared throughout Sophocles' play.

χρῆν δ' εὐθὺς εἶναι τήνδε τοῖς πᾶσιν δίκην,
ὅστις πέρα πράσσειν γε τῶν νόμων θέλοι,
κτείνειν· τὸ γὰρ πανοῦργον οὐκ ἂν ἦν πολύ.
(1505–7)

> This is the punishment that should come at once to everyone who likes to act against the law – death. Then there would be little crime.

Surely not all modern audiences unanimously condone this endorsement of the death penalty, as the Sophoclean passage does. Yet the power of the emotional conditioning that they had undergone did evoke at least one group of modern audience members' unanimous endorsement of the killings. At the 1983 staging of the play by Cacoyannis in Epidauros, as Orestes spoke his closing words before leading Aegisthus off stage to kill him, the audience sounded its approval with an enthusiastic, spontaneous round of generalized applause.[576]

In Aeschylus, Orestes ignores the bloodied body of Clytemnestra, virtually (and perhaps, as I have suggested, literally) hiding it behind the bloodied garment that his mother used to ensnare his father. In Sophocles, Clytemnestra's corpse also remains hidden from her children's eyes after her death: after the off-stage killing, her corpse is never within her matricidal children's sight or the audience's. When the *eccyclêma* is rolled out with her corpse on it, it is covered with a cloth, which keeps it removed from view. The spectators do not ever see the mother's lifeless body through her children's eyes – a lens that might risk evoking their pity or the spectators' and elicit *pathos*.[577]

---

[576] On the caution required in defining *one* audience response as naïve; see e.g., Goldhill 2012, ch. 2.

[577] The scene in which Electra and the Chorus recount the killing of Agamemnon early on in the play provides a significant point of comparison with Clytemnestra's death. Removed in time though it is, Electra and the Chorus members recall the scene of Agamemnon's death in a manner that makes the killing vividly present in the audience's mind, focusing on his body and his voice. Electra describes (97–102) how Clytemnestra and Aegisthus split his skull with a bloody axe, "as woodcutters fell an oak," while the Chorus evokes the king's actual cries:

οἰκτρὰ μὲν νόστοις αὐδά
οἰκτρὰ δ' ἐν κοίταις πατρῴαις,
ὅτε οἱ παγχάλκων ἀνταία
γενύων ὡρμάθη πλαγά.
(193–6)

> Pitiful was the cry heard at his homecoming, and pitiful the cry as your father lay on his couch, when the stroke of the brazen axe tore straight into him.

The situation is as follows: Orestes (in disguise) has lured his mother's lover to the scene under the false pretense that he will be able to see his (Orestes') dead body and thus verify with his own eyes that the last threat to his and Clytemnestra's rule over Argos has been effectively removed by a fortuitous accident, as the false messenger account has alleged. Aegisthus eagerly requests that the covering be removed from the corpse that he believes to be Orestes' so that he can relish proof of the destruction of the threat to this throne and make all his subjects witness the fact that he is now the uncontested ruler of Argos:

οἴγειν πύλας ἄνωγα κἀναδεικνύναι
πᾶσιν Μυκηναίοισιν Ἀργείοις θ' ὁρᾶν,
ὡς εἴ τις αὐτῶν ἐλπίσιν κεναῖς πάρος
ἐξῇρετ' ἀνδρὸς τοῦδε, νῦν ὁρῶν νεκρὸν
στόμια δέχηται τἀμά, μηδὲ πρὸς βίαν
ἐμοῦ κολαστοῦ προστυχὼν φύσῃ φρένας.
(1458–63)

I tell you to open the doors and to reveal the sight to all the Mycenaeans and the Argives, so that if anyone was previously buoyed up by vain hopes centered on this man, he may now see him a corpse and accept my bridle, and not need violent chastisement from me to teach him sense.

The tyrant imagines that he is about to stage a display that would confirm his rule over Argos. In fact, he is the one on display: Orestes and Electra are watching him, and so are the audience members.[578] Orestes enjoins him to lift the covering off the body himself, for "it is not mine but yours to look on this and to speak loving words!" (αὐτὸς σὺ βάσταζ'. οὐκ ἐμὸν τόδ', ἀλλὰ σόν, | τὸ ταῦθ' ὁρᾶν τε καὶ προσηγορεῖν φίλως, 1470–1). No need to call Clytemnestra, Orestes adds with seething sarcasm; she is already near. Dramatic tension builds leading up to Aegisthus's discovery of the corpse's identity; the audience already knows whose body it is, of course, but the reaction that its revelation is going to elicit from Clytemnestra's lover and fellow tyrant promises to be appreciable, particularly because of the element of surprise that the revelation will comprise.[579] Ac-

---

The pity they voice for Agamemnon provides an opportunity for them to express pity and support of Electra, and to stress her suffering and the outrageous treatment she endures because of her mother. No such pity is ever expressed for Clytemnestra.

578 There is great irony to the wording that Aegisthus uses to express his wish that the covering be lifted from the corpse for all to see it: he inadvertently points to the metaphorical covering that is about to be removed from his own eyes when he discovers the true identity of the corpse in question.

579 Aegisthus expects to rejoice (χαίρειν), 1456.

cordingly, all eyes are on Aegisthus as he looks down upon the queen in the moment when he lifts the *kalumma* from the covered body.

This is the only point at which Clytemnestra's body is seen after she is killed – and Aegisthus is the only one who sees it. The point of focus is not her body itself but Aegisthus's response to the sight of her corpse — a response that is being watched by Orestes, Electra, and the spectators, and which spotlights the queen's culpability. Instead of having her children see the body directly, Sophocles has Orestes and Electra look on and watch while Aegisthus sees her lifeless body. Their perception of their mother's death is mediated by the horrified gaze of her complicit lover; the focus is on the latter's incriminating emotional response to the sight, rather than on her mangled body itself. The revelation of Clytemnestra's dead body to him (and only him) provides an opportunity to call to the matricides' and the audience's minds the incriminating ties that bound the two to each other when she still lived and, hence, the violation that she committed of her ties to her husband and children through her affair. On seeing Clytemnestra's corpse, Aegisthus cries out in grief and dismay: "Ah! What is this I see?" (οἴμοι, τί λεύσσω; 1475). His extreme distress underscores the bond between the adulterous lovers and provides justification for the matricide that has just been committed and the tyrannicide that is to follow. His dismay stems from the nature of his relationship to Clytemnestra: they were lovers, partners in crime, and fellow tyrants.

Aegisthus's death follows soon thereafter. He is to be seen and heard no more ("Let him say no more," μηδὲ μηκύνειν λόγους, 1484; "Set [him] ... out of our sight," ἀλλ' πρόθες ... ἄποπτον ἡμῶν, 1487–9). Just as Clytemnestra's murder was only perceived in relation to Agamemnon's, so is Aegisthus's. Orestes orders him to go where Agamemnon was slaughtered (1495–6), so he can meet his doom in the same place where the act for which he is being punished was committed.

Euripides' *Electra:* Motherhood destroyed

In his *Electra*, Euripides revisits Clytemnestra's execution at the hands of her own children by – quite literally – making his audience see the matricide from a different viewpoint.[580] In Euripides, after the siblings commit the deed,

---

[580] On Euripides' engagement with Aeschylean tragedy and the prominent ways in which his poetics display a self-conscious awareness of his indebtedness to his predecessors, see Torrance 2011; she discusses metapoetry in Euripidean more broadly in Torrance 2013.

they engage in an alternative lament (*kommos*) with the Chorus, in which they report their deed to each other and to the audience and simultaneously reenact it through gestures and movements.[581] As they revisit the scene that has just taken place offstage, they become, in effect, spectators to their own deed. Their vision of the deed as they watch it *a posteriori, qua* spectators, challenges the preconceptions and values in the name of which they acted.[582] In the process of reenacting the scene of Clytemnestra's death and putting it before their own and the spectators' eyes in its stark and horrific reality, they look at their mother's body, both literally (onstage) and as they view it through their retelling, with the newfound lucidity granted by their retrospective lens. Only then do they come to realize the full moral and human cost at which obtaining revenge for their father has come.[583] Their vision of and relationship to Clytemnestra's body bears directly on their assessment of the matricide and on their perception (as well as the audience's) of the morally, socially, and religiously problematic nature of the killing that they have committed.[584]

Unlike the other two tragedians, Euripides makes the siblings who avenge their father by killing Aegisthus and Clytemnestra perceive these deaths as distinct, not as two parts of a justified whole. In his play, Orestes' and Electra's perceptions and treatments of the two bodies distinguish sharply between the justified killing of Aegisthus and the far more troublesome death of Clytemnestra at their hands. One of the significant decisions that Euripides makes in this respect is to follow Aeschylus by putting the murder of Aegisthus *before* that of Clytemnestra, in contrast to Sophocles' very deliberate choice to have Clytemnestra's death precede Aegisthus'. The death of the queen is thus the culminating point of Euripides' play.

The aftermath of the slaughter of the adulterer and tyrant Aegisthus in Euripides is treated as unequivocally as it is in Sophocles. For the murderers, it evokes a strong sense of vindication, nothing more. A messenger relays the ac-

---

581 On words and gestures of lament (including ritual lament) and grief in Greek tragedy, see Medda 2013, 1–24.
582 On the complexity of the experience of performers on the Athenian stage, as one of estrangement or reincarnation, see Lada-Richards 1997.
583 Iakov argues that the siblings are psychologically fragmented and even contradictory, in a reflection of the deep crisis of the time when the play was produced (Iakov in Markantonatos and Zimmermann 2012, 121–38). On Euripides' use of structure and dramatic composition as means of introducing such reversals and surprises as we have here and regarding the greater challenges that the more open structures of his plays pose to his audience, see Mastronarde 2010, ch. 3, with bibliography.
584 I offer a longer discussion the *kommos* of Euripides and especially of the role of the siblings' reenactment of their deed in Allen-Hornblower 2015.

count of the death to Electra. The murder takes place in a field where Aegisthus is in the process of offering sacrifices to the gods. As he leans over the entrails of a sacrificial animal, he reads signs of ill omen that point to the imminent return of Agamemnon's son, Orestes. In fact, Orestes is standing right behind Aegisthus, wearing a disguise and claiming to be a Thessalian on his way to sacrifice to Olympian Zeus at the Alpheus (781–2). Every one of Aegisthus's words as he prepares for his sacrifice makes his hostility to the children of Agamemnon blatantly obvious. He openly states his enmity in the presence of the very target of his hostile wishes. By underlining his culpability and enmity just moments before he is killed, his words invite Orestes to consider the death he is about to inflict as both necessary and justified.

Aegisthus addresses several wishes to the gods, asking for divine favor in preserving his and Clytemnestra's prosperity, while praying that Orestes and Electra may continue to endure their miserable condition, thus providing Orestes (and the audience) with grounds for indignation (*to nemesan*) on at least two counts:[585] pain on seeing the undeserved good fortune of the bad (Aegisthus' and Clytemnestra's)[586] and pain at the undeserved misfortune of the good (Agamemnon's children, who, insofar as they have committed no harm and merely seek to avenge their father, can be called "good").[587] Addressing the "nymphs of the rocks," Aegisthus voices the wish that his "bitterest personal foe and enemy to [his] house" should fare badly.[588] In other words, he is asking the gods that Orestes and Electra should meet with ill fortune, as the messenger spells out when he relates Aegisthus's words to Electra after the murder has taken place: "meaning Orestes and you" (805–8). Unbeknownst to Aegisthus, his prayer is pointing up his enmity (ἔχθιστος ... πολέμιος, 832–3) toward the children of the king whose power he has usurped and whose wife he has taken as his mistress, even as one of these children is standing right behind him.[589]

---

[585] On the different sorts of indignation as categorized by Aristotle, see above, n. 415.

[586] Compare the *Choephori*, where the Chorus describes the painful experience of witnessing the unjust rewarded while the victims of injustice remain unavenged (lines 639–45).

[587] See Arist., *Rh.* 1452b36–53a4, and Belfiore 1992, 229–30.

[588] In the *Choephori*, Electra articulates a similar prayer at Agamemnon's tomb, though hers is a prayer for good fortune for herself and Orestes and evil for Aegisthus and Clytemnestra (138–51).

[589] The siblings' misery is familiar to the audience at this point: Electra in particular has repeatedly underscored her deplorable condition and degrading marriage to a farmer, as well as the unjust treatment reserved for Orestes, barely saved from death by his sister when Aegisthus contrived to have him killed. See e.g., Electra's speech to Orestes in disguise (300–31).

Right after he speaks his incriminating prayer, Aegisthus is attacked and dealt a deadly blow by Orestes. The messenger reports Aegisthus's extremely violent death in lavish and grisly detail. Orestes clobbers him from behind, striking him "in the spine and smashing his vertebrae" till "his whole body from head to toe convulsed and writhed in a bloody death agony" (842–3). As a modern audience, it is tempting to assume that such a brutally painful death would have (or should have) elicited some form of sympathy. In fact, it is far more likely that it is meant to indulge the sort of satisfaction that stems from revenge. Aristotle writes that "revenge is pleasant ... and victory is pleasant too, not only for those who are competitive but for everyone; for there arises a sense [or image: *phantasia*] of superiority, for which everyone has a passion."[590] This is just one example of an accepted standard of Greek popular morality, according to which there is satisfaction in seeing death rightfully dealt to one's enemies.[591] The graphic details concerning Aegisthus's slow agony after the hideous smashing of his spine are, I believe, indulging the audience's sense of vengeful pleasure. Despite its extreme brutality, Aegisthus's death is meant to elicit the feeling that Justice has been done, a feeling that is all the more probable as the audience has been conditioned to experience a third facet of *to nemesan* by this point: pleasure at the deserved misfortune of the bad – the sort of misfortune that does not evoke, but actually excludes, pity.[592]

The context in which Aegisthus is killed – after uttering such egregiously incriminating words – condones the feeling of justice felt by Orestes in eliminating a tyrant who is a direct and hostile threat to his own person.[593] Other internal audiences to the killing (in addition to Orestes) are also present and corroborate this sense of just revenge. Several servants of the house witness the murder of their master Aegisthus; initially, they take up arms against Orestes and his accomplice Pylades. The point of portraying such a fleeting initiative on their part is to show how quickly – indeed, immediately — their hostility toward Orestes is reduced to nought when the son of Agamemnon reveals his true iden-

---

[590] See Konstan 1999, 9, translating Arist., *Rh.* 1.11.13–14. Konstan quotes from the *Rhetoric* in pointing up the distinctly pleasurable experience of the audience in watching the gory death inflicted by Hecuba on Polymestor to avenge her son's death in Euripides' play bearing the queen of Troy's name.
[591] See Dover 1974, ch.4, "oneself and others" esp. 180–4.
[592] See Arist., *EE* 3.7.1233b24–6. On "justified indignation" and how it expels pity, see Arist., *Rh.* 2.9.1387a2 and Moles 1984, esp. 327 ff.
[593] Aegisthus is offering a sacrifice to propitiate the gods in his favor and bring harm to Agamemnon's children. This serves as a vivid reminder, both to Orestes and to the audience, of his shameless usurpation of power and his continued wielding of such power over Argos.

tity to them.⁵⁹⁴ In an instant, the servants shift to joy and celebration, "rejoicing and hallooing." They proceed to crown Orestes as the murdered Agamemnon's successor and avenger, who has rightfully obtained the position that was his by birth (854–5). Their joy spreads to the Chorus members, who leap in joyful dance "like fawns" (859–65), and then on to the principal addressee of the account, Electra, who feels "free to open [her] eyes" at last (868). It is reasonable to assume that this ripple effect also spread to the external audience, which at this point has been led to share in a sense of justified indignation and can enjoy the tragic pleasure that lies in seeing revenge duly accomplished.

Orestes and Electra continue to indulge their sense of vindication and their pleasure in revenge after the murder of Aegisthus, as they contemplate with relish the various ways they could mistreat his body. Both siblings take joy in the thought of desecrating the adulterer's remains and toy with the idea of impaling him on a stake and giving him up to wild animals (895–8). Urged to carry on by Orestes, Electra casts aside her hesitations about gloating over the corpse of her enemy for fear it might be considered *hybris* by some (902) and draw envy (φθόνος) onto her. He dismisses any qualms on the basis that "harming enemies" brings no censure (903, 905–6). Accordingly, she launches into a tirade in which she expresses pure delight as she stands over the dead body of her mother's lover, with the gratification to be expected from one who has been rehearsing a vengeful speech long since but never had the power to deliver it to the wrongdoer's face, as she is able to do now.⁵⁹⁵ The tyrant's severed head is a subject for rejoicing, as the Gorgon's head was for Perseus (856).⁵⁹⁶ While abuse of an enemy's body pushes the limits of acceptable behavior,⁵⁹⁷ it is not clear to what extent the siblings' delight here is portrayed as a transgression; at any rate, no one else present offers a word of reproach, and there is not a word encouraging moderation uttered by the Chorus. What we can say with certainty is that, aside from indulging the tragic pleasure that stems from victorious revenge (perhaps to an extreme degree), the primary function of the siblings' delight in

---

594 An old servant of the house recognizes his rightful master and verifies his identity at 852–3.
595 The extreme nature of Electra's character in such scenes has led many critics to dismiss her as lacking in a basic, common humanity with which the audience may identify; see e.g., Conacher 1967, 201 ff. Kitto 1939, ch. 12 calls Electra "a middle-aged virago" (351). Her reaction in the aftermath of Clytemnestra's death, as we will see, calls for a more nuanced assessment of her character.
596 On the possibly derogatory implications of the parallels drawn between Orestes and Aegisthus, and Odysseus and Perseus throughout the play, see Goff 1991; Cropp 2013.
597 As noted by Blundell 1989, 55 ff.; also noted by Cropp 2013, *ad* 905–6.

the aftermath of Aegisthus's death is the contrast that it sets up with their reaction to Clytemnestra's death.

The transition from Aegisthus's murder to Clytemnestra's is fairly swift. Orestes deals summarily and dismissively with the corpse of his mother's lover, ordering his servants to carry it off into the darkness and hide it from sight for fear Clytemnestra might discover what has happened when she arrives at Electra's hut according to plan. At this point, Clytemnestra comes into view. Orestes' ambivalence regarding the murder he is about to commit – matricide – begins from the moment Clytemnestra appears on stage and comes within his line of sight. Euripides highlights the emotional impact that Clytemnestra's presence has on her son from the start. From the moment he catches sight of her, his words foreground what he sees in her: the maternal body that gave birth to him. He dwells on the physical bond between them with some insistence: "No, I see the one that has engendered me, that gave me birth," (οὔκ, ἀλλὰ τὴν τεκοῦσαν ἥ μ' ἐγείνατο, 964). The very redundancy of his words provides a constant reminder of the blood ties between him and his mother and of the fact that she gave him life through birth. He hesitates and turns to Electra: "What, then, shall we do? Shall we really slay *our mother?*" (τί δῆτα δρῶμεν; μητέρ' ἦ φονεύσομεν, 967). Electra rejects Orestes' wavering, but the words she employs to egg her brother on actually call attention to the power exerted by the mere sight of his mother's body on her brother: "Surely you are not seized by pity since you caught sight of your mother in person?" (μῶν σ' οἶκτος εἷλε, μητρὸς ὡς εἶδες δέμας, 968). Clytemnestra's presence puts the incontrovertible corporeal reality of the queen before Orestes' eyes – and he sees in her not the murderer of Agamemnon or lover of Aegisthus primarily, but his mother.[598] In killing her, he will be taking the life of the one who gave him his own: "How can I kill her, who nurtured me and bore me?" (πῶς γὰρ κτάνω νιν, ἥ μ' ἔθρεψε κἄτεκεν, 969). The motif of childbirth, present from the moment Clytemnestra appears, forms a backdrop to the entire scene and will take on considerable significance after Clytemnestra's death, as we are about to see.

Euripides presents his audience with an Orestes in whose eyes his mother's identity is defined, first and foremost, by the act of having given birth to him, not by what she has done (kill Agamemnon). The sight of Clytemnestra's body leads Orestes to begin to recognize the sacred nature of a child's bonds to his mother

---

[598] On the ambivalence of the young male character of Orestes in light of other Euripidean instantiations of the same type, see Mastronarde 2010, 280–306. Mastronarde points up Orestes' discomfort with the role of avenger of his father assigned to him by the mythological tradition and highlights the challenges to certain aristocratic ideals of male achievement that Euripides puts forward in Orestes' unease.

and to waver at the prospect of committing matricide. The acknowledgment and recognition that Clytemnestra is his mother sets in motion the process that reaches its climax in the excruciating realization, after he kills her, of how profoundly unnatural and morally reprehensible the act of matricide is. Already now, Orestes openly questions Apollo's oracle, stressing its lack of wisdom and its immorality and even wondering aloud if Apollo was really the one who voiced it and not "some avenging demon who had taken on the guise of the god." In the end, he condemns Phoebus's oracle as simply wrong (οὔ τἂν πιθοίμην εὖ μεμαντεῦσθαι τάδε, 981).[599]

Electra, however, goads her brother on with relentless coaxing, ultimately convincing him to commit the unspeakable deed (962–87). In doing so, she fulfills the role that was given to Pylades in Aeschylus's *Choephori*.[600] Orestes' persistent reluctance throughout the argument with his sister prepares the audience for the overwhelming emotions that will take hold of him (and Electra) immediately after the bloody murder of his mother. His hesitations stem from concerns regarding the exile and pollution with which he will have to pay for the shedding of his mother's blood, but also from the moral qualms that come with the recognition that he simply should not kill his own mother (μητέρ', ἣν οὐ χρῆν, κτανεῖν, 973).

Electra's retorts all markedly avoid ever acknowledging their mother's presence and physicality and the relationship that binds them to her: every utterance on her part relentlessly reverts back to one single, obsessive mental image – the vision of Clytemnestra killing her father (970, 974, 976, 978, 984).[601] She invokes the will of Apollo and the moral necessity of avenging their father, which she returns to like a mantra ("avenging your father," πατρὶ τιμωρῶν σέθεν, 974; "our father's vengeance," πατρῴαν τιμωρίαν, 978). When Orestes heads into the home of Electra and the farmer to whom she has been married to wait for their mother and execute the god's order, yielding to a combination of injunctions, threats, and accusations of cowardice, all spoken by his sister, he reveals his sense that the act he is about to commit is both awesome and awful with a

---

[599] For the questioning of Apollo's moral sanity, see lines 971, 973, 979, and 981.
[600] Conacher 1967, 203 ff. points out the noteworthy distinction between Aeschylus's matricides (including Electra), who are guided by divine command; Sophocles' Electra, who is motivated by heroic ideals of a breadth that goes "beyond the ordinary human level;" and Euripides' Electra, who is guided, not by "divine commands or absolute ideals of loyalty," but by a less noble and merely personal hatred of her mother.
[601] On the *stichomythia* here, see Schwinge 1968, 85–100.

marked *polyptoton*: δεινοῦ δ' ἄρχομαι προβήματος, | καὶ δεινὰ δράσω γ' ("it is a dreadful task I am beginning and I am about to do dreadful things," 985–6). The deed is a trial, he says, and a bitter one at that (πικρὸν, 987).[602]

Clytemnestra arrives in her carriage, and an *agôn* between Electra and her mother ensues. The queen proffers justifications in her defense that the audience expects: they are the very same ones voiced by her in Aeschylus and Sophocles – namely, Agamemnon's murder of Iphigenia and the insulting presence of his concubine, Cassandra.[603] Electra levels all the accusations at her mother that she had earlier mentioned in Clytemnestra's absence: her killing of Electra's father, Agamemnon; her adulterous affair with Aegisthus; and the miserable condition to which she has subjected both of her children.[604] Euripides also veers significantly away from Aeschylus's and Sophocles' portrayals of the queen, however. His version of Agamemnon's widow is a far cry from the gloating, vindictive, and perverse queen of Aeschylus. As Electra hurls one accusatory and venomous remark after another at her, Clytemnestra voices a combination of self-reproach and regret, which makes her increasingly worthy of sympathy in the audience's eyes:

... καὶ γὰρ οὐχ οὕτως ἄγαν
χαίρω τι, τέκνον, τοῖς δεδραμένοις ἐμοί.
οἴμοι τάλαινα τῶν ἐμῶν βουλευμάτων·
ὡς μᾶλλον ἢ χρῆν ἤλασ' εἰς ὀργὴν πόσει.
(1105–10)

In fact, my child, I'm not so very glad at what I've done. Alas! How foolish I was in my planning, how excessive the anger I nursed against my husband!"[605]

The queen's words evoke a sense of conscious fallibility on her part. This helps to give her character nuance and finesse and humanizes her in the spectators' eyes.[606]

---

602 The contrast between the two siblings contributes to characterize Orestes as timid and marked by uncertainty, and Electra as determined and vindictive; see Grube 1941, 302–6; also Conacher 1967 *passim*.
603 See lines 1018–29 and 1030–40.
604 Lines 1060–96.
605 The order of the lines is problematic; see Cropp 2013 and Jebb 1894, both *ad loc*. Sophocles' Clytemnestra takes an antithetically unapologetic stance (*El.* 549–51).
606 See Cropp: "Here Euripides makes Clytemnestra, if not sympathetic, at least vulnerable and ordinary in her anxiety to please both Electra and Aegisthus... . She is very different from Aeschylus' or Sophocles' Clytemnestra ... and from hybristic victims such as Aegisthus... . Her regrets foreshadow her children's later remorse" (Cropp 2013, *ad* 1102–46).

Some have suggested that the subtler portrayal of Clytemnestra, particularly her emotional ambivalence toward the murder of Agamemnon, is essential to making her children regret their deed after they kill her.[607] However, if it is in fact the case that, as Cropp suggests, "her regrets foreshadow her children's later remorse,"[608] we should not assume that her expression of regret is only or even mainly what influences her children's assessment of their mother's deed (killing their father) and the justice (or lack thereof) of the matricide. Such a nuanced version of Clytemnestra certainly points up Euripides' enrichment of his characters' psychological depth (in comparison to, say, Sophocles' Clytemnestra) and his prominent use of his characters' emotional responses to explore this psychological depth.[609] Yet it bears emphasizing that it is not Clytemnestra's more appealing character traits and her own disapproval of the act that she has committed that make her children consider her execution morally and humanly wrong in the end.[610] It is rather, purely and simply, the fact that a mother has been killed by her own children. An unsympathetic Clytemnestra would be just as deserving of the horror that her children display as the more human one that we have here, as is clear from their reactions to her execution in its aftermath.

There is considerable irony to the fact that Electra lures her mother into her humble country abode with the false news that she has just given birth to a child (1124).[611] Her lie brings to the fore the motifs of maternity and childbirth once more, which Electra uses here to manipulative ends.[612] Electra's words as she follows Clytemnestra into the house convey her joy at the prospect of sacrificing her mother to the gods by sending her to meet her death, in just requital for her father's slaughter; these words are, of course, only heard by the audience (1139–46). Inside, Orestes waits. A choral ode follows, in which the Chorus of young

---

[607] Kamerbeek 1974, in his commentary on Sophocles' *Electra*, contrasts Sophocles' Clytemnestra with Euripides' and links the queen's regret in Euripides with the children's remorse.

[608] See above note.

[609] On Clytemnestra's dissatisfaction with herself as a naturalistic touch, see Kitto 1939, 356–7.

[610] For one thing, Orestes is not present when she voices her regrets, and he is the one most struck by the abomination of the matricide after the fact.

[611] Aegisthus has married the princess to this peasant so as to ensure that she might not have any noble offspring who could grow up to claim their right to the throne of Argos as descendants of the deceased king Agamemnon. The farmer himself provides this information when he speaks the play's prologue. He also mentions that Electra is still a virgin (44).

[612] Mossman 2001 examines the gendered nature of both Clytemnestra and Electra's speech in Euripides' *Electra*. On the psychological implications of this lie and its place in the portrayal of Electra's character, see Hall 2006, 60–98.

women recounts in vivid terms the killing of Agamemnon by Clytemnestra, reproducing in direct speech the actual words spoken by the king to his ruinous wife (1151–4). The ode makes reference to requital (ἀμοιβαὶ κακῶν), the shifting winds within the house (μετάτροποι πνέου- | σιν αὖραι δόμων, 1146–7), and justice (δίκα, 1155); all point to the murder that is about to take place and to the chain of causality that has led to it, including Clytemnestra's adultery (1156). The overarching theme of the song is clear: her killing is just punishment.

All of a sudden, the Chorus is interrupted by Clytemnestra's death cries: "Children, in the gods' name, do not kill your mother!" (ὦ τέκνα, πρὸς θεῶν, μὴ κτάνητε μητέρα, 1165).[613] The metrical interruption marks the momentousness of the murderous act under way and the shift in mood that attends it.[614] In stark contrast to the image of Clytemnestra with which the Chorus members left off, envisioning the queen in the powerful and destructive stance of wielding an axe and likening her to a lioness, the most supreme of hunters (1163), Clytemnestra's final words reveal her as a vulnerable woman, hunted down and unarmed. In an attempt to save her life, she appeals to the nature of the relationship between her killers and herself, begging them, her children (ὦ τέκνα), to spare her, their mother (μητέρα). The Chorus members then adopt a radically different tone from their preceding song: they bewail Clytemnestra's fate and pity her (ὤιμωξα κἀγὼ πρὸς τέκνων χειρουμένης, "I too wail for you, overpowered as you are by your own children," 1168; σχέτλια μὲν ἔπαθες, "cruel are the things you have endured," 1170), despite the unholy deeds that she has committed, which they acknowledge (ἀνόσια δ' εἰργάσω, "yet you did unholy things <to your husband>," 1170). From this point on, references to retribution and to the gods as justification for the murder of Clytemnestra rapidly disappear from both the Chorus's and the characters' lines. Increasingly, the siblings' focus shifts to the body of Clytemnestra, and the horrific nature of the act of matricide becomes ever more manifest, to their eyes and to ours.

The door to Electra's house opens, and the corpses of Aegisthus and Clytemnestra are displayed in the doorway. The mere sight of Orestes and Electra standing over the two bodies, with blood visible everywhere, carries significance for the audience. First, the onstage display of the matricides near their mother's and her lover's bodies is a conspicuous visual echo of the scene of the *Agamemnon* in which Clytemnestra stands triumphantly over her husband's and his concubine's corpses. As we have seen, Aeschylus was the first to exploit the poten-

---

[613] As in Sophocles, Euripides' Clytemnestra cries out in a manner that echoes the cries of Agamemnon in Aeschylus.
[614] Her words, screamed offstage, interrupt the flow of dochmiacs (mostly) in the final choral ode with the sudden introduction of iambs.

tial for connecting the two murders (Agamemnon's and Clytemnestra's) visually and causally: his trilogy includes just such a visual echo, when Orestes is shown standing over Clytemnestra's and Aegisthus's bodies in the second play, the *Choephori*. Euripides' scene thus not only echoes the murder of Agamemnon and the Cassandra by Clytemnestra as it is portrayed in Aeschylus but also invites comparison with the Aeschylean version of the aftermath of the murder of Clytemnestra (and Aegisthus).[615] However, the visual echo of the *Agamemnon* and *Choephori* is where the parallel ends; or rather, that very parallel brings out all the more the distinctions between the dramatists' vastly different portrayals of the aftermath of Clytemnestra's death.

The way in which the murder of Clytemnestra is reported in Euripides is both unexpected and supremely effective. Resorting, as the ancient tragedians had to, to words in order to report to the audience (and any internal addressees) the violent act that could not be shown onstage, Euripides has the very ones who committed the murder describe it, just as Aeschylus had Clytemnestra herself report the killing of Agamemnon to the Chorus and audience. Unlike Clytemnestra in Aeschylus, these killers do not gloat. Following Clytemnestra's death, Orestes and Electra painfully regret what they have just done and engage in a long lament over their mother's dead body, along with the Chorus. They stand over her corpse and verbally (as well as physically) reenact the entire scene of their mother's death at Orestes' own hands; as they envision what they have just seen, so too does the audience. Their emotional response is the focal point of the entire closing scene preceding the arrival of the Dioscuri. Their reactions center on precisely what Athena and Apollo had dismissed in the trial scene of Aeschylus's *Eumenides:* the maternal body, in its concrete physicality, as a giver of life.[616]

The description of the death of Clytemnestra in Euripides is unusual in several ways, including its mode of delivery: song. Following Clytemnestra's death, a *kommos* begins (1172–1237), a song of lamentation, in which Orestes (and Electra to a lesser degree, though the attribution of some lines is uncertain) and the Chorus sing in response to one another. There is a *kommos* in Aeschylus's *Choephori* as well, but it precedes the killing of Clytemnestra, and its purpose is quite the opposite from the present one: it is a lament for the dead Agamemnon and an attempt on the part of his children to summon their father's powers

---

[615] On the likely use of the wheeled platform in Euripides' *Electra* and for other remarks concerning the staging, see Cropp 2013 *ad loc.*
[616] Segal 1985 and Murnaghan 1988 both emphasize the importance of Clytemnestra's corporeality in the eyes of her children in Euripides' version of her death, in contrast to the denial of that corporeality in the other two playwrights' versions; see also Vickers 1979.

so he can aid them in avenging him and bringing about the death of their mother, Clytemnestra. The *kommos* in Euripides reflects the profound shift of focus in his characters' perspective, in contrast to Aeschylus's. Here, the *kommos* is also sung by Orestes and Electra, but rather than leading up to, preparing for, and anticipating Clytemnestra's death, it follows it. Instead of a lament calling upon their dead father at his tomb, it is a lament over the lifeless body of their mother, whom they have just stabbed to death. They do not seek to summon any particular power through their song; they simply dwell helplessly on the deed they have done, in graphic visual detail.

For the entire length of the sung exchange between the matricides and the Chorus, the siblings provide a narrative of the queen's death and describe their responses to it, both at the time that they killed her and in the present time of their narration, moments after they have committed the deed. The *kommos* thus combines within it two different speech genres of Greek tragedy. On the one hand, the sung exchange (*amoibaion*) between the siblings and the Chorus recounts the death as it happened and thus provides the information usually included in a messenger speech. On the other hand, this messenger speech is part of a sung performance: specifically, a song of lamentation.[617] Lamentation and messenger speech become one, with two additional, extraordinary twists: the messenger speech is spoken by the very perpetrators of the deed being reported and the lament is sung by the very murderers of the person being lamented.

The murderers (primarily Orestes, although scholars disagree about the attribution of the lines throughout the exchange)[618] report each step of the killing to one another and to the Chorus in slow, painstaking detail with a combination of dismay and horror. In Aeschylus, Orestes' speech and averted gaze following the murder enabled him to ignore, to a significant extent, the human cost of his action and the sheer horror of killing one's mother; Euripides forces his characters, as it were, to look on at their own deed as spectators by having them bear witness to and recount what they have just done. Extreme distress takes hold of them as they retell, and verbally and physically reenact, the most pathetic moments of the murder scene "through dance, gesture and words."[619] In doing this, they undergo the agonizing experience of "viewing" their mother's body as it is attacked by her children. As he begins to recount the actual killing, Orestes asks

---

[617] Regarding the *epikêdeion* as the funeral song sung over the body of the dead, cf. Procl. quoted in Phot., *Bibl.* 321a30.
[618] See below, n. 620.
[619] Roisman and Luschnig 2011, *ad loc*. For a discussion and comparison of mimetic actions in ancient Greek drama and ritual, see Segal 1993, especially the sub-section of ch. 2 on "Tragedy, song, and ritual."

the Chorus (and, presumably, Electra), "*Did you see* how the poor woman thrust her breast from her robes in the midst of the slaughter?" (κατεῖδες οἷον ἁ τάλαιν' ἔξω πέπλων | ἔβαλεν ἔδειξε μαστὸν ἐν φοναῖσιν, 1206–7). One of the siblings includes several visual details regarding Clytemnestra's gestures: how she put her hand to Orestes' face, how she clung to his cheeks, and how he, in turn, dropped his sword, melting when he saw the "limbs that bore [him and Electra] pressing to the ground" (πρὸς πέδωι | τιθεῖσα γόνιμα μέλεα; τακόμαν δ' ἐγώ, 1208–9).[620] When the Chorus expresses disbelief that anyone could look their own mother in the eye while dealing her a deadly blow, Orestes confirms that the sight was so unbearable that he was only able to carry it out by veiling his eyes:[621]

ἐγὼ μὲν ἐπιβαλὼν φάρη κόραις ἐμαῖς
φασγάνωι κατηρξάμαν
ματέρος ἔσω δέρας μεθείς.

(1221–3)

I threw my cloak about my eyes
And began the sacrifice with my sword,
Thrusting it into my mother's throat.

Electra admits that she continued to egg him on and "grasped the sword" with him at that point; the acuteness of her regret at her gesture, whether it was virtual or actual, is clear (1218–26).[622]

---

620 The attribution of the lines is problematic; Denniston 1939 follows Wilamowitz in attributing 1206–9 to Electra. Cropp 2013, on the other hand, states that it is "quite clear" that these lines are Orestes' but does not provide any argumentation for his certainty. For reasons to accept Seidler's τακόμαν here, see Mastronarde 1979, 70.
621 In doing so, Orestes is also avoiding the binding that comes with supplication; on supplication in general (including the important role of touch), see Gould 1973, 85–90. On characters veiling themselves in Greek drama as a sign of grief or that they see themselves as polluted, see Cairns 2011. In Orestes' case here, the veiling could be interpreted as a combination of both: he wants to avoid his mother's gaze and the pollution that would come with acknowledging her status as a suppliant; at the same time, that veiling could be seen as prefiguring the grief we are about to see him display in the aftermath of the killing. It is also worth bearing in mind Orestes' apprehension and heightened sense of shame at the prospect of meeting Clytemnestra's father and his grandfather Tyndareus, and especially his fear at the thought of meeting the latter's gaze (and judgment), in *Orestes* 460–1 (see the quotation with which I opened the chapter and n. 621). On shame and 'face,' see Dover 1974, esp. 236 ff.
622 Critics disagree on whether Electra physically participated in the deed, as 1224–5 suggest if taken literally. Whether she actually "grasped the sword" or not, the claim stresses her involvement in the killing and her resulting sense of guilt. Internal indications point to the lack of differentiation between the two siblings when it comes to their responsibility in killing their moth-

Euripides clearly had noted how, in Aeschylus (and, perhaps, in Sophocles, if the latter's play preceded his), the matricides' physical disengagement was central to their ability to consider the killing of their mother coldly, mainly if not strictly as a deserved punishment. His matricidal pair comes to recognize the sacred ties of kinship to their mother as they watch the spectacle of her physical body enduring the unspeakable. The marked use of terms referring to the act of watching (and not wanting to watch) Clytemnestra as she died, the numerous instances in which her killers refer to touching her (and avoiding her touch), and the concrete references to her body parts and movements as her helpless limbs fell to the ground in supplication – all turn the matricides into closeup eyewitnesses to the deed, as they do the Chorus members and the audience. The precise visual and tactile detail made possible by the closeup vantage point from which they experienced it draws the audience into the scene's physicality, making the spectators watch the scene with the same directness and proximity to the vulnerable maternal body of Clytemnestra as the children who actually perpetrated the monstrous deed. The reenactment even includes sound: we hear the desperate plea that Clytemnestra addressed to Orestes now spoken by him, as he somewhat eerily adopts the voice of the mother whom he has just killed and whose supplication he rejected: τέκος ἐμόν, λιταίνω ("My child, I beseech you!" 1215).

By presenting their deed from the perspective of onlookers ("Did you see … ?"), the siblings express an increasing sense of distance and alienation from their own action. It is as though they were seeing someone else commit the violation; the way they recount the deed puts them in the position of bystanders taking in each violent movement required to kill the supplicating Clytemnestra in all its raw atrocity, at a point when they are just as powerless to prevent the event from unfolding as the audience members sitting in the theater. The audience's and the matricides' perspectives fuse into one single, powerless, and paralyzed gaze. In their verbal and physical reenactment of the scene, the siblings' language and gestures lead them to gradually rediscover the very "corporeal inextricability" of their lives and bodies with their mother's, which their Sophoclean and Aeschylean counterparts so vividly deny.[623]

---

er: Clytemnestra's final, desperate plea is addressed to both of her children (1165), and the Chorus begins to cry for her as both of her children are overpowering her (1168).

623 See Murnaghan 1988, where she focuses on Orestes' denial of his physical relationship to his mother in the *Oresteia* and his concealment of his mother's body through his speeches in Aeschylus (she briefly discusses Euripides at 36). Compare Orestes' retrospective assessment of his deed in Euripides' *Orestes*, where, as Cairns notes, "the emphasis is on Orestes' intellectual apprehension of his crime" (Cairns 1993, 304). In the *Electra*, by contrast, Euripides em-

As they embrace the stance of spectators to their deed, the siblings' assessment of its morality and justice shifts as well. Orestes claims to have acted "in reprisal for [his] pains" (1181) but asks that Earth and Zeus bear witness to the bloody, "defiling deeds" wrought by his own hand (1177–82).[624] Pointing to the dead body of Clytemnestra (and not, presumably, that of Aegisthus) rolled out on the *eccyclēma*, he voices a sense of shame (and pollution) when he wonders "what host, what pious man will look at [him]" now that he has killed his mother (τίς εὐσεβὴς | ἐμὸν κάρα προσόψεται | ματέρα κτανόντος; 1196–7).[625] While the Chorus addresses Clytemnestra's corpse and tells her that she "justly atoned for murder of the children's father" (πατρὸς δ' ἔτεισας φόνον δικαίως, 1189), it also singles out Electra as the motor behind what they call "unholy, dreadful things" and reproaches her with coercing her "unwilling brother" into doing them (1204–5). The audience is made to perceive the deed, in keeping with the matricides' assessment, as an abomination that is humanly and morally wrong: the siblings' actions are "defiling" (in Orestes' words, μυσαρά 1179) and "lamentable" (in Electra's words, δακρύτα, 1182), even if just in principle (the Chorus's words, πατρὸς δ' ἔτεισας φόνον δικαίως, 1189), and have given rise to "grievous miseries" (the Chorus, ἄλαστα μέλεα, 1187–8).

The very spectacle that the siblings present to the audience when they first emerge from the cottage and reappear onstage after killing their mother helps to convey in visual terms the unnaturalness of their deed. The Chorus calls attention to their appearance: they are drenched in gore, "fouled with their mother's newly shed blood" (μητρὸς νεοφόνοις ἐν αἵμασιν, 1172). Aegisthus's and Clytemnestra's bodies lie in the doorway. As Clytemnestra's bloodied children stand over their mother's equally bloodied body, the audience is presented with a perversion of the tableau that typically follows childbirth. In a horrid reversal of the natural course of events, what the spectators see is not maternal blood covering

---

phasizes the "affective consequences" of Orestes' awareness. While Cairns (*ibid.*) points out that, in *Orestes*, Euripides "separates the element of retrospective conscience from its effects and manifestations," in the *Electra* we might say that he blends the cognitive together with the emotional and even the physical, as the moment of realization and its impact are joined together, and the gestures of mournful reenactment combine with the (intellectual) vision that the matricides cast upon that reenactment.

624 Contrast Aeschylus's *Choephori*, where Orestes calls on gods (all-seeing Sun) to witness what he considers to be the *justice* of his deed, 984–6.

625 Compare Orestes' concern with meeting Clytemnestra's father Tyndareus's gaze in Euripides' *Orestes* 43 and 460–1 respectively; see my earlier mention of these lines above n. 621 in connection with Orestes' veiling his eyes before he kills his mother. On the mixture of fear of disapproval (external judgment) with his own, internal recognition of his having fallen short of meeting the obligations owed to *philoi*, see Cairns 1993, 297–8.

the bodies of infants to whom a mother has given new life; it is maternal blood covering the bodies of children who have taken their mother's life away from her.[626] There are verbal references to childbirth as well, which are equally deserving of our attention, as they contribute to our understanding of the visual tableau that the scene presents: a mother and her children, all covered in her blood.

We have seen how the motif of childbirth emerges from the moment Clytemnestra comes into view and tinges Orestes' perception of her, forming a leitmotiv throughout the following scenes. While Orestes acknowledges the bond that links him to his mother from the instant he sees her, Electra does so for the first time only after her mother's death, experiencing a revelation of sorts as she shifts from the stance of insistent goad and catalyst of the murder to that of horrified spectator to what she and her brother have done.[627] When she blames herself for the killing, she notes the nature of the physical violation that she urged Orestes to commit on their behalf, by referring to her own birth:

δακρύτ' ἄγαν, ὦ σύγγον', αἰτία δ' ἐγώ.
διὰ πυρὸς ἔμολον ἀ τάλαινα ματρὶ τᾶιδ',
ἅ μ' ἔτικτε κούραν.
(1182–4)

"Lamentable indeed [are these deeds], my brother, and I am the one to blame. I burned with ruthless hatred for my mother here, she who gave birth to me, her daughter."[628]

The Chorus further insists on the birth motif when they address the dead queen's corpse, defining her as one who "gave birth" to murderers:

ἰὼ τύχας †σᾶς τύχας† (1185)
μᾶτερ τεκοῦσ'
ἄλαστα μέλεα καὶ πέρα
παθοῦσα σῶν τέκνων ὑπαί.

"Alas for your fortune, mother who bore ... suffering grievous miseries and more at your own children's hands," 1185–8).[629]

---

626 This was noted by Goff, in passing: "It is possible to read a reference to birth itself in the scene" (Goff 1991, 265).
627 Also noted by Denniston 1939 ad loc.
628 Translation based on Cropp 2013.
629 The text here is problematic; see Cropp 2013, ad loc.

In his *Agamemnon*, Aeschylus depicts Clytemnestra as a mother in whose eyes the intimate bond she had with her daughter Iphigeneia remains forever associated with the act of having given birth to her. This conscious insistence on the physical bond that defined her relationship to Iphigeneia bears directly on her sense of the justice there was in killing Agamemnon to avenge her daughter. It was rightful retribution for the sacrifice of Iphigeneia at his hands because he had slaughtered her child, destroying her "birth pang" (ὠδίς):

> ἔθυσεν αὐτοῦ παῖδα, φιλτάτην ἐμοὶ
> ὠδῖν', ἐπῳδὸν Θρῃκίων ἀημάτων.
> (1417–8)

He sacrificed his own child, the darling offspring of my birth pangs, as a spell to charm the winds of Thrace.

In stating that Agamemnon sacrificed her child, "the darling offspring of [her] birth pangs" (ἔθυσεν αὐτοῦ παῖδα, φιλτάτην ἐμοὶ | ὠδῖν'), the queen employs a term that could be used in reference to a child, but was primarily used to designate the travails of giving birth.[630] The bodies of child and mother become poetically undifferentiated in this dense metaphor: ὠδίς, "birth pang," denotes a deep-seated, corporeal attachment, as epitomized by the pain of labor.[631] The

---

[630] Ὠδίς in Aeschylus was used to designate the child in her relationship to her mother: see Dumortier 1935, 27–8.
[631] On the power of ὠδίς (*ôdis*) to evoke the visceral and potent nature of the attachment between mother and daughter in Clytemnestra's eyes, see Loraux 1990, 62–3; on the metaphorical uses of *odynê* and *ôdis*, see Loraux 1990, 67 ff. Concerning the evocation of birth pangs as a poetic tool, see also Holmes 2007. The importance of pain in giving birth as the basis for the mother-child bond as it is presented in Euripides was not lost on Jean Giraudoux, the early 20th century French novelist, essayist, diplomat, and playwright. In his drama, *Electre*, he has Clytemnestra trace the *lack* of a physical or emotional bond between Electra and herself to the time when she gave birth to her daughter. There was, she says, no pain involved: "Où veux-tu en venir? Tu veux m'entendre dire que ta naissance ne doit rien à mon amour, que tu as été conçue dans la froideur? Sois satisfaite. Tout le monde ne peut pas être comme ta tante Léda, et pondre des oeufs. Mais pas une fois tu n'as parlé en moi. Nous avons été des indifférentes dès ta première minute. Tu ne m'as même pas fait souffrir à ta naissance" ("What are you getting at? Do you want to hear me say that your birth was not in any way the result of an act of love – that you were conceived in cold dispassion? Be satisfied. Not everyone can be like your aunt Leda and lay eggs. But not once did you speak inside me. We were indifferent to each other from the moment you were conceived. You did not even make me suffer when I gave birth to you"). Translation mine.

root of the attachment and inviolable bond between mother and child stems (at least in part) from the suffering inherent in the act of giving birth.[632]

Euripides uses the pain of childbirth to point up both the bond between mother and child and the pain that comes with the destruction of that bond, to particular effect: his Chorus make reference to birth pangs when it describes the painful impact his mother's death has an Orestes. Orestes describes how he "melted" when his mother bared her breast to him and pointedly refers to his mother in physical terms that define her as the one who bore him: he melted, he says, from seeing her body collapse as her "limbs that are life-giving" (γόνιμα μέλεα, 1209) fell to the ground. In response, the Chorus members express their sympathy for his pain by exclaiming:

σάφ' οἶδα· δι' ὀδύνας ἔβας,
ἰήιον κλύων γόον
ματρὸς ἅ σ' ἔτικτεν.

(1210-2)

I know well *the pains* you went through, as you heard the wailing cry of the mother who gave you birth!

By defining Clytemnestra as "the one who gave birth to [Orestes]" (ματρὸς ἅ σ' ἔτικτεν, 1212), the Chorus members stress the extent to which matricide is a violation. The word that they use to describe "the pains [Orestes] went through" also corroborates our sense of the violation that has taken place: it is the standard word for labor pains, ὀδύναι.[633] In a feat of poetic compression, the term *odynai* summarizes the interconnectedness of the harm inflicted on the maternal body with the pain that this harm evokes in its perpetrator: Orestes is the offspring of the very body that he has destroyed. That the description of his pain at killing her verbally echoes hers at giving birth to him draws attention to the horrific paradox of matricide. At the close of the scene, Orestes' words again encapsulate the unnatural paradox inherent in his and Electra's deed – Clytemnestra gave life to those who took hers – with the added pathos that he is addressing his dead

---

[632] On the power of giving birth and the role of the pain that it entails in bonding mother to child, see also E., *IA* 917-8 and E., *Ph.* 355-6 (on which, see Mastronarde 1994 *ad loc.*). Aristotle later offered two explanations for the bond created between mother and child in the process of giving birth, one of which corroborates the notion that the pain of labor is central to establishing that bond: "Mothers love their children more for these reasons: the process of engendering offspring is more painful, and they know better that the children are their own," (διὰ ταῦτα δὲ καὶ αἱ μητέρες φιλοτεκνότεραι· ἐπιπονωτέρα γὰρ ἡ γέννησις, καὶ μᾶλλον ἴσασιν ὅτι αὐτῶν, *EN* 1168a25-6).

[633] The significance of the birth motif throughout *Electra* is noted by Hall 2006, 60-98.

mother directly as he articulates it: "So you bore children to be your murderers!" (φονέας ἔτικτες ἆρά σοι, 1229).⁶³⁴

As he revisits the perpetration of matricide and the aftermath of Clytemnestra's death at the hands of her children, Euripides deliberately makes use of a garment in connection with Clytemnestra's body, just as his predecessor Aeschylus did and as Sophocles does too; but the effect is the opposite from the one achieved by the other two dramatists. The parallel makes even clearer the very different light in which Euripides' matricides see their mother's body and assess their deed. In Aeschylus, as in Sophocles, a garment conceals Clytemnestra's body, whether figuratively (and perhaps literally) in Aeschylus or literally in Sophocles. In the *Choephori*, after killing Clytemnestra, Aeschylus's Orestes displays the garment that Clytemnestra used to kill Agamemnon and uses it as a point of focus that "cloaks" the slaughter of his own mother in the vestment of justice, enabling him (and the audience) to avert his (and their) eyes from his mother's corpse and to focus on the just principles in the name of which he, the Chorus, Electra, and Pylades believe him to have acted and in the name of which he is acquitted in the *Eumenides*. In Sophocles, Orestes covers his mother's body with a cloth and conceals it from his (and our) sight: it remains covered from the time of her death, never to be seen or described in its bloodied state by her children. When the cloth is lifted, Clytemnestra's body is uncovered only briefly, but it is not seen by Orestes or Electra, or the audience. Instead, the incriminating gaze of Aegisthus mediates the matricides' and our indirect perception of their mother's body: as the adulterer lifts the cloth, sees the corpse, and recognizes Clytemnestra, he realizes that he must now meet his own impending doom at the hands of Orestes, reminding us of his and the queen's shared culpability, soon to be reflected in their shared doom (1475–8). Her body serves as a tangible sign of her guilt and of the justice of her punishment.

Euripides' use of garments also involves hiding and covering Clytemnestra's body, but in his case, the concealing garments actually draw attention to her corporeal presence and to the horror of matricide, both during the killing and after the fact. The first mention of a garment used to conceal Clytemnestra from sight occurs when the Chorus highlights the specific moment in which Orestes prepared to kill his mother. As the Chorus members imagine the glances that he and Clytemnestra must have exchanged, they simply cannot conceive of a son withstanding the sight of the death of his mother at his own hands:

τάλαινα. πῶς <δ'> ἔτλας φόνον
δι' ὀμμάτων ἰδεῖν σέθεν

---

634 See Foley 2001, 234–5.

ματρὸς ἐκπνεούσας;

(1218-20)

Poor wretch! How could you bear to set your eyes upon your mother as she bled and breathed her last?

Orestes confirms that the sight of his victim was too piteous to bear. So much so, in fact, that he threw a cloak over his eyes before dealing his mother a fatal blow ("I threw my cloak about my eyes and began the sacrifice with my sword, thrusting it into my mother's throat," 1221-3).[635] Orestes covers his eyes to hide Clytemnestra's body from his sight. His gesture marks the son's recognition of the violation that he is committing even as he commits it, while the graphic nature of the details he provides — how he thrust his sword into his mother's throat – gives the audience a glimpse of the horror that he could not bring himself to see.

After Clytemnestra's death, Euripides uses another garment to conceal her body in a manner that distinguishes his matricidal characters from their counterparts in Aeschylus and Sophocles. Orestes orders his sister to "take this robe and cover our mother's limbs" before he addresses his mother's corpse directly, with words that suggest pity and acknowledge the monstrous abnormality before him: "Ah! You gave birth to your own murderers!"

λαβοῦ, κάλυπτε μέλεα ματέρος πέπλοις
<καὶ> καθάρμοσον σφαγάς.
φονέας ἔτικτες ἆρά σοι.

(1227-9)

Electra obeys his order, drawing attention to the act of shrouding the body of her mother: ἰδού, φίλαι τε κοὐ φίλαι | φάρεα τάδ' ἀμφιβάλλομεν ("There, I am putting this cloak over the one loved and not loved," 1230-1). The language Electra uses as she covers Clytemnestra's body highlights the tension at the core of her children's relationship to her; her body is "dear and not dear at once" (φίλαι τε κοὐ φίλαι), but the very act of covering the body is dutiful preparation for it to be laid out and a final mark of filial respect for motherhood destroyed.

The final, dismissive blow dealt to the notion that there was any righteousness to the matricides' deed comes when even the divine justification for killing Clytemnestra – obeying Apollo's oracle — is questioned. Castor, with the partic-

---

635 Quoted above, p. 236.

ular authority of a *deus ex machina*,⁶³⁶ rejects the grounds for the matricide in decrees that seem all the more radical and definitive because of their brevity: Apollo's oracle was not wise (1246); the Kêres (here identified with the Erinyes) will pursue Orestes, but Pallas Athena will ward them off with a mere gesture (holding up her *aegis*, 1252–7); and when Orestes faces trial for murder, he will be acquitted, not because what he did was just, but because Apollo will take the blame for the murder himself: Λοξίας γὰρ αἰτίαν | ἐς αὑτὸν οἴσει, μητέρος χρήσας φόνον, ("for Loxias will take the blame upon himself, since it was his oracle that advised your mother's murder," 1266–7).⁶³⁷ There is a slightly different strain of human helplessness that shines through these many references to the misguided nature of the oracles and decisions of the divine – one equally if not more despairing than the pervasive sense we are given in Aeschylus of an underlying divine order to all human endeavors. The play highlights the "inscrutability of the divine purpose" and the unpredictable mutability of mortals' fortune — both expressions of an earlier, archaic view that lives on, even in this Euripidean play that critics often date to the last decade of the fifth century.⁶³⁸

Euripides' *Electra* is a play in which "breathtaking horror and regret" take center stage.⁶³⁹ The siblings' visual reenactment of Clytemnestra's death and the wave of regret attending it offer an interesting alternative to the vision of the Erinyes that torments Orestes at the end of Aeschylus's *Choephori*. In Euripides, Orestes' focus on his mother's body and his (and Electra's) prominently featured emotional response to her death make clear that it is not solely because of fear of the external consequences of his deed – pollution and divine punishment, embodied by the Furies (or Erinyes), who avenge the shedding of the blood of kin — that he feels such powerful moral and emotional qualms about killing his mother, both before and after the deed.⁶⁴⁰ The Erinyes' threats

---

636 As we have seen, Orestes already questioned Apollo's oracle far earlier but allowed himself to be convinced by Electra's arguments regarding of the necessity of submitting to divine will and of avenging one's father.
637 Translation here is E. P. Coleridge (New York 1938).
638 Lloyd 2013 offers a useful overview of the opposing, traditionalist and ironic readings of Euripides, with bibliography, and gives due attention to the traditional world-view that we hear voiced in the tragedian's plays (especially in connection with the motif of the mutability of fortune). Though other voices do "echo contemporary speculation" (Lloyd-Jones 1971, 147), it would be misguided to overlook the more archaic world-views and assume that Euripides simplistically espouses any one view expressed by his characters (Lloyd 2013, 208).
639 Roisman and Luschnig 2011, 222.
640 It is not clear that the Erinyes that begin to haunt Orestes immediately after he has committed his deed in the closing scene of Aeschylus's *Choephori* are solely a manifestation of pollution

and bloodthirsty pursuit of the matricide that we see in the *Choephori* and at the beginning of the *Eumenides* would be somewhat redundant in Euripides in light of the overwhelming emotional disarray of Orestes and Electra. The siblings' recognition of the horrible nature of what they have done largely eliminates the need for punitive divine pursuit; the divinities are mentioned only in passing at the end, as a nuisance that will be dealt with through Athena's intervention.[641]

Gellie states, "all the driving forces that were in the Aeschylus plays are in his *Electra* but they are on the edge of the play. They are there so that we will notice that they have been pushed aside and that other forces have taken their place... It is Euripides' view... that people respond only to human ... pressures... that we are governed... by the need to manage our emotions."[642] There are no Erinyes with eyes dripping with blood, casting a thirsty and reproachful gaze upon the matricides in Euripides' *Electra*. Rather, his characters are given a chance to take a hard look at themselves. They see their action for what it is on a moral and human level, by taking in its physicality at a most basic level. It is by having the matricides reenact the murder through words and gestures that Euripides puts the body of their mother before their eyes and the audience's. Only then, looking upon the maternal body and watching themselves commit the killing from the standpoint of spectators, do they grasp the full moral and human cost of having avenged their father; only then do they understand the unnatural, abhorrent nature of the deed that they have committed.

---

and preclude any notion of internalized guilt on his part (on "shame culture" as opposed to "guilt culture," see Dodds 1951, 28–63, *versus* Williams 1993). At the same time, in Euripides, Orestes' reluctance does stem in part from concerns regarding the judgment (divine punishment) and consequences (exile) that will result from his action, not solely from considerations of the unconscionable nature of the deed itself. The issue of the role of the Erinyes in Aeschylus hinges on our very understanding of the role of the divine and its interaction with the ancient Greek individual's mind; it is beyond the purview of the present study to attempt to solve it, but Feder 1980, 80, summarizes the complexities of the issue well: "The threatening fantasy figure is both a personified force incorporating social prohibitions and punishments and an internalized agent of control by guilt and fear."

641 Moreover, according to Castor's report, the Furies do not consider Orestes to be polluted. On pollution in the *Oresteia*, see Meinel 2015, ch. 3. Williams 1993 differentiates between guilt, which can be defined as an emotion concerned with the victims of one's actions, and shame, which is concerned with one's own and others' perceptions of the self; if we espouse these definitions, then it might be said that Euripides stresses the siblings' *guilt* as opposed to their shame (Williams 1993, ch. 4, especially 87 ff.).

642 The above quotation is part of Gellie's argument that Euripides' great innovation in his *Electra* is to take events that belong in the high level of myth and tragedy, and to contrast these with procedures that are "kept at the lower level of common behavior" (Gellie 1981, 1 and 3, respectively).

A strange consequence of the siblings' painful acknowledgment of their own transgression is that it partly rehabilitates them in the audience's eyes. As the characters themselves recognize the monstrous and immoral nature of their deed, Euripides humanizes them by having them stress their regret for what they have done. While this regret does not exculpate them of their horrendous deed, it considerably enhances the pathos of their situation. The horror of the killing, but even more so the horror of its impact on the siblings, shows them in the act of enduring a sort of pain that makes them worthy of our pity.

By stressing the importance of the siblings' verbal and visual recognition of Clytemnestra's body *qua* maternal body and featuring it prominently as the medium through which they (and the audience) come to recognize the true abomination of their deed, Euripides explicates what was implicit in Aeschylus and perhaps hinted at in Sophocles: how staunch adherence to abstract principles entails a narrowly restricted vision, which involves deliberate and questionable omissions. He invites his audience to consider the stark visual evidence that his fellow playwrights make their characters avoid. The more peripheral the maternal body remained to Orestes and Electra's vision in the other dramatists' potrayals, the more apt the siblings were to execute her without any ensuing qualms, as they do to a degree (though not without some ambivalence) in Aeschylus and with full confidence in Sophocles.

There is no need for Furies to pursue the siblings at the end of Euripides' play as they do Orestes at the end of Aeschylus's *Choephori*. We find no external intervention that signals to the matricides how misguided and tainted the action they have taken was. Instead, they themselves realize on their own, as their gaze shifts, how much the implications and consequences of their deed had eluded them until then. The source of their changed stance is psychological and internal, as it were, as their realization stems not from the act of envisioning something external (vengeful goddesses with eyes dripping blood chasing after their blood in turn), but from their own outlook onto the dead body before them, and the act that led to that body being no more than a lifeless corpse. In Euripides, the characters' realization of their own limits (and errors) comes from a peculiar, dramatized form of introspection, whereby the characters examine and judge what they have done by externalizing it for each other, and for the audience, through reenactment.

Chapter Four: Neoptolemus Between Agent and Spectator in Sophocles' *Philoctetes*

> "Every one admits how praiseworthy it is in a prince to keep faith, and to live with integrity and not with craft. Nevertheless our experience has been that those princes who have done great things have held good faith of little account, and have known how to circumvent the intellect of men by craft, and in the end have overcome those who have relied on their word."
>
> — Niccolò Macchiavelli, *The Prince*, chapter XVIII[643]

This final chapter focuses on the central character in a play produced by Sophocles late in his career, in 409 BC: the *Philoctetes*. The *Philoctetes* is a play that focuses not so much on Philoctetes' suffering but on the different reactions that his suffering elicits: the witnesses to the eponymous hero's suffering and their responses to it are as prominently featured as the suffering itself, if not more so, and with good reason, given that their responses bear directly on the evolution of the play's plot and Philoctetes' fate. My focus is on the figure of Neoptolemus, one of the play's two protagonists (the other being the eponymous hero himself). He offers an interesting variation from the agents-turned-spectators examined in the previous chapters. He does not shift from one status (that of agent) to the other (that of spectator of the consequences of his action); rather, he alternates between the two for the better part of the work under consideration. At the start of the play, the wily Odysseus entrusts the youth with a mission: tricking the wounded Philoctetes into boarding his ship so the Greeks can bring him to Troy with them, as they must if they are to take the city, according to an oracle. Odysseus exits the stage and proceeds to monitor the play-within-the-play that he has staged from the sidelines, as an offstage playwright and director of sorts. Meanwhile, Neoptolemus obediently goes on to play the part that has been assigned to him, delivering his (mostly false) lines to his designated interlocutor in order to gain his trust and attain the goal that has been prescribed to him: to get the suffering man to board his ship under false pretenses. As he witnesses the spectacle of Philoctetes' suffering firsthand, however, Neoptolemus plays his deceitful role with increasing difficulty. At the sight of his victim's plight, he gradually relinquishes the role of obedient agent devoted to carrying out Odysseus's agenda and becomes an (often completely silent) observer for long stretches of time, in an onstage illustration of *aporia* that suggests his great inner turmoil, until he finally strays from his prescribed script altogether, and espouses a new role, in keeping with what he has come to see as his true nature.

Scholars have discussed and debated at some length the central turning points of Neoptolemus's emotional and moral evolution in the face of his interlocutor's pain, asking mainly when they occur, and why. My contribution centers on how the act of witnessing Philoctetes'

---

[643] Translated by E.K. Marriott; online project Gutenberg edition of Macchiavelli's *The Prince*, http://www.gutenberg.org/files/1232/1232-h/1232-h.htm, 2006.

pain has a significant impact on Neoptolemus and on how that impact (and the ensuing shifts in his stance) are conveyed to the audience. In a play where words are principally a means for Neoptolemus to manipulate his interlocutor in order to implement Odysseus's stratagem and advance the Greeks' agenda, every spoken utterance is suspect. Words cannot be trusted, and each of Neoptolemus's (and even the Chorus's) speeches are notoriously ambiguous, and their degree of genuineness often indiscernible. The playwright has other means of communicating the young man's inner turmoil and transformation to the audience, along with the shifts in the relationship that develops between the two protagonists, by way of extralinguistic means: namely, through sounds. Throughout the chapter, one of the main points of my investigation is to show how the playwright resorts to sounds in order to relate both Philoctetes' pain and Neoptolemus's (sincere) responses to it and in order to mark the critical moments in which true *philia* between the two protagonists comes to be reestablished on solid grounds.

In the works I have analyzed until now, when poets make their protagonists adopt the stance of spectator to the actions they committed earlier, they enable the latter to acquire some form of knowledge or insight regarding the nature and consequences of these actions — but only too late. The status of helpless observer that these protagonists are made to embrace is, I have argued, a poetic instantiation of the very nature of the human condition. The late nature of their learning is as systematic as it is deliberate: the characters remain painfully unable to put it to use. Their lives are defined by a fundamental powerlessness at their core, with the added pathos that they are put in a position in which they are able to realize and recognize their limits by looking upon what they have done, with newfound lucidity perhaps, yet nought to do but endure.[644]

Sophocles' *Philoctetes* presents its audience with a variation on the above scheme in several respects. It, too, focuses on a protagonist who undergoes a significant transformation and evolution when he is put in the position of observing Philoctetes, as well as the consequences of his own actions (and especially of his interactions with the sufferer). However, in this particular drama, the agent-turned-spectator in question (Neoptolemus) is given a chance to act on the knowledge that he acquires as an observer, before it is too late.

Sophocles produced the *Philoctetes* late in his career, at the very end of the fifth century BC. In that year – 409 BC – the spectators at the City Dionysia had barely recovered from the Four Hundred's *coup d'état* two years prior, and the political context and general ambiance was one of division and distrust after repeated, unpredictable, and rapid shifts in power from one political party to another. Social cohesion had suffered a great blow. Fear of treason on the part of any individual or group must have been at the forefront of every audience mem-

---

[644] Clytemnestra in Aeschylus's *Agamemnon* is the exception in that it is with delight that she looks upon what she has done, but that very delight points up her lack of lucidity.

ber's mind. It is this divisive distrust, along with the values and attitudes needed to confront it and maintain a functional and cohesive *polis*, which Sophocles invites us to consider in his *Philoctetes*.[645]

The story of the *Philoctetes* is well known: nine years before the start of the play, while the Greeks were on their way to Troy, the nymph Chryse inflicted a serpent bite on Philoctetes' foot because of an inadvertent transgression on his part. The wound has festered ceaselessly since then, tormenting him with intermittent bouts of intense pain. Because the symptoms of his suffering were (allegedly) disruptive to the proper functioning of the rest of the community, the Greeks opted to abandon Philoctetes on nearby Lemnos while they continued on to conquer Ilium. At the point when the play begins, however, they have just heard from the Trojan seer Helenus that Priam's city will only fall if Philoctetes rejoins their ranks, equipped with the bow he has received from Heracles.[646] In response, Odysseus hatches a plan: Achilles' young son Neoptolemus should befriend and beguile the abandoned hero with a false account of his own betrayal by the Greeks and thereby entice Philoctetes to board his ship under the pretense that Neoptolemus will provide him a safe journey to his home in Malis.

With this play, we are faced with a fascinating dramatic exploration of the novel sort of perspective and awareness that come with the protagonist's embrace of the status of observer. The entire tragedy centers on a hero in pain: Philoctetes.[647] Yet the dramatist focuses his audience not so much on the eponymous hero's suffering *per se*, but on how the spectacle of that suffering is perceived by the other characters in the play (especially the young Neoptolemus), and how they react to it.[648] The play zeroes in on the transformation that the young

---

[645] Ringer 1998, ch. 6 discusses the importance of the immediate political, social, and military context to our understanding of the *Philoctetes* (see especially 101–3), and argues that the dramatist "uses theatrical character and situation as an allegory for a society in profound crisis." Beer, 2004 135 ff. examines the *Philoctetes* in its historical context, and underscores how much it must be understood as a political drama that puts the fortunes of the polis front and center.

[646] See lines 603–21. Lines 66–9 expressly state that Neoptolemus must have Philoctetes' bow in his possession, but the oracle is ambiguous regarding whether Philoctetes himself, or just his bow, is necessary for the Greeks to conquer Troy (see e.g., Gill 1980 and Roberts 1989). Winnington-Ingram 1980 (ch. 12) examines the relevance of the bow question and its ambiguity as essential to the economy of the play, its reversals, and its suspense.

[647] Throughout this chapter, I follow Avezzù's text (Pucci et al. 2003). My translation is largely based on Lloyd-Jones 1994. An earlier version of parts of this chapter was published in Allen-Hornblower 2013, where I look at Sophocles' *Philoctetes* from a comparative angle, with a particular focus on André Gide's reception of Sophocles in his *Philoctète*.

[648] Wilson (1941, 273) notes that the play's interest centers on "the latent interplay of character, on a gradual psychological conflict," something that led it to be rather unpopular and dis-

man undergoes, and the actions he undertakes, when he is forced by Philoctetes' bouts of agony to suspend (at least temporarily) his participation in the plot he has been dutifully carrying out, and is put in the position of observer. Winnington-Ingram describes the play as one in which "the lasting effects of a cruel act are displayed."[649] We might add that it is a play in which those lasting effects are viewed, evaluated, and (eventually) acted upon by an internal spectator: Neoptolemus.

Unlike the other characters that I have considered up to this point, Neoptolemus does not go from being an active participant in the action to being a mere onlooker considering its aftermath. He is not powerless to change the outcome of his initiative; rather, he is faced with a choice. For (roughly) the first half of the play, Neoptolemus is an agent. As long as he implements Odysseus's plan, he is playing the role assigned to him by the son of Laertes: Odysseus is the virtual playwright and stage director of a play-within-a-play, which features Neoptolemus as its principal actor, and which is intended to trick Philoctetes, whose reactions (trust and friendship) are also anticipated and planned, unbeknownst to the victim of the plot.[650] When bouts of searing pain assail Philoctetes and interrupt the flow of Neoptolemus's conversation with him, however, the young man can no longer carry out his mission, nor act out his fake role. He strays from the lines that have been assigned to him, going off script with cries of *aporia*.[651] For the audience, watching the *Philoctetes* in these moments involves watching Neoptolemus witness Philoctetes' suffering, and watching him evolve as a result of what he sees. During these crucial turning points in the play, the young man is in limbo, wavering in "a kind of agonized suspension" between the status of agent, carrying out the mission entrusted to him by Odysseus, and that of spectator.[652]

---

regarded by critics leading up to the twentieth century. Cf. Taplin 1971, 26: "It is a play of relationships and communication, not of great deeds."

649 Winnington-Ingram 1980, 280 (and all of ch. 12).

650 The entire play is built around this metatheatrical premise of a play-within-a-play, with its own internal spectators constituting an audience on stage; on this, see e. g., Falkner and Ringer (both 1998); Lada-Richards 2009, with bibliography; also Goldhill 2009, 27–47. On metatheater in Sophoclean drama in general, see chapter 2, n. 289.

651 Critics disagree as to whether Neoptolemus plays his deceptive role up until that point with relish or reluctance; see Winnington-Ingram 1980, 285 n. 19.

652 See Halliwell 2002, 212, where he discusses the ways in which pity lends itself particularly well to the theatrical experience because the pitier is one who is in the position of an observer and witness, rather than a participant in the action. In his examination of metatheater in *Philoctetes*, Ringer notes the particular nature of Neoptolemus's shifting status, and the important role it plays in his evolution: "Neoptolemus is a surprising combination of internal actor, a char-

What does Neoptolemus see from the observer's standpoint, and how does what he sees effect change in him, his course of action, and his relationship to Philoctetes? First, there is the spectacle of Philoctetes' pain. The mere act of watching Philoctetes endure great suffering is a powerful factor of change onto itself, because of the pity it evokes (from Neoptolemus, at least). Yet watching Philoctetes interact with him also puts before Neoptolemus's very eyes a model of heroic integrity, nobility, and humanity with which he is naturally inclined to identify, and has only grudgingly renounced. In Philoctetes, Neoptolemus sees more than a sufferer; he sees a better, truer version of himself.[653] As the play progresses, he is not only increasingly frozen, physically and verbally, by the spectacle of Philoctetes' agony; he is also more hesitant to continue the play-acting that he has been putting on, because the integrity of his victim and interlocutor leads Neoptolemus to value Philoctetes' judgment and friendship more and more. Moving away from the utilitarian perspective inculcated in him by Odysseus, he feels a growing sense of shame that is directly tied to the lens through which he now reevaluates his own deeds — a lens that is increasingly aligned with Philoctetes' viewpoint: namely, an uncompromising stance of unshakable integrity. As Neoptolemus comes to respect and admire the hero as a father figure and role model, the spectacle of his own trickery, which he knows Philoctetes will soon uncover, becomes unbearable in his own eyes. By watching Philoctetes, he is given the opportunity to measure the impact that his actions and decisions have on the sufferer, on their relationship, and on his own sense of integrity.

Contrary to the characters we have examined until now, Neoptolemus is not one who is powerless, looking upon the outcome of his actions when it is too late. Instead, the turning point for him comes when he anticipates how his action is going to be seen from the viewpoint of Philoctetes, a man he has come to respect and admire, after he successfully carries out the mission entrusted to him by Odysseus. Neoptolemus does not so much witness the aftermath of his actions *a posteriori* as he foresees how that aftermath will be seen, through the eyes of his victim.

By casting Neoptolemus in the role of spectator, by prominently displaying his hesitation – but also and especially his power to choose between opposite moral choices – and by depicting the transformation that the young man undergoes as a result of being a spectator to Philoctetes' suffering, Sophocles leads the

---

acter playing a "role" within his role and onstage audience to Philoctetes' suffering" (Ringer 1998, 104).

653 Regarding Neoptolemus's return to a nature that was his all along, see Fulkerson 2006 (below, n. 689).

audience to reflect on their own role as spectators of suffering, including outside of the theater. As he makes them watch Neoptolemus react to the sight of Philoctetes before him and observe the evolving relationship between the play's two protagonists,[654] Sophocles challenges his audience to ponder a range of social and ethical questions along with Achilles' son, including which values and attitudes need to be upheld in human interactions between *philoi*; what emotional response and form of action pain should evoke from conscientious onlookers; and what the consequences and potential benefits of a compassionate response (or lack thereof) are for the sufferer, his witness, and the community at large.[655]

There is, however, a major potential obstacle to the audience's being able to perceive whether and when Neoptolemus's response to the spectacle before him does evolve. From the time he agrees to take part in Odysseus's plan at the beginning of the play, the youth's words and stance are rife with ambiguity, often leaving both the Chorus and the audience at a loss as to where he stands.[656] Deceit plays such a central role from the start of the play that it is difficult to detect when Neoptolemus is telling the truth and when he is lying. As the young man and his subservient sailors obligingly carry out Odysseus's plan, they are playing a (sham) role, doing or saying whatever they assume might be most effective in hoodwinking the wounded Philoctetes in order to promote Odysseus's agenda and (allegedly, at least) the reason of state. Throughout the tragedy, *logos* serves primarily as a channel for deceit and, ironically, as something of an obstacle to true communication between the characters.[657] Even the Chorus's words are implicated: some of the choral utterances are designed to aid in carrying out Odysseus's plan, and one even includes a fake religious utterance, in a brief, sung

---

[654] Both Philoctetes and Neoptolemus share the status of protagonist in this play, as many scholars have noted.

[655] The social, ethical, and political role of pity within Greek tragedy has been amply discussed. On the moral and practical outcomes of emotions (pity in particular) and the importance of Neoptolemus's emotional and moral evolution, see Lada-Richards 1993 and Hawkins 1999, as well as Sternberg 2005 and Visvardi 2007 and 2015, each with bibliography. The moral questions at the core of the *Philoctetes* are narrowly intertwined with the emotional process through which Neoptolemus is morally educated over the course of the play; see e.g., Knox 1964; Alt 1967, 122 ff.; Whitman 1951, 175 ff.; Nussbaum 1976, 1986, 1999; Aultman-Moore 1994; Gibert 1995; Worman 2000; Konstan 2001; Fulkerson 2006; Apfel 2011; and Austin 2011, as well as, more recently, Fulkerson 2013, 66–79. Concerning the ethical and social implications of (Neoptolemus and the Chorus's) pity, see Blundell 1989.

[656] Even Neoptolemus himself at times does not quite seem to know in which direction he is leaning, and the true meaning of some of his utterances is as obscure as his judgment is muddled and confused.

[657] Podlecki 1966 reads the *Philoctetes* as a "case-study in the failure of communication" and focuses on the power of *logos* to bring about such a breakdown.

ode.[658] Neoptolemus's and the sailors' ambiguous words and their constant shifting between allegiance to Odysseus and pity toward Philoctetes create misunderstandings among the participants in the plot themselves, leaving the audience equally uncertain as to which lines are meant sincerely and which are not.[659] As a result, the process of watching the *Philoctetes* and of watching the witnesses to his pain as they react to it is, to a large extent, a guessing game,[660] and commentators often disagree regarding the veracity of a given statement and the potential double meaning of any expression, which may be intended by the speaker to be understood in one way by Philoctetes and in another by those who are complicit in seeking to dupe him.[661]

Yet if Sophocles' play invites its audience to watch Neoptolemus as he watches and reacts to Philoctetes, then it is of the utmost importance that they should be given some pointers as to how and when the human interactions between Philoctetes and the witnesses to his pain, and Neoptolemus especially, are genuine.[662] It is particularly important that the audience be able to perceive the crucial turning points in Neoptolemus's emotional and moral evolution, as well as the stimuli that spark that evolution. It is likely because of the problematic use of the spoken word, or *logos*, on the part of the play's *dramatis personae*

---

[658] This egregious example of a staged performance of false emotion is the Chorus's highly problematic and much-discussed perjured oath (391–402), which it utters immediately following another false tale from Neoptolemus, in which he tells Philoctetes of the dishonor that he, too, allegedly endured among the Greeks (343–90). Regarding the blasphemous oath, see Bers 1981 and, more recently, Fletcher 2011, ch. 2.

[659] The internal audience formed by the Chorus is left wondering about the veracity of any statement on the part of their leader, Neoptolemus, while they themselves, through their own frequently ambivalent words, make their allegiance to Odysseus's cause or Philoctetes' often indecipherable. I explore one such example, which occurs in lines 833–8, below.

[660] Seale 1982 explores the abundant use of staging and other visual effects in the *Philoctetes* to maintain suspense and surprise the audience.

[661] See, for instance, Pucci *et al.* 2003, 231 *ad* 582–90. Even Neoptolemus's silences leave the audience uncertain as to where he stands — and that is precisely the point (see recently Goldhill 2009, 38–55). There are some exceptions, including, first and foremost, those words uttered when Philoctetes is not on stage (as in the case of the *parodos*, examined later). Others include, but are not limited to, when characters utter an aside that is not intended to be heard by the other characters (although what is and is not an aside is not always straightforward) or when they inadvertently voice spontaneous reactions, whose display does not contribute to and might even hinder the implementation of their scheme. In such instances, the audience has no reason to doubt the sincerity of their responses or to suppose that they are the fruit of calculation.

[662] The question is, of course, that of when the other Greeks are being genuine; Philoctetes, in true Achillean fashion, is entirely genuine throughout.

that Sophocles resorts to another means of conveying the important shifts in the dynamic between the two main characters. One of the central goals of this chapter is to examine that means.

In what follows, I bring to the fore how Sophocles uses sounds – descriptions of sounds, the actual production of sounds, and the depiction of varying reactions to sounds – to depict the key turning points in the relationship between Philoctetes and those who witness his pain, and the major milestones in Neoptolemus's transformation. In a play where words (*logos*) most often serve to deceive,[663] sounds fulfill a unique dramatic function on the level of internal communication, by enabling communication among the characters of the play, and on the level of external communication, between the characters and the audience. These sounds play a crucial role, not only in conveying the nature, intensity, and complexity of Philoctetes' pain to those who witness it (internal and external audiences alike), but also in communicating Neoptolemus's responses to it. While, as audience members, we cannot trust the youth's actual words at any given point, we can rely on his visceral responses and cries to convey the gradual emotional and moral transformation that he undergoes as he sees Philoctetes suffer and as he measures the impact that his actions and decisions have on the sufferer, on their relationship, and on his own sense of integrity. Like the spectacle of Philoctetes' suffering, sounds have an irreducible, inherent "truth" to them in this play; they are not contrived or manipulated to carry out an agenda but, rather, spontaneous expressions of actual feelings and pain, which reveal fundamental truths about those who utter them, as well as those who perceive them.

The first part of this chapter explores how Sophocles uses references to the sounds of Philoctetes' environment to stress the hero's pain and its powerful impact on its audience, even before the hero comes onstage for all to see. Beyond the strictly physical, there is a broader, social origin to his pain, which stems from his isolation, and an important function fulfilled by the natural soundscape of the island on which he has been abandoned, especially at the start of the play, is to bring to the fore this social dimension of his suffering.[664] Philoctetes' loneliness is expressed as a longing for a witness and especially for an interlocutor to

---

[663] Podlecki 1966; Rose 1976.
[664] Philoctetes' isolation has been explored at some length, particularly with regard to the hero's gradual sense of identification with his natural surroundings (and its beasts). His isolation is a central motif throughout the play; see e. g., Biggs 1966, Nussbaum 1999, Worman 2000, and Goldhill 2012, especially 124–5. On the sense of alienation and dehumanization that stems from this isolation, see also Knox 1964, 117 ff.; Rose 1976, Segal 1981, 292 ff., 470; and Taplin 1987.

hear him and perhaps answer his cries.⁶⁶⁵ The fact that his loneliness and longing are expressed through sounds and echoes prepares the audience for the considerable importance that is later given to the actual echoes that Neoptolemus voices when the lens through which he sees Philoctetes and himself changes dramatically.

The subsequent section of the chapter examines Sophocles' use of the sounds made by the suffering Philoctetes, and the reactions (and sounds!) that they elicit, as a means of mapping and implicitly ranking the discrete ethical dispositions of those who witness his suffering, according to their responses. By contrasting the different responses, the tragedy spotlights the process by which Neoptolemus eventually comes to uphold the heroic moral standards of his father, Achilles, and to establish truthful bonds of friendship with Philoctetes. I devote particular attention to the crucial turning points in the young protagonist Neoptolemus's evolution, which are partly communicated to the audience by way of vocal signs of his own moral pain — the first hints that the establishment of a true relationship of *philia* between him and the eponymous hero is (still) possible.

The healing presence of a witness and interlocutor

The most immediately obvious choice that Sophocles makes to highlight the suffering associated with Philoctetes' isolation is to make Lemnos a deserted island.⁶⁶⁶ The result is that, in Sophocles' portrayal, Philoctetes' abandonment by his fellow Greeks has amounted not just to his exclusion as an individual from the community of his *philoi*, but also to an effective denial of his suffering.⁶⁶⁷ Without any form of social recognition or external witness to his pain, it is as though that pain did not exist, other than in and for the sufferer.⁶⁶⁸

---

665 In featuring, first, the absence of any interlocutor for Philoctetes, and then, the different possible human responses to his suffering on the part of his witnesses, the play brings the social dimensions of suffering to the fore. The social aspects of Philoctetes' pain are an important component of his suffering. His pain also affects his social interactions with others, by eliciting their pity (or not), as we will see.
666 This is a deliberate and significant deviation from the Lemnos of the other *Philoctetes* plays, produced by Aeschylus and Euripides: both included a Chorus of Lemnians. Perrotta 1935, ch. 7 emphasizes the centrality of this isolation motif and the suffering that it causes Philoctetes, and compares this choice on Sophocles' part with the other two tragedians'.
667 According to Odysseus's account, Philoctetes made loud cries and was a nuisance to the entire community of his fellow Greeks. Yet, as Odysseus himself is aware, in abandoning Phil-

Starting in the *parodos* of the play, the Chorus prepares the audience for the considerable importance that they and Neoptolemus are about to have (including in the suffering hero's eyes) as the only ones in ten years to witness Philoctetes' suffering.[669] The group of Neoptolemus's sailors are standing by Philoctetes' cave together with their young leader, and examining the hero's dwelling place in his absence.[670] They look upon Philoctetes' environment and the visible signs of his disease, and they imagine the dreadful, solitary life he has been forced to lead since being rejected by his peers nine years prior.[671] Achilles' son notes the concrete consequences for the sufferer of having no one at his side: there was no one to provide him with medicinal aid to relieve his pain.[672] The Chorus members dwell rather on the pain that has stemmed from his isolation, and his aching desire for the compassionate presence of a fellow human being.[673] They express their understanding of the harrowing nature of Philoctetes' seclusion when they first voice pity for the hero, stressing the excruciating nature of his affliction, but also harping to a notable degree on the pain he no doubt felt from having had to endure it alone, with no compassionate witness at his side:[674]

---

octetes, the Greeks are guilty of a grave violation of *philia* (see Blundell 1989). The play itself lays particular stress on this violation by dwelling on its consequences for Philoctetes.

668 This is why Neoptolemus's affectation that he has not heard of Philoctetes and his excruciating wound elicits such pain on Philoctetes' part (lines 254–316).

669 Perrotta 1935, 413 ff. contrasts the play's prologue, which, he states, puts forward Philoctetes' future mission at Troy, with the *parodos*, which accentuates his suffering. The very same man the gods have beaten down, they now elevate once more, P. notes, comparing e.g., Oedipus in *Oedipus at Colonus*. I discuss this reversal at greater length in a chapter in a forthcoming volume on Disgust, edited by Lateiner and Spatharas (Allen-Hornblower 2016).

670 The *parodos* is a "shared parodos" (see Kitzinger 2008, 80 ff.): it consists of several exchanges between the Chorus (their parts in sung stanzas) and Neoptolemus (his parts in anapests). After convincing Achilles' son to enact his plan, Odysseus has exited the scene, for fear Philoctetes may recognize him. Inoue 1979 offers a short discussion of a sound word at the beginning of the *Philoctetes*; she does not consider the *parodos*.

671 See lines 150–200.

672 For Neoptolemus' reaction, see lines 164–8. The audience is later informed that the hero has found an herb that helps to alleviate his pain (645–50).

673 Cf. Rose 1976, 60: "At a time when Euripides, Aristophanes, and perhaps others were exploring the idea of a life full of peaceful isolation from man in the friendly company of beasts, Sophocles seems to have been at pains to emphasize the horrors of real, total isolation from human society."

674 In line 171, the absence of a σύντροφον ὄμμα does not signify that Philoctetes has "no companion to look on" (Lloyd-Jones); rather, it signals the *absence of a friendly onlooker*: "l'assenza di un occhio amico" (Pucci in Pucci et al. 2003, 12 ad loc.).

Χο. οἰκτίρω νιν ἔγωγ', ὅπως,
μή του κηδομένου βροτῶν
μηδὲ σύντροφον ὄμμ' ἔχων,
δύστανος, μόνος αἰεί,
νοσεῖ μὲν νόσον ἀγρίαν
. . . .
οὗτος πρωτογόνων ἴσως
οἴκων οὐδενὸς ὕστερος,
πάντων ἄμμορος ἐν βίῳ
κεῖται μοῦνος ἀπ' ἄλλων
στικτῶν ἢ λασίων μετὰ
θηρῶν, ἔν τ' ὀδύναις ὁμοῦ
λιμῷ τ' οἰκτρὸς ἀνήκεστ' ἀμερίμ-
νητά τ' ἔχων βάρη.
ἁ δ' ἀθυρόστομος
Ἀχὼ τηλεφανὴς πικραῖς
οἰμωγαῖς ὑπακούει.
(169–73, 180–90)

I pity him, in that with none among mortals to care for him
and with no companion to look after him, miserable, always alone, he suffers from a cruel sickness
. . . .
This man, inferior, perhaps, to none of the houses of the first rank,
lies without a share of anything in life, far from all others, with beasts dappled or hairy,
and pitiably in his pain and hunger he endures afflictions incurable and uncared for.
And she whose mouth has no bar, Echo, appearing far off, responds to his bitter cries of lamentation.

Though they have neither come face to face with Philoctetes nor heard his cries, Neoptolemus's men construe a mental tableau of the hero's solitude, mainly by picturing the soundscape that defined his existence. They start by noting the absence of an onlooker: there is no one to watch over him (169–70).[675] They then shift from sight (ὄμμα) to sound, and go on to imagine him voicing desperate cries of pain that remain unanswered in the midst of the wild and barren environment surrounding him. How bitter the disembodied Echo, "human sound dehumanized,"[676] must have been – an ironic acknowledgment of his cries that underlines, through its presence, the absence of any human response, by making

---

[675] Note the conspicuous repetition of μόνος line 172, which occurs again at 183. Biggs 1966 notes the specificity of Philoctetes' situation in comparison with other Sophoclean heroes: while isolation may be the "standard heroic problem" resulting from self-sufficiency, in Philoctetes' case, "a new tone is evident. Constant repetition of *monos, eremos* emphasize *loneliness*."
[676] The quote is from Austin 2011, 83.

the emptiness around him resound with nothing but the reverberation of his own voice. The Chorus is an especially effective channel for harping on Philoctetes' deprivation of any form of human communication. Their very mode of expression provides a poignant contrast to the picture of solitude that they are conjuring up: even as they sing about the lack of any human response to Philoctetes' voice, they do so as a collective entity, echoing one another in antiphonal responsion from *strophe* to *antistrophe* and reinforcing each other's meter, rhythm, themes, and emotions, through song.[677] Their song itself is a reflection of the communal nature of the choral body and thus offers a meaningful contrast with Philoctetes' lonesome cries, which can only pathetically echo themselves.[678]

From the moment he enters the stage, Philoctetes makes constant references to the absence of any human presence to witness his pain, foregrounding how great a source of suffering it has been for him, and putting it on a par with the physical pain that he has to endure.[679] In his initial exchange with Neoptolemus following the *parodos*, he repeatedly proclaims his overwhelming joy at hearing the mere sound of a human voice.[680] Companionship, he says, would have alleviated his burden: any witness, by his sheer presence, would share in

---

[677] Kitzinger's commentary of the passage (2008, 83) calls attention to the meaningful contrast through which the Chorus conveys the solitude of Philoctetes' voice:

> The adjectives ... describe [Echo's] meaningless voice and her physical distance from the one she echoes. The lack of another's physical and meaningful presence, which Echo metaphorically represents, stands in stark contrast to the Chorus members' own echoing of each other in song ... the Chorus feels in a particular way the desolation and futility of a disconnected voice that only echoes itself.

Some thematic connections between *strophe* and *antistrophe* further contribute to the echoing effect within the choral song, thus providing an even clearer foil for Philoctetes' isolation.

[678] The connection between the echo motif and music, as well as the contrast these two create with isolation, is pinpointed by Nussbaum 1999, 258:

> The Chorus is at the same time describing its own activity and its absence in the outcast's life, thus making the audience vividly aware of the role of music in civic affairs. The spectators are right now hearing articulate sounds that denote fellowship, religion, civic discourse. In Philoctetes' world, those humane noises are absent.

[679] See, for example, lines 169–73. In lines 265–9, the adjective *erêmos* occurs twice in the space of just four lines.

[680] See lines 219–35. Both Philoctetes and the Chorus underline the important role played by the social acknowledgment of an individual's pain: both suggest that any compassionate presence actually contributes to lessening the pain (while also making direct assistance possible, by providing the sufferer with healing herbs, 697–9).

his pain and make it more bearable. The absence of a witness has, conversely, made his pain worse: οὐχ ὅστις ἀρκέσειεν, οὐδ' ὅστις νόσου | κάμνοντι συλλάβοιτο (281-2).[681] Later in the play, when Neoptolemus pretends to head back to his ships, Philoctetes falls at the youth's knees in supplication, begging the Greeks not to desert him, desperate at the thought of being left again to endure his plight alone. His pleading words pointedly underscore his dread of solitude with a hendiadys:

προσπίτνω σε γόνασι, καίπερ ὢν
ἀκράτωρ ὁ τλήμων, χωλός. ἀλλὰ μή μ' ἀφῇς
ἐρῆμον οὕτω χωρὶς ἀνθρώπων στίβου
(485-7)

I fall to my knees before you, helpless though I am in my misery, and lame: but please, do not leave me thus, deserted, far from where any man treads.

Conversely, after he loses consciousness in the face of an especially acute bout of pain, Philoctetes awakens to find Neoptolemus still at his side, and effusively expresses his gratitude for the young man's aid, aid that consists of his sheer presence (867-71). The sound of a human voice (ὦ φέγγος ὕπνου διάδοχον, 867) in Philoctetes' mouth becomes a synecdoche for faithful companionship and is deemed salutary (μεῖναι παρόντα καὶ ξυνωφελοῦντά μοι, 871).[682]

Toward the middle of the play, Philoctetes decides to allow Neoptolemus to touch the bow he received from Heracles, as a token of (what he believes to be) their by then firmly established friendship.[683] He heads into his cave to fetch it, accompanied by Neoptolemus. Meanwhile, the Chorus of sailors launches into the only choral *stasimon* that is exclusively sung and danced by the Chorus (aside from two short interludes). In it, they marvel at how Philoctetes could have borne his condition – not so much his pain *per se*, but *being alone* as he listened to the waves beating the shore around him. The desolate soundscape that has surrounded him for nine years is a spatial and aural expression of the excruciating experience he has undergone, one of complete social isolation:

---

[681] Later, after he loses consciousness in the face of an especially acute bout of pain, Philoctetes awakens to find Neoptolemus still at his side and effusively expresses his gratitude for the young man's aid, an aid that consists of his sheer presence (867-71).
[682] On companionship as a cure, see Biggs 1966, 231, and lines 167 ff., 195, and 280 ff.
[683] For the significance and symbolism of the bow and its role in depicting the various stages of Neoptolemus and Philoctetes' relationship, see an overview (with bibliography) in e. g., Johnson 1988, 117 n. 1, and Kosak 1999.

τόδε <δ'αὖ> θαῦμά μ' ἔχει,
πῶς ποτε πῶς ποτ' ἀμφιπλήκτων
ῥοθίων μόνος κλύων, πῶς
ἄρα πανδάκρυτον οὕτω
βιοτὰν κατέσχεν·
ἵν' αὐτὸς ἦν πρόσουρος, οὐκ ἔχων βάσιν,
οὐδέ τιν' ἐγχώρων
        κακογείτονα,
παρ' ᾧ στόνον ἀν-
    τίτυπον <τὸν> βαρυβρῶτ'
    ἀποκλαύσειεν αἱματηρόν·
                (687–95)[684]

But at this I wonder, how, how did he listen alone to the waves that beat the shore around him, and endure a life so full of tears? Where he himself was his only companion, with no one coming to him, not a single neighbor nearby for him in his troubles, to whom he might lament, with groans inviting a response, the sickness that devoured him, thirsty for blood.

The sounds that surround Philoctetes create a sense of vast emptiness, while his own cries highlight the yearning for social acknowledgment that lies at their core. The singular noun-epithet στόνος ἀντίτυπος in particular epitomizes Philoctetes' desperate longing for human company.[685] The attention paid to the soundscape that has surrounded him helps to point up the social origin of his pain, and to underscore his need for an interlocutor.

Interestingly, at the close of the play, Philoctetes makes reference to the soundscape around him as he redefines his relationship to his natural environment on Lemnos in more ambivalent terms. It is especially noteworthy that he uses the very same combination (στόνος ἀντίτυπος) that we noted in the choral passage above, which occurs once more at a crucial juncture, as he speaks his last words (1460). By that point, Philoctetes' relationship to the Greeks has shifted; he no longer believes that Neoptolemus and his sailors are his benefactors, at least not for the mere sake of helping a friend; he knows that they are serving the

---

[684] The text is somewhat problematic; see Pucci *ad loc.* for discussion.

[685] Translators have struggled to render the significance and range of the epithet ἀντίτυπος. The adjective is most often used to describe either a blow being repelled or any shape or form that corresponds to an original through which it was created (e.g., a stamp to the die); it is later used as a substantive, to mean "image." Cf. *LSJ* A.2.c., which includes (late) examples of ἀντίτυπος meaning "reproduction, copy." Thus, Lloyd-Jones's "with groans inviting a response" emphasizes not the fact that Philoctetes' groans *create* an echo but the fact that they call for a response – and receive none; cf. Jebb 1898: "with no one ... near him while he suffered, in whose ear he could pour forth the lament, awaking response." Compare Buschor 1979 *ad loc.*: "Kennt keine Antwort der Seufzer." Pucci in Pucci *et al.* 2003, *ad loc.* glosses in a similar vein in his commentary: "ἀντίτυπον: significa 'che invita risposta.'"

army's agenda, albeit, in the end, with good intentions toward him. The sounds referred to in the closing lines uttered by the hero reflect this change. What his isolation has come to mean to Philoctetes by then, when he is about to reintegrate the community that betrayed him (on Heracles' orders), is ambiguous. As he bids Lemnos farewell, Philoctetes evokes the sounds the island, in a wistful reminiscence that spotlights for the last time the themes of solitude and isolation that lie at the core of the play, but casts them in a slightly different light. Philoctetes mentions his own voice along with the sounds of the island once again (using the noun-epithet combination στόνος ἀντίτυπος) in a manner that suggests ambivalence on his part, both toward the community of the Greeks and toward the island where he spent so many miserable years. The blending of his voice with the echoes from the mountain of Hermes reflects the extent to which he has come to see his own uncompromising, heroic identity as inseparable from the island, and conveys the sense of loss and alienation that his departure entails:[686]

> καὶ κτύπος ἄρσην πόντου προβολῆς
> ...
> πολλὰ δὲ φωνῆς τῆς ἡμετέρας
> Ἑρμαῖον ὄρος παρέπεμψεν ἐμοὶ
> στόνον ἀντίτυπον χειμαζομένῳ
>   (1455, 1458–60)

[Farewell], strong sound of the sea beating on the promontory...
And often the mountain of Hermes brought back to me a groan answering my voice as the storm assailed me!

Pain and its perceiver

Philoctetes' shouts of agony in the central scene of the tragedy (730 ff.) have received much attention, and with good reason;[687] yet it is as early as the *parodos* that the depiction of the spectacle offered by Philoctetes in his pain begins. Strikingly, the impact of his pain and its power to elicit intense responses are underscored, in an indirect and unexpected manner, before the hero even enters the stage. Also foregrounded from the start are the variety of possible reactions to his suffering. Before the sight of Philoctetes begins the process of causing Neo-

---

686 For more on this matter, see Allen-Hornblower 2013.
687 On Philoctetes' shouts and the depiction of his pain more broadly in that central scene, see for instance, Segal 1981, 292–361; Blundell 1989; Worman 2000; Pucci in Pucci *et al.* 2003, 245–53 *ad loc.*; Budelmann 2006; and Nooter 2012, 124–46.

ptolemus to waver, the poetics of the play suggest the wide range of disparate possible responses that his suffering can elicit through the noteworthy disparity in how the suffering man *sounds* to those who hear him.

The sounds emitted by Philoctetes and the reactions that they elicit contribute to mapping the emotional predispositions and values of the characters who hear him, and to distinguishing the two poles between which Neoptolemus will come to vacillate. On the one hand, there is the aloof and unfeeling detachment of Odysseus, whose perceptions are warped by his deliberately distancing himself from the victim and his symptoms, whom Odysseus keeps carefully out of his perceptive field.[688] On the other hand, there is the compassionate, spontaneous outburst of the Chorus of sailors, who initially experience and express an overwhelming sense of pity at the mere sound of Philoctetes approaching, as they recognize the human voice beneath his seemingly inhuman cries. The mapping of the characters' values according to their perception of and reactions to sounds sets the stage for the audience's understanding of how much the impact of the spectacle of human suffering varies according to the perceiver. It highlights a key element to our understanding of Neoptolemus's later evolution: that human suffering impacts the witnesses to that suffering to varying degrees, depending on that observer's character and nature (or *physis*). Neoptolemus is eventually changed by the act of watching Philoctetes suffer because of his intrinsic nobility;[689] not so Odysseus, whose different values influence and guide his perceptions.

At the start of the play, Neoptolemus reacts with dismay (and perhaps a bit of disgust) at the sight of Philoctetes' humble abode. On seeing his rags covered in pus drying in the sun, miserable signs of a pathetic existence, he cries out:

ἰοὺ ἰού· καὶ ταῦτά γ' ἄλλα θάλπεται
ῥάκη, βαρείας του νοσηλείας πλέα.[690]

(38–9)

---

[688] Odysseus's deliberate avoidance of any form of contact with Philoctetes is not unsimilar, in the emotional distance it enables, from Orestes' careful avoidance of any visual contact with Clytemnestra's corpse in Aeschylus' *Choephori*, which I discussed in chapter 3.

[689] On Neoptolemus's wavering and remorse and how his evolution marks a return to his true Achillean self, see Fulkerson 2006, where she puts Neoptolemus's moral maturation in terms of his "discovering what it means to have the *physis* he has;" see also Fulkerson 2013, 66–79. As F. notes, Neoptolemus is not being transformed so much as he is gradually embracing behavior that is true to the nature he has inherited from his father. This is made clear from the poetics of the play; see also Blundell 1987, 1988.

[690] On the significance of different interjections in Greek tragedy, see Biraud 2009.

Ah! Ah! And here is something else, rags drying in the sun,
Covered in pus from some grievous sore!

In the *parodos*, after he agrees to obey Odysseus's orders to trick Philoctetes, Neoptolemus is quick to dismiss the wounded hero's suffering. He brings into play the all-too-hastily and conveniently reached assumption that it must have been willed by the gods. The very reference to divine sanction (191–200) is, perhaps, a telltale sign that he is trying to stifle his scruples.[691] On the other hand, the Chorus members experience a powerful emotional reaction in this same *parodos*, first to the visual evidence of the wretched lifestyle that Philoctetes has been forced to lead, then to the actual sounds the man makes in his suffering, as he first approaches them.[692] After being horrified at the visible markers of Philoctetes' pitiful existence, the sailors' emotion intensifies when they begin to hear his cries. They then launch into what Austin calls "the longest ode in all of Greek poetry dedicated to a single sound."[693] They are, at this point, not spectators (in a visual sense) as much as they are an audience, listening to the sound of a human voice and responding to it in song with their own. I begin with the strophe:

ΣΤΡ.
Χο. εὔστομ' ἔχε, παῖ.
Νε.   τί τόδε;
Χο.   προὔφάνη κτύπος,
φωτὸς σύντροφος ὡς τειρομένου <του>,
ἤ που τῇδ' ἢ τῇδε τόπων.
βάλλει, βάλλει μ' ἐτύμα φθογγά
        του στίβον κατ' ἀνάγκαν
ἕρποντος, οὐδέ με λάθει
βαρεῖα τηλόθεν αὐδὰ

---

691 I return to this below.
692 See Kitto 1956, 111–2; Gardiner 1987, 18. For the sailors' nascent feeling of pity earlier on seeing the rags and other visible traces of the miserable and isolated existence Philoctetes has been leading, see lines 150–200. The Chorus believes that Philoctetes' suffering is undeserved and therefore worthy of its pity: see Kitzinger 2008, 76, with a discussion of Arist., *Rh.* 2.8. 1385b13–6. For an illuminating summary of Aristotle's views on pity and pain, see Konstan 2001, 128–36; see also Konstan 2006, 201–8. On the convenient notion of "merit-based pity" in reference to the Aristotelian definition of pity, see Sandridge 2008 (mentioned above in chapter 3, n. 541). Regarding the role of the senses, and sight in particular, in provoking pity, already pointed up by Aristotle (*Rh.* 2.8.1386a34), see Sternberg 2005, 25–43.
693 Austin 2011, 86 ff.

τρυσάνωρ· διάσημα γὰρ θροεῖ.[694]

(201–9)

Cho. Be quiet, boy. Neo. What is it?
Cho. A sound appeared
One that sounds like the companion of a man in distress – this way, I think, or that.
It strikes me, it strikes me! The true
voice of one who treads along his path under constraint, and the burdensome cry from far
off of a man in distress ... it does not escape me:
clearly he is uttering a lament.

While in the climactic pain scene at the center of the play (730–820), the protagonist's cries and physical collapse are (mainly) what convey the extremity of his suffering to Neoptolemus and the audience, in this first encounter, Sophocles introduces Philoctetes' pain by steering the audience's attention toward his cries' *effects* on the internal audience. Neither the Chorus members nor the audience can see the hero at this point. While sight often plays the prominent role in eliciting pity (in tragedy as well as other genres),[695] here the sailors' pity is elicited primarily by sounds, which they experience with increasing intensity before that object of pity (Philoctetes) even comes into view for them and the audience to see.[696] We have no indication (such as stage directions or internal references made by the Chorus) of whether any sounds were actually produced offstage for the audience to hear.[697] It is likely that the audience was presented with the Chorus's song itself and no more.[698]

---

[694] The variant θρηνεῖ ("he is singing a dirge") is adopted by some editors; see e.g., Lloyd-Jones-Wilson 1990, following Dawe.
[695] On pity and sight, see above, n. 692. While scholars have debated the sincerity of this pity, Kitzinger's arguments for taking the pity at face value are compelling (see Kitzinger 2008, 75 n. 13).
[696] In her discussion of the role of "hearing" alongside seeing in provoking pity, Sternberg uses "hearing" to refer to the pitier's perception of articulate and intelligible speech (*logos*) – not sounds and inarticulate cries, as we have here (Sternberg 2005, 25–36). I am grateful to Guido Avezzù's question in response to an earlier version of this paper given on the occasion of a Sophocles conference organized in Torino in 2010, in which he raised the question of why Sophocles uses sounds as opposed to sight in this play to evoke (and convey) emotion.
[697] On internal references to sounds offstage and onstage in Greek tragedy, see Edmunds 2002 (regarding Aeschylus's *Septem contra Thebas*). Seidensticker 2006, 106 ff., discusses the use of cries offstage and onstage in Greek tragedy as a means of depicting violent actions unfit for the stage.
[698] The production of cries offstage is not necessary and would likely detract from the Chorus's powerful words themselves. It is tempting to imagine that some form of musical accompaniment to the Chorus's song, by adopting a certain cadence or pitch, might have stood in for Philoctetes' cries; but this can only remain speculative.

Indirect though it is, this first impression of Philoctetes in his suffering is remarkably vivid. The Chorus members' depiction conveys the severity of Philoctetes' pain by foregrounding the sounds' impact on them. In so doing, the Chorus provides the audience with a lens through which the hero's pain is represented in all its harshness.[699] Of equal if not greater importance is the succession of terms that the sailors use to describe what they hear: the progression from κτύπος to φθόγγα to αὐδά to θροεῖ reflects the Chorus members' growing feeling of pity as Philoctetes draws nearer, and helps to characterize them as deeply compassionate.[700] It is worth pausing to analyze the small but significant shift that each term introduces in relation to the one preceding it.

The choral description begins with a remarkable *synaesthesia* that conveys the sailors' surprise at what they hear, "a sound appeared" (προὐφάνη κτύπος) — a twist almost unique in its metaphorical density.[701] The initial noun used here, κτύπος, typically designates any sound produced by an inanimate source (the beating of horses' hooves, a clap of thunder, the rumor of a brook, a knock on a door). A notable shift follows with the term φθόγγα, whereby the sailors indicate that what they perceive, unmistakably, is a voice (ἐτύμα

---

[699] The bibliography on the Chorus in Greek tragedy and its function is enormous, and limitations of space do not allow for an extensive account of the range of scholarly positions on the question. On Sophoclean choruses and Sophocles' dramatic technique in general, see e.g., Burton 1980 and Gardiner 1987; also Visvardi 2015, with bibliography. For an overview of the use of the Chorus as internal audience and model for the external audience, in the context of a broader critical discussion of the political function of tragic performances in classical Athens, see Murnaghan 2012 (esp. 224–32) with relevant bibliography. Regarding attending theatrical performances as part and parcel of a voting citizen's political duties, see the bibliography in Goldhill 2012, 38 n. 2. On the unusual characteristics of the Chorus in Sophocles' *Philoctetes* in relation to other Sophoclean choruses, see Schein 2013, 18–20. On the Chorus's role in connection with Neoptolemus's moral and emotional evolution over the course of the play, see also above n. 655, with additional bibliography.

[700] The Chorus does not continue in this sympathetic vein throughout the play. The very next time it sings, its song is the false oath that I mentioned above, designed to trick Philoctetes into believing Neoptolemus's equally fabricated account of his having been cheated out of Achilles' armor by Odysseus and the Atreids (391–402). On the Chorus's multiple identities and the related question of its share in the action of Sophocles' extant plays, see Murnaghan 2012, 220–35; on its shifting role in the *Philoctetes*, including as a "character" that highlights some important characteristics of the main actors, see Kitzinger 2008, 71–135.

[701] To my knowledge, there is only one other instance of synaesthesia to be found in Greek tragedy, in Aeschylus's *Septem contra Thebas*. It also occurs in the *parodos*. The Chorus, on hearing the shouts and clatter of armor of the Argive army, declares: "I see the clatter" (κτύπον δέδορκα, 103). For a discussion of the latter passage, see Edmunds 2002, 107 ff. On synaesthesia and the ancient senses, see Butler and Purves 2013.

φθογγά)⁷⁰² – that is, a sound uttered by a sentient being. It is a voice, moreover, that clearly communicates the painful struggle of the one producing it (του στίβον κατ' ἀνάγκαν ἕρποντος). The progression continues with αὐδά (βαρεῖα τηλόθεν αὐδά τρυσάνωρ), a term that is used strictly in reference to the *human* voice and, on occasion, to song.⁷⁰³ The shift from φθογγά to αὐδά marks the crucial moment in which the Chorus members perceive the human being behind the sounds they are hearing, as they are reminded by his wretched condition of the humanity that they share with him as fellow mortals who are equally vulnerable to the twists and turns of fate.⁷⁰⁴ This is one of the first examples we have of the irreducible genuineness of cries in this play, and of their paradoxical ability to enable communication, though they are inarticulate. Segal's observations regarding the scene of Philoctetes' onstage agony hold true for the present passage as well: his "broken cries imply a kind of natural language, reduced to the level of bestial howl but at least free of manipulative rationalism" that "in its very rawness and wildness ... can touch a chord of instinctive communication."⁷⁰⁵ I would

---

702 Φθόγγα commonly designates sounds (including voices) produced by *animate* beings, whether human or animal. Nooter also notes the gradual humanization of Philoctetes' voice here (Nooter 2012, 126–7). See Chantraine s.v. κτύπος, φθογγά, and αὐδή. Concerning the voice in ancient Greece (and the evocative power of silences), see Lachenaud 2013.

703 See Krapp 1964, 24, regarding the highly specific semantic range of αὐδή in Homeric poetry. Both Clay and Ford (Clay 1974, 131ff.; Ford 1992, 174–9) note that the use of αὐδή in Homer is reserved for mortals; it distinguishes humanly intelligible utterances from animal noises and divine speeches alike. The use of the term αὐδή here points up the cries' potential ability to establish a form of communication between the sufferer and his witnesses, despite the fact that no articulate speech is perceived. (I say potential, because the nature and character of the witness is a key element in enabling the establishment of communication; an unfeeling observer such as Odysseus can ignore the humanity of the sufferer entirely, and preclude any sort of exchange between them as a result).

704 Earlier, the Chorus explains that its pity is based on the understanding that the suffering of any mortal is (potentially) shared by all human beings, because of the vulnerability inherent in the human condition: see lines 177–9. On the pitier's perception of his own vulnerability in relation to the fate of the pitied, see Arist., *Rh.* 2.8.1385b13–16. Cf. Johnson and Clapp 2005, 127: "Compassion ... is premised on an understanding of the common inheritance of suffering shared by all human beings." The Chorus's expression of pity for Philoctetes thus constitutes an acknowledgment of their shared humanity. The example of Odysseus at the start of Sophocles' *Ajax* is another illustration of how much this acknowledgment of shared humanity is the basis and premise for the experience of pity on the part of the pitier.

705 Segal 1981, 335. Ringer 1998, 108–9 pays due attention to the importance of Philoctetes' entrance cry as an "unscripted, inarticulate howl" that he likens to (and contrasts with) other characters' entrance speeches, in that the scream's "protorealistic effect" sets the eponymous hero apart from all others who are "acting," while Philoctetes never does. This cry is a mark

simply stress in addition that these cries *can* touch a chord of instinctive communication, but that they do not necessarily. Whether or not they do depends, in fact, on the listener, in whose reactions Sophocles provides a wealth of information concerning that listener's character, nature, and values, as we are about to see, not just in the case of the Chorus, but of Odysseus and Neoptelemus as well.

Accompanying the progression in the terminology used by the sailors to describe Philoctetes' cries from less to more human are semantic and metaphorical shifts that indicate the increasingly powerful impact of these cries on the Chorus members themselves. After the sound of his cries "appears" to them, his voice "strikes" them (βάλλει βάλλει μ' ἐτύμα φθογγά).[706] The web of metaphors broadens: from sight and sound, it expands to touch, with the emphatically positioned and twice-repeated verb βάλλει. The image (along with the alliteration in labial occlusives) helps to give the otherwise invisible pain of the hero a concrete, almost tangible existence: by saying that the sound "strikes" them, the Chorus members make the audience picture it traveling from the sufferer to them like a weapon.[707] The language suggests that the cries' impact is so strong that it causes the witnesses to experience pain themselves in turn, metaphorically if not literally[708] — a most evocative expression of pity.[709] The audience's impres-

---

of his sincerity. The same will be true, as we will see, of Neoptolemus's cry when he can neither bear himself nor his acting stance any longer.

706 On the ancient Greeks' conception of pity as an emotion that stems from an external source and "enters into" the pitier, see Sternberg 2005, 37–40; cf. Herder on the ability of a plaintive tone to "cut through the organs of [the listener's] body ... like an arrow" (Herder 1772, quoted below).

707 In his *Treatise on the Origin of Language* (*Abhandlung über den Ursprung der Sprache*, first published in 1772), the eighteenth-century German philosopher Herder questions the notion of a radical opposition between human language and primeval cries. (He has Greek tragedy in mind: Philoctetes is specifically mentioned at the beginning of his essay.) Herder places the inarticulate cry within the system of language precisely because of its power to elicit strong emotions: "Wer ists, dem bei einem zuckenden, wimmernden Gequälten, bei einem achzenden Sterbenden, auch selbst bei einem stohnenden Vieh, wenn seine ganze Maschine leidet, dies Ach nicht zu Herzen dringe?" ("Who is he who – in the presence of a convulsive whimpering victim of torment, at the bedside of a moaning fellow in the throes of death ... when the entire machinery of his body suffers, does not feel how this Ah touches his heart?"). He goes on to challenge Diderot's allegation that the blind are less receptive to pain by emphasizing the power of sounds to elicit pity: "Jeder Klageton geht ihm um so inniger und scharfer, wie ein Pfeil, zum Herzen! (...) Grausen und Schmerz fahrt durch seine Glieder" ("Every plaintive tone, like an arrow, goes the more keenly, the more penetratingly to his heart! (...) Horror and pain cut through the organs of his body," Herder [1772] 1987, esp. 260–1). For more on Herder's reflections and their relevance to *Philoctetes*, see Weissberg 1989, with bibliography.

708 Compare the terms used by Philoctetes himself to describe the pain's progressive invasion of his body, which denote piercing, penetration, and violation of his physical integrity (see lines

sion of the affective power of Philoctetes' cries reaches a culminating point at the close of the strophe when, though no actual words are articulated, the sailors come to perceive the sounds emitted by him as a quintessentially human song of suffering: what they are hearing, they say, is a distinct lament: διάσημα γὰρ θροεῖ.[710]

We see from the Chorus's description that Philoctetes' inarticulate cries are neither inhuman nor incapable of establishing communication ("infected" though he and his language may be by his disease).[711] Rather, they are equivocal, "so human yet so inhuman."[712] His cries have the capacity to touch his fellow

---

742–6 and 785–92 and Worman 2000). Pucci in Pucci et al. 2003,187–8 ad loc. points up the etymological relationship between τείρω, the verb used to describe how the sufferer himself is "pierced" (τειρομένου), and the epithet τρυσάνωρ (from τρύω) that the chorus uses to describe his voice (209). The latter offers two potential meanings, as Pucci underlines: a subjective one ("che dice il dolore di un uomo") and an objective one ("che addolora un uomo," which applies to the pain's effect on the Chorus).

709 A full discussion of the concept and semantic range of "pity" in English in comparison with the Greek terms it encompasses would reach beyond the limits of the present study, as would an examination of English terms inadequately used to express the Greek notions encompassed by the words ἔλεος, οἶκτος, and the like. For our present purposes, I simply wish to call attention to the fact that the pity voiced by the Chorus is not pity as it was defined by Aristotle in his *Rhetoric*, where pain is a part of the experience of pity solely because of the expectation of harm to oneself (for Aristotle's definition, see ch. 2 n. 406 and Konstan 2001). Rather, the Chorus's pity is closer to the sympathy denoted by the *sun-* compounds Aristotle later used in his *Nicomachean Ethics*, where the very definition of a friend is "one who suffers and rejoices along with his *philos*" (Arist., *EN* 9.4.11566a7–8). On the distinctions between pity and experiencing another's pain as one's own, as established by Aristotle, see Konstan 2001, 128–36. Stanford's translation of the Greek concept of οἶκτος (which is the term used by the Chorus in this play – along with related verbs – when it expresses pity) as "compassionate grief" is more appropriate than our English term "pity," with its demeaning connotations (Stanford 1983, 24). On the various Greek words for pity, see also Burkert 1955. For a discussion of our modern notion of "pity" in relation to the Greek words ἔλεος and οἶκτος, see Johnson 1980, 1–9; Konstan 2001; and Johnson and Clapp 2005,154–5. Regarding the distinction between pity and compassion in the *Philoctetes* in particular, see Konstan 2001, 51–4.

710 The text here is disputed. Avezzù retains the manuscripts' γὰρ θροεῖ, and Cerri translates this as "è distinto il lamento" (for both, see Pucci et al. 2003, 32 ad 209). The variant θρηνεῖ (the poetical term for mourning, as noted by Nooter 2012, 126), adopted by Lloyd-Jones and Wilson, following Dindorf's conjecture, also denotes lament (see Lloyd-Jones and Wilson 1990 ad loc.). θροεῖν is a variant of θρηνεῖν at S., *Aj.* 582.

711 On the degree to which Philoctetes' disease "infects" his language, see Worman 2000.

712 Austin 2011, 87. I agree with Austin that the cries always contain a kernel of humanity. See also Segal's assessment of the power of Philoctetes' cries over Neoptolemus in the scene of the hero's onstage agony, which applies to the present passage as well: "Those terrible bestial shrieks in fact are the first steps toward a genuine human communication. When he hears

Greeks by "remind[ing] both character and audience ... of Philoctetes' essential humanity."[713] Whether they do so or not depends on who is listening to him. Odysseus's very different perception of and reaction to these same cries, to which I turn below, is a testament to the degree to which the cries' pitiable nature is determined by the perceiver and makes the Chorus's compassionate disposition here all the more distinctive.[714]

The more the Chorus members perceive the human component in the voice of the suffering hero, the more their song humanizes him in the audience's eyes.[715] At the same time, the more they reveal a growing feeling of pity toward him, the more their own humane disposition becomes manifest.[716] The depiction of the hero's pain, by focusing the audience on the reactions of its witnesses, thus also functions as an effective mode of characterizing the Chorus members themselves.[717]

Throughout the *parodos*, the Chorus members are singing – even as they describe Philoctetes' cries as a form of song. When they feel his pain "striking"

---

these cries, Neoptolemus must confront the reality of what he is doing to a fellow human being, never more human than when he lies ... in agony" (Segal 1981, 333–5). Knox and Podlecki, on the other hand, lay too much stress on "the obliteration of all traces of humanity" in Philoctetes' cries in the same climactic pain scene (quote from Knox 1964, 131; Podlecki 1966, 235).

713 Nussbaum 1999, 268. (Nussbaum is making reference to Philoctetes' articulate language, however.) Nooter discusses Philoctetes' growing poetic ability and lyricism as the play progresses (Nooter 2012, 124–46); my point here is to draw attention to the power of his inarticulate cries to affect others as well.

714 Both Odysseus's and Neoptolemus's descriptions of Philoctetes' living conditions include language that associates the sufferer with beasts: see lines 26–49 and Buxton 1982, 118–20. There is recurrent imagery throughout the *Philoctetes* that portrays the eponymous hero's disease as a beast that perpetually threatens his very humanity (see Worman 2000 and Térasse 2001), including in Philoctetes' own words (e.g., lines 785–8).

715 Nussbaum believes that by singing his misery, the sailors are "putting Philoctetes back into the human community" (Nussbaum 1999, 259). Though it experiences pity, the Chorus does not take any action as a result, in part because of its choral status: see Gardiner 1987, 18; Blundell 1989, 195; and Kitzinger 2008, 82. On pity and action, see Sternberg 2005.

716 Aristotle emphasizes the evaluative dimension of pity and points up the fact that it is characteristic of good people; see Konstan 2001, 128–33. On suffering and sympathy in Greek tragedy as a measure of the humanity of a given character, see Vickers 1979, 70 ff.

717 According to Burton's reading, the *parodos* consists of distinct sections, each conveying different moods: thus, lines 169–90 convey pity, while those that follow mark a "return to alert suspense" and "action" (Burton 1980, 227–31). The Chorus does regard Philoctetes with some wariness (see line 136, expressing distrust, and line 156, expressing dread at potential hostility); but I see no such clear division of moods by section. Rather, it seems to me that there are constant variations in the Chorus's mood throughout the *parodos*, with pity dominating in the lines just examined. See my further discussion below.

them, their song *about* pain becomes a song *of* pain; Philoctetes' lament (if not his actual suffering) becomes their own. As the Chorus becomes a mouthpiece for the sufferer in singing its "lamentation for Philoctetes' suffering,"[718] the sympathetic nature of its emerging feeling of pity is reflected in the fact that their mode of expression is the same as the one that they characterize his cries as being – a lamentation. Their entrance song provides a sounding board for Philoctetes' pain that both acknowledges it and literally gives it voice.

In the *antistrophe*, Sophocles continues to make the sailors' perception of the sounds produced by Philoctetes in his pain a central point of focus:

ANT.
Χο. ἀλλ' ἔχε, τέκνον.
       Νε. λέγ' ὅ τι.

Χο. φροντίδας νέας·
ὡς οὐκ ἔξεδρος, ἀλλ' ἔντοπος ἀνήρ,
οὐ μολπὰν σύριγγος ἔχων,
ὡς ποιμὴν ἀγροβάτας,
ἀλλ' ἤ που πταίων ὑπ' ἀνάγκας βοᾷ τηλωπὸν ἰω-
άν, ἢ ναὸς ἄξενον αὐ-
γάζων ὅρμον· προβοᾷ γὰρ αἴλινον.[719]
          (210–8)

ANT.
Cho. But take, my son ...
       Neo. What?! Tell me!
Cho. New counsels! For he is not far from home; no, the man is in this very place -
not playing the music of Pan's pipe as would a shepherd roaming the wild;
but stumbling, rather, he cries out a far-sounding scream ...
either under some sort of constraint, or because he can see the harbor that is hostile to any
ship's anchorage; for he is crying out a dirge.

Here, the sailors attempt to define what they are hearing through a negative simile that describes what Philoctetes does *not* sound like: οὐ μολπὰν σύριγγος ἔχων, | ὡς ποιμὴν ἀγροβάτας ("not playing the music of Pan's pipe, as would a shepherd roaming the wild").[720] Rather, he is "crying out a dirge" (προβοᾷ

---

[718] Austin 2011, 84.
[719] The text of this line poses metrical problems; see my discussion below.
[720] The rather enigmatic comparison has perplexed scholars. Some (e.g., Segal 1981, 297 ff. and Pucci in Pucci *et al.* 2003, 188 *ad loc.*) take the description of the wanderer producing the "music of Pan's pipes" (μολπὰν σύριγγος) as separate from and intended to form a contrast with the following line (ὡς ποιμὴν ἀγροβάτας), which they believe is meant to underscore Phil-

γὰρ αἴλινον).⁷²¹ The purpose of the extended negative simile is not to contrast the figure of the shepherd with that of the hero *per se* but to contrast the different types of sounds that they produce. The cheerful music played by an errant shepherd (an early pastoral motif) serves as a foil to the desperate note at the core of the suffering man's cries.⁷²²

The closing line of the Chorus's song is problematic. The manuscripts' τι δεινόν (in lieu of αἴλινον) does not offer exact responsion with the corresponding line in the strophe as it appears in the manuscripts (line 209, ending with θροεῖ).⁷²³ Lachmann's conjecture, αἴλινον ("dirge," 218), is appealing: it contributes to portraying Philoctetes' tone as pathetic, while also continuing the motif introduced at the close of the preceding strophe, where the Chorus concludes that it is hearing a lament – that is, that Philoctetes' cries are a form of plaintive song.⁷²⁴ If the conjectured αἴλινον is adopted, the strophe ends on a very different note from the one struck by τι δεινόν ("something terrible"), which appears in the manuscripts. An ending that describes Philoctetes' cry as "something terrible" would indicate an abrupt shift in the Chorus's stance, from pity for the sufferer to fear of him, thus marking a shift on the sailors' part from a strong sense of identification with the sufferer to one of distance and alienation from him –

---

octetes' wildness (ἀγροβάτας would be a reference to his savage allure and gait). It is true that Philoctetes has come to identify with his wild environment and its beasts (he lives among animals, 184–5) as a result of his loneliness and disease (see above, n. 714); but lines 213 and 214 function together, and both refer to the shepherd of the simile.

721 Or a terrible shout: τι δεινόν. On the problematic nature of the text here, see below p. 274. For more on the significance of δεινόν (if the Chorus's entrance song does end in this way), see Austin 2011, 86–7.

722 In Homer already, the *syrinx* (or panpipe) is played by two shepherds (*Od.* 18.526). The insistence on the difficulty with which Philoctetes moves about, which is mentioned twice, corroborates the audience's sense of his deplorable condition (κατ' ἀνάγκαν ἕρποντος in the *strophe* and πταίων ὑπ' ἀνάγκας βοᾷ in the *antistrophe*).

723 Scholars are divided on this issue. Avezzù follows Lachmann's emendation of τι δεινόν in favor of αἴλινον: προβοᾷ γὰρ αἴλινον (Pucci *et al.* 2003, 32). Others (see Lloyd-Jones and Wilson 1990, 183–84) prefer the alternative προβοᾷ τι δεινόν (or τι γὰρ δεινόν, Jebb 1898).

724 Line 209, quoted earlier: διάσημα γὰρ θροεῖ. In her discussion of the Linos song and of its connections with lament, Alexiou describes the αἴλινος as a cry of a dual nature: the term can refer to a cry of grief or to one of joy and victory (Alexiou [1974] 2002, 57 and 218 n. 10). Nooter notes that the epic term ἰωάν in the present *antistrophe* (line 216–7) further characterizes Philoctetes' cry as "lament itself" (Nooter 2012, 126–7). Pucci's translation of the ending of both *strophe* and *antistrophe* reflects the thematic continuity that is maintained if the αἴλινον hypothesis is correct: διάσημα γὰρ θροεῖ, "è distinto il lamento," and προβοᾷ γὰρ αἴλινον, "intona proprio un lamento!" (Pucci in Pucci *et al.* 2003, 31–3, *ad loc.*).

just before Philoctetes enters the stage.[725] The conjectured αἴλινον, on the other hand, emphasizes to the very end of the choral song the human note that the Chorus members perceive at the heart of Philoctetes' cries and points to the compassionate nature of their response.[726]

With the Chorus's song, the audience catches a glimpse of one possible reaction to Philoctetes in his pain: one involving pity. The Chorus members here present a model of the humane and moral behavior of the compassionate bystander, which Neoptolemus will eventually follow later in the play, with significant implications for his own subsequent actions and for his relationship to Philoctetes. Therein lies the reason for Sophocles' choice to feature the sailors' compassionate response so prominently. Their response is dependent on their ability to recognize the humanity of the sufferer and to perceive the humanity beneath Philoctetes' bestial cries.

The Chorus's predisposition to pity "set[s] the emotional tone" for Neoptolemus, who will shake off Odysseus's cynical influence after the turning point of Philoctetes' onstage agony at the center of the play.[727] In the young man's case, it is the sight of Philoctetes' suffering, as well as having the chance to witness the nobility and worth of the sufferer, that will lead him to abandon his own playacting and deceit. As we will see, when Neoptolemus reacts to Philoctetes' pain (and to his own misconduct toward the old man), the "sound effects" continue, but with a shift from the sounds emitted by Philoctetes in his pain to those emitted by Neoptolemus. At this early point in the play, however, the young man has been convinced by Odysseus to give priority to glory over honor.[728] As long as he is actively implementing the plan that Odysseus has conceived, he is able to keep pity and human feeling at bay. The greater good on behalf of which Odys-

---

[725] If the Chorus is indeed expressing fear here, it is immediately proven wrong, if not ridiculed, by Philoctetes' warm enthusiasm as he greets his fellow Greeks (219 ff.).
[726] It is not to be excluded, however, that the Chorus's reaction to Philoctetes should in the end be ambivalent and injected with some degree of wariness mixed with pity, at the key moment that precedes his entrance onstage. Though rapid, such a radical change would not be implausible, given how inconstant the Chorus proves to be throughout the rest of the tragedy. If there is such an evolution in the Chorus's perception of Philoctetes' cries, it would further emphasize the fickle nature of the sailors. The Chorus of tragedy is not a character and is known for its shifting judgment and ambivalence. It cannot be reduced to one coherent ethical or psychological stance. In the *Philoctetes*, its members sometimes behave as though they were a *bona fide* character, as when they express their opinion and seek to influence Neoptolemus's decisions; but their positions are often contradictory, at times within one and the same song: see e.g., Murnaghan 2012, 220–35.
[727] The quote is from Visvardi 2007, 170.
[728] For Odysseus's seductive argumentation, see lines 81–5 and 96–119.

seus tells him he must act and the recognition that he supposedly will receive from the community make Neoptolemus willing to let go of his moral qualms, at least for the time being. The Chorus's reaction does not have any impact on his relationship to Philoctetes — yet. As for the Chorus members, they neither prompt Neoptolemus to act differently, nor take any action themselves. The choral song merely illustrates the genuine, compassionate relationship that could exist between the young man and Philoctetes, their (initial) reaction to Philoctetes' pain setting an exemplary standard for Neoptolemus. The young man will follow suit only later in the play. As we will see, it is not just coming face to face with Philoctetes' acute pain and witnessing his agony firsthand that will prompt him to change, but the noble character of the sufferer itself. For now, however, he continues to play the main role in the implementation of Odysseus's plan: that of beguiler and betrayer of Philoctetes.

A blind eye and a deaf ear: The averted gaze and selective hearing of Odysseus

The Chorus's song in the *parodos* reflects the sort of sympathy and emotional identification with the sufferer that can arise in an impartial witness, who sees (and hears!) a fellow Greek who has been left to face great pain in complete solitude. Despite the repellent symptoms of Philoctetes' disease, the Chorus members still acknowledge both the intensity of his pain and the humanity of the sufferer: they recognize in him a fellow human, a *philos* in pain. The same cannot be said of Odysseus; his stance is the very antithesis of the sailors'. From his very first words at the start of the play, Odysseus deliberately maintains a noteworthy distance between himself and Philoctetes, both physically and figuratively speaking, and he continues to do so throughout the drama, presenting Neoptolemus with a model of behavior toward which he gravitates for the first half of the play, swayed by the skilled speaker's seductive and persuasive promises of fame. This distance is what enables him to dehumanize Philoctetes and facilitates the unfeeling pragmatism with which he handles every interaction with the man, directing Neoptolemus to do the same. That he should be so preoccupied with maintaining such a careful distance from the sufferer indirectly and paradoxically suggests his awareness of, or at any rate draws attention to, the power of human interaction – be it through sight, sound, or touch – to evoke feeling and to make the humanity of even a seemingly bestial and disgusting sufferer apparent. If it were not so powerful, then Odysseus would not need to go to such lengths to avoid direct contact with his fellow Greek.

Take Odysseus's description of Philoctetes' cries in the opening lines of the play, for example:

Ἀκτὴ μὲν ἥδε τῆς περιρρύτου χθονὸς
Λήμνου, βροτοῖς ἄστιπτος οὐδ' οἰκουμένη,
ἔνθ', ὦ κρατίστου πατρὸς Ἑλλήνων τραφεὶς
Ἀχιλλέως παῖ Νεοπτόλεμε, τὸν Μηλιᾶ
Ποίαντος υἱὸν ἐξέθηκ' ἐγώ ποτε –
ταχθεὶς τόδ' ἔρδειν τῶν ἀνασσόντων ὕπο –
νόσῳ καταστάζοντα διαβόρῳ πόδα·
ὅτ' οὔτε λοιβῆς ἡμὶν οὔτε θυμάτων
παρῆν ἑκήλοις προσθιγεῖν, ἀλλ' ἀγρίαις
κατεῖχ' ἀεὶ πᾶν στρατόπεδον δυσφημίαις,
βοῶν, ἰύζων. ἀλλὰ ταῦτα μὲν τί δεῖ
λέγειν;

(1–12)

This is the shore of the sea-girt land of Lemnos, untrodden by mortals and uninhabited. Here it was, Neoptolemus, son of Achilles, you who were reared as the son of the noblest father among the Greeks, that I once put ashore the Malian, son of Poeas – I was ordered to do this by those in command – whose foot was oozing from a disease that was eating it away; for we could not pour libations or sacrifice in peace: he filled the entire camp with savage, ill-omened cries, screaming and shouting. But why must I speak of these things?

Odysseus's words present a stark and telling contrast with the Chorus members' perception and depiction of Philoctetes' cries. He begins his account of the abandonment of Philoctetes with a rather idyllic description of the island (τῆς περιρρύτου χθονὸς | Λήμνου, "the sea-girt land of Lemnos").[729] He proceeds to portray the wound on Philoctetes' foot in terms that stress its repulsive aspect (it oozes, καταστάζοντα) and associate his disease, and hence the sufferer it afflicts, with the animal realm (διαβόρῳ: the disease "devours" him).[730] Of particular interest to me here is the way in which Odysseus describes the sounds Philoctetes produced as a result of his wound. In his pain, Odysseus claims, Philoctetes voiced cries that were inhuman (ἀγρίαις, "savage") and unfavorable (δυσφημίαις). These noisy manifestations of Philoctetes' agony were, he says, unbearable and disruptive to the point of making sacrifices to the gods impossible for his fellow

---

[729] We may well suspect that the rosy depiction of Lemnos is intended to diminish Odysseus's and the other Greeks' culpability in the eyes of Neoptolemus. Nooter 2012, 125, notes the artificial nature of Odysseus's positive spin here.
[730] On Philoctetes' disease as a threat to his very identity, see n. 714.

Greeks.[731] Odysseus thus provides Neoptolemus with a plausible (albeit disputable and morally questionable) reason for why the Greeks abandoned one of their own on a deserted island and continued on their expedition to Troy without him, despite his experiencing obvious, severe, and undeserved suffering.[732]

Odysseus's account leaves us under the impression that the manifestations of Philoctetes' torment constituted an impediment to the proper carrying out of indispensable communal activities: he describes "savage" shouts creating unbearable noise and threatening the other Greeks' well-being, because propitiating the gods became, allegedly, unfeasible. In depicting Philoctetes thus, the son of Laertes provides Neoptolemus with a (disputable) excuse for the Greeks abandoning one of their own. Philoctetes was, according to Odysseus, an obstacle to the harmony and proper functioning of the community and was, accordingly, expelled. Odysseus's focus is solely on what he claims to have been the deleterious effects of the cries for the community, without any concern for the human suffering that caused these cries or any consideration of the ethical and social questions that the suffering of a *philos* raises for the rest of the community. By remaining alien and external to Philoctetes' suffering, Odysseus calls attention to his incapacity – or, rather, his unwillingness – to acknowledge and feel another's pain. This lack of human feeling is what led the Greeks to a greater violation of *philia:* abandoning Philoctetes and sailing on to Troy.[733]

---

[731] It is revealing of how grossly exaggerated this claim is that, after Helenus's oracle has been pronounced (declaring Philoctetes and his bow essential to the taking of Troy, 603–21), Philoctetes' pain and his cries of suffering are no longer even mentioned as a threat or hindrance to proper religious observances.

[732] Pucci in Pucci *et al.* 2003,157 *ad loc.* dismisses Odysseus's pseudoreligious excuses offhand and foregrounds the moral crime that abandoning Philoctetes actually represents – which is precisely what Odysseus is trying to cover up as best he can. Kitto points out that Odysseus glosses over some rather obvious, more humane alternatives: for instance, the Greeks could very well have sent Philoctetes home to Malis (Kitto 1956, 103–4). Pucci also stresses the blameworthiness of Neoptolemus's complicit acceptance of Odysseus's facile explanation: the young man, he says, should raise more questions (and eyebrows) (Pucci *et al.* 2003, 159 *ad loc.*). Neoptolemus's rather simplistic conception of divine sanction notwithstanding (see lines 191–200), it is clear that Philoctetes' suffering is undeserved, both through Odysseus's and Philoctetes' accounts of the origins of his supernatural wound, which resulted from his inadvertently stumbling into the sacred realm of Chrysê. On the different characters' relationship to the divine in this play, including Odysseus's utilitarian use of the gods as "the appendage of his own purposes," and Neoptolemus's evolving relation to the gods' purposes, see Segal 1977.

[733] It is possible that Odysseus cuts off his own speech because dwelling on Philoctetes' plight might give rise to pity – if not in his own heart, then in Neoptolemus's. Perrotta 1935, 409 believes that pity arises when he pronounces these words, though P. does not specify whose – only the spectator's, he says, is certain.

There is a wide discrepancy between Odysseus's and the Chorus's perceptions and depictions of Philoctetes' cries of pain, as well as between their different reactions to these cries. This disparity shows that Philoctetes' condition and symptoms are bestial and his presence detrimental only to the extent that his interlocutors perceive them to be.[734] While the Chorus's words and song are revealing of its members' compassionate disposition and of their ability to recognize the humanity and vulnerability that they share with Philoctetes, the way in which Odysseus describes the plight of a fellow Greek is consistent with and revealing of his general conception of human beings (*philoi* though they may be) as mere tools.[735]

The figure of Odysseus in the *Philoctetes* is a "degenerate descendant of the Homeric hero," in the words of Knox: he is a stereotypical representative of cynical fifth-century (Athenian) politicians, well versed in the sophistic manipulation of *logos* and empty rhetoric.[736] He deliberately spurns any heroic code or "standard of conduct of any kind," for "he is for victory, by any and every means."[737] The obtuseness of Odysseus's utilitarian frame of mind and his ap-

---

[734] This is not to say that the pain Philoctetes experiences does not threaten to dehumanize him. In fact, Philoctetes himself makes numerous references to his disease as a beast: see Segal 1981, 470 n. 38, for an exhaustive list of references to such occurrences; regarding the alienation that comes with such suffering, see also above, n. 714.

[735] On Odysseus's "instrumental view of human relations" (see lines 86–119) in contrast to Philoctetes' view, see Linforth 1956, 103–5. Nussbaum 1976, 35 ff., stresses Odysseus's inability "to make crucial distinctions between men and inanimate objects;" see also Segal 1981, 328–61; at 333–5, Segal describes how the arts of speech as Odysseus practices them "betray civilized values." Gardiner 1987, 20, contrasts the Chorus with Odysseus: "The Chorus ... clearly contrast with <Odysseus> in the humaneness of their consideration of Philoctetes' physical circumstances and their awareness that his existence must be a miserable one; there has been no such sign of humaneness in Odysseus." Cf. Austin: "Of suffering Odysseus had not a word to say" (Austin 2011, 84). Regarding Odysseus's initially successful attempt to convert Neoptolemus to his utilitarian views of human interactions, see the bibliography concerning the moral education of the young man in n. 655 Cairns (1993, 252–3) casts Neoptolemus's moral dilemma in terms of one that opposes "co-operative and competitive aspects of his concern for honour."

[736] Knox 1964, 124. On the ambiguous relationship between contemporary depictions of sophists and Odysseus's cunning use of *logos* to advance his agenda in the *Philoctetes*, see also Podlecki 1966; Rose 1976; Segal 1981; Blundell 1989; Ringer 1998 ch. 6; Worman 2000. De Romilly 1995, 97–109, revisits the question of the play's portrayal of Odysseus and the fifth-century demagogue he epitomizes from a slightly different angle; she argues that the drama does not so much embrace a counterposition to the sophists' as it highlights the questions most acutely raised by the intellectual climate of the time.

[737] The quote is also from Knox (see above note). *Logos* can be broadly defined here as "rational discourse and thought." Apfel 2011, 312–23, offers an overview of past scholarly discussions

proach to social, civic, and political matters are reflected in his conception and use of words and fellow humans as tools to meet certain ends. This is a fifth-century take on the shape-shifting and adaptable Odysseus *polytropos* of Homeric epic and of the *Odyssey* in particular: in the *Philoctetes,* the dexterous wielder of words of epic becomes a slicker, more contemporary version of himself, one who is strongly evocative of the fifth-century sophists.[738] His reduction of *logos* to the status of a malleable tool and his moral relativism disconnect him from any concern or quest for truth and are directly correlated with a lack of consideration for the intrinsic worth of human bonds within a community of *philoi*.[739]

Odysseus's response to Philoctetes' pain thus reflects a narrow conception of the value of human relationships and of communication in general. His deliberate choice to ban any form of (literal and metaphorical) physical interaction with Philoctetes at various points in the play is noteworthy.[740] While the audience's sense of the Chorus's humanity emerges when they witness the sailors' perceptive sensitivity to the nuances of Philoctetes' cries, conversely, Odysseus is repeatedly shown to remain blatantly and purposefully deaf and insensitive to those around him.[741] He has, it seems, numbed himself to the point of being unable to experience pain in response to what he perceives. He speaks some telling

---

which view Odysseus in the *Philoctetes* as the epitome of the hardhearted, pragmatic politician and deceitful master of sophistic rhetoric. Apfel herself proposes a more positive interpretation of Odysseus's character in the play (with which I cannot agree, for reasons that become clear in what follows).

738 The growing influence of sophistry at the time is also conveyed through the figure of Odysseus as he is portrayed in Euripides' plays, particularly the *Hecuba*, in which he is depicted in a highly negative light. Sophocles' *Ajax*, on the contrary, offers up an entirely different and even antithetical version of the tragic Odysseus we see in the *Philoctetes:* in that play, he is a profoundly compassionate and humane internal spectator to the plight of a fellow human being, Ajax. Regarding the varied usage of the traditional character of Odysseus in the culture of democratic Athens, see Suksi 2009.

739 This lack of concern for the truth eventually leads to the breakdown of social bonds and the failure of communication. On this matter, see e.g., Segal 1981, Podlecki 1966, Blundell 1987, and Worman 2000.

740 The empty shell Odysseus comes to represent is aptly encapsulated by Knox 1964, 125: "For Odysseus there is no heroic standard, no point of reference at all, no identity." Compare also Nussbaum 1976, 33; she describes Odysseus's "... lack of concern" resulting "in his appearing an oddly faceless, mechanical *persona*."

741 This brings to mind the connection that Aristotle makes in the *Nicomachean Ethics* between the degree of ethical rectitude in one's nature and one's ability to experience pleasure and pain at the right things: "The character must somehow preexist with an affinity for *aretê*, loving what is *kalos* and feeling discomfort at what is shameful" (179b29–31). The passage is quoted by Blundell 1988, 146, in reference to the gradual shaping of Neoptolemus's *physis*.

lines in this regard early on in the play, when he counsels the young Neoptolemus on how to gain Philoctetes' trust through deceit:

λέγων ὅσ' ἂν
θέλῃς καθ' ἡμῶν ἔσχατ' ἐσχάτων κακά.
τούτῳ γὰρ οὐδέν μ' ἀλγυνεῖς· εἰ δ' ἐργάσῃ
μὴ ταῦτα, λύπην πᾶσιν Ἀργείοις βαλεῖς.
(64–7)

> And you may add as many of the most extreme insults against me as you please, for by that you will give me no pain, but if you fail to do it, you will give grief to all the Argives.

Odysseus's words link his cynicism to a total lack of sensitivity – one that precludes his ability to feel pain, including the metaphorical, moral agony of shame (τούτῳ γὰρ οὐδέν μ' ἀλγυνεῖς) that will later cause Neoptolemus to cry out.

One might consider the possibility that Odysseus is providing a genuine account (in his own warped view) of Philoctetes' abandonment, rather than crafting a tale destined to exculpate himself and his fellow Greeks in the eyes of Neoptolemus, if it weren't for his blatant eagerness to move on from the topic: "But why must I speak of these things?" (ἀλλὰ ταῦτα μὲν τί δεῖ | λέγειν, 11–12). The intentional brevity of his account and his calculated *aposiopesis* are telling signs of unease and of some degree of disingenuousness on his part.[742] We might well venture to suggest that his portrayal of Philoctetes' cries of pain is, at the very least, exaggerated. Later in the play, when Odysseus wants to force him to board the Greek ships, Philoctetes voices his skepticism at the legitimacy of the reasons put forward by Odysseus for abandoning him, which he calls a mere pretext (1031–4). In fact, Odysseus's swift and cold depiction of the abandonment of Philoctetes is symptomatic of every human interaction in which he engages. He considers neither the humanity nor the identity of his interlocutor; only his own agenda and his interlocutor's role in serving it come into play.[743]

In order to maintain a coldly utilitarian stance in every human interaction and in order for his manipulative agenda to play out smoothly, Odysseus remains at a calculatedly safe remove from any sort of human touch or contact with Phil-

---

[742] For this reason, I do not believe, as Knox suggests (1964, 186 n. 1), that Odysseus is "delicately" omitting to mention the stench of the hero's wound (which Philoctetes subsequently mentions himself, 1032); the omission is more likely due to Odysseus's desire to shift away from the incriminating account of the abandonment to another topic: his plan of deceit.

[743] On Odysseus's self-serving immorality masquerading as devotion to the public good, see especially Blundell 1989, 184 ff.

octetes. To the extent that it is possible, he also remains out of sight, by having Neoptolemus interact with Philoctetes instead and even ordering the young man to send out scouts to make sure no encounter between himself and the wounded hero will occur:

> τὸν οὖν παρόντα πέμψον ἐς κατασκοπήν,
> μὴ καὶ λάθῃ με προσπεσών.
> (45–6)
>
> So send the man you have with you to look out, lest he should suddenly fall upon me.[744]

He does not confront his prey (Philoctetes) directly but uses Neoptolemus as a shield, as Philoctetes later points out in his rage (πρόβλημα σαυτοῦ παῖδα τόνδ', 1008). When Philoctetes threatens to commit suicide later in the play, Odysseus does not even deign to prevent the old hero whom he has pushed to such despair from doing so; this would involve direct physical contact. He has two of his men stop Philoctetes in his stead.[745]

Odysseus never looks upon Philoctetes' suffering directly. His character maintains a physical distance and avoids any human interaction involved in the execution of his plan. Instead, he plays the role of behind-the-scenes playwright and stage director of a playlet, in which he assigns the role of protagonist to Neoptolemus.[746] It is Odysseus's carefully maintained distance that enables him to disregard Philoctetes' suffering and the Greeks' earlier betrayal of him and to encourage Neoptolemus to do the same, in view of what he claims to be the greatest priority: the reason of state and collective victory at Troy, in the name of which he spurns a "standard of conduct of any kind."[747] Like Orestes in Aeschylus's *Choephori*, he focuses on abstract principles and an invisible form of good and neglects the human body before him. His claims to patriotic fervor and his bombastic invocation of Neoptolemus's necessary self-sacrifice for the

---

744 Odysseus also feels justified fear that Philoctetes should see him, and prudently exits the scene, lest he be recognized by Philoctetes and shot by his "inescapable arrows that convey death" (ἰούς <γ'> ἀφύκτους καὶ προπέμποντας φόνον, 105).
745 That there are two men intervening is apparent from the dual at 1003. Odysseus is not saving Philoctetes from death out of concern for him, of course, but because he must be brought to Troy.
746 The only time Odysseus does take the sight of the suffering hero into account is when he contemplates displaying Philoctetes to the Greek army as a trophy, a tangible sign of his successful mission (944). Here again, his vantage point is that of a stage director, while he reduces Philoctetes to no more than a stage prop in the spectacle of his own glorious success as the one who retrieved the man needed to take Troy.
747 Knox 1964, 124.

good of the community (see especially lines 96–122) are a pendant to his lack of emotional responsiveness to Philoctetes. His deliberate choice to interact with the sufferer as little as possible is both what leads and enables him to ignore Philoctetes' humanity and dignity entirely.

Seale contrasts "the careful distance of Odysseus" with the subsequent close contact Neoptolemus has with Philoctetes:

> The spatial distinction provides the measure for the degrees of personal involvement which are explored.... . The physical location of Odysseus on the margins of the action is actually one of the striking external features of the drama and admirably illustrates the detachment and caution of his role. Neoptolemus, by contrast, is implicated in the action.[748]

Neoptolemus's role is, indeed, the active and involved role of agent: he is the protagonist in a play-within-a-play designed by Odysseus.[749] But this role involves close contact, as Seale notes, and Neoptolemus will find himself evolving as a result of it, especially when he takes on the unexpected role of spectator to Philoctetes' pain and character during the hero's bouts of agony.

Neoptolemus's alignment with Odysseus's plan at the start of the play is, interestingly, cast in terms that equate the numbing of his moral sensitivities with a lack of feeling that might be understood both literally and figuratively, on both the physical and the emotional level.[750] When Neoptolemus initially displays strong resistance to the son of Laertes' limited and unethical conception of human exchange and his strictly utilitarian view of language, the young man mentions the *pain* that words of deceit cause him. They are, he suggests, just as harmful as the deeds he is required to carry out by making use of false words intended to trick his addressee:

> ἐγὼ μὲν οὓς ἂν τῶν λόγων ἀλγῶ κλύων,
> Λαερτίου παῖ, τούσδε καὶ πράσσειν στυγῶ·
> ἔφυν γὰρ οὐδὲν ἐκ τέχνης πράσσειν κακῆς,
> οὔτ' αὐτὸς οὔθ', ὥς φασιν, οὑκφύσας ἐμέ.
>
> (86–9)
>
> Whatever words I feel pain hearing, son of Laertes, these I also hate to put into practice! It is my nature to do nothing by treacherous conniving; neither do I, nor, I am told, did my father.[751]

---

748 Seale 1982, 29.
749 On the metatheatrical dimensions of this internal playlet, see above, n. 289.
750 Later, his moral pain will translate into a physical one, as we will see.
751 My translation here is based on Schein's commentary (2013, 136 *ad loc.*).

Central to the act that Neoptolemus is asked to put on is the use of deceit. Deceit involves a discrepancy between word and action that goes against his natural penchant for forthrightness and truth, both of which are chief components of the heroic *ethos* he inherited from his father, Achilles. Neoptolemus's words here are reminiscent of Achilles' words in the embassy scene of the *Iliad*, in which the hero professes his scorn for the likes of Odysseus:

> ἐχθρὸς γάρ μοι κεῖνος ὁμῶς Ἀΐδαο πύλῃσιν
> ὅς χ' ἕτερον μὲν κεύθῃ ἐνὶ φρεσίν, ἄλλο δὲ εἴπῃ.
> (9.312–3)
>
> As hateful to me as the gates of Hades
> is the one who says one thing, but hides another in his heart.[752]

By collaborating in Odysseus's deceitful scheme, Neoptolemus realizes, he would forsake the heroic ideal voiced by Achilles in book 9 of the *Iliad*: one of congruence between word and deed, which amounts to a congruence between appearance and reality. At this early stage, rather than forsake his *physis*, Neoptolemus considers using outright force in getting Philoctetes to come to Troy, believing it would be preferable to the duplicitous act he is being asked to put on. But Heracles' inescapable arrows are in Philoctetes' possession, and force is not an option. The idea of playing a central role in the conquest of Troy wins out in the face of what is presented to him as no more than a brief bout of shamelessness:

> νῦν δ' εἰς ἀναιδὲς ἡμέρας μέρος βραχὺ
> δός μοι σεαυτόν, κᾆτα τὸν λοιπὸν χρόνον
> κέκλησο πάντων εὐσεβέστατος βροτῶν.
> (83–5)
>
> Now give yourself to me for a few hours of shamelessness, and later for the rest of time be called the most dutiful of mortals!

---

[752] Neoptolemus's statements in lines 86–9 and his subsequent remarks (βούλομαι δ', ἄναξ, καλῶς | δρῶν ἐξαμαρτεῖν μᾶλλον ἢ νικᾶν κακῶς, 94–5) have, since Antiquity, prompted commentators to quote this passage from *Iliad* 9. Thus, the scholiast on *Philoctetes* 94 writes: εἰσάγει δὲ αὐτὸν ὁ Σοφοκλῆς τὸν τοῦ πατρὸς λόγον λέγοντα κτλ. On the heroic ideal within the *Philoctetes* and the indebtedness of the play to the Homeric figure of Achilles, see e.g., Rabel 1997 and Schein 2006. The latter brings to light the pervasive allusions to both the *Iliad* and the *Odyssey* throughout the play and their role in generating a sense of tension for the audience between the epic paradigms and values epitomized by the Homeric versions of Odysseus and Achilles, and the fifth-century "tragic" versions of the characters. See also Schein 2012.

Neoptolemus is swayed by Odysseus's seductive rhetoric. The son of Laertes promises him eternal renown in carefully chosen terms redolent of the very sort of nobility Achilles would condone: "You will be called clever, and at the same time valiant" (σοφός τ' ἂν αὐτὸς κἀγαθὸς κεκλῇ' ἅμα, 119).[753]

The staged play-within-a-play can now begin: with his eyes set on the prospect of obtaining recognition from the entire Greek army, Neoptolemus embraces what Odysseus has cunningly labeled as the Greek cause, though it is with the prospect of individual glory that he lures the young man. And so it is that Neoptolemus renounces all sense of shame, for the time being at least: "Let it be! I will do it, casting off all shame!" (ἴτω· ποήσω, πᾶσαν αἰσχύνην ἀφείς, 120).[754] He, too, begins to use *logoi* as mere tools to reach his goal, in keeping with Odysseus's teachings. According to the latter, human interactions and verbal exchanges are simply geared toward achieving one's own objectives by all means necessary, without any regard for truth or for the intrinsic and communal value of genuine interpersonal exchanges between true friends, based on trust and the mutual recognition of both interlocutors' humanity and dignity.

Even after he sets aside any sense of shame and starts to implement Odysseus's plan, Neoptolemus continues to preserve a sense of the sort of integrity that he naturally aspires to embrace, especially as he watches Philoctetes consistently abide by it with uncompromising steadfastness. At various key points in the play, the poetics suggest the transformative power exerted on Neoptolemus by the act of watching Philoctetes and of observing the consequences of his ploy as they play out at the hero's expense. The audience watches Neoptolemus as he watches and evaluates Philoctetes' behavior in the face of searing agony — a shaming template against which the youth cannot help but see his own behavior fall short, with increasing discomfort. While an abundance of language referring to the act of watching underscores the power of the spectacle of suffering to change its young witness, sounds play a crucial role in conveying Neoptolemus's hesitation and transformation to the audience.

---

753 Compare Odysseus's devious use of these terms at 79–86, and contrast with their use in a genuine sense by Philoctetes at 473–81; for the similarity and a comparison between the two, see Schein 2013, 203 *ad* 473 ff.

754 Odysseus's amoral code has a destructive impact on the community, in contrast to the one that Neoptolemus gradually comes to espouse once again. Thus, the young man's evolution involves "a ... complex negotiation between what is due to himself and what is due to others" (Fulkerson 2006, 52). On Greek ethical life as communal, see Gill 1996.

Watch yourself, young man

From the start of the play, it is clear that Odysseus has mapped out Neoptolemus's act carefully, and has even thought out alternative scenarios, should the need arise. In their initial exchange, he tells Neoptolemus that, if matters seem to move along too slowly between him and Philoctetes, and the plan's implementation seems to linger, he (Odysseus) will send in a third actor, a man disguised as a sea captain, who will tell a cunning tale that will corroborate Neoptolemus's tall tale and fake act, and thus help the Greeks hoodwink Philoctetes into boarding Neoptolemus's ship.[755] After the Chorus enjoins Neoptolemus to pity Philoctetes, a false merchant sent by Odysseus arrives (542) and delivers to Neoptolemus the fabricated news that the Argives are on their way to Lemnos in pursuit of him, and that Odysseus and Diomedes have set off in pursuit of "another man," who turns out to be Philoctetes.[756] This is a notoriously ambiguous passage, in which every exchange between Neoptolemus and this false merchant is laden with double meaning. Neoptolemus asks the false merchant to "speak openly" (581) before him and Philoctetes, whom he refers to as his "great friend;" he invites the merchant to conceal none of the things that he has heard concerning Odysseus's alleged plan. To this, the merchant replies, with equal ambiguity, that Neoptolemus should "watch what he is doing."[757] Neoptolemus retorts that he has, in fact, been watching what he has been doing carefully, and for a while now:

> Ἐμ. ὅρα τί ποιεῖς, παῖ.
>   Νε. σκοπῶ κἀγὼ πάλαι.
> Ἐμ. σὲ θήσομαι τῶνδ' αἴτιον.
>   Νε. ποιοῦ λέγων.
>   (589–90)
>
> Mer. Watch what you are doing, my son!
>   Neo. I have been watching closely indeed for a long time.

---

[755] Odysseus spells out this back-up plan at 126–31. There is a (perhaps playful) metatheatrical and self-referential dimension at play here. It is well known that Aristotle credits Sophocles with the introduction of a third actor to the tragic stage: here, his character, Odysseus, plans for the introduction of a third actor within his own play-within-a-play, in addition to Neoptolemus and Philoctetes and the Chorus, who are already onstage. In fact, that third actor will be a merchant, who comes accompanied by a fourth (mute) sailor (542).
[756] See 542–627.
[757] Easterling 1997, 170, discusses some of the multiple possible meanings of each of the characters' replies and notes the ambiguity of the expression in Greek, "watching oneself."

> Mer. I shall hold you responsible for this!
> Neo. Fine, do that! But speak![758]

Neoptolemus perhaps means that he has been watching (σκοπῶ) what he has been doing for a while in the sense that he has been carefully implementing Odysseus's plan, manipulating Philoctetes with false tales and, now, false displays of his trustworthiness. But his words could also mean that he has been watching what he has been doing from a moral standpoint.[759]

Later, when Philoctetes is asleep, and Neoptolemus is in possession of the bow that Philoctetes has entrusted to him, the young man is in a position to make the next move: the hero has given him his trust, his friendship, and his sole means of subsistence. He considers what he will say now, the next step in the plan being to get Philoctetes on board his ship. The Chorus underlines the crucial turning point at which Neoptolemus finds himself:

> ὦ τέκνον, ὅρα ποῦ στάσῃ,
> ποῖ δὲ βάσῃ,
> πῶς δέ σοι τἀντεῦθεν
> φροντίδος. ὁρᾷς ἤδη.
>
> (833–5)
>
> My son, watch where you stand, where you go, and what your next thought from hence will be. You see already!

Then once more, at 861–2, the Chorus again uses language that refers to the act of watching in an ambiguous manner: "Look, see if your speech suits the moment!" (ὅρα, βλέπ' εἰ καίρια | φθέγγῃ·) To them, this exhortation suggests the cautious, calculating execution of Odysseus's plan, but it also reminds the audience of the hesitation that comes with observation, because watching, for Neoptolemus, also means perceiving the morally commendable nature of his victim and the morally reprehensible nature of his own choices with respect to Philoc-

---

[758] Reinhardt 1933 describes the incapacity for words to be understood by either party as a polyphony in which true communication becomes impossible. Cf. Pucci 2013, 231 *ad loc.*
[759] Easterling 1997, 170, suggests this as well:

> The audience may take [these words], if they wish, as a hint that Neoptolemus has been feeling qualms about the propriety of deceiving the trusting Philoctetes. On the other hand, it could "simply" mean "Don't worry; I am carrying out Odysseus' orders and playing my part well." What is important here is that the ironic play with the dramatic medium is intimately related to the central issues of *Philoctetes*: truth and lies, loyalty and treachery, honour and self-interest, the conflicting needs, and the conflicting rhetoric, of individuals and groups.

tetes.⁷⁶⁰ Soon after this, the audience is given tangible vocal signs that Neoptolemus can stand his own duplicity no more.

The sounds of Neoptolemus's moral awakening

For the first part of the play, Neoptolemus embraces the worldview of Odysseus, or at least the mode of human interaction that it prescribes. The cunning speaker has successfully convinced the young man that what brings great influence, as well as recognition from others, is a pragmatic, utilitarian approach to human interactions in which the word, *logos*, is king, granting as it does the power to manipulate one's interlocutors to achieve one's ends. When Odysseus encourages Neoptolemus to tell lies that "bring salvation" (108–11) in the opening exchange between the two men, Neoptolemus already shows his moral scruples and indignation. He imagines that he will not be able to bear Philoctetes' gaze as he delivers falsehoods: "With what kind of face will one be able to utter these words?" (πῶς οὖν βλέπων τις ταῦτα τολμήσει λακεῖν, 110).⁷⁶¹ Later, when these moral scruples become overpowering, we see Neoptolemus return to the same idea: it is the anticipation of the spectacle of his own shameful conduct as it will be viewed by Philoctetes (sc., with horror and indignation at his betrayal) that causes him to reveal the entire plot to the hero (αἰσχρὸς φανοῦμαι, 906).

I wish to focus here on two main points regarding the connections that exist between the spectacle of Philoctetes' agony, its impact on Neoptolemus, and the latter's response. The first is the question of what sways Neoptolemus as he watches Philoctetes suffer — the motives for his evolution. The second is the question of the means by which the dramatist conveys to the external audience how and when Neoptolemus is swayed. As we have seen, while Philoctetes is still onstage, the spectators simply cannot trust any of what Neoptolemus says, as his

---

760 The role in which Odysseus is cast in the internal mini-drama at the start of Sophocles' *Ajax* is comparable, in that he occupies a double status that reminds the audience of what they share with him: "The spectator, as the role of Odysseus demonstrates, cannot remain uninvolved: simultaneously participating in a spectacle and watching it, he is forced to comprehend his double status as both player and audience. In other words, he is de facto complicit in the events he has come to see represented" (Dobrov 2001, 68–9).
761 Schein 2013, 140–1 *ad loc.*, underlines Neoptolemus's strong sense of the shameful nature of his own conduct already at this early stage, and makes the compelling suggestion that Neoptolemus "perhaps reflects a desire to distance himself from the shame that might be seen *in his own eyes*" (italics mine). On the internalization of the gaze of others as an important component of shame, see Williams 1993, ch. 4 and below, p. 290ff.

words may be intended to deceive the hero. They can, however, measure the intensity of Philoctetes' onstage display of agony and its impact on Neoptolemus in other ways, and they are even afforded glimpses (perhaps we might call them "sound bites") that reflect Neoptolemus's inner turmoil and evolution, long before his actions illustrate it.

Before I turn to the "sound bites" that reflect the emergence of a genuine friendship between the two men, it is useful to turn back to an earlier passage in the drama, where Philoctetes describes what he (at that point mistakenly) perceives to be an affinity of minds and values between him and Achilles' son, by way of a musical metaphor. It is early in the play, shortly after Philoctetes comes on stage and he and Neoptolemus meet for the first time. The young man, following Odysseus's recommendation (lines 54–69), has told the fabricated tale of his own betrayal at the hands of Odysseus and the Atreids. He seeks to represent himself as one who shares in Philoctetes' hatred of them so as to secure the hero's trust and friendship.[762] The stratagem works superbly.[763] Presuming, as Neoptolemus intended him to, that he has found one whose plight and humiliation match his own, Philoctetes takes the young man's story of being cheated out of his father's armor (which is, in fact, Ajax's story) to be a solid basis for *philia* between them. The language that he uses to describe his satisfaction in the friendship that stems from shared enmity is rich in imagery:

> Φι. ἔχοντες, ὡς ἔοικε, σύμβολον σαφὲς
> λύπης πρὸς ἡμᾶς, ὦ ξένοι, πεπλεύκατε,
> καί μοι προσᾴδεθ' ὥστε γιγνώσκειν ὅτι
> ταῦτ' ἐξ Ἀτρειδῶν ἔργα κἀξ Ὀδυσσέως.
> (403–6)
>
> You have sailed here, strangers, with a pain that clearly dovetails with mine, and your tale harmonizes with my own: I recognize these as the actions of the sons of Atreus and Odysseus!

---

762 Shared enmity toward common wrongdoers establishes *de facto* friendship. Regarding common objects of hatred as a basis for the ritualized friendship of *philia*, see e.g., Segal 1981, 332, and Blundell 1989, 196. Neoptolemus himself describes this bond later (ἐγὼ μὲν αὐτοῖς δυσμενής· οὗτος δέ μοι | φίλος μέγιστος, οὕνεκ' Ἀτρείδας στυγεῖ, 585–6).

763 Though we may well assume Neoptolemus's story to be entirely fictitious, it is in fact impossible to know whether there is a kernel of truth to the tale or whether it has been entirely invented by Neoptolemus. Scholars see varying possible degrees of veracity in the account: see Pucci 2003 *ad loc.* on 343–90, with bibliography. Visser 1998, 89, also provides an overview of various scholarly positions touching on this question, as does Calder III 1971, 389–407.

In the translation above, I use the term 'dovetails' to refer to the way in which Philoctetes imagines how his suffering and resulting disposition toward the Greeks are shared by Neoptolemus, because of the slights they have incurred at the hands of the same enemies.[764] The term σύμβολον in Greek actually refers to a physical object that Philoctetes uses metaphorically to convey the compatibility of their stories, dispositions, and values with a concrete visual image. It is an appropriate physical object to suggest the harmony of minds that goes hand in hand with an emerging friendship: in its original use, the object served as "a material indication of identification or agreement" that "may have begun as a private practice as a reminder of *xenia* or ritualized friendship."[765] The practice in question involved two individuals or groups breaking an object in two for each to keep one of the two halves, which could later be used as a token of recognition and a reminder of a relationship of *philia* that had been previously established between individuals.[766] Here, Philoctetes uses the σύμβολον to describe in palpable terms how he and Neoptolemus are bound by a ritualized *philia* (or so he thinks) – not because of past *xenia*, but because of a shared experience of painful exclusion and dishonor (λύπη, 404) suffered at the hands of the very same enemies.

Following the concrete image of the σύμβολον, the power of a story to establish a relationship is then conveyed by a musical metaphor: "And your tale harmonizes with my own: I recognize these as the actions of the sons of Atreus and Odysseus!" (καί μοι προσᾴδεθ' ὥστε γιγνώσκειν ὅτι | ταῦτ' ἐξ Ἀτρειδῶν ἔργα κἀξ Ὀδυσσέως, 405–6).[767] There are only very few attestations of προσᾴδω ("to harmonize with") from the classical period.[768] The only instance other than the one we have here in which the word is used metaphorically in a way that denotes

---

[764] The Chorus later vouches for the authenticity of Neoptolemus's tale through feigned distress and a false oath.
[765] See *OCD* s.v. "σύμβολον." Regarding the use of σύμβολα in ritualized friendship, see Herman 1987, 59 ff.
[766] We have examples of the familiarity of the meaning of σύμβολον and its metaphorical usage from the classical period, including the famous instance in which it is used in the humorous theory of creation offered up by Aristophanes in Plato's *Symposium* (191d): each human being is said to be "perpetually in search of his corresponding σύμβολον," or other half.
[767] Literally, "you *harmonize with me*."
[768] Of the three we have in addition to this Sophoclean instance, two are literal instances which explicitly refer to singing, either unaccompanied or in harmony with an instrument. One such occurrence is found in Aristophanes, where it is used absolutely to express the act of "singing the songs in a tragedy" (Ar., *Eq.* 401). In one of two Platonic occurrences, it is also used literally, in a context where reference is made to music and "singing to the reed" – that is, singing to the tune of, in harmony with the reed: Pl., *Lg.* 670b.

"singing in harmony with, chiming in" is in Plato's *Phaedrus*, where it contributes to defining an agreement as a meeting of the minds.[769] In our passage, the metaphor illustrates how a story can be a performative utterance of sorts: it can both reflect and express the like-mindedness of two individuals, who thus figuratively "sing to the same tune." It is as though form (each of their stories, described as songs) reflected content (the slight that they both suffered — or so Philoctetes has been led to believe – at the hands of the Greeks). To Philoctetes, their tales harmonize with one another. The musical metaphor reflects his perception of what he considers to be a natural compatibility between his disposition and values (integrity and trust) and Neoptolemus's, in the face of a common, disloyal enemy (the Greeks that have betrayed them).[770] Philoctetes' words here would be an apt description of the choral song in the *parodos*, wherein the Chorus sang a song of lamentation. At that point, the sailors' mode of expression was an actual song in which they sang the pain that they felt in response to Philoctetes' own "song" of pain (as expressed through his cries), and thereby demonstrated the sympathetic nature of their emerging feeling of pity. Here, on the contrary, there is great pathos in Philoctetes' enthusiastic appraisal of the harmony that he imagines connects him with his interlocutor, because we know that this harmony is fake.[771] Yet this language also foreshadows the genuine mutual understanding and shared values that eventually unite the two men and turn Neoptolemus against Odysseus.

As time goes by and Philoctetes' trust in him increases, Neoptolemus's own duplicity becomes increasingly unbearable to him. He comes to a point where he can no longer stand to be just the sort of man that his own father, Achilles, Philoctetes' dear friend, loathed more than anything.[772] The process leading up to that breaking point and the decisive moments in which Neoptolemus's emotional responses readjust his moral compass are revealed to the audience long before they are spelled out to Philoctetes by Neoptolemus's actual words.

The depiction of a character's inner (emotional and psychological) world always comes with its challenges, especially within the dramatic genre, in which

---

769 Pl., *Phdr.* 86e: ἔπειτα [δὲ] ἀκούσαντας ἢ συγχωρεῖν αὐτοῖς ἐάν τι δοκῶσι προσᾴδειν, ἐὰν δὲ μή, οὕτως ἤδη ὑπερδικεῖν τοῦ λόγου, "And then, after we have heard them, we can either agree with them, *if they seem to strike the proper note*, or, if they do not, we can proceed to argue in defense of our reasoning" (translation based on Fowler 1953).
770 Another (true) source of friendship between the two men are the friends that they share — most importantly, Neoptolemus's now dead father, Achilles (329–35).
771 Ringer 1998, 112 remarks that Philoctetes' reference to the Chorus's song (προσᾴδω) "self-consciously hints at the artificiality of the Chorus's false performance."
772 See the earlier quotation of Hom., *Il.* 9.312–3.

there is no omniscient narrator providing the audience with additional, "objective" information regarding the workings of a character's inner thoughts.⁷⁷³ These difficulties are compounded in the *Philoctetes* because, as we have seen, for the better part of the play (until Neoptolemus's confession at 915– 26), all of the characters (other than Philoctetes himself) are directly involved in executing Odysseus's plan of deceit. Neoptolemus is the only one whose feigned innocence is credible in Philoctetes' eyes, because he is Achilles' son and because he was not part of the initial expedition of Greeks who abandoned him on Lemnos. That is also the reason why Odysseus has made him the primary actor in the mini-play in which he has asked him to play a key role, and why we, as an audience, have trouble knowing when and whether his words are genuine.

Sounds, as we have seen, play a prominent role in conveying the dynamics of interpersonal relationships within the play. First off, they are central in conveying the lack of any companionship that causes Philoctetes so much pain, as we have seen in the choral descriptions of his desperate isolation. Sounds also play an essential role in relating the powerful impact of Philoctetes' cries on the Chorus members, and in differentiating between characters according to their widely differing reactions to his suffering. We have just seen how a sound metaphor is used by Philoctetes when he mistakenly assumes that Neoptolemus is his friend, based on his story of having also been slighted by the Atreids and Odysseus. Sounds continue to play an important role in depicting the evolving relationship between the play's two protagonists, by pinpointing the key moments of Neoptolemus's internal transformation. Sophocles portrays – indeed, foregrounds – the milestones in Neoptolemus's ethical maturation and communicates that inner evolution to the audience by a means that reaches beyond the semantic content of words *per se*.

The moment toward the middle of the play in which Neoptolemus directly witnesses Philoctetes' onstage agony for the first time is a crucial turning point in the young man's relationship to the wounded hero.⁷⁷⁴ The actual *result* of Neoptolemus's evolution is clear from the various decisions he makes and the

---

773 The spectators are never given a guarantee of authenticity regarding any characters' words, which are the sole source of information that they are given in drama. Even asides and monologues are sometimes problematic, as we have no stage directions indicating whether they are soliloquies, or whether another character is still present onstage, overhearing what is being said. The audience is not given any indication as to whether a character intends her words to be overheard or not.
774 Zerba 2012, 55 notes how Neoptolemus' inner turmoil, which she calls *psychomachia*, is "brought about when the role-playing Neoptolemus as actor becomes an onstage *theatês*, or spectator, of Philoctetes' suffering."

actions he undertakes later on, including his pivotal decision to reveal the truth to Philoctetes about the Greeks' deceptive plan and his blatant disobedience of Odysseus's orders (915). The emotional *process* of Neoptolemus's moral awakening and his changing emotional responses to the spectacle of Philoctetes' suffering in the climactic scene of his agony that lead to the above decision, are what I wish to focus on here.

As Philoctetes' pain assails him with unbearable ferocity, the hero gradually loses the ability to articulate actual words and then to speak at all, before losing consciousness altogether. Communication between him and Neoptolemus, who stands by and looks on as he writhes in agony, is hindered. Instead, he barks out shouts of pain in a series of increasingly inarticulate, onomatopoeic outbursts.[775] These cries have received considerable attention already from other scholars.[776] I turn my attention to Neoptolemus's subsequent articulation of his reaction to them: his own silences and cries, both of which reflect his increasing "moral pain."[777]

When Philoctetes sinks to the ground and falls unconscious, overpowered by his illness (820), Neoptolemus has an ambiguous exchange with the Chorus, leaving the sailors (and the audience) unsure once more as to where he stands in

---

[775] See lines 750–4:

Νε. τί δ' ἔστιν οὕτω νεοχμὸν ἐξαίφνης, ὅτου
τοσήνδ' ἰυγὴν καὶ στόνον σαυτοῦ ποῇ;
Φι. οἶσθ', ὦ τέκνον;
              Νε. τί ἔστιν;
                    Φι. οἶσθ', ὦ παῖ;
                          Νε. τί σοί;
οὐκ οἶδα.
                    Φι. πῶς οὐκ οἶσθα; παππαπαππαπαῖ.

[776] Among other things, the passage I quote in the previous footnote has been seen as reduction of Philoctetes' language to a subhuman level. For the extralinguistic nature of Philoctetes' cries, see e.g., Blundell 1989; Worman 2000, 24ff.; and Pucci 2003, *ad loc*. Later scholars' fruitful reflections on the cries can be contrasted with earlier interpretations, which seem to misunderstand the point of these extrametrical lines (Dawe simply emended them [1978, 128]). Philoctetes' stammered interjections are actually rich in meaning; among other things, they contain a pun referring to the infancy (*in-fans*) to which the suffering hero is being forced to revert: παῖ (Worman 2000).

[777] On Neoptolemus's "moral pain" in this particular passage, see Aultman-Moore 1994. Scholars have tried to pinpoint the exact moment at which Neoptolemus begins to feel this pain but have not come to any sort of agreement. See Fulkerson 2006, 51 n. 11, for an assessment of past opinions and bibliography regarding the matter.

relation to the hero.[778] After he regains consciousness, Philoctetes' pain has abated somewhat; the young man's agitation, on the other hand, continues to increase steadily. At this point, Neoptolemus has been leading the hero toward the Greek ships. He realizes that as soon as Philoctetes catches sight of them, he will understand that he has been tricked. Not only is the Greeks' scheme about to be discovered by Philoctetes, but so is Neoptolemus's own, active role in it. His betrayal and the false, deceitful persona he has embraced will be exposed: the young man Philoctetes has come to trust and love will be revealed as a traitor. At this prospect, Neoptolemus comes to such a point of agony that he finally blurts out:

> Νε. παπαῖ· τί δῆτ' <ἂν> δρῷμ' ἐγὼ τοὐνθένδε γε;
> Φι. τί δ' ἔστιν, ὦ παῖ; ποῖ ποτ' ἐξέβης λόγῳ;
> Νε. οὐκ οἶδ' ὅπῃ χρὴ τἄπορον τρέπειν ἔπος.
> (895–7)
>
> Ne. Ah! What am I supposed to do from here on?
> Phi. What is it, child? Where are you going with these words?
> Ne. I don't know in which direction to turn my words – I am stuck.

The young man's outburst makes manifest the irrepressible wave of emotion that overwhelms him at this point. His statement is muddled, in a direct and genuine reflection of his confused frame of mind. His cry escapes him, and he fumbles to give Philoctetes an explanation when the latter inquires about it, answering with enigmatic words (οὐκ οἶδ').

Neoptolemus goes on to provide increasingly revealing explanations for his distress, ostensibly addressed to Philoctetes, but which are highly illuminating for the audience as well. In these explanations, it becomes clear that it is not just the spectacle of Philoctetes' agony that leads Neoptolemus to waver. Though his intensifying feeling of pity for the suffering hero plays a major role, there is another dimension to the spectacle before him that leads him to reconsider his stance. In watching Philoctetes, he is directly exposed to his father's heroic values, enacted before him by Philoctetes' combination of forthrightness and trust. The impact that the spectacle of Philoctetes' pain has on him is linked to the noble nature that he perceives in the hero and the new lens it leads him to cast on himself.

When he comes to after collapsing, Philoctetes is overwhelmed with gratitude that Neoptolemus and his sailors have not fled and left him to his disease,

---

[778] The chorus expresses its confusion and concern regarding Neoptolemus's unclear stance in lines 833–8.

as all others have before. As far as he is concerned, Neoptolemus is the first to have pitied him and remained with him. Despite having witnessed the repulsive aspects of his malady and its symptoms at their most extreme, Neoptolemus and his men are still at his side (869–76). Philoctetes commends the young man for what he takes to be an unmistakable sign of trustworthiness, reliability, and friendship: only a noble nature sprung from noble ancestors (ἀλλ' εὐγενὴς γὰρ ἡ φύσις κἀξ εὐγενῶν, 874) would endure a spectacle so thoroughly unpleasant to witness. Even Philoctetes realizes that his loud screams and the stench of his swelling and suppurating wound are repulsive (876). The audience knows better: Neoptolemus has remained close by not, or at least not mainly, out of concern or pity for the hero but in order to carry out the mission that serves Odysseus's and his own interest and (if we are to believe Odysseus's claims earlier in the play) the collective interest of the Greeks: taking the hero with them to Troy. Philoctetes does not know of this agenda nor of Neoptolemus's ulterior motives, and so, as the two men begin making their way toward the ship that Philoctetes wrongly believes will take him home at long last, he lavishes praise on Neoptolemus for having endured the disgusting symptoms of his bout of pain.

When he hears Philoctetes' expressions of gratitude, Neoptolemus feels with special acuteness the disparity between the deceitful role that he has taken on since the start of the play and the person Philoctetes believes him to be: Achilles' worthy son and heir. The undeserved praise that Philoctetes bestows on him serves as a harrowing reminder for Neoptolemus of the gulf between the moral standards that his nature (*physis*) beckons him to follow and the utilitarian code that he has espoused for the sake of glory. Every aspect of his existence has become "distasteful" (902) because of the dissonance between his *physis* and his actions, as he later explains, albeit cryptically:

> ἅπαντα δυσχέρεια, τὴν αὑτοῦ φύσιν
> ὅταν λιπών τις δρᾷ τὰ μὴ προσεικότα.
> (902–3)
>
> All is disgust when one leaves one's own nature
> and does things that misfit it![779]

At the height of Philoctetes' agony, just before the old man collapsed to the ground unconscious, Neoptolemus had fallen silent, prompting Philoctetes ask about his sudden speechlessness, at which point the youth had given the hero

---

[779] I discuss Neoptolemus's self-directed moral disgust here and the language he uses to express it more at length in a chapter of the forthcoming volume on disgust edited by D. Lateiner and D. Spatharas in the Oxford University Press "Emotions of the Past" series.

a puzzling explanation: "I have been in pain long since, lamenting for your woes" (ἀλγῶ πάλαι δὴ τἀπὶ σοὶ στένων κακά, 806). The claim that he has been "in pain" (ἀλγῶ) because of Philoctetes' woes invites the audience to consider the spectacle of Philoctetes' torture to be the basis for Neoptolemus's own malaise. What he is describing here, it seems, is the experience of a growing surge of pity on seeing Philoctetes' miserable condition reach an excruciating level of intensity. But "long since" (πάλαι) suggests that Neoptolemus is now experiencing with heightened potency an emotion that has actually been eating away at him in a more latent form since long before the bout of agony that he has just witnessed began.[780] A few lines later, Neoptolemus repeats the same formula, while providing further explication regarding the source of his pain: "It is not the thought that I will desert you, but rather the thought that I will take you on a journey that will cause you grief, that has long pained me" (λιπὼν μὲν οὐκ ἔγωγε, λυπηρῶς δὲ μὴ πέμπω σε μᾶλλον, τοῦτ' ἀνιῶμαι πάλαι, 913).[781] Beyond the pain inherent in the experience of pity, which is due to the anticipation of the possibility of a similar suffering in oneself, Neoptolemus is clearly experiencing another sort of pain.[782] It is perhaps in part the sort of shared suffering characteristic of *philoi* – one that finds its closest equivalent in the definition of a friend in the *Nicomachean Ethics* as "one who suffers and rejoices along with his *philos*" (Arist., *NE* 9.4.11566a.7–8).[783] Neoptolemus identifies with the hero

---

780 Winnington-Ingram 1980, 284 and Lesky 1983, 172 give due attention to the importance of πάλαι; the former suggests that Neoptolemus's pity may have begun at the same time as the Chorus's, when the young man first caught sight of Philoctetes. Perrotta 1935, 423 n. 2 remarks that this later statement of Neoptolemus's would not affect how the audience would have interpreted Neoptolemus's stance in the earlier scenes, since they could not have anticipated this later declaration; for all intents and purposes, in the earlier part of the play, he says, Neoptolemus is pitiless, for we have no reason to lend any feelings to characters that are not openly expressed at the time that they are experienced.
781 Along the same lines, Neoptolemus later declares that even the emotion of pity that has overcome him is not actually new: ἐμοὶ μὲν οἶκτος δεινὸς ἐμπέπτωκέ τις | τοῦδ' ἀνδρὸς οὐ νῦν πρῶτον, ἀλλὰ καὶ πάλαι (965–6). This pity stems from Neoptolemus's intrinsic knowledge that any human being who withholds such pity from a helpless and ailing individual "is forgetting or denying the limits of mortal existence" (Heath 1999, 149). The model of the pitier who always bears these limits in mind is the Sophoclean figure of Odysseus in the *Ajax*; see above, pp. 110.
782 Aristotle's definition in the *Rhetoric* 2.8, which I quoted ch. 2 n. 406, bears repeating here: "Let pity, then, be a kind of pain in the case of an apparent destructive or painful harm of one not deserving to encounter it, which one might expect oneself, or one of one's own, to suffer, and this when it seems near" (transl. Konstan 2001).
783 See Neoptolemus's above explanation, ἀλγῶ πάλαι δὴ τἀπὶ σοὶ στένων κακά. It is the fact that he is causing harm to his *philos* that brings harm upon Neoptolemus in turn.

— with his values and with his outlook — and this is what leads to the young man's painful sense of shame (on which more in a moment).

Neoptolemus's pity is both a sign and a consequence of his developing a sense of the like-mindedness that binds him to Philoctetes: he realizes the humane and heroic values that they share and that he is betraying those values, on behalf of Odysseus, and for sake of the Atreids' victory at Troy. The latter are enemies to Philoctetes; if he and Neoptolemus are friends, they should be the young man's enemies as well (see lines 1382–6).[784] But there is, in fact, more to Neoptolemus's pain than pity, as he himself goes on to point out. When Philoctetes asks him to explain his mysterious outcry (παπαῖ, 895), Neoptolemus says, "I shall be seen as shameful: that is what has been paining me for a long time" (αἰσχρὸς φανοῦμαι· τοῦτ' ἀνιῶμαι πάλαι, 906).

Philoctetes' pain evokes Neoptolemus's pity, but equally if not more important are the hero's nature and values, which the young man has seen him illustrate from their very first exchange: absolute trust, unwavering allegiance to friends, and complete integrity. Just now, in the face of a pain so excruciating that it makes him lose consciousness, he has displayed great dignity and a proud endurance that evoke Neoptolemus's respect and awe. Neoptolemus's perception of the old man has shifted, as has his perception of what it is right for him to do. He has come to feel how much the values illustrated by Philoctetes in his every interaction are in keeping with his own true *physis:* before his eyes the suffering man has offered examples of the virtues of an Achillean *physis:* forthrightness, a readiness to display trust and friendship, and fortitude in the face of undeserved pain.[785]

---

[784] On common enemies as a basis for friendship, see above, n. 762.
[785] The Chorus earlier stresses the pitiable nature of the sight offered by Philoctetes, which they explicitly link to the fact that his pain is undeserved:

ἄλλον δ' οὔτιν' ἔγωγ'
  οἶδα κλυὼν οὐδ' ἐσιδὼν μοίρᾳ
τοῦδ' ἐχθίονι συντυχόντα θνατῶν,
ὃς οὔτε τι ῥέξας τιν', οὔτε νοσφίσας,
ἀλλ' ἴσος ἐν <γ'> ἴσοις ἀνήρ,
ὤλλυθ' ὧδ' ἀναξίως.

(681–5)

But there is none other among mortals whom I have heard of or have looked upon who has met with more hateful a destiny than this man, who having done nothing to anyone, done no murder, but being a just man among just men, was perishing thus undeservedly.

That fortitude and continued trust concomitantly evoke the young man's growing shame and discomfort at his own conduct,[786] both of which are all-important in leading him to abandon Odysseus's scheme. The more laudable and trusting Philoctetes shows himself to be, the more Neoptolemus senses the harrowing discrepancy between the hero's character and the deceiving role that he has agreed to take on at the hero's expense. His victim's (unfounded) gratitude toward him makes Neoptolemus dread the imminent moment when his duplicity will be exposed and his shamefulness revealed (αἰσχρὸς φανοῦμαι).[787] The contradiction between Neoptolemus's behavior up to this point – following Odysseus's orders – and what his true nature commands him to do becomes a source of unbearable moral pain for him, particularly in light of the unqualified trust Philoctetes has put in him (entrusting him with his bow), a trust which marks out Neoptolemus as a worthy *philos* in accordance with the heroic code of honor, in stark contrast to what we know to be Neoptolemus's successful show of duplicity.[788]

Neoptolemus's shame increases as the integrity of his victim causes him to value Philoctetes' judgment more and more. This sense of shame is directly tied to the lens through which he now evaluates his own deeds — a lens that is now becoming aligned with Philoctetes' own.[789] As the young man ceases to consider

---

On Neoptolemus's Achillean *physis*, see e.g., Blundell 1987, 1988, Nussbaum 1979, Fulkerson 2013. For an insightful and nuanced perspective of Achilles' hatred of deceit as context-specific and Neoptolemus's perhaps naïve moral rigor, see Heath 1999, 142–3. Blundell 1988, Heath 1999 and Gibert (1995, 146 ff.) rightly stress the fact that not all of Neoptolemus's (righteous) principles and the actions that he takes as a result can be traced back to Achilles, since it is not entirely clear what Achilles would do in his situation. Rather, it is the "moral force of <Neoptolemus's> traditional character" that drives him to change camps and his behavior in the play (Gibert 1995, 147).

786 See Jebb *ad loc.* for the noble fortitude with which Philoctetes endures his pain.
787 The Greek φανοῦμαι is, I think, deliberately ambiguous and significant here: it can be taken to mean either that Neoptolemus will *seem* to be shameful or that he will be *revealed* as shameful, the former implying that he actually is not, the latter that he is. Whether or not he is remains to be proven, in his words (disclosing the plot to its victim) and deeds (acting in accordance with Philoctetes' interests).
788 Neoptolemus's pain has become all the more acute as he has just been entrusted with Philoctetes' bow, making the discrepancy between the hero's noble trust and upholding of *philia*, on the one hand, and the counterfeit version of *philia* Neoptolemus himself has been reciprocating with, on the other, all the greater.
789 Regarding self- and other-regarding aspects of the experience of shame in ancient Greek culture and their relationship to concepts of conscience, see Cairns (1993). Williams 1993 also addresses self- and other-directed aspects of shame; see especially ch. 4, "Shame and Autonomy," where he discusses the ability of the Greek term *aidôs* to cover both of our modern

his actions from the Greek army and Odysseus's conveniently self-serving perspective, he imagines how he will appear to the one whom he has come to respect and admire as a father figure and role model.[790]

As Neoptolemus's gaze, outlook, and sense of self increasingly align with Philoctetes', he feels pain because he is about to be revealed as shameful (906) in the eyes of one whose opinion he values. Of course Neoptolemus means "in Philoctetes' eyes" here, but the anticipation of Philoctetes' view of his (Neoptolemus's) actions for what they have been until now (deceitful), and the anticipation of the outrage with which Philoctetes will see the Greek ships (which amount to evidence that he is being taken to Troy despite himself) become unbearable in Neoptolemus's own eyes.[791] Up to this point, he has embraced duplicity: his behavior and words have not been in keeping with his values and aspirations.[792] These values and aspirations are in line with Philoctetes', and Neoptolemus's pain stems, in short, from an increasing feeling of alienation from his own true nature.

The audience has watched Neoptolemus watch Philoctetes; now they watch him cast a new lens onto his own actions, putting himself in the position of Phil-

---

notions of shame and guilt. Dover 1974 also discusses Greek notions of conscience in connection with shame (esp. ch. 5, "Sanctions"). Shame can be experienced not just at the prospect of others' judgment of one's actions, but in one's own eyes: see below, n. 793. Cairns 1993, 260 ff. underlines how Neoptolemus' feeling of *aidôs* stems not just from the prospect of Philoctetes' disapproval here, but also "on the basis of standards which have become part of <his> character" (261).

790 Wilson 1941, 295 notes the combination and complementarity of pity and admiration that lead Neoptolemus to begin shifting away from participating in Odysseus's scheme, as the young man comes to treat the wounded elder "simply as another man, whose sufferings elicit his sympathy and whose courage and pride he admires."

791 On the pain involved in the experience of shame that stems from "fear of disgrace," see Konstan 2006, ch. 4, esp. at 109:

> In addition to feeling pity, Neoptolemus has come to respect the rough nobility and endurance of Philoctetes; he is now capable of regarding the man he is manipulating not as a stranger but as a friend... . In proportion to his positive regard for Philoctetes, Philoctetes' judgment of his conduct is increasingly important to him. Aristotle ... maintained that 'we feel shame before those people whom we take seriously,' for it is their opinion of us that we care about. Neoptolemus' shame is sharpened because the vice in his character, as exhibited by the action performed contrary to his own principles, has now been made manifest to a morally serious witness.

On shame in ancient Greek culture in connection with the notion of 'face' and saving face in particular, see Dover 1974, 217 ff.

792 On Neoptolemus's remorse and its key function within the play's plot, see Fulkerson 2013, 66–79.

octetes as witness. It is no longer the prospect of seeming glorious in the eyes of all the Greeks (119) that impels Neoptolemus. His utmost desire at this point is to be genuine in the eyes of the one man whom he has come both to pity and respect, as a fellow human plagued with suffering and as a worthy *philos*, a man of uncompromising integrity, unshakable nobility and aspirations, and absolute trustworthiness.[793] The dual nature of Neoptolemus's agony – stemming as it does from a combination of pity with shame – is pointed up by Philoctetes shortly hereafter, when he explicates the nature and source of Neoptolemus's pain to Odysseus:

> δῆλος δὲ καὶ νῦν ἐστιν ἀλγεινῶς φέρων
> οἷς τ' αὐτὸς ἐξήμαρτεν οἷς τ' ἐγὼ 'παθον
> (1011–2)
>
> And you can see now how he is pained
> by his crime *and* by my suffering!

So much, then, for the basis and motives for Neoptolemus's emotional and moral transformation; I want to turn now to the poetics that Sophocles employs to reveal the young man's inner turmoil. In having Neoptolemus cry out παπαῖ (895), Sophocles makes him utter the very same cry as Philoctetes.[794] This deliberate and significant verbal parallel spotlights how much the pain that Neoptolemus experiences here both echoes and is caused by the pain that he has witnessed. παπαῖ is an unambiguous vocal signpost marking the point at which Neoptolemus can no longer bear to witness the spectacle of Philoctetes' acute pain, nor his own role in the face of such pain. It is the first external sign we are given of the young man's emerging remorse. By echoing Philoctetes, Neoptolemus conveys the alignment of their views and the disgust and shame that he feels for his own actions and words as an executor of Odysseus's plan. The verbal echo points to the changing dynamic between the two characters as the kindred nature of their spirits emerges.

With his visceral outburst, Neoptolemus begins to redefine himself in the audience's eyes as a *philos* to Philoctetes.[795] The same can be said of the verb Neo-

---

[793] On the concern for another that prevails in Neoptolemus's experience of shame (as opposed to self-regarding or self-promoting goals that shame may push one to pursue), see Cairns 1993 and 2005 (esp. 311–12). Cairns also discusses the affinity between Philoctetes' and Neoptolemus's "ethical suppositions," and stresses the power that sheer contact with the like-minded Philoctetes has on the young man's transformation (Cairns 1993, 253).
[794] Noted by Knox 1964, 132 (et al.).
[795] Winnington-Ingram notes the importance of these markers of authentic response on Neoptolemus's part, in a play where Sophocles continuously intrigues his audience with silences

ptolemus uses to describe his own pain, ἀνιᾶσθαι (τοῦτ' ἀνιῶμαι πάλαι, 906), which seldom occurs in the extant Sophoclean corpus. The only other occurrence of the verb in the *Philoctetes* is spoken by the eponymous hero himself, when he describes his misery after the Greeks departed from the island, leaving him all alone to face his suffering: "When I looked all around me, I could find nothing present but my pain" (πάντα δὲ σκοπῶν | ηὕρισκον οὐδὲν πλὴν ἀνιᾶσθαι παρόν, 282–3). As with Neoptolemus's cry παπαῖ, the young man's reuse of a rare term employed earlier by Philoctetes connects the old man's suffering with his own moral pain, suggesting the emergence of a bond between them.[796] It implies the very sort of harmony of minds that Philoctetes had (rightly, it turns out) imagined existed between them earlier, which he defined in concrete terms as a σύμβολον σαφὲς λύπης (403–4) when he heard Neoptolemus express hostility toward the Atreids and Odysseus. Furthermore, as Neoptolemus echoes Philoctetes' cries of pain and defines his own moral pain with a term that directly echoes the one used by Philoctetes to describe the pervasive agony of his malady, the audience hears the human echo to Philoctetes' pain, the στόνος ἀντίτυπος (693), for which the hero had so longed.[797] Neoptolemus's response to Philoctetes' pain fulfills the role that the young man's tall tale was intended to. At the time, Philoctetes thought they were singing to the same tune (καί μοι προσᾴδεθ', 405). They are now actually doing so, as Neoptolemus's cries echo (and dovetail with) Philoctetes', and reveal to the audience how much his ethical compass has shifted.

The use of a cry to convey Neoptolemus's inner moral transformation to the audience is not merely dramatically effective but one of only two reliable ways for the latter to be able to discern Neoptolemus's veritable disposition at this stage. For even if Philoctetes were to leave the stage or fall back into an unconscious state, should Neoptolemus use the mediation of words to describe his changing inclination, there would be no way for the internal or the external audience to gauge their authenticity or the genuineness of his pain. An open declaration of friendship or pity on Neoptolemus's part at any point in this scene would inevitably be suspect, in light of the audience's knowledge of the young man's participation in the overarching plan to deceive Philoctetes by be-

---

and deception, leaving them wondering and guessing where the young man stands: "Neoptolemus, <has> to preserve the façade of deception... it is not until the pressure has become fully effective that we are allowed to see its effects at all. We cannot *know* how he is reacting from moment to moment" (W.-I. 1980, 283).

796 This echo is noted by Schein in his 2013 commentary, *ad loc*.
797 On Philoctetes' στόνος ἀντίτυπος, a "groan inviting a response" which the Chorus evokes early on in the *parodos*, see above, p. 260.

coming his friend. Because of its visceral, spontaneous nature and its lack of an intended addressee, the cry functions as a revealing aside. While it is uttered in Philoctetes' presence, it does not rouse his suspicion (though he will eventually come to question Neoptolemus about it, as well as about his long silence), but it does alert the audience to the inner workings of Neoptolemus's moral maturation. Having Philoctetes overhear Neoptolemus's reactions enables him to understand later on what it is the young man has been experiencing all along.[798]

In recognizing his affinity with Philoctetes, Neoptolemus is beginning to demarcate himself from the likes of Odysseus. That this demarcation should be articulated in terms of the *pain* he experiences is significant and consistent with the portrayal, earlier on in the play, of Odysseus's propensity to act in a deceitful manner, with total disregard for truthfulness. We saw earlier how Odysseus's questionable moral standards, according to which the ends justify the means, are also couched in terms that evoke moral suffering — or rather, a lack thereof.[799] The son of Laertes positions himself early in the play as the polar opposite of Achilles when he states with pride that he is not one who suffers from any qualms in implementing whatever means are necessary to reach his goals, including saying one thing and doing another (τούτῳ γὰρ οὐδέν μ' ἀλγυνεῖς, 66). Conversely, Neoptolemus discovers the moral imperatives and actions that the suffering of *philoi* requires when he see Philoctetes suffer and experiences moral pain in response. Moments after his cry reveals his shifting allegiance to the audience, Neoptolemus unveils his participation in the scheme to Philoctetes, making the dramatic importance of the scene as a whole clear.[800] His cries and cryptic explanations have prepared the audience for his about-face, and given them access to the motives that lead him to reveal all to Philoctetes.

---

798 See 1011–2, quoted above: δῆλος δὲ καὶ νῦν ἐστιν ἀλγεινῶς φέρων | οἷς τ' αὐτὸς ἐξήμαρτεν οἷς τ' ἐγὼ 'παθον, "And you can see now how he is pained by his crime *and* by my suffering!"
799 Earlier in the play, Odysseus was clearly distinguished as one who does not experience pity: the play appears to suggest that those who do not suffer along with others through the experience of pity are not moral. See Aristotle's *Nicomachean Ethics* (179b29–31) on the correlation between the degree of ethical rectitude in one's nature and one's ability to experience pleasure and pain at the right things (quoted above, n. 741).
800 In his 2013 commentary, Schein (*ad* 894–7) notes that the lines in which Neoptolemus cries out in pain "mark clearly the key moment of reversal in the dramatic action."

How to "act?"

Watching Philoctetes and witnessing his suffering comes to inform the way in which Neoptolemus chooses to use words: he abandons playacting in favor of speaking the truth.[801] Ironically, it is just as the audience is given good reason to consider Neoptolemus (and his words) to be truly trustworthy that Philoctetes no longer does. Neoptolemus's cries precede his unveiling of the Greeks' plan to the hero. That revelation, in turn, shatters the *philia* between them, for Philoctetes has no reason to believe anything he says anymore, and in fact has good reason to suspect any of his words are untrue and spoken with an underlying agenda (919–26). Actions, not words, are necessary for regaining Philoctetes' trust and reestablishing a relationship of *philia* with him on grounds that are not insincere. To regain the hero's trust, Neoptolemus will have to go beyond renouncing playacting. Instead of carrying out another's agenda and behaving in a manner that is alien his nature, he must act in accordance with what his inner disposition impels him to do. He must cease to "act" – as in, play a part – and begin to act, as in, take action.

Neoptolemus's moral agony is only the first step, though a crucial one, along that path. He has not made any decision that might change his course of action, only a decision regarding his words. From the time he unveils the Greeks' plan to Philoctetes on, the audience has no reason to doubt the veracity of his words, since they know that he no longer has any reason to lie. But Sophocles maintains the suspense for his audience regarding the young man's next move by having him keep silent. For one hundred lines (974–1074), Neoptolemus remains on stage but says absolutely nothing.[802] He vacillates still, as he did before the scene of agony began to affect him.[803] When he speaks again for the first time, briefly, there is a palpable tension in his words. He mentions his pity

---

[801] See Zerba 2012, 53: "Neoptolemus... <is> a character whose scripted role diverges from the moral action he finally chooses. The distancing of actor from role opens a space in which the inner self, shadowy and incipient at first, emerges as an alienated other capable of critiquing the spectacle of which he is a part."

[802] Neoptolemus lapses into a pained silence at several points. Philoctetes is the one who makes that silence conspicuous when he inquires as to its cause, first at lines 740–1 (οὐκ ἐρεῖς, ἀλλ' ὧδ' ἔσῃ | σιγηλός;) and then again lines 804–5: τί φῄς, παῖ; τί φῄς; τί σιγᾷς; ("What are you saying, boy? What are you saying? Why are you silent?"). Seale 1982 discusses Neoptolemus's silences at various points in the play in his chapter on *Philoctetes*; Goldhill and Lada-Richards also discuss these silences and the suspense that they maintain (both in Goldhill and Hall 2009). On heroic silences followed by outbursts, see Montiglio 2000.

[803] For his earlier hesitations, see lines 779–81: γένοιτο δὲ πλοῦς οὔριός τε κεὐσταλὴς ὅποι ποτὲ | θεὸς δικαιοῖ χὠ στόλος πορσύνεται, on which see Pucci 2003, 216–7.

once again, fearing, it seems, that he might be said (sc. by Odysseus) to be "too full of it" (1074). For the time being, he merely allows his sailors to remain at Philoctetes' side and keep him company while the preparations are made for the Greeks' ship to depart for Troy. At this point, the plot against him has been revealed to Philoctetes, and the Greeks have the bow in their possession, so their plan is to abandon him, now bowless and doomed to die, while they go on to conquer Ilium (1075–80).[804]

Why the continued silence — and wavering – on Neoptolemus's part? He still considers that a powerful necessity (πολλὴ κρατεῖ | τούτων ἀνάγκη, 920–1) requires him to obey the orders he has received: τῶν γὰρ ἐν τέλει κλύειν | τό τ' ἔνδικόν με καὶ τὸ συμφέρον ποεῖ ("Justice and policy cause me to obey those in command," 925–6). Only later does he complete his about-face by taking action in a manner that reveals his true Achillean nature, not just in word, but in actual deed. Only in *acting*, that is, in taking action (as opposed to his earlier playacting) does Neoptolemus rehabilitate himself in the eyes of Philoctetes, when he finally abandons not just deceit, but the implementation of Odysseus's plan altogether: first, by returning the bow to Philoctetes; then, by agreeing to sail the old man home, despite his belief that it is both in the hero's interest and willed by the gods that Philoctetes should accompany the Greeks and conquer Troy with them. These two concrete initiatives on Neoptolemus's part are what it takes for Philoctetes to believe in his trustworthiness once again and for the *philia* between the two men to be reborn on solid ground. At this point, Heracles' intervention as a *deus ex machina* is necessary to guarantee Philoctetes' presence at Troy and make the reestablished *philia* between two individuals both a new basis for a more solid community and a condition of that community's salvation. Were it not for this divine intervention, they would, presumably, sail back to Malis.[805]

There are multiple reversals in the plot and surprises leading up to Neoptolemus's two significant actions. The dramatic action proceeds in fits and starts, and the plot reversals are reflected onstage in the characters' movements — as they set off for the ships, as Philoctetes rushes toward the cliff to kill himself, as Odysseus jumps into the scene *in extremis* to prevent Neoptolemus from returning the bow to Philoctetes, and so on.[806] Throughout these reversals, Neo-

---

[804] Regarding the ambiguity of the oracle concerning whether Philoctetes and his bow, or just Philoctetes, are necessary to conquer Priam's city, see above, n. 646.

[805] Of course, the mythical tradition suggests that this was never an option: the audience knows that, in the end, Philoctetes was at Troy.

[806] Regarding significance of stage actions and gestures in the play, see especially Taplin 1977, *passim*, 1978, 131–3, and 1987; also Seale, 1982, 26–55.

ptolemus's prolonged onstage silences continue to offer signs of his growing ambivalence and of his continuing inner turmoil: he is clearly wavering and in pain.

Before the key actions and words noted above (the restitution of the bow, the agreement to sail back to Malis, and Heracles' intervention), there are several important utterances spoken by Philoctetes that deserve our attention, in which the hero makes reference to the power exerted by the sight of his suffering on others. These remind the audience of how much the spectacle of Philoctetes' pain continues to have the potential to affect Neoptolemus and ultimately shape his actions, while also drawing attention to what causes the delay in his taking significant action.

When Neoptolemus appeals to justice and the orders of his superiors as reasons that compel him not to return the bow to Philoctetes and when he continues to encourage him to come to Troy, Philoctetes tries to make the young man change his mind by every possible means. Within the space of just one speech, Philoctetes curses him, shames him, and then supplicates and begs him. We know he is unsuccessful at this point when he specifically notes how Neoptolemus has averted his gaze and removed Philoctetes from his line of sight, turning away from the obligations that come with acknowledging a suppliant:[807]

> οἴ' ἠπάτηκας· οὐδ' ἐπαισχύνῃ μ' ὁρῶν
> τὸν προστρόπαιον, τὸν ἱκέτην, ὦ σχέτλιε;
> . . . .
> ἀλλ' ὡς μεθήσων μήποθ', ὧδ' ὁρᾷ πάλιν.
> (929–30, 935)

> How you have deceived me! Are you not even ashamed to look upon the suppliant who turned to you, you wretch?
> . . . .
> But he looks away, as though he will never let [the bow] go.

Neoptolemus remains silent, his hesitation soon reaching a climactic point of *aporia*. Philoctetes draws attention to this silence, which he interprets to be a sign of Neoptolemus's unwavering adherence to Odysseus's plan: "What do you say? You are silent! I am nothing, miserable one!" (τί φῄς; σιωπᾷς. οὐδέν εἴμ' ὁ δύσμορος, 951). But Neoptolemus's subsequent cries show that Philoctetes has completely misinterpreted this silence; in fact, the youth is overwhelmed with pity at this point (ἐμοὶ μὲν οἶκτος δεινὸς ἐμπέπτωκέ τις | τοῦδ' ἀνδρός,

---

[807] On supplication in general (including the important role of contact and the gaze), see Gould 1973, 85–90. On *aidôs* and shame as factors in eliciting proper behavior in the context of supplications, see Cairns 1993.

"As for me, a strange pity for this man has fallen upon me," 965–6). After having been mute, he now remains immobile; he is completely frozen about what to do or say next:

οἴμοι, τί δράσω; μή ποτ' ὤφελον λιπεῖν
τὴν Σκῦρον· οὕτω τοῖς παροῦσιν ἄχθομαι.
(969–70)

What am I to do? I ought never to have left Scyros; such is the grief I feel at what is before me!

Turning to his sailors, he utters the quintessential tragic formulation of *aporia*, asking them, "What are we to do, my men?" (τί δρῶμεν, ἄνδρες, 974).[808]

When Odysseus announces that Philoctetes must accompany the Greeks to Troy and that he will be forced to do so if he does not willingly agree to it (982–3), Philoctetes reaches the depths of despair. He no longer possesses his sole means of defending himself and of surviving on the island alone, and he is now entirely at his arch-enemy's mercy: his bow is in Odysseus's hands, because he entrusted it to Neoptolemus, who has refused to give it back to him.[809] The hero's physical autonomy and the uncompromising stalwartness with which he has adhered to his heroic values are about to be violated through the use of force. To prevent this, the hero attempts to kill himself: death is preferable to aiding those who are guilty of betraying him yet again, and have added insult (the plan to dupe him) to injury (their initial abandonment of him ten years prior). Odysseus puts a stop to Philoctetes' desperate plan to throw himself to his death from a cliff by having two of his men seize him, thereby regaining physical control over Philoctetes' person, as well as his destiny (1001–3).

At this point, Philoctetes' words draw the audience's attention to the pitiable sight he offers. In doing so, he provides the audience with some indication of the disparity between Odysseus and Neoptolemus, especially in how they actually view the hero and respond to the sight of him. Neoptolemus has just unambiguously expressed his pain at what is before him (οὕτω τοῖς παροῦσιν ἄχθομαι, "such is the pain I feel at the present situation," 970), and Philoctetes comes to understand that the youth betrayed him because he was obeying orders

---

[808] We are reminded of when Orestes turns to Pylades in the *Choephori*, just before killing his mother, when the sight of her bared breast, a tangible symbol of her maternity, causes him to waver in the execution of Apollo's will: "Pylades, what should I do? Should respect prevent me from killing my mother?" (Πυλάδη, τί δράσω; μητέρ' αἰδεσθῶ κτανεῖν, 899).

[809] Neoptolemus does so because of a continued sense of duty to his superiors and because of the oracle; see above.

(1010). He takes note of the fact that Neoptolemus is greatly pained by what he has done, a moral agony which makes his integrity obvious to Philoctetes and leads the hero to consider the young man to be his equal in worth, while he considers Odysseus inferior to Neoptolemus (ἀνάξιον μὲν σοῦ, κατάξιον δ' ἐμοῦ, <Neoptolemus is> "too good for you, good enough for me," 1009). He underlines for the spectators the visible signs that he perceives (and which they, in all likelihood, cannot, if only because of the masks the actors are wearing) of Neoptolemus's moral pain and shows that he understands the underpinnings of Neoptolemus's response. He contrasts the young man's disposition with his addressee's (Odysseus's) lack of scruple and expresses his understanding of the complex nature of the young man's experience of pain as one that stems from a combination of two emotions: pity for the hero, and shame at his own behavior (lines 1011–2, quoted above). I mention these lines again because Philoctetes' words are worth dwelling on: they contrast different modes of viewing. On the one hand, there is the impact that the sight of him has on Neoptolemus ("He is pained … by my suffering!"). On the other, there is the obvious lack of any such impact on Odysseus, whose vision, as described by Philoctetes, is murky, muddled by the many layers of calculation and cunning that make him perceive the world around him as though only partially and indirectly, through the shadowy contours of his agenda:

> ἀλλ' ἡ κακὴ σὴ διὰ μυχῶν βλέπουσ' ἀεὶ
> ψυχή νιν ἀφυᾶ τ' ὄντα κοὐ θέλονθ' ὅμως
> εὖ προὐδίδαξεν ἐν κακοῖς εἶναι σοφόν.
> (1013–5)
>
> But your evil mind, looking out from its recesses, skillfully taught him,
> inept pupil and unwilling as he was, how to be cunning in doing evil.[810]

In his continued desperation, Philoctetes invokes other witnesses, whose reactions he imagines would be different: the gods. He (briefly) calls upon them to avenge him and provide him with healing; for if they can see the spectacle of his pitiable life, then surely they will feel the pity that Odysseus does not, and which Neoptolemus *does* feel, but without converting it into any form of action:

> ἀλλ', ὦ πατρῴα γῆ θεοί τ' ἐπόψιοι,
> τείσασθε τείσασθ' ἀλλὰ τῷ χρόνῳ ποτὲ

---

[810] Schein 2013, 274 *ad loc.*, comments on the reference to the "recesses" through which Odysseus's mind looks out and perceives the world around him by noting that it "suggests both the kind of spying the audience has just witnessed on the part of Odysseus, as he lurked near the cave and eavesdropped … and an ingrained shiftiness of mind or soul."

ξύμπαντας αὐτούς, εἴ τι κἄμ' οἰκτίρετε.
ὡς ζῶ μὲν οἰκτρῶς, εἰ δ' ἴδοιμ' ὀλωλότας
τούτους, δοκοῖμ' ἂν τῆς νόσου πεφευγέναι.
(1040–4)

O native land and gods that look upon it, punish them, punish all of them, late but surely, if you feel any pity for me! For my life is pitiable; but if I were to see them ruined, I would seem to have escaped my sickness!

As he voices his desire for revenge, Philoctetes calls attention to the pitiable nature of the spectacle he offers (εἴ τι κἄμ' οἰκτίρετε. | ὡς ζῶ μὲν οἰκτρῶς). He wishes the roles were reversed and that, rather than be the object of spectacle, he might be the pitiless spectator of his enemy's suffering, gloating over Odysseus as the son of Laertes does over him:[811]

ἰδοίμαν δέ νιν,
τὸν τάδε μησάμενον, τὸν ἴσον χρόνον
ἐμὰς λαχόντ' ἀνίας.
(1113–5)

And may I see him,
Him who contrived this scheme, for the same extent of time
Doomed to my agony!

Witnessing Philoctetes' pain has not yet led Neoptolemus to take action in support of him (namely, by returning his bow to him).

In an especially pathetic moment, the sufferer, abandoned once more to his own devices, but this time also to his death, imagines the bow as a spectator to it all – the bow that has been taken away from him by the Greeks, who are now leaving him once more. He envisions this bow playing the role of a just and compassionate witness to his suffering and of indignant spectator to the evils he is enduring at the hands of the Greeks:

ὦ τόξον φίλον, ὦ φίλων
χειρῶν ἐκβεβιασμένον,
ἦ που ἐλεινὸν ὁρᾷς, φρένας εἴ τινας   (1130)
ἔχεις, τὸν Ἡράκλειον
ἄθλιον ὧδέ σοι
οὐκέτι χρησόμενον τὸ μεθύστερον,
ἀλλ' ἐν μεταλλαγᾷ <χεροῖν>
πολυμηχάνου ἀνδρὸς ἐρέσσῃ,   (1135)
ὁρῶν μὲν αἰσχρὰς ἀπάτας,

---

811 We are reminded of Heracles' wishes to see Deianeira suffer in the *Trachiniae*; see ch. 2.

> στυγνόν τε φῶτ' ἐχθοδοπόν,
> μυρί' ἀπ' αἰσχρῶν ἀνατέλ-
> λονθ' ὃς ἐφ' ἡμῖν κάκ' ἐμήσατ' ἔργων.
> (1128–39)

> O beloved bow, bow that was forced out of my loving hands, *you look with pity*, I think, if you have any feeling, upon the unhappy friend of Heracles who shall never use you anymore, but you are plied instead in the grasp of a cunning man, *looking on his shameful deceptions and on the loathsome enemy*, who contrived against me innumerable evils that arise from shameful deeds![812]

It is an apt personification, because of the bow's many associations with friendship and trust: Heracles, after all, entrusted the bow to Philoctetes when the latter took pity on the great hero, when he saw him burning alive on his funeral pyre.

Neoptolemus has been able to continue to follow orders and to give priority to his sense of obligation toward the Greek army because he has, temporarily, averted his gaze and thus avoided the power exerted by the sight of Philoctetes' plight. Odysseus betrays his awareness that the spectacle of human suffering has the power to weaken Neoptolemus's resolve to adhere to the plan to take the bow and abandon Philoctetes, when he warns the young man *not to look at him*:

> χώρει σύ· μὴ πρόσλευσσε, γενναῖός περ ὤν,
> ἡμῶν ὅπως μὴ τὴν τύχην διαφθερεῖς.
> Φι. ἦ καὶ πρὸς ὑμῶν ὧδ' ἔρημος, ὦ ξένοι,
> λειφθήσομαι δὴ κοὐκ ἐποικτερεῖτέ με;
> (1068–71)

> Od. You, get on your way. Do not look at him, noble though you are, so that you do not destroy your luck!
> Phi. Shall I really be left here thus desolate by you too, strangers? And shall you have no pity for me?

By telling Neoptolemus *not* to look at Philoctetes, Odysseus draws attention to the power of the spectacle of the human sufferer to evoke Neoptolemus's pity. Accordingly, it is to Neoptolemus's pity that Philoctetes appeals in the lines that immediately follow. Odysseus explicitly associates the act of looking at Philoctetes with Neoptolemus's nobility when he instructs him not to look, "noble though [he is]." The present tense of the imperative (μὴ πρόσλευσσε) suggests that Neoptolemus is looking at Philoctetes and does not take his eyes off the

---

[812] The italics in the Greek text (and the translation) are mine, for emphasis.

hero, even as he reluctantly and hesitantly walks away.[813] The implication of the concessive clause ("noble though you are") is that abandoning a man deserving of pity, such as Philoctetes, is ignoble. That Odysseus should recognize the ignoble character of the deed and yet should carry on with his plan and persist in inveigling Neoptolemus into participating in it provides us with a clear measure of his ruthlessness.

Clearly, what Neoptolemus has witnessed continues to haunt him after he exits the stage. When he returns, he is chased by Odysseus, who cannot prevent him from taking matters into his own hands and becoming an active agent once again — not one defined and guided by Odysseus's agenda, but one who acts in keeping with what his nature dictates. At this point, he appears to have access to a broader vision, which enables him to see beyond the here and now and understand what is best both for him and for Philoctetes: "What I see is best for you and me if it is accomplished" (ἃ σοί τε κἀμοὶ λῷσθ' ὁρῶ τελούμενα, 1381). When Philoctetes proves completely inflexible, Neoptolemus puts his obligations toward a *philos* before what he considers to be best for both of them: he agrees to sail Philoctetes back to Malis (1402), though this will be harmful to Philoctetes (who will not be cured of his disease), to the Greek army (that will not conquer Troy), and to Neoptolemus (who will acquire no glory at Ilium as a result). The youth's hesitations have ceased as he has come to consider the importance of honoring the duties of *philia*, and this consideration ultimately wins him over (see lines 1246 and 1251).[814] That is when Heracles appears to them in a *deus ex machina* and enjoins Philoctetes to aid his fellow Greeks.

The play's "happy ending" is notoriously problematic.[815] It leaves no doubt that Philoctetes' reintegration is divinely sanctioned. Heracles' *deus ex machina* offers a final and definitive sign of divine endorsement of Philoctetes' rejoining the expedition to Troy and reintegration into the community of his peers: Heracles makes clear that, by joining in the collective endeavor, Philoctetes will bring about the conditions necessary for both the Greeks' victory at Troy and for the healing of his malady.[816] His being reunited with his peers can be taken as a return to the civilized world[817] and a result of "the divine impulse of Philoctetes

---

813 This is noted by Schein 2013, 282 *ad loc.*
814 Taplin 1971, 36 notes that Neoptolemus's decision to change his actions and behavior has taken shape offstage. Gibert 1995, 149 n. 91 underlines how the location of this momentous decision offstage hints at its inwardness.
815 I use quotation marks because of the difficulty of interpreting the ending.
816 See lines 1437–8.
817 There is great ambiguity throughout the play regarding which of the two worlds — Philoctetes' or the Greeks' — is the more "civilized": see Segal 1981, ch. 10.

himself."⁸¹⁸ But it could just as well be the gods imposing their will on the hero.⁸¹⁹ Regardless, though Philoctetes has until this point been adamantly refusing to join the Greeks and leave Lemnos, there is some joy in his reply to the divinized hero, when he accepts the divine will.⁸²⁰

The outcome of the drama marks the culmination of the important and positive role played by Neoptolemus's ability to recognize Philoctetes' humanity and acknowledge his suffering. On an individual level, this has enabled him to reconcile with what he has intuited to be his true nature all along; on an interpersonal level, it establishes a true and trusting friendship between the two protagonists. Philoctetes acknowledges both of these results:

ξύμφημι. τὴν φύσιν δ' ἔδειξας, ὦ τέκνον,
ἐξ ἧς ἔβλαστες, οὐχὶ Σισύφου πατρός,
ἀλλ' ἐξ Ἀχιλλέως, ὃς μετὰ ζώντων ὅτ' ἦν
ἤκου' ἄριστα, νῦν δὲ τῶν τεθνηκότων.
                                                  (1310–3)

I agree! You showed the nature, my son, of the stock you come from, having not Sisyphus for father, but Achilles, who had the greatest fame while he was among the living and has it now among the dead.

Neoptolemus's embrace of the values of forthrightness and respect inherited from his father and embodied by Philoctetes has proven to be beneficial not only to his relationship with Philoctetes but to the community as a whole, as Philoctetes' rejoining of the Greek expedition to Troy will allow for its victory. In the play's closing, it is Philoctetes' turn to renounce the negative aspects of his past behavior, tempering his uncompromising heroic belief system in favor of more contemporary democratic ideals and "new, socially relevant heroic pos-

---

818 Whitman 1951, 188.
819 See Easterling 1978, 222–8. Whitman 1951, 172–89 discusses the difficulties of the play's ending by paying close attention to Philoctetes' relationship to the community as a hero of uncompromising integrity, faced with a divine edict that ultimately tempers the self-destructiveness inherent in (and indeed necessary) to his heroic nature.
820 See lines 1409–44. On the problematic ending of the play, see Hawkins 1999 (esp. 356–7), Schein 2001, Jouanna 2003, and Hawthorne 2006, with bibliography. One possible interpretation of the ending is to see it as a positive depiction of the rightful reintegration of the hero into the community of his peers; however, the *deus ex machina* and Philoctetes' acceptance of Heracles' divine will can also be understood as a falsely happy ending, intended to stress just how little freedom mortals have in light of their necessary subservience to the gods' whims and desires. For an overview of both positions, see for instance, Easterling 1978 and Kirkwood 1994, each with bibliography. On the difficulties posed by Philoctetes' change of mind regarding going to Troy, see Gibert 1995, 143 ff.

sibilities."⁸²¹ By accepting a collaborative role in the taking of Troy, Philoctetes emphasizes the importance of *"philia*, the virtue of collaboration, cooperation, and mutual benefit."⁸²² The play's ending highlights the benefits that stem from belonging to a civic community and devoting oneself to the common good.⁸²³

By the end of the *Philoctetes*, the audience is filled with hope that Neoptolemus has gotten back in touch with his true, noble nature, returning to action after pondering its potential outcomes from the careful stance of an observer, and choosing the ethical course in the end. Watching the youth watch Philoctetes and embrace more ethical and humane values and behaviors as a result in this drama is, no doubt, a means of pointing up for the external spectators the qualities of the ideal witness to a *philos's* suffering in life outside the theater proper. As Neoptolemus goes from agent to spectator, and back to being an actively involved and enlightened agent once more, Sophocles ends his play on a seemingly optimistic and promising note. Unlike Achilles, Deianeira, or Orestes and Electra (in Euripides), he does not look on at the outcome of his actions without being able to take any action: he anticipates the outcome of his initiative, and changes his actions as a result.

But for how long does Neoptolemus continue to act in a manner that is enlightened by his observations? Heracles' divine pronouncement at the end of the play also contains a warning: Philoctetes and Neoptolemus should show reverence to the gods when they conquer Troy. That reverence, he goes on to state, lives on forever in the reputation of mortals after their death (1439–44). This is likely an allusion to the tradition, according to which Neoptolemus impiously and pitilessly murdered Priam when the aged king of Troy had placed himself

---

821 The quote is from Schein 2005, 44, in the context of a broader discussion of the play's characters' (changing) relationships to divinity. On *philia* and its role in Greek society and in Sophocles, see e.g., Blundell 1989, 31ff., and Edmunds 1996, 117–28. Regarding the negative aspects of the heroic value system which Philoctetes thus rejects, see Winnington-Ingram 1980, 297. He equates Philoctetes' "heroic resentment of injury and hatred of enemies" in its extreme version with "the negative aspect of the [heroic] code," which has come to occupy "the whole of his emotion" before Heracles' intervention. Regarding the Homeric aspects of the hero's heroic values, see Schein 2006.
822 Hawkins 1999, 356.
823 Cairns 1993, 254–5 discusses the "cooperative side" of the code of honor that Philoctetes demands, and that Neoptolemus ultimately embraces. Yet the play's ending is problematic, and Ringer 1998 ch. 6 rightly underscores how the *deus ex machina* is a "contrived resolution" that "deliberately evades the issues raised by all that has gone before" (Ringer 1998, 104).

under the divine protection of Zeus by clinging to an altar as a suppliant.[824] If an allusion to the tradition is indeed underlying this warning, then by calling to the audience's mind Neoptolemus's future behavior as they knew it from that tradition, the closing of the play underscores the possibility for the young man to return to the malleability and fickleness he earlier embraced; it is a chilling suggestion of "the precariousness of the youth's ability to abide by principles he seems to have accepted, and the fragility of the moral education he receives on Lemnos."[825] After stressing throughout the play the interconnectedness between the act of observing and that of recognizing Philoctetes' humanity, and after underlining how that recognition enables the preservation of interpersonal ties and human dignity in the interest of all, Sophocles reminds his audience of how easily a man can lose sight of the humanity of others when caught up in the heat of the action and the pleasure of victory. Neoptolemus could well go back to being a mere agent once more, rather than a careful observer. The tradition tells us, he will.

---

824 The young man's impiety at the sack of Troy was notorious (Easterling 1978, 39; Taplin 1987, 76); regarding this ultimate failure on the youth's part and its ancient sources, see Schein 2011a, 83.

825 Kyriakou 2011, 248. Zerba 2012, 62–3 underscores the ironic turn of the play's closing lines and the shadow of doubt it casts upon its ending, and Neoptolemus's future behavior especially.

Bibliography

Aceti, C. (2008), "Sarpedone fra mito e poesia," in: Aceti, C. / Leuzzi, D. / Pagani, L. (eds.), *Eroi dell'Iliade. Personaggi e strutture narrative*, Rome, 1–270.
Adkins, A. (1960), *Merit and Responsibility; A Study in Greek Values*, Oxford.
Alden, M. (2001), *Homer Beside Himself : Para-narratives in the* Iliad, Oxford.
Alexiou, M. (1974), *The Ritual Lament in Greek Tradition*, Cambridge (2nd ed. [2002] P. Roilos (ed.), Lanham, MD.
Allan, W. (2005a), "Tragedy and the Early Greek Philosophical Tradition," in: J. Gregory (ed.), *A Companion to Greek Tragedy*, Oxford, 71–82.
Allan, W. (2005b), "Arms and the Man: Euphorbus, Hector, and the Death of Patroclus," in: *Classical Quarterly* 55, no. 1, 1–16.
Allen-Hornblower, E. (2012), "Revisiting the Apostrophes to Patroclus in *Iliad* 16," in: *Donum natalicium digitaliter confectum Gregorio Nagy septuagenario a discipulis collegis familiaribus oblatum* (Festschrift in honor of Professor Gregory Nagy), 2012 (26 pp.) [see http://nrs.harvard.edu/urn3:hul.ebook:CHS_Bers_etal_eds.Donum_Natalicium_Gregorio_Nagy.2012]
Allen-Hornblower, E. (2013), "Sounds and Suffering in Sophocles' *Philoctetes* and Gide's *Philoctète*," in: *Studi Italiani di Filologia Classica* 11, no. 1, 5–41.
Allen-Hornblower, E. (2014), "Gods in Pain: Walking the Line Between Divine and Mortal in Iliad 5," *Lexis* 32, 28–57.
Allen-Hornblower, E. (2015), "The *kommos* in Euripides' *Electra*," in: G. Moretti / C. Pepe (eds.), *Le parole dopo la morte: forme e funzioni della retorica funeraria nella tradizione greca e romana*, Labirinti 158, Trento, 2015, 37–58.
Allen-Hornblower, E. (2016), "Moral Disgust in Sophocles' Philoctetes," in: D. Lateiner / D. Spatharcus, *Disgust. Emotions of the Past Series*, Oxford.
Alt, K. (1967), "Schicksal und φύσις im *Philoktet* des Sophokles," in: *Hermes* 89, 141–74.
Anderson, M. (ed.) (1965), *Classical Drama and its Influence: Essays presented to H. D. Kitto*, London.
Apfel, L. (2011), *The Advent of Pluralism: Diversity and Conflict in the Age of Sophocles*, Oxford.
Armstrong, J. (1958), "The Arming Motif in the *Iliad*," in: *The American Journal of Philology* 79, no. 4, 337–54.
Arnott, G. (1981), "Double the Vision: A Reading of Euripides' *Electra*," in: *Greece & Rome* 28, no. 2, 179–92.
Aultman-Moore, L. W. J. (1994), "Moral Pain and the Choice of Neoptolemus: *Philoctetes* 894," in: *Classical World* 87, 309–10.
Austin, N. (1999), "Anger and Disease in Homer's *Iliad*," in: J. Kazazis / A. Rengakos (eds.), *Euphrosyne: Studies in Ancient Epic and its Legacy in honor of Dimitris N. Maronitis*, 11–49.
Austin, N. (2011), *Sophocles'* Philoctetes *and the Great Soul Robbery*, Madison, WI.
Bakker, E. (1993), "Discourse and Performance: Involvement, Visualization and 'Presence' in Homeric Poetry," in: *Classical Antiquity* 12, no. 1, 1–29.
Bakker, E. (1997), "Storytelling in the Future: Truth, Time, and Tense in Homeric Epic, in: E. Bakker / A. Kahane (eds.), *Written Voices, Spoken Signs: Tradition, Performance, and the Epic Text*, Cambridge, MA, 11–36.

Bakker, E. (2005), *Pointing at the Past: From Formula to Performance in Homeric Poetics*, Washington, DC.
Bakker, E. (2009), "Homer, Odysseus, and the Narratology of Performance," in: J. Grethlein / A. Rengakos (eds.), *Narratology and Interpretation: The Content of Narrative Form in Ancient Literature*, Berlin, 117–36.
Bakker, E. (2013), *The Meaning of Meat and the Structure of the* Odyssey, Cambridge.
Baltes, M. (1983), "Zur Eigenart und Funktion von Gleichnissen im 16. Buch der *Ilias*," in: *Antike und Abendland* 29, 36–48.
Barrett, J. (2002), *Staged Narrative: Poetics and the Messenger in Greek Tragedy*, Berkeley.
Barrett, J. (2014), "Narratological approaches to Greek tragedy," in: H. M. Roisman (ed.), *The Encyclopedia of Greek Tragedy*, Chichester, UK, 877–82.
Barlow, S. (1971),*The imagery of Euripides: a study in the dramatic use of pictorial language*, London.
Bassett, S. E. (1930), "The Pursuit of Hector," in: *Transactions and Proceedings of the American Philological Association* 61, 130–49.
Bassett, S. E. (1938), *The Poetry of Homer*, Berkeley.
Beck, D.. (2012), *Speech Presentation in Homeric Epic*, Austin, TX.
Beer, J. (2004), *Sophocles and the Tragedy of Athenian Democracy*, Westport.
Belfiore, E. (1983), "The Eagles' Feast and the Trojan Horse: Corrupted Fertility in the Agamemnon," in: *Maia* 35, 3–12.
Belfiore, E. (1992), *Tragic Pleasures. Aristotle on Plato and Emotion*, Princeton, NJ.
Belfiore, E. (2000), *Murder among Friends: Violations of philia in Greek tragedy*, Oxford.
Benveniste, E. (1969), *Le vocabulaire des institutions indo-européennes*, Paris.
Bers, V. (1981), "The Perjured Chorus in Sophocles' *Philoctetes*," in: *Hermes* 109, 500–4.
Biggs, P. (1966), "The Disease Theme in Sophocles' *Ajax*, *Philoctetes* and *Trachiniae*," in: *Classical Philology* 61, 223–35.
Biraud, M. (2009), *Les interjections du théâtre grec antique : étude sémantique et pragmatique*, Paris.
Block, E. (1982), "The Narrator Speaks: Apostrophe in Homer and Virgil," in: *Transactions of the American Philological Association* 112, 7–22.
Block, E. (1986), "Narrative Judgment and Audience Response in Homer and Virgil," in: *Arethusa* 19, no. 2, 155–69.
Blundell, M.W. (1987), "The Moral character of Odysseus in *Philoctetes*," in: *Greek, Roman, and Byzantine Studies* 28, 307–29.
Blundell, M.W. (1988), "The *phusis* of Neoptolemus in Sophocles' *Philoctetes*," in: *Greece and Rome* 35, 137–48.
Blundell, M.W. (1989), *Helping Friends and Harming Enemies: A Study in Sophocles and Greek Ethics*, Cambridge.
Boedeker, D. (1984), *Descent from Heaven: Images of Dew in Greek Poetry and Religion*, Chico, CA.
Bonnafé, A. (1989), "Clytemnestre et ses batailles: Éris et Peithô," in: R. Etienne / M.-T. Le Dinahet / M. Yon (eds.), *Architecture et poésie dans le monde grec: Hommage à Georges Roux*, Lyon, 149–57.
Bouvier, D. (2002), *Le Sceptre et la lyre: l'Iliade ou les héros de la mémoire*, Grenoble.
Bowra, C. M. (1930), *Tradition and Design in the* Iliad, Oxford.
Brook, A. (2014), *Ritual Poetics in the Plays of Sophocles*, PhD Diss., Toronto.

Budelmann, F. (2006), "Körper und Geist in tragischen Schmerz-Szenen," in: B. Seidensticker / M. Vöhler (eds.), *Gewalt und Ästhetik. Zur Gewalt und ihrer Darstellung in der griechischen Klassik*, Berlin, 123–48.
Budick, S. / Iser, W. (1989), *Languages of the Unsayable: The Play of Negativity in Literature and Literary Theory*, New York.
Burgess, J. (2009), *The Death and Afterlife of Achilles*, Baltimore.
Burkert, W. (1955), "Zum Altgriechischen Mitleidshegrieff," PhD Diss., Erlangen.
Burton, R. (1980), *The Chorus in Sophocles' Tragedies*, Oxford.
Bushnell, R. (2005), *A Companion to Tragedy*, Oxford.
Buschor, E. (1979), *Aiskhylos. Sophokles. Euripides. Gesamtausgabe der griechischen Tragödien*, Zürich.
Butler, S. / Purves, A. (eds.) (2013), *Synaesthesia and the Ancient Senses*, Durham, UK.
Buxton, R. (1982), *Persuasion in Greek Tragedy: a Study of Peithô*, Cambridge.
Buxton, R. (2007), "Tragedy and Greek Myth," in: R. Woodard (ed.), *The Cambridge Companion to Greek Mythology*, Cambridge, 166–89.
Cairns, F. (1993), *Aidôs: The Psychology and Ethics of Honour and Shame in Ancient Greek Literature*, Oxford.
Cairns, D. (2005), "Values," in: J. Gregory, (ed.), *A Companion to Greek Tragedy*, Oxford, 305–20.
Cairns, D. (2013), *Tragedy and Archaic Greek Thought*, Swansea.
Calame, C. (2005), "The Tragic Choral Group: Dramatic Roles and Social Functions," in: R. Bushnell, (ed.), *A Companion to Tragedy*, Oxford, 215–33.
Calder III, W. M. (1971), "Sophoclean Apologia: *Philoctetes*," in: *Greek, Roman, and Byzantine Studies* 12, 153–74.
Carawan, E. (2000), "Deianira's Guilt," in: *Transactions of the American Philological Association* 130, 189–237.
Cawthorn, K. (2008), *Becoming Female: The Male Body in Greek Tragedy*, London.
A. Chaniotis (ed.) (2012), *Unveiling Emotions: Sources and Methods for the Study of Emotions in the Greek World*, Stuttgart.
A. Chaniotis / P. Ducrey (eds.) (2013), *Unveiling Emotions II. Emotions in Greece and Rome: Texts, Images, Material Culture*, Stuttgart.
Chatman, S. (1990), *Coming to Terms: The Rhetoric of Narrative in Fiction and Film*, Ithaca.
Chatman, S. / van Peer, W. (eds.) (2001), *New Perspectives on Narrative Perspective*, Albany.
Chong-Gossard, J. (2008), *Gender and Communication in Euripides' Plays: Between Song and Silence*.
Clay, J. S. (1974), "Dêmas and Audê: the Nature of Divine Transformation in Homer," in: *Hermes* 102, 129–36.
Cohen, D. (1991), *Law, Sexuality, and Society: the Enforcement of Morals in Classical Athens*, Cambridge.
Coleridge, E. (tr.) (1938), *Euripides Orestes*, New York.
Collins, D. (1998), *Immortal Armor. The Concept of Alkê in Archaic Greek Poetry*, Maryland.
Conacher, D. J. (1967), *Euripidean Tragedy: Myth, Theme, and Structure*, Toronto.
Conacher, D. J. (1997), "Sophocles' *Trachiniae*: Some Observations," in: *Transactions of the American Philological Association* 118, 21–34.
Cropp, M. (2013, first published 1988), *Euripides:* Electra, Warminster, UK.
Crotty, K. (1994), *The Poetics of Supplication: Homer's* Iliad *and* Odyssey, Ithaca, NY.
Culler, J. (1977), "Apostrophe," in: *Diacritics* 7, no. 4, 59–69.

Damen, M. (1989), "Actor and Character in Greek Tragedy," in: *Theatre Journal* 41, 316–40.
Davies, M. (1991), *Sophocles. The Trachiniae*, Oxford.
De Jong, I. (1987), *Narrators and Focalizers: The Presentation of the Story in the Iliad*, Amsterdam.
De Jong, I. (1991), *Narrative in Drama: The Art of the Euripidean Messenger-Speech*, Leiden.
De Jong, I. (2009), "Metalepsis in ancient Greek literature," in: J. Grethlein / A. Rengakos (eds.), *Narratology and Interpretation: The Content of Narrative Form in Ancient Literature*, Berlin, 87–115.
De Martino, F. (1977), "Omero fra narrazione e mimesi (Dal poeta ai personaggi)," in: *Belfagor* 32, 1–6.
Denniston, J. D. (1939), *Euripides. Electra. Edited with introduction and Commentary*, Oxford.
Denniston, J. D. / Page, D. (1957), *Aeschylus: Agamemnon*, Oxford.
Di Benedetto, V. (1994), *Nel Laboratorio di Omero*, Torino.
Di Benedetto, V. / Medda, E. (eds.) (1997), *La Tragedia sulla scena: la tragedia greca in quanto spettacolo teatrale*, Turin.
Diggle, J. (2005), "The Violence of Clytemnestra," in: J. Dillon / S. E. Wilmer (eds.), *Rebel Women: Staging Ancient Greek Drama Today*, London, 215–21.
Dobrov, G. (2001), *Figures of Play: Greek Drama and Metafictional Poetics*, Oxford.
Dodds, E. (1951), *The Greeks and the Irrational*, Berkeley.
Dodds, E. (1960), "Morals and Politics in the *Oresteia*," in: *Proceedings of the Cambridge Philological Society* 6, 19–31.
Dover, K. (1974), *Greek Popular Morality in the Time of Plato and Aristotle*, Berkeley.
Dué, C. (2002), *Homeric Variations on a Lament by Briseis*, Lanham, MD.
Dué, C. (2006), *The Captive Woman's Lament in Greek Tragedy*, Austin.
Dumortier, J. (1935), *Le Vocabulaire médical d'Eschyle et les écrits hippocratiques*, Paris.
Dundes, A. (1981), *The Evil Eye: A Folklore Casebook*, New York.
Dunn, F. (2012a), "Metatheatre and Crisis in Euripides' *Bacchae* and Sophocles' *Oedipus at Colonus*," in: A. Markantonatos / B. Zimmermann (eds.), *Crisis on Stage: Tragedy and Comedy in Late Fifth-Century Athens*, Berlin, 359–76.
Dunn, F. (2012b), "Sophocles and the Narratology of Drama," in: J. Grethlein / A. Rengakos (eds.), *Narratology and Interpretation: The Content of Narrative Form in Ancient Literature*, Berlin, 337–56.
Dutoit, E. (1936), *Le Thème de l'adynaton dans la poésie antique*, Paris.
Easterling, P. E. (1977), "Character in Sophocles," in: *Greece & Rome* 24, 121–9.
Easterling, P. E. (1978), "Philoctetes and modern criticism," in: *Illinois Classical Studies* 3, 27–39.
Easterling, P. E. (1982), *Sophocles: Trachiniae*, Cambridge.
Easterling, P. E. (1996), "Weeping, Witnessing, and the Tragic Audience: Response to Segal," in: M. S. Silk (ed.), *Tragedy and the Tragic: Greek Theatre and Beyond*, Oxford 173–81.
Easterling, P. E. (1997), "Form and Performance," in: P. E. Easterling (ed.), *The Cambridge Companion to Greek Tragedy*, Cambridge, 151–77.
Eck, B. (2012), *La Mort rouge: homicide, guerre et souillure en Grèce ancienne. Collection d'Études anciennes. Série greque*, 145, Paris.
Edmunds, S. (1990), *Homeric Nêpios*, New York.
Edmunds, L. (1996), *Theatrical Space and Historical Place in Sophocles' Oedipus at Colonus*, Lanham, MD.

Edmunds, L. (2002), "Sounds Off Stage and On Stage in Aeschylus, *Seven Against Thebes*," in: A. Aloni / E. Berardi / G. Besso / S. Cecchin (eds.), *I Sette a Tebe. Dal mito alla letteratura. Atti del Seminario Internazionale*, Bologna, 105–15.

Elmer, D. / Bonifazi, A. (2011), "Composing Lines, Performing Acts: Clauses, Discourse Acts, and Melodic Units in a South Slavic Epic Song," in: E. Minchin (ed.), *Orality, Literacy and Performance in the Ancient World*, Leiden, 89–109.

Elmer, D. (2013), *The Poetics of Consent. Collective Decision Making and the* Iliad, Baltimore.

Falkner, T. (1993), "Making a Spectacle of Oneself: The Metatheatrical Design of Sophocles' *Ajax*," in: *Text and Presentation: Journal of the Comparative Drama Conference* 14, 35–40.

Falkner, T. (1998), "Containing Tragedy: Rhetoric and Self-Representation in Sophocles' *Philoctetes*," in: *Classical Antiquity* 17, no. 1, 25–58.

Falkner, T. (2005), "Engendering the Tragic *Theatês*: Pity, Power, and Spectacle in Sophocles' *Trachiniae*," in: R. Sternberg (ed.), *Pity and Power in Classical Athens*, Cambridge.

Feder, L. (1980), *Madness in Literature*, Princeton.

Fenik, B. (1968), *Typical Battle Scenes in the* Iliad. *Studies in the Narrative Techniques of Homeric Battle Description, Hermes Einzelschriften* 21, Wiesbaden, Germany.

Ferrari, G. (1997), "Figures in the Text: Metaphors and Riddles in the *Agamemnon*," in: *Classical Philology* 92, 1–45.

Finan, T. (1979), "Total Tragedy and Homer's *Iliad*," in: *The Maynooth Review*, 71–83.

Fletcher, J. (2011), *Performing Oaths in Classical Greek Drama*, Cambridge.

Fludernik, M. (1993), "Scene shift, Metalepsis, and the Metaleptic Mode," in: *Style* 37, 382–400.

Foley, H. (1975), *Ritual Irony: Poetry and Sacrifice in Euripides*, Ithaca, NY.

Foley, H. (1981), "The Conception of Women in Athenian Drama," in: H. Foley (ed.), *Reflections of Women in Antiquity*, New York, 127–68.

Foley, H. (2001), *Female Acts in Greek Tragedy*, Princeton, NJ.

Ford, A. (1992), *Homer: the Poetry and the Past*, Ithaca, NY.

Frame, D. (2009), *Hippota Nestor*, Cambridge, MA.

Franchet d'Esperey, S. (2006), "Rhétorique et poétique chez Quintilien: à propos de l'apostrophe," in: *Rhetorica* 25, 163–85.

Fränkel, E. (1950), *Aeschylus:* Agamemnon, Oxford.

Friis Johansen, H. (1964), "Die *Electra* des Sophokles. Versuch einer neuen Deutung," *Classica et Medievalia* 25, 8–32.

Frontisi-Ducroux, F. (1986), *La Cithare d'Achille: essai sur la poétique de* l'Iliade, Rome.

Fulkerson, L. (2006), "Neoptolemus grows up? 'Moral development' and the Interpretation of Sophocles' *Philoctetes*" in: *Cambridge Classical Journal* 52, 49–61.

Fulkerson, L. (2013), *No Regrets: Remorse in Classical Antiquity*, Oxford.

Fuqua, C. (1980), "Heroism, Heracles, and the *Trachiniae*," in: *Traditio* 36, 1–81.

Gagné, R. (2013), *Ancestral Fault in Ancient Greece*, Cambridge.

Gagné, R. / Hopman, M. (eds.) (2013), *Choral Mediations in Greek Tragedy*, Cambridge.

Gardiner, C. (1987), *The Sophoclean Chorus: A Study of Character and Function*, Iowa City.

Garvie, A. F. (1986), *Aeschylus'* Choephori, Oxford.

Gasti, H. (1993), "*Sophocles'* Trachiniae: *a Social or Externalized Aspect of Deianeira's Morality*," in *Antike und Abendland* 39, 20–8.

Gellie, G. (1981), "Tragedy and Euripides' *Electra*," in: *Bulletin of the Institute of Classical Studies* 28, 1–12.

Genette, G. (1980, first published 1972), *Figures III. Discours du récit*, Paris.
Genette, G. (1983), *Nouveau Discours du Récit*, Paris.
Genette, G. (2004), *Métalepse. De la Figure à la fiction*, Paris.
Gibert, J. (1995), *Change of Mind in Greek Tragedy*, Göttingen.
Gill, C. (1980), "Bow, Oracle, and Epiphany in Sophocles' *Philoctetes*," in: *Greece and Rome* 27, 137–46.
Gill, C. (1996), *Personality in Greek Epic, Tragedy, and Philosophy: The Self in Dialogue*, Oxford.
Goff, B. E. (1991), "The Sign of the Fall: the Scars of Orestes and Odysseus," in: *Classical Antiquity* 10, vol. 2, 259–67.
Goheen, R. (1955), "Aspects of Dramatic Symbolism: Three Studies in the *Oresteia*," in: *American Journal of Philology* 76, 113–37.
Golder, H. / Prevear, R. (1999), *Sophocles Aias (Ajax)*, New York.
Goldhill, S. (1984), *Language, Sexuality, Narrative: The* Oresteia, Cambridge.
Goldhill, S. (1991), "Violence in Greek Tragedy," in: J. Redmond (ed.), *Violence in Drama, Themes in Drama* 13, Cambridge, 15–34.
Goldhill, S. / Hall, E. (eds.) (2009), *Sophocles and the Greek Tragic Tradition*, Cambridge.
Goldhill, S. (2012), *Sophocles and the Language of Tragedy*, Oxford.
Gould, J. (1973), "Hiketeia," in: *Journal of Hellenic Studies* 93, 74–103.
Goward, B. (1999), *Telling Tragedy: Narrative Technique in Aeschylus, Sophocles and Euripides*, London.
Gregory, J. (2002), "Euripides as Social Critic," in: *Greece & Rome* 49, no. 2, 145–62.
Gregory, J. (2005), *A Companion to Greek Tragedy*, Oxford.
Gregory, J. (2014), "Tragedy and Archaic Greek Thought by Douglas Cairns" (Review), in: *Classical Journal* 109, no. 4, 506–9.
Grethlein, J. / Rengakos, A. (eds.) (2009), *Narratology and Interpretation: The Content of Narrative Form in Ancient Literature*, Berlin.
Griffin, J. (1976), "Homeric Pathos and Objectivity," in: *Classical Quarterly* 26, no. 2, 161–87.
Griffin, J. (1978), "The Divine Audience and the Religion of the *Iliad*," in: *Classical Quarterly* 28, no. 1, 1–22.
Griffin, J. (1980), *Homer on Life and Death*, Oxford.
Griffith, R. (1998), "Corporality in the Ancient Greek Theatre," in: *Phoenix* 52, no.3/4, 230–56.
Griffith, M. (2009), "The poetry of Aeschylus (in its traditional contexts)," in: P. Jouanna / F. Montanari (eds.), *Eschyle à l'aube du théâtre occidental*, Entretiens 55, Geneva, 1–49.
Grube, G. (1941), *The Drama of Euripides*, London.
Guidorizzi, G. (2013), *Il Compagno dell'anima : i Greci e il sogno*, Milano.
Hall, E. (2006), *The Theatrical Cast of Athens: Interactions between Ancient Greek Drama and Society*, Oxford.
Hall, E. (2009) "Deianeira deliberates," in: S. Goldhill / E. Hall (eds.), *Sophocles and the Greek Tragic Tradition*, Cambridge, 69–96.
Halliwell, S. / Innes, D. / Russell, D., et al., (eds.) (1995), *Poetics of Aristotle*, ed. and transl. S. Halliwell; Longinus, *On the Sublime*, transl. W. Fyfe, rev. D. Russell; Demetrius, *On Style*, ed. and transl. D. Innes, based on W. Rhys Roberts, Cambridge, MA.
Halliwell, S. (2002), *The Aesthetics of Mimesis: Ancient Texts and Modern Problems*, Princeton.

Hawkins, A. H. (1999), "Ethical Tragedy and Sophocles' *Philoctetes*," in: *Classical World* 92, no. 4, 337–57.
Hawthorne, K. (2006), "Political Discourses at the End of Sophokles' *Philoktetes*" in: *Classical Antiquity* 25, 243–76.
Heath, M. (1987), *The Poetics of Greek Tragedy*, Stanford.
Heath, M. (1999), "Sophocles' *Philoctetes*: A Problem Play?" in: in: J. Griffin (ed.), *Sophocles Revisited. Essays presented to Sir Hugh Lloyd-Jones*, Oxford.
Heath, J. (1999a), "Disentangling the Beast: Humans and Other Animals in Aeschylus' *Oresteia*," *Journal of Hellenic Studies* 119, 17–47.
Heiden, B. (1989), *Tragic Rhetoric: An Interpretation of Sophocles'* Trachiniae, New York.
Heiden, B. (2008), *Homer's Cosmic Fabrication: Choice and Design in the* Iliad, Oxford.
Henrichs, A. (2000), "*Drama* and *Dromena*: Bloodshed, Violence, and Sacrificial Metaphor in Euripides," in: *Harvard Studies in Classical Philology* 100, 173–88.
Henrichs, A. (2010), "What is a Greek God?" in: J. N. Bremmer / A. W. Erskine (eds.), *The Gods of Ancient Greece: Identities and Transformations*, Edinburgh Leventis Studies 5, Edinburgh, 19–40.
Henry, R. M. (1905), "The Use and Origin of Apostrophe in Homer," in: *Classical Review* 19, no. 1, 7–9.
Herder, J. G. (1987), first published 1772 "Über den Ursprung der Sprache," in: W. Pross (ed.), *Herder und die Anthropologie der Aufklärung*, Munich, 253–318.
Herington, J. (1986), "The Marriage of Earth and Sky in Aeschylus' *Agamemnon* 1388–1392," in: M. Cropp / E. Fantham / S. E. Scully (eds.), *Greek Tragedy and its Legacy: Essays presented to D. J. Conacher*, Calgary, 27–33.
Herman, G. (1987), *Ritualised Friendship and the Greek city*, Cambridge.
Hirschberger, M. (2012), "The Fate of Achilles in the *Iliad*," in: F. Montanari / A. Rengakos / C. Tsagalis (eds.), *Homeric Contexts: Neoanalysis and the Interpretation of Oral Poetry*, Berlin, 185–96.
Holmes, B. (2007), "*The* Iliad*'s Economy of Pain*," in: *Transactions of the American Philological Association* 137, no. 1, 45–84.
Holmes, B. (2010), *The Symptom and the Subject: the Emergence of the Physical Body in Ancient Greece*, Princeton.
Hopman, M. G. (2013), "Chorus, Conflict and Closure in Aeschylus' *Persians*." in R. Gagné / M. G. Hopman (eds.), *Choral Mediations in Greek Drama*. Cambridge, 58–77.
Iakov, D. (2012), "Fragmenting the Self: Society and Psychology in Euripides' *Electra* and *Ion*," in: A. Markantonatos / B. Zimmermann (eds.), *Crisis on Stage: Tragedy and Comedy in Late Fifth-Century Athena*, Berlin, 121–38.
Inoue, E. (1979), "Sight, Sound and Rhetoric: *Philoctetes* 29ff.," in: *American Journal of Philology* 100, 217–27.
Ieranò, G. (2011), "Bella come in un dipinto:" la pittura nella tragedia greca," in: L. Belloni / A. Bonandini / G. Ieranò / G. Moretti (eds.), *Le Immagini nel testo, il testo nelle immagini: rapporti fra parole e visualità nella tradizione greco-latina*, Trento, 241–65.
Janko, R. (1992a), *The Iliad: A Commentary*, vol. 2, books 13–16, Cambridge.
Janko, R. (1992b), *The Iliad: A Commentary*, vol. 6, books 20–24, Cambridge.
Jebb, R. C. (1883–1900), *Sophocles : The Plays and Fragments*, 7 vols., Cambridge.
Johnson, J. F. (1980), "Compassion in Sophocles' 'Philoctetes:' A Comparative Study," PhD Diss., Austin, TX.

Johnson, J. A. (1988), "Sophocles' *Philoctetes:* Deictic Language and the Claims of Odysseus," in: *Eranos* 86, 117–21.
Johnson, J. F. / Clapp, D. (2005), "Athenian Tragedy: An Education in Pity," in: R. Sternberg (ed.), *Pity and Power in Ancient Athens*, Cambridge, 123–64.
Jouan, F. (1983), "Réflexions sur le rôle du protagoniste tragique," in: *Théâtre et spectacles dans l'antiquité. Actes du colloque de Strasbourg, novembre 1981*, 63–80.
Jouanna, J. (2003), "La doppia fine del *Filottete*: rotture et continuità," in: G. Avezzù (ed.), *Il drama sofocleo. Testo, lingua, interpretazione*, Stuttgart, 151–74.
Judet de la Combe, P. (2001), *L'Agamemnon d'Eschyle: Commentaire des Dialogues*, Villeneuve d'Ascq, France.
Judet de la Combe, P. (2012), "Le théâtre, au-delà de la metathéâtralité. Sur la fin de l'*Electre* d'Euripide," in: *Lexis* 30, 341–53.
Kakridis, J. (1949), *Homeric Researches*, Lund.
Kamerbeek, J. (1963), *The plays of Sophocles*, 2: *Trachiniae*, Leiden.
Kamerbeek, J. (1974), *The Plays of Sophocles*, 5: *the Electra*, Leiden.
Kamerbeek, J. (1980), *The plays of Sophocles*, 6: *Philoctetes*, Leiden.
Kannicht, R. (ed.) (2004), *Tragicorum Graecorum Fragmenta. Vol. 5. Euripides*, Göttingen.
Karydas, H. (1998), *Eurykleia and her Successors: Female Figures of Authority in Greek Poetics*, Lanham, MD.
Kelly, A. (2012), "The Mourning of Thetis: 'Allusion' and the Future in the *Iliad*," in: F. Montanari / A. Rengakos / C. Tsagalis (eds.), *Homeric Contexts: Neoanalysis and the Interpretation of Oral Poetry*, Berlin, 221–68.
Kim, J. (2000), *The Pity of Achilles: Oral Style and the Unity of the* Iliad, Lanham, MD.
Kirk, G. S. (1985), *The Iliad: A Commentary*, vol. 1, books 1–4, Cambridge.
Kirkwood, G. M. (1941), "The Dramatic unity of Sophocles' *Trachiniae*," in: *Transactions of the American Philological Association* 72, 203–11.
Kirkwood, G. (1958), *A Study of Sophoclean Drama*, Ithaca, NY.
Kirkwood, G. (1994), "Persuasion and Allusion in Sophocles' Philoctetes," in: *Hermes* 122, 425–36.
Kitto, H. D. F. (1939), *Greek Tragedy*, London.
Kitto, H. D. F. (1956), *Form and Meaning in Drama*, London.
Kitzinger, R. (2008), *The Choruses of Sophokles'* Antigone *and* Philoktetes: *A Dance of Words*, Boston.
Kitzinger, R. (2012), "The Divided Worlds of Sophocles' *Women of Trachis*," in: K. Ormand (ed.), *A Companion to Sophocles*, Oxford, 111–25.
Knox, B. M. W. (1964), *The Heroic Temper. Studies of Sophoclean Tragedies*, Berkeley.
Konstan, D. (1999), "Pity and Self-Pity," in: *Electronic Antiquity* 5, no. 2, http://scholar.lib.vt.edu/ejournals/ElAnt/V5N2/konstan.html.
Konstan, D. (2001), *Pity Transformed*, London.
Konstan, D. (2005), "Aristotle and the Emotions," in: V. Pedrick / S. Oberhelman (eds.), *The Soul of Tragedy: Essays on Athenian Drama*, Chicago, 13–26.
Konstan, D. (2006), *The Emotions of the Ancient Greeks: Studies in Aristotle and Classical Literature*, Toronto.
Kosak, J. C. (1999), "Therapeutic Touch and Sophocles' *Philoctetes*," in: *Harvard Studies in Classical Philology* 99, 93–134.
Krapp, H. J. (1964), *Die akustischen Phänomene in der Ilias*, PhD Diss., Munich.
Kyriakou, P. (2001), "Warrior vaunts in the *Iliad*," in: *Rheinisches Museum*, n.s. 144, 250–77.

Kyriakou, P. (2006), *A Commentary on Euripides' Iphigeneia in Tauris*, Berlin.
Kyriakou, P. (2011), *The Past in Aeschylus and Sophocles*, Berlin.
Lachenaud, G. (2013), *Les Routes de la voix: l'Antiquité grecque et le mystère de la voix*, Paris.
Lada-Richards, I. (1993), "Empathic Understanding: Emotions and Cognition in Classical Dramatic Audience-Response," in: *Proceedings of the Cambridge Philological Association* 39, 94–140.
Lada-Richards, I. (1997), "'Estrangement' or 'Reincarnation'?: Performers and Performance on the Classical Athenian Stage," in: *Arion* 5, 66–107.
Lada-Richards, I. (2009), "The players will tell all: the dramatist, the actors and the art of acting in Sophocles' *Philoctetes*," in: S. Goldhill / E. Hall (eds.), *Sophocles and the Language of Tragedy*, Oxford, 48–68.
Lang, M. (1989), "Unreal Conditions in Homeric Narrative," in: *Greek, Roman, and Byzantine Studies* 30, 5–26.
Lateiner, D. (2002), "Pouring Bloody Drops (*Iliad* 16.459): The Grief of Zeus," in: *Colby Quarterly* 38, 42–61.
Lattimore, R. (1951), *The Iliad*, Chicago.
Lebeck, A. (1971), *The Oresteia: A Study in Language and Structure*, Cambridge, MA.
Ledbetter, G. (1993), "Achilles' Self-address: *Iliad* 16.7–19," in: *American Journal of Philology* 114, no. 4, 481–91.
Lesky, A. (1983), *Greek Tragic Poetry*. Translated by Matthew Dillon, New Haven.
Létoublon, F. (2005), "La Patroclie, exploits et mort du héros (*Iliade* XVI)," in: *L'information littéraire* 57, 3–11.
Leuzzi, D. (2008), "La morte dell' eroe nell'*Iliade*: scene e sequenze narrative," in: C. Aceti / D. Leuzzi / L. Pagani (eds.), *Eroi dell'Iliade. Personaggi e strutture narrative*, Rome, 271–326.
Linforth, I. (1956), "*Philoctetes*: the play and the man," in: *University of California Publications in Classical Philology* 15, 95–156.
Lloyd, M. (2005), *Sophocles: Electra*, London.
Lloyd, M. (2013), "The Mutability of Fortune in Euripides," in: D. Cairns (ed.), *Tragedy and Archaic Greek Thought*, Swansea, 205–26.
Lloyd-Jones, H. (1970), *Agamemnon, Choephoroe, Eumenides*, 3 vols, Berkeley.
Lloyd-Jones, H. (1971), *The Justice of Zeus*, Berkeley.
Lloyd-Jones, H. (ed. and transl.) (1994), *Sophocles*, vol. 2, Cambridge, MA.
Lloyd-Jones, H. / Wilson, N. G. (1990), *Sophoclea: Studies on the Text of Sophocles*, Antica 4, Oxford.
Lombardo, S. (tr.) (1997), *Homer: Iliad*, Indianapolis.
Lonsdale, S. (1990), *Creatures of Speech: Lion, Herding, and Hunting Similes in the Iliad*, Stuttgart.
Loraux, N. (1985), *Façons Tragiques de Tuer une Femme*, Paris.
Loraux, N. (1990), *Les Mères en Deuil*, Paris.
Loraux, N. (1995), *The Experiences of Tiresias: The Feminine and the Greek Man*, transl. P. Wissing, Princeton, NJ.
Lord, A. (2000, first published 1960), *The Singer of Tales*, Cambridge.
Louden, B. (1993), "Pivotal Contrafactuals in Homeric Epic," in: *Classical Antiquity* 12, vol. 2, 181–98.

Lourens, M. (2013), *Tragic Views of the Human Condition: Cross-cultural Comparisons between Views of Human Nature in Greek and Shakespearean tragedy and the Mahabharata and Bhagavadgita*, New York.
Lovatt, H. (2013), *The Epic Gaze: Vision, Gender and Narrative in Ancient Epic*, Cambridge.
Lowenstam, S. (1981), *The Death of Patroklos: A Study in Typology*, Königstein.
Lynn-George, M. (1996), "Structures of Care in the *Iliad*," in: *Classical Quarterly*, n.s., 46, no. 1, 1–26.
Lyons, D. (2012), *Dangerous Gifts: Gender and Exchange in Ancient Greece*, Austin.
Mac Donald, M. (1978), *Terms for Happiness in Euripides*, Göttingen.
Mac Leod, C. (1982), *Iliad XXIV*, Cambridge.
MacLeod, L. (2001), *Dolos and Dikê in Sophokles'* Elektra, Leiden.
March, J. (2001), *Sophocles*. Electra, Warminster, UK.
Markantonatos, A. (2002), *Tragic Narrative: A narratological study of Sophocles'* Oedipus at Colonus, Berlin.
Markantonatos, A. / Zimmermann, B. (eds.) (2012), *Crisis on Stage: Tragedy and Comedy in Late Fifth-Century Athens*, Berlin.
Marks, J. (2010), "Context as Hypertext: Divine Rescue Scenes in the *Iliad*," in: *Trends in Classics* 2, vol. 2, 300–22.
Marseglia, R. (2013), *Le Rôle dramatique de la vue et de l'ouïe dans la tragédie d'Euripide*, PhD Diss., Paris.
Martin, R. (1983), *Healing, Sacrifice, and Battle : Amêchania and Related Concepts in Early Greek Poetry*, Innsbruck.
Martin, R. (1989), *The Language of Heroes: Speech and Performance in the* Iliad, Ithaca, NY.
Mastronarde, D. (1979), *Contact and Discontinuity: Some Conventions of Speech and Action on the Greek Tragic Stage*, Berkeley.
Mastronarde, D. (1994), *Euripides: Phoenissae*. Cambridge.
Mastronarde, D. (2010), *The Art of Euripides*, Cambridge.
Matthews, V. J. (1980), "Metrical Reasons for the Apostrophe in Homer," in: *Liverpool Classical Monthly* 5, 93–9.
McCall, M. (1972), "The *Trachiniae*: Structure, Focus, and Heracles," in: *American Journal of Philology* 93, 142–63.
McCoy, M. (2013), *Wounded Heroes: Vulnerability as a Virtue in Ancient Greek Literature and Philosophy*, Oxford.
McClure, L. (1999), *Spoken like a Woman: Speech and Gender in Athenian Drama*, Princeton.
McClure, L. (2012), "Staging Mothers in Sophocles' *Electra* and *Oedipus the King*," in: K. Ormand (ed.), *A Companion to Sophocles*, Oxford, 367–80.
Medda, E. (2013), *La Saggezza dell'illusione: studi sul teatro greco*, Pisa.
Meinel, F. (2015), *Pollution and Crisis in Greek Tragedy*, Cambridge.
Mills, S. (2000), "Achilles, Patroclus and Parental Care in Some Homeric Similes," in: *Greece and Rome* 47, no. 1, 3–18.
Minchin, E. (1991), "Speaker and Listener, Text and Context: Some Notes on the Encounter of Nestor and Patroklos in *Iliad* 11," in: *Classical World* 84, no. 4, 273–85.
Minchin, E. (2011), "'Themes' and 'Mental Moulds:' Roger Schank, Malcolm Willcock and the Creation of Character in Homer," in: *Classical Quarterly* 61, no. 2, 323–43.
Mirto, M. S. (2007), *La morte nel mondo greco: da Omero all'età classica*, Roma.
Mitchell-Boyask, R. (2008), *Plague and the Athenian imagination: Drama, History, and the Cult of Asclepius*, Cambridge.

Mitchell-Boyask, R. (2012), "Heroic Pharmacology: Sophocles and the Metaphors of Greek Medical Thought," in: K. Ormand (ed.), *A Companion to Sophocles*, Oxford, 316–30.
Moles, J. L. (1979), "A Neglected Aspect of *Agamemnon* 1389–92," in: *Liverpool Classical Monthly* 4, 179–89.
Moles, J. (1984), "Philanthropia in the *Poetics*," in: *Phoenix* 38, no. 4, 325–35.
Montanari, F. / A. Rengakos / C. Tsagalis (eds.) (2012), *Homeric Contexts: Neoanalysis and the Interpretation of Oral Poetry*, Berlin.
Montiglio, S. (2000), *Silence in the Land of Logos*, Princeton.
Morgan, K. (1992), "*Agamemnon* 1391–1392: Klytaimnestra's defense foreshadowed," in: *Quaderni Urbinati di Cultura Classica* 42, 25–7.
Morrell, K. (1996–7), "The Fabric of Persuasion: Clytaemnestra, Agamemnon, and the Sea of Garments," in: *Classical Journal* 92, 141–65.
Mossman, J. (1995), *Wild Justice: a Study of Euripides' Hecuba*, Oxford.
Mossman, J. (2001), "Women's Speech in Greek Tragedy: The Case of Electra and Clytemnestra in Euripides' *Electra*," in: *Classical Quarterly, N.S.* 51, no. 2, 374–84.
Most, G. (2003), "Anger and pity in Homer's *Iliad*," in: *Yale Classical Studies* 32, 50–75.
Moulton, C. (1977), *Similes in the Iliad and Odyssey*, Hypomnemata 49, Göttingen.
Mueller, M. (1984), *The Iliad*, London.
Muellner, L. (1976), *The Meaning of Homeric εὔχομαι through its formulas*, Innsbruck.
Muellner, L. (1996), *The Anger of Achilles: Mênis in Greek Epic*, Ithaca, NY.
Muellner, L. (2012), "Grieving Achilles," in: F. Montanari / A. Rengakos / C. Tsagalis (eds.), *Homeric Contexts: Neoanalysis and the Interpretation of Oral Poetry*, Berlin, 197–220.
Muller, Y. (2011), "Le maschalismos, une mutilation rituelle en Grèce ancienne?" in: *Ktèma* 36, 269–96.
Munteanu, D. L. (2012), *Tragic Pathos: Pity and Fear in Greek Philosophy and Tragedy*, Oxford.
Murnaghan, S. (1988), "Body and Voice in Greek Tragedy," in: *The Yale Journal of Criticism* 1, 23–43.
Murnaghan, S. (1999), "The Poetics of Loss in Greek Epic," in: M. Beissinger / J. Tylus / S. Wofford (eds.), *Epic traditions in the contemporary world: the poetics of community*, Berkeley, 203–20.
Murnaghan, S. (2012), "Sophocles' Choruses," in: K. Ormand (ed.), *A Companion to Sophocles*, Oxford, 220–35.
Nagy, G. (1974), *Comparative Studies in Greek and Indic Meter*, Harvard Studies in Comparative Literature 33, Cambridge, MA.
Nagy, G. (1979), *The Best of the Achaeans: Concepts of the Hero in Archaic Greek Poetry*, Baltimore.
Nagy, G. (1983), "On the Death of Sarpedon," in: C. Rubino / C. Shelmerdine (eds.), *Approaches to Homer*, Austin, 189–217.
Nagy, G. (1990), *Pindar's Homer: the Lyric Possession of an Epic Past*, Baltimore.
Nagy, G. (1996), *Poetry as Performance. Homer and Beyond*, Cambridge.
Neal, T. (2006), *The Wounded Hero: Non-Fatal Injury in Homer's Iliad*, Bern.
Nooter, S. (2012), *When Heroes Sing: Sophocles and the Shifting Soundscape of Tragedy*, Cambridge.
Nussbaum, M. (1976), "Consequences and Character in Sophocles' *Philoctetes*," in: *Philosophy and Literature* 1, 25–53.

Nussbaum, M. (1986), *The Fragility of Goodness: Luck and Ethics in Greek Tragedy and Philosophy*, Cambridge.
Nussbaum, M. (1996), "Compassion: The Basic Social Emotion," in: *Social Philosophy* 13, 27–58.
Nussbaum M. (1999), "Invisibility and Recognition: Sophocles' *Philoctetes* and Ellison's *Invisible Man*," in: *Philosophy and Literature* 23, no. 2, 257–83.
O'Daly, J. P. (1985), "Clytemnestra and the Elders: Dramatic technique in Aeschylus, *Agamemnon* 1372–1576," in: *Museum Helveticum* 42, 1–19.
Ormand, K. (1996), *Exchange and the Maiden: Marriage in Sophoclean Tragedy*, Austin.
Ormand, K. (ed.) (2012), *A Companion to Sophocles*, Oxford.
Pagani, L. (2008), "Il codice eroico e il guerriero di fronte alla morte," in: C. Aceti / D. Leuzzi / L. Pagani (eds.), *Eroi dell'Iliade. Personaggi e strutture narrative*, Rome, 327–418.
Parker, R. (1983), *Miasma: Pollution and Purification in Early Greek Religion*, Oxford.
Parker, R. (1999), "Through a glass darkly: Sophocles and the Divine," in: J. Griffin (ed.), *Sophocles Revisited. Essays presented to Sir Hugh Lloyd-Jones*, Oxford, 11–30.
Parry, A. (1972), "Language and Characterization in Homer," in: *Harvard Studies in Classical Philology* 76: 1–22.
Parry, M. (1928), *L'épithète traditionnelle dans Homère*, Paris, reprinted in: A. Parry (ed.) (1971), *The Making of Homeric Verse: The Collected Papers of Milman Parry*, Oxford.
Pedrick, V. / Oberhelman, S. (eds.) (2005), *The Soul of Tragedy: Essays on Athenian Drama*, Chicago.
Peradotto, J. (1964), "Some Patterns of Nature Imagery in the *Oresteia*," in: *American Journal of Philology* 85, 378–93.
Peradotto, J. (1969), "The Omen of the Eagles and the HYOS of Agamemnon," in: *Phoenix* 23, 237–63.
Perrotta, G. (1931), *Le Donne di Trachis*, Bari.
Perrotta, G. (1935). *Sofocle*, Milan.
Pickard-Cambridge, A. (1968), *The Dramatic Festivals of Athens*, Oxford.
Podlecki, A. (1966), "The Power of the Word in Sophocles' *Philoctetes*," in: *Greek, Roman, and Byzantine Studies* 7, 233–50.
Podlecki, A. (1989), *Aeschylus*. Eumenides, Warminster, UK.
Porter, J. (ed.) (1999), *Constructions of the Classical Body*, Ann Arbor, MI.
Pozzi, D. (1994), "Deianeira's Robe: Diction in Sophocles' *Trachiniae*," in: *Mnemosyne* 47, no. 5, 577–85.
Pucci, P. / Avezzù, G. / Cerri, G. (eds.) (2003), *Sofocle: Filottete*, Milan.
Pulleyn, S. (1997), "Erotic Undertones in the Language of Clytemnestra," in: *Classical Quarterly*, n.s., 47, no. 2, 565–7.
Rabel, R. (1997), "Sophocles' *Philoctetes* and the interpretation of *Iliad* 9," in: *Arethusa* 30, 297–307.
Rabel, R. (1998), *Plot and Point of View in the Iliad*, Ann Arbor.
Rabinowitz, N. (1992), "Tragedy and the Politics of Containment," in: A. Richlin (ed.), *Pornography and Representation in Greece and Rome*, Oxford, 36–52.
Radermacher, L. (1914), *Sophokles. Vol. IV*, Berlin.
Ready, J. (2011), *Character, Narrator and Simile in the Iliad*, Cambridge.
Redfield, J. (1975), *Nature and Culture in the Iliad: the Tragedy of Hector*, Chicago.
Rehm, R. (1994), *Marriage to Death: The Conflation of Wedding and Funeral Rituals in Greek Tragedy*, Princeton.

Reinhardt, K. (1933), *Sophokles*, Frankfurt.
Reinhardt, K. (1961), *Die Ilias und ihr Dichter*, Göttingen, Germany.
Revermann, M. (2006), "The Competence of Theatre Audiences in Fifth- and Fourth-Century Athens," in: *Journal of Hellenic Studies* 126, 99–124.
Richardson, S. (1990), *The Homeric Narrator*, Nashville.
Richardson, N. (1993) *The Iliad: A Commentary*, vol. 6, books 21–24, ed. G.S. Kirk, ed., Cambridge.
Ringer, M. (1998), *Electra and the Empty Urn: Metatheater and Role Playing in Sophocles*, Chapel Hill.
Rinon, Y. (2008), "A Tragic Pattern in the *Iliad*," in: *Harvard Studies in Classical Philology* 104, 45–91.
Roberts, D. (1984), *Apollo and His Oracle in the* Oresteia, Göttingen.
Roberts, D. (1989), "Different Stories: Sophoclean Narrative(s) in the *Philoctetes*," in: *Transactions of the American Philological Association* 119, 161–76.
Roisman, H. M. / Luschnig, C. A. E. (2011), *Euripides'* Electra: *A Commentary*. Norman, OK.
Roisman H. M. (2014), *The Encyclopedia of Greek Tragedy*, ed. H. M. Roisman, Chichester, UK.
Romani, S. (2004), *Nascite speciali: usi e abusi del modello biologico del parto e della gravidanza nel mondo antico*, Alexandria.
de Romilly, J. (1958), *La Crainte et l'angoisse dans le théâtre d'Eschyle*, Paris.
de Romilly, J. (1995), *Tragédies grecques au fil des ans*, Paris.
Rose, P. W. (1976), "Sophocles' *Philoctetes* and the Teachings of the Sophists," in: *Harvard Studies in Classical Philology* 80, 49–105.
Rose, P. W. (1992), *Sons of the Gods, Children of Earth: Ideology and Literary Form in Ancient Greece*, Ithaca, NY.
Rossi, L.E. (ed.) (1977), *Due seminari romani di Eduard Fraenkel. Aiace e Filottete di Sofocle*, Rome.
Rutherford, R. (1982), "Tragic Form and Feeling in the *Iliad*," in: *Journal of Hellenic Studies* 102, 145–60.
Rutherford, R. (2012), *Greek Tragic Style. Form, Language, Interpretation*, Cambridge.
Sandridge, N. (2008), "Feeling Vulnerable, but Not Too Vulnerable: Pity in Sophocles' *Oedipus Coloneus*, *Ajax*, and *Philoctetes*," in: *Classical Journal* 103, 433–48.
Saunders, K. (1999), "The Wounds in *Iliad* 13–16," in: *Classical Quarterly*, n.s., 49, no. 2, 345–63.
Saunders, K. (2004), "Frölich's Table of Homeric Wounds," in: *Classical Quarterly* 54, no. 1, 1–17.
Schadewaldt, W. (1943), *Iliasstudien*, Leipzig.
Schadewaldt, W. (1965), *Von Homers Welt und Werk*, Stuttgart.
Schein, S. (1984), *The Mortal Hero: An Introduction to Homer's* Iliad, Berkeley.
Schein, S. (1997), "Divinity and Moral Agency," in: A. Lloyd, *What is a God? Studies in the Nature of Greek Divinity*, London, 123–39.
Schein, S. (2001), "Heracles and the Ending of Sophocles' *Philoctetes*," in: *Studi Italiani di Filologia Classica* 19, 38–52.
Schein, S. (2005), "Divine and Human in Sophokles' *Philoktetes*," in: S. Oberhelman / V. Pedrick (eds.), *The Soul of Tragedy: Essays on Athenian Drama*, Chicago, 26–46.
Schein, S. (2006), "The *Iliad* and *Odyssey* in Sophocles' *Philoctetes*. Generic Complexity and Ethical Ambiguity," in: J. Davidson / F. Muecke / P. Wilson (eds.), *Greek Drama III: Essays in Honour of Kevin Lee*, London, 129–40.

Schein, S. (2011a), "Language and Dramatic Action in the Prologue of Sophocles' *Philoktetes*," in: *Dioniso: rivista di studi sul teatro antico*, n.s., 1, 79–96.
Schein, S. (2011b), "The Language of Hatred in Aeschylus and Sophocles," in: *Mètis New Series* 9, 69–80.
Schein, S. (2012), "Sophocles and Homer," in: K. Ormand (ed.), *A Companion to Sophocles*, Oxford, 424–39.
Schein, S. (2013), *Sophocles: Philoctetes*, Cambridge.
Schopenhauer, A. (1891), *The Art of Literature: A Series of Essays*, selected and transl. by T. Saunders, London.
Schwinge, E. (1968), *Die Verwendung der Stichomythie in den Dramen des Euripides*, Heidelberg.
Scodel, R. (1984), *Sophocles*, Boston.
Scodel, R. (2002), *Listening to Homer: Tradition, Narrative, Audience*, Ann Arbor, MI.
Scott, W. C. (2009), *The Artistry of the Homeric Simile*, Hanover, NH.
Seaford, R. (1994), *Reciprocity and Ritual: Homer and Tragedy in the Developing City-State*, Oxford.
Seale, D. (1982), *Vision and Stagecraft in Sophocles*, Chicago.
Sébillote-Cuchet, V. (2003), "Cris de femmes, cris d'hommes. Éléments de critique pour l'interprétation du cri en Grèce ancienne," in: D. Lett / N. Offenstadt (eds.), *Haro! Noël ! Oyé ! Pratiques du cri au Moyen-Age*, Paris, 205–16.
Segal, C. (1977), "Philoctetes and the Imperishable Piety," in: *Hermes* 105, 133–58.
Segal, C. (1981), *Tragedy and Civilization. An interpretation of Sophocles*. Cambridge, MA.
Segal, C. (1982), *Dionysiac Poetics and Euripides' Bacchae*, Princeton.
Segal, C. (1985), "Tragedy, Corporeality and the Texture of Language: Matricide in the Three Electra Plays," in: *Classical World* 79, 1, 7–23.
Segal, C. (1992), "Time, Oracles and Marriage in the *Trachiniae*," in: *Lexis* 9/10, 63–91.
Segal, C. (1993), *Euripides and the Poetics of Sorrow: Art, Gender, and Commemoration in* Alcestis, Hippolytus *and* Hecuba, Durham, NC and London.
Segal, C. (1995), *Sophocles' Tragic World: Divinity, Nature, Society*, Cambridge, MA.
Segal, C. (1996), "Catharsis, audience, and closure in Greek tragedy," in: M. Silk (ed.), *Tragedy and the Tragic: Greek Theatre and Beyond*, Oxford, 149–72.
Segal, C. (2000), "The Oracles of Sophocles' *Trachiniae*: Convergence or Confusion?" in: *Harvard Studies in Classical Philology* 100, 151–71.
Seidensticker, B. (2006), "Distanz und Nähe: Zur Darstellung von Gewalt in der griechischen Tragödie," in: B. Seidensticker / M. Vöhler (eds.), *Gewalt und Ästhetik. Zur Gewalt und ihrer Darstellung in der griechischen Klassik*, Berlin, 91–122.
Serghidou, A. (2010). *Servitude tragique : esclaves et héros déchus dans la tragédie grecque*, Besançon.
Sewell-Rutter, N. J. (2007), *Guilt by Descent: Moral Inheritance and Decision Making in Greek Tragedy*, Oxford.
Sidgwick, A. G. (1890), *Aeschylus Agamemnon*, Oxford.
Silk, M. (ed.) (1996), *Tragedy and the Tragic: Greek Theatre and Beyond*, Oxford.
Sinos, D. (1975), *Achilles, Patroklos, and the Meaning of Philos*, Innsbruck.
Slatkin, L. (1991), *The Power of Thetis: Allusion and Interpretation in the* Iliad, Berkeley.
Slatkin, L. (2007), "Notes on Tragic Visualizing in the *Iliad*," in: C. Kraus / S. Goldhill / H. Foley / Jas Elsner (eds.), *Visualizing the Tragic. Drama, Myth, and Ritual in Greek Art and Literature. Essays in Honour of Froma Zeitlin*, Oxford, 19–34.

Snell, B. (1953), *The Discovery of the Mind in Greek Philosophy and Literature*, New York.
Sommerstein, A. (2008), *Aeschylus: Oresteia*, Cambridge.
Sommerstein, A. (2010), *Aeschylean Tragedy*, London.
Sorum, C. E. (1978), "Monsters and the Family: The Exodos of Sophocles' *Trachiniae*," in: *Greek, Roman, and Byzantine Studies* 19, 59–73.
Stanford, W. (1972), *Ambiguity in Greek Literature: Studies in Theory and Practice*, London.
Stanford, W. (1983), *Greek Tragedy and the Emotions: An Introductory Study*, London.
Stevens, E. (1944), "Some Attic Common Places of Pity," in: *The American Journal of Philology*, 65, no. 1, 1–25.
Sternberg, R. (2005), *Pity and Power in Ancient Athens*, Cambridge.
Stieber, M. (2006), "Beflowered with Beauty: The Imagery of *Ag.* 659–60," in: *Scripta Israelica Classica* 25, 25–49.
Strauss Clay, J. (2011), *Homer's Trojan Theater: Space, Vision, and Memory in the* Iliad, Cambridge.
Suksi, A. (2009), "Odysseus in Democratic Athens," PhD Diss., Toronto.
Taplin, O. (1971), "Significant Actions in Sophocles' *Philoctetes*," in: *Greek, Roman, and Byzantine Studies* 12, no. 1, 25–44.
Taplin, O. (1977), *The Stagecraft of Aeschylus: the Dramatic Use of Exits and Entrances in Greek Tragedy*, Oxford.
Taplin, O. (1978), *Greek Tragedy in Action*, Berkeley.
Taplin, O. (1987), "The Mapping of Sophocles' *Philoctetes*," in: *Bulletin of the Institute of Classical Studies* 34, 69–77.
Taplin, O. (1992), *Homeric Soundings*, Oxford.
Térasse, S. (2001), "Pathologie et bestialité: une représentation métaphorique de la maladie dans les tragédies de Sophocle," in: *Anthropologica* 33-4, 47–59.
Thumiger, C. (2009), "Metatheatre in modern and ancient fiction," in: *Materiali e Discussioni per l'Analisi dei Testi Classici* 63, 9–58.
Torrance, I. (2011), "In the footprints of Aeschylus: Recognition, allusion, and metapoetics in Euripides," in: *American Journal of Philology* 132, 177–204.
Torrance, I. (2013), *Metapoetry in Euripides*, Oxford.
Van Brock, N. (1959), "Substitution rituelle," in: *Revue Hittite et Asianique* 65, 117–46.
Vellacott, P. (1984), *The Logic of Tragedy*, Durham.
Vernant, J. P., Vidal-Naquet, P. (1972), *Mythe et Tragédie en Grèce ancienne*, Paris.
Vickers, B. (1973), *Towards Greek Tragedy: Drama, Myth, Society*, London.
Vickers, B. (1979), *Comparative Tragedy*, London.
Visser, T. (1998), *Untersuchungen zum Sophokleischen Philoktet*, Stuttgart.
Visvardi, E. (2007), "Dancing the Emotions: Pity and Fear in the Tragic Chorus," PhD Diss., Stanford.
Visvardi, E. (2015), *Emotion in Action: Thucydides and the Tragic Chorus*, Leiden.
Waldock, A. (1951), *Sophocles the Dramatist*, Cambridge.
Weil, S. (1941), *L'Iliade ou le poème de la force*, Marseille.
Weissberg, L. (1989), "Language's Wound: Herder, Philoctetes, and the origin of speech," in: *Modern Language Notes* 104, 548–79.
Wheeler, G. (2003), "Gender and Transgression in Sophocles' "Electra," in: *Classical Quarterly* 53, no. 2, 377–88.
Whitman, C. (1951), *Sophocles: A Study of Heroic Humanism*, Cambridge, MA.
Whitman, C. (1958), *Homer and the Homeric Tradition*, Cambridge, MA.

Williams, B. (1993), *Shame and Necessity*, Berkeley.
Wilson, E. (1941), *The Wound and the Bow: Seven Studies in Literature*, Boston.
Wilson, D. (2002), *Ransom, Revenge, and Heroic Identity in the* Iliad, Cambridge.
Wilson, E. (2004), *Mocked with Death: Tragic Overliving from Sophocles to Milton*, Baltimore.
Winnington-Ingram, R. P. (1948), "Clytaemnestra and the Vote of Athena," in: *Journal of Hellenic Studies* 68, 130–47.
Winnington-Ingram, R. P. (1965), "Tragedy and Greek Archaic Thought," in: M. J. Anderson (ed.), *Classical Drama and its Influence: Essays presented to H. D. Kitto*, London, 29–50.
Winnington-Ingram, R. P. (1980), *Sophocles: An Interpretation*, Cambridge.
Winnington-Ingram, R. P. (1983), *Studies in Aeschylus*, Cambridge.
Wohl, V. (1998), *Intimate Commerce: Exchange, Gender, and Subjectivity in Greek Tragedy*, Austin.
Wohl, V. (2010), "A Tragic Case of Poisoning: Intention between Tragedy and the Law," in: *Transactions of the American Philological Association* 40, 33–70.
Worman, N. (2000), "Infection in the Sentence: The Discourse of Disease in Sophocles' Philoctetes," in: *Arethusa* 33, 1–36.
Xanthou, M. (2015), "Maternal figures in the Stesichorean blueprint: Althaea, Callirhoe and the Lille Queen," in: *Quaderni Urbinati di Cultura Classica, forthcoming* 2015.
Yamagata, N. (1989), "The Apostrophe in Homer as Part of the Oral Technique," in: *Bulletin of the Institute of Classical Studies* 36, 91–103.
Yoon, F. (2012), *The Use of Anonymous Characters in Greek Tragedy: The Shaping of Heroes*, Leiden.
Zeitlin, F. (1965), "The Motif of the Corrupted Sacrifice in Aeschylus' *Oresteia*," in: *Transactions of the American Philological Association* 96, 463–508.
Zeitlin, F. (1978), "The Dynamics of Misogyny. Myth and Mythmaking in the *Oresteia*," in: *Arethusa* 11, 149–84.
Zerba, M. (2012), *Doubt and Skepticism in Antiquity and the Renaissance*, Cambridge.
Zyroff, E. (1971), *The Author's Apostrophe in Epic from Homer Through Lucan*, Baltimore.

Index

absence   12, 16, 18, 29, 31, 34, 41, 43–45, 48f., 51, 54, 57, 59, 62f., 65–69, 71–75, 78–79, 81f., 88, 91, 94f., 102, 108, 110, 112, 118–119, 126, 133f., 139, 142f., 155, 158, 163, 166, 183, 203–204, 208, 211, 217–218, 220f., 226, 229–231, 242, 255–259, 267, 276, 298, 301
Achelous   105f., 116, 118, 144, 169
Achilles   6, 9–11, 16–18, 21f., 25–27, 30–32, 35–40, 43–45, 48–56, 59, 61, 63–65, 68–93, 96, 139f., 249, 252, 255f., 265, 274, 281f., 288f., 292, 294, 299, 308f.
– Achilles' voice   18, 72f., 78, 80–82
– achos and Achilles   51 n. 138
– and his mother Thetis. *See* Thetis
– death of Achilles   25, 65, 91f.
act   2, 4–8, 11, 13, 16, 20f., 26, 31, 41, 50, 82, 90, 92, 94–96, 99, 101, 108, 112, 121–123, 127f., 133f., 139, 156, 160, 163, 165, 171f., 174–178, 181f., 184, 186f., 189–193, 195, 197f., 200, 203f., 207–211, 216, 218, 220, 222, 224, 229f., 232–234, 237, 239f., 243, 245–248, 250f., 262, 273, 281–284, 287, 299f., 306f., 309f.
– acting   2, 8, 142, 187, 251, 266f., 295, 301
– actor   125, 144, 154, 174, 199, 214, 250, 265, 283, 289, 300, 304
– reenact   185, 200, 224, 234f., 245
reenactment   84, 172, 208, 225, 237, 244, 246
Adamas   67
address   18, 38, 46–49, 55f., 59–61, 63, 68, 73, 76, 78–80, 86, 89, 164, 173, 187, 215, 226, 238f., 243, 295
adynaton   194. *See* imagery
Aegisthus   156
in Aeschylus   180, 182, 184, 199, 201–207, 209
in Sophocles   212–216
in Sophocles and Euripides 218–229, 231–233, 238, 242
Aeschylus   8, 10f., 97, 113, 125, 127, 142, 171f., 176–178, 181f., 185, 189f., 192, 194f., 198–201, 203, 208–210, 212, 216, 218–220, 222, 225, 230f., 233–246, 255, 262, 264f., 279
– *Agamemnon* 10–12, 16, 113, 177–185, 187–197, 199–201, 203–207, 209, 213, 217–220, 222, 224–227, 229, 231–234, 239f., 242, 248
– *Choephori*   172, 196, 201, 204, 208, 216, 218f., 226, 230, 233f., 238, 242, 244, 246, 262, 279, 303
– *Eumenides*   199f., 208f., 234, 242, 244
Agamemnon   10–12, 16
Agamemnon in the *Iliad*   21, 44, 51, 57f., 60–63, 73f., 77, 80, 82f., 86, 90
Agamemnon and Cassandra in Aeschylus 125, 127, 171f.
Agamemnon in Aeschylus. *See Agamemnon*
agency   8, 10f., 16, 83, 94, 97, 104, 107, 109, 116f., 130f., 135f., 140, 142, 152, 157, 162, 166f., 172, 185–188, 190, 200, 205–207, 236, 242, 244f., 295
agent   2–5, 7–16, 18, 21, 49, 81, 92, 94, 97, 106, 110, 117, 120, 131, 138, 140, 143f., 147, 166, 169–172, 174f., 182, 188f., 198f., 215, 244, 247f., 250, 253, 280, 307, 309f.
aidôs   36, 115, 139, 202, 207, 213, 215, 219, 295, 302. *See* respect, shame
Ajax
Ajax in the *Iliad*   28, 31, 67f., 90
Ajax in Sophocles. *See* Sophocles' *Ajax*
alienation   6, 9, 94, 130, 212, 237, 254, 261, 271, 276, 296
Andromache   21, 25, 36, 41f., 44, 53
anger   21, 26–7, 32, 44f., 53, 64, 73, 80, 83, 86, 93, 119, 122, 126, 133–4, 148, 151, 160, 189, 197, 214, 231, 279. *See* emotion
anonymous observer   23–4, 34, 42, 45, 67, 133, 173. *See* eyewitness, spectator
Antilochus   56, 58f., 86
Aphrodite   27f., 31, 62, 107, 115, 117–119, 126f., 140, 142–144, 152, 157, 162f., 169, 192. *See* Cypris

Index

Apollo 27, 29, 31, 33, 35–38, 45, 49, 52, 54, 62–72, 78–82, 84, 89, 91, 200, 202–204, 208–210, 212, 214, 229 f., 234, 243, 303
apostrophe 18, 46–50, 52, 54–63, 65 f., 71–76, 78–81, 86–89. See metalepsis
archaic thought 8, 16, 97, 137, 141, 188, 195, 244
Ares 37, 62, 65, 86
aristeia 27, 32, 34 f., 44, 49, 55, 62, 70, 79, 90. See Diomedeia; Patrocleia
Aristophanes 256, 287
Aristotle 2, 5, 19, 110, 150, 156, 160, 211, 226 f., 241, 263, 268 f., 277, 283, 293, 296, 299
– *Nicomachean Ethics* 268, 277, 293, 299
– *Poetics* 2, 19
– *Rhetoric* 156, 227, 268, 293
Artemis 163, 197
Astyanax 44
atê 170, 195. See anger
Athena 23, 27 f., 31, 37–39, 46, 58 f., 70, 73, 81, 86, 110 f., 124, 139, 199, 208 f., 234, 243, 245
audience 1–14, 16, 18–21, 23–25, 27, 29, 35, 38, 41 f., 46–48, 50 f., 55–57, 59–61, 64–67, 69–76, 78–81, 84, 86–89, 92–98, 100 f., 104, 106–108, 111, 113 f., 119, 122–124, 126, 128, 130–134, 136, 138, 141, 145 f., 149–152, 154–157, 160, 163 f., 168, 170–179, 181 f., 184–186, 188–190, 195, 198–206, 208–216, 218 f., 221–234, 237 f., 242 f., 245 f., 248–256, 258, 262–265, 267, 269, 271 f., 281 f., 284 f., 288–293, 296–304, 309 f.
– external audience 2–4, 15, 24, 131, 136, 154, 157, 204, 228, 254, 265, 285, 298
– internal audience 1–3, 19, 34, 45, 57, 128, 131, 157, 178, 190, 227, 253, 264 f.

beauty 36, 39, 105–107, 113–116, 119 f., 144, 169
bias 7, 10, 13, 175, 177. See perspective
body 4, 26, 28, 30, 32–34, 36, 39–41, 43 f., 49, 54 f., 58, 61, 68 f., 83, 86, 90, 93, 130–131, 146, 150, 152–156, 167, 171 f., 176, 182, 188, 194, 199 f., 202–212, 214 f., 217–219, 222–226, 228 f., 233 f., 237 f., 240–246, 254, 258, 264, 267, 276 f., 279 f., 287, 303
bystander 2, 120, 130, 237, 272. See anonymous observer; eyewitness; spectator; internal audience

Cassandra 43, 113, 125, 127 f., 181–184, 197 f., 203 f., 219, 231, 233
causation 138, 140, 142 f., 148, 150, 187. See agency; responsibility
Cebriones 49, 54
characterization 91, 176, 195, 198, 222, 232, 267, 272–273
choice 15, 17, 48, 81, 83, 91, 103, 142, 172, 182, 211, 225, 250 f., 255, 272, 277, 280, 284
Chorus 1, 9, 13, 99, 104–108, 118 f., 122, 124, 126, 129, 135, 137, 140–146, 148 f., 152, 157 f., 164, 167–169, 177–184, 186–190, 194, 196–198, 201, 204–208, 212, 214, 218–220, 222, 224, 226–228, 232–239, 241 f., 248, 252 f., 255 f., 258 f., 262–274, 276 f., 283 f., 287–290, 293 f., 298
Clytemnestra 5, 10, 12, 16, 113, 123, 125, 127, 159, 171 f., 177–210, 212–225, 228–245, 248, 262
communication 250, 252, 254, 258, 266–268, 277, 284, 290
community 32, 44, 88, 93, 160, 249, 252, 255, 261, 269, 273, 275, 277, 280, 282, 301, 307–309
companionship 258 f., 289
compassion 1, 43–4, 48, 90, 94, 97–8, 101-3, 107–9, 114, 136, 151, 216, 252, 256, 258, 262, 265–266, 268–9, 272–3, 276–7, 305. See pity; *suggnômosynê*; sympathy
conscience 1, 171, 210, 237, 295
corpse 8, 21, 26–28, 30, 33–36, 39 f., 43, 53, 58, 60, 68, 86, 91, 155, 160, 163, 171, 175 f., 182, 184, 187, 194, 200 f., 203 f., 206, 210, 212, 222–224, 228, 233 f., 238 f., 242 f., 246, 262. See body
Creon 178, 185
Culler, Jonathan 47 f.

culpability   132, 140, 159, 201, 224, 226, 242, 274. See responsibility
Curse   132, 147 f., 162, 171, 188 f., 196, 198, 209, 302
Cypris   1, 118–129, 140–146, 157–9, 169. See Aphrodite

dactylic hexameter   37, 39, 61, 67, 69, 73
δαίμονι ἶσος   62–65
death   3, 9 f., 10, 12, 16, 18 f., 21, 24–39, 40 f., 41–47, 49–58, 55, 57 f., 60–84, 86, 88 f., 91 f., 96, 102–105, 115 f., 118, 120, 125, 127, 129–137, 139–151, 155 f., 162–164, 166 f., 171–178, 182–186, 189–202, 204–207, 209–222, 223 f., 241 f., 267, 279, 303, 305, 309.
deceit   38, 113, 124, 252, 272, 278, 280 f., 289, 294, 301
Deianeira   9 f., 16, 94–110, 112–157, 159–171, 174, 178, 188, 305, 309
– and Ajax   124, 138–40, 160, 168–9
– and Cassandra, 127
– and Hector   103, 115, 139–140
– and Hippolytus   162–3
– and Oedipus   100, 168
– and Odysseus   110–112
– suicide of   145 f.
diegesis   12, 46, 49, 61
– heterodiegetic   6, 12, 174
– homodiegetic   6 f., 12, 130, 174
– intradiegetic   61, 75, 79
Diomedeia   27
Diomedes   27–30, 62, 283
Diomedes and Patroclus   63
disease   115, 117 f., 122, 142, 144, 256, 268 f., 271, 273 f., 276, 291, 307. See illness
disgust   256, 262, 292, 297
divine   1, 3, 5, 11, 16 f., 19, 25–30, 32, 34, 43, 45, 62, 67, 70 f., 80, 82, 86, 91, 96–98, 106 f., 109–112, 115, 118, 126, 137, 140, 142, 144, 152, 158, 165 f., 169 f., 172, 187 f., 203, 226, 230, 243–245, 263, 266, 275, 301, 307–309
divine detachment   1, 26, 146, 168

echo   14, 53, 56, 61, 86, 108, 168, 187, 203, 209, 213, 219, 233, 241, 244, 255, 257 f., 260 f., 297 f. See sounds
echthroi   19, 26, 39, 42
Electra 10, 16
– in Aeschylus   156, 171–4, 177, 179, 182, 191
– in Euripides   12, 18, 158, 173–174, 179, 184, 202, 217–222, 224–226, 228–233, 235–246, 309
– in Sophocles   173–174, 179, 199–200, 206, 210–217
emotion   1–5, 24, 26, 41, 48, 69, 116, 121, 128, 130, 134, 136, 146, 156 f., 162, 173–175, 178, 181, 190, 201, 211, 230, 245, 252 f., 258, 263 f., 267, 291–293, 304, 309
– and cognition   16, 22, 110, 238
– and morality   171, 176, 210
– emotional effect   2 f., 19, 48 f., 145
– emotional lens   20, 42, 45 f., 76
– emotional and physical proximity   3, 47, 66, 81, 145–7, 237
– emotional response   2, 4, 6, 12 f., 19, 25 f., 29, 38, 68, 114, 140, 172, 178, 184 f., 194, 208, 218, 224, 232, 234, 244, 252, 288, 290
enargeia   20, 47, 72
Epeigeus   49
epiphanies   27, 126, 143
epistemic limitations   13, 94, 100. See also fallibility
epithet   260 f., 268
formulaic epithet   34, 36, 50, 52, 62, 64, 85 f.
Erinyes   157, 189, 193, 199, 203, 208, 215, 220, 243–246. See also Furies
Eros   117, 121
erôs   106, 114 f., 118 f., 137, 140, 143
Euripides   15, 17, 115, 117, 142, 163, 171–173, 177 f., 182 f., 185, 199 f., 210, 212, 218 f., 224 f., 227, 229–238, 240–246, 255 f., 277, 309
– *Electra*   172, 182, 191, 199, 206, 210–215, 217–222, 224–226, 228–233, 235–245
– *Hecuba* 178, 227, 277
– *Hippolytus* 162 f., 169

– *Medea* 113, 178, 185
Eurytus 107
Evenus 121
eyes 1, 3, 7, 9f., 13, 16, 18, 20f., 23–25, 27–29, 35, 37f., 41f., 45, 54, 71, 76, 78, 84, 87f., 92, 96–98, 103–105, 107f., 116, 125–131, 134f., 137, 139f., 142, 144–146, 150f., 153–158, 160f., 164–166, 169–172, 175, 178, 181f., 184f., 190, 200, 202, 206, 208, 210–212, 214, 216, 218, 222f., 225, 228f., 231, 233f., 236, 238–240, 242f., 245f., 251, 256, 269, 274, 278, 282, 285, 289, 294–297, 301, 306
eyewitness 1, 20, 34, 100, 107, 118, 125, 130f., 142, 145f., 148, 152, 173, 175, 237

fallibility 5, 10f., 15–17, 38, 48, 53, 71f., 82–84, 86, 90, 94, 96f., 101f., 104, 106, 110–112, 117, 122–124, 129, 135, 137, 139, 148–152, 160, 162–164, 231, 246
fate 15–17, 21, 29, 31–32, 35, 37f., 41, 47, 51f., 53, 70, 72f., 76, 82f., 84, 87, 89, 91–92, 94–96, 98, 100–102, 105, 108f., 112, 118, 122f., 129, 133–135, 137, 140, 142, 147, 149–152, 165–168, 178, 185, 202, 211, 219, 233, 247, 266
fear 2, 19, 26, 37, 60, 69, 79, 99f., 104–106, 109–112, 116, 118f., 121, 129, 134–136, 144, 158, 187, 214, 216, 220, 228, 236, 238, 244, 248, 256, 271f., 279, 296
fertility 186, 193, 197–201
focalization 2, 6f., 13, 18, 23f., 37, 69, 72, 76, 78, 87, 95, 174f.
forces 10f., 16f., 90, 94, 97f., 105, 109, 116, 123, 137, 148, 152, 172, 188, 190, 198f., 235, 245
formulaic diction 21f., 26, 37, 50f., 54f., 62, 67, 73, 126, 293
fortune 98, 100, 103, 109, 111, 114–115, 123, 170, 239, 244
Furies 203, 208, 215, 221, 244–6

garment 124, 126–8, 151, 177, 191, 205–7, 209, 241–3, 321. *See* robe
gaze 1–3, 5f., 13, 20, 23, 35, 38, 67f., 80f., 85, 92, 95, 97, 105, 108, 111, 119–121, 124, 127, 132, 136f., 144, 153–155, 165, 169, 171, 176f., 200, 204f., 209f., 224, 235–238, 242, 245f., 273, 285, 296, 302, 306
gender 97, 107, 118, 140, 152f., 178, 180, 184, 188
Genette, Gérard 6, 46f., 74, 174
gesture 4, 12, 14, 36, 132, 145, 176, 178, 181–183, 195, 198, 202, 206, 210, 212, 214, 219, 225, 235–237, 243, 245, 301
Glaucus 29f., 32–34, 45, 68, 74
– and Sarpedon 65
god 8, 15f., 19, 21, 24–27, 29, 31f., 37–39, 43, 45, 52, 56, 58f., 61–68, 70–73, 77, 80, 83f., 86, 92, 94, 105, 109, 111f., 114–119, 121, 124–126, 131, 136, 138, 142, 152, 157f., 163, 166–169, 188, 192, 198, 200, 202f., 207–209, 214, 218, 220, 225–227, 230, 232f., 238, 243, 256, 263, 274f., 301, 304f., 307–309
grief 19f., 23–4, 26, 32, 36f., 40, 42–44, 51, 69, 82, 86f., 91, 98, 104, 109, 153, 158, 162f., 174, 197, 212, 215f., 224, 236, 268, 271, 278, 293, 303

Harpalion 67
hatred 126, 133f., 136, 156, 162, 164f., 192, 195, 213, 216, 230, 239, 286, 294, 309
Hector 2, 20f., 27f., 30f., 34–46, 49, 52–56, 59–61, 65, 67–70, 72f., 83–86, 88, 92f., 103, 115, 139f.
– death of Hector 3, 36, 41, 44, 65, 69, 86
Hecuba 178, 227, 277
– in the *Iliad* 3, 21, 25, 36, 40, 53
– in Euripides' *Hecuba* 178, 227, 277
Helen 27, 44, 69, 187
helplessness 5, 10f., 13–16, 18, 21, 25, 28, 30–33, 47, 55–56, 71f., 81f., 88f., 91f., 94–98, 100, 104f., 109f., 111, 116, 118, 121f., 129–131, 135, 137, 140, 144, 146f., 148, 150, 152f., 157, 164–166, 168–170, 177, 244, 248, 265
Hera 29–32, 37, 53, 81, 192
Heracles 9, 94–97, 100–109, 112–122, 124–167, 169, 249, 259, 261, 281, 301, 305–309
Heraclidae 158

Hermes   43, 261
hero   10, 16, 18–21, 25, 28–33, 35–38, 42–49, 53, 55, 57–60, 62f., 65–68, 70–72, 76, 78, 81–84, 87–95, 97, 100, 102, 105–108, 115, 119–122, 125, 127, 129–134, 138, 140f., 149–154, 156–158, 160, 162, 164–166, 173, 177, 181, 184, 215, 247, 249, 251, 254–257, 261, 263–269, 271, 276, 278–282, 284–286, 289–295, 298, 300–304, 306–309
Hesiod *Theogony*, 193
Homer   2, 19f., 24, 36, 47, 75, 78, 87, 92, 266, 271
Homeric poet   3, 9, 12, 19f., 22f., 47, 67, 70f., 74f., 78, 96
Homeric question   22
hope   44, 104, 117, 126, 136, 214, 223, 309
human condition   5, 11, 15, 27, 94, 96f., 101, 108, 157, 168, 248, 266
humanize   157, 231, 246, 257, 266, 269, 273, 276
Hydra   123, 165
Hyllus   94, 96f., 100, 104, 117, 123, 127f., 130–136, 138, 140, 144, 146–170

identification   89, 221, 254, 271, 273, 287, 293
identity   24, 77f., 89f., 113f., 116, 129f., 184, 204, 217f., 223, 227, 229, 261, 274, 277f.
ignorance   53, 81, 86f.
illness   142, 290. *See* disease
imagery   12, 14, 27, 89, 142, 171–173, 177, 182, 184f., 189f., 192–196, 198f., 240, 267–9, 286–289
– metaphor 27, 89, 114, 118, 142, 150, 184, 192–196, 203, 223, 240, 258, 265, 267, 277f., 286–289
– simile   36, 57, 59, 85, 197, 270f.
– synaesthesia 265
indignation   68, 160, 178, 214, 226–228, 285.
innocence   52, 117, 125, 133–135, 140, 142, 148, 154, 159f., 162–164, 289
intent   73, 83, 104, 107, 113, 117, 123–125, 130f., 135, 138, 152, 157, 159–164, 179, 261, 278

internal observer   2. *See* anonymous observer, eyewitness, internal audience, spectator
Iole   101, 103f., 113–116, 120, 125, 137, 141–143, 150, 157–158
irony   9, 51, 77, 85, 95, 102–104, 108, 110, 112, 118, 125, 128, 134, 158, 189, 213, 223, 232
isolation   21, 33f., 38, 45, 68, 70, 74, 109, 112, 119, 129, 135, 137, 146, 148, 163, 167, 173, 207f., 214, 217, 219, 254–261, 273, 289, 298, 303
– isolation of Patroclus at his death   21, 38, 45, 70, 74,
– isolation of Philoctetes on Lemnos   256–257, 259–260, 298, 303

justice   1, 15, 27, 151–155, 171, 176, 183, 186, 190, 198, 200, 203–211, 214, 220, 227, 232, 237–240, 242, 301f.

kleos   19f., 28–9, 30, 32, 37, 44, 50, 55, 63, 70, 73, 77, 80–82, 87, 90, 108, 123, 126, 131, 138–140, 150, 156, 165, 181, 272f., 282, 292, 295, 307–309
knowledge   87, 92, 97–104, 107f., 111–114, 121f., 143f., 152, 162, 165–168, 174–190, 223f., 248, 293, 298, 300. *See* late learning

lament   20, 40, 42f., 51, 53, 55, 57f., 80, 86f., 91, 142f., 149, 158, 166, 187, 203, 205, 207, 213, 217, 224f., 234f., 260, 264, 268, 270f., 288, 293
language   4, 30, 78, 84, 91, 171, 173, 178–181, 184–186, 188f., 191, 194–198, 210f., 215, 237, 243, 266–269, 280, 282, 284, 286, 288, 290, 292
late learning   4, 6, 8–11, 14, 16, 34, 71, 84, 86f., 92, 97–100, 102, 104, 107, 111f., 121–123, 126, 128f., 137, 147f., 151, 159, 166f., 248
lens   7f., 10, 18, 21, 71, 76, 101, 131, 145f., 148, 151, 170, 175, 191, 222, 251, 255, 265, 291, 295f. *See* emotional lens

logos 252, 254, 264, 276f., 285. *See* persuasion
love 3, 21f., 35, 40, 58f., 73, 80f., 94, 104f., 112f., 115, 117f., 120f., 137, 140–166, 212, 240, 291, 306. *See* Eros, erôs

Melanippus 58–61
Meriones 67, 90
message 125, 218
messenger speech 1, 7, 11f., 124f., 171–178, 185, 194, 198, 200, 213, 235
– messenger 1, 7, 11f., 113f., 125, 133, 171–178, 182, 185, 194, 198, 200f., 215f., 218, 223, 225f.
metalepsis 18, 46–48, 61f., 66, 74f., 81, 88
metanarrative 12, 172, 189f., 194f.
metatheater 15, 102, 250, 280, 283
metatheatrical 102, 250, 280, 283
monster 105, 124, 137, 141, 143, 148, 150, 152f., 165f., 206
morality 103, 171, 176, 210f., 227, 230, 237, 278
mortality 15f., 18, 26, 29, 32, 82, 84, 88, 91, 93. *See* death
mother 28, 36, 40, 51, 80, 83–86, 91, 132f., 135, 140f., 144, 147–149, 151, 155f., 158, 160f., 167f., 172, 177, 193f., 195, 197, 199–222, 224f., 228–245, 303
motherhood 36, 186, 199, 207, 224, 243
mourning 36, 40, 42, 55, 91, 158, 197, 215, 268. *See* grief
murder 7, 10, 16, 27, 31, 34, 39, 49, 51, 55–57, 69, 84, 90f., 113, 127f., 131, 133, 155, 165, 171–173, 175–179, 181–204, 206, 208–211, 213–215, 218–222, 224–236, 238f., 241–245, 294, 303
murderer 7, 12, 171f., 174–177, 190, 200, 205, 221, 225, 229, 233, 235, 239, 241, 243
music 55, 195, 258, 264, 270f., 286–288

narrative 2, 6f., 11f., 18–21, 31f., 40, 46f., 50, 57–61, 66–68, 74, 79–81, 84, 87f., 90, 92, 134, 172–175, 177f., 182, 189f., 215, 235. *See* diegesis
narratology 6, 74f.

narrator 6f., 9, 11f., 14, 18–21, 23, 34, 46, 48, 52, 57, 60, 66, 69f., 72, 74–80, 83, 86, 89f., 130, 171f., 174f., 288
Neoptolemus 17, 178, 247–260, 262–265, 267–269, 272–310
Nessus 121, 123, 127f., 137, 140–144, 147f., 150, 152, 161–166
Nestor 50, 77f.
νήπιος 52, 55, 85
nosos 114f., 150
nurse 1, 98, 132, 135, 140–149, 155, 157, 164, 168, 174, 178, 202, 212f., 216

Odysseus
– in Sophocles' *Ajax* 98, 110–112, 116, 138, 140, 159
– in Sophocles' *Philoctetes* 247–253, 255f., 262f., 265–267, 269, 272–290, 292–307
Oechalia 107, 109, 114, 142
Oedipus 100, 168, 256
Oeneus 157
oiktos See compassion; pity
oracle 98, 100, 141, 165–6, 200, 203, 229–30, 243–4, 247, 249, 275, 301, 303
oral poetics 22
Orestes 10, 156, 171f., 177, 182, 193, 195, 212–230, 232–239, 241–246, 262, 279, 303, 309
– and Clytemnestra 10, 113, 184, 193, 211f., 217, 219f., 223, 225f., 233, 238, 242
– and Electra 10, 171f., 177, 199f., 210, 212, 218, 220f., 223–226, 228, 230, 232–235, 241, 244–246, 309
– and Pylades 217, 242. *See* Pylades
– in Aeschylus's *Oresteia* 182, 193, 195, 199–210
– in Euripides' *Electra* 10, 16, 156, 200, 220f., 232, 245
– in Sophocles' *Electra* 210f.

pain 3, 5, 11, 15, 17, 21, 23f., 25–6, 28f., 31, 33, 40f., 51, 69, 88, 93–6, 98f., 101–2, 104–106, 110, 113, 117, 121, 127–8, 129–138, 140, 143f., 146, 148–157, 160, 163, 166, 168–170, 174, 182f., 208, 211, 215, 217, 222, 226f., 238f., 245, 247f.,, 278–

280, 282, 285 f., 288–299, 301–306, 308 f.
- moral pain   255, 280, 290, 295, 298 f., 304
Paris   27 f., 67
passive   9, 39, 78, 81 f., 94, 99, 105, 119–121, 124, 126, 129, 136 f., 168
past   4, 6–8, 13 f., 47 f., 72, 94–96, 99, 104, 112, 116, 119, 127, 131, 165, 171, 173, 176, 182, 186 f., 190, 195, 198, 200, 212, 287, 290, 292, 308
pathos   4–5 f., 10, 18, 20, 25, 29, 35 f., 38, 41, 45, 47, 49, 53, 63, 71, 76, 80, 81, 84, 88, 100, 105, 123, 126, 128 f., 134, 139, 144, 149–152, 156 f., 162, 170, 178, 209, 217, 222, 235, 241, 246, 248, 262, 271, 288, 305
Patroclus   9 f., 18, 21, 23, 25, 28–36, 39, 43–60, 62–93, 107
- Patrocleia   46, 49 f., 88, 90
- Patroclus as *alter ego* of Achilles   18, 25, 65, 77–8, 88–90
Peleus   31, 36 f., 51 f., 56, 63, 73, 90
Pentheus   15
perception   8, 12–14, 19, 54, 69 f., 93 f., 99 f., 108, 110, 121 f., 153, 156, 159 f., 164 f., 176, 185 f., 188, 198, 204, 212, 219, 224 f., 239, 242, 245, 262, 264, 266, 269 f., 272, 274, 276, 288, 294
performance   1, 6, 13 f., 22, 47 f., 74 f., 81, 124–127, 171, 185, 221, 235, 253, 265, 288
interperformative reference, 177, 209
personification   117, 245, 306
perspective   1–4, 7–9, 11, 13 f., 20, 53, 70, 76, 102, 107 f., 110, 118, 121, 130 f., 145, 167, 171, 174–5, 182, 185, 234, 237, 249, 251, 279, 294, 296
persuasion   36, 161–2, 273
Phaedra   162–163
philia   24 f., 35, 80, 94, 96, 104, 107, 114, 116–120, 122, 124 f., 127, 133 f., 136 f., 139, 142 f., 150, 159, 161–165, 199, 201, 203 f., 212 f., 220–224, 228 f., 233, 240, 287, 291, 295, 300, 307, 309. *See* philoi, philos

Philoctetes   17, 98, 136, 157, 247–310
- Philoctetes' bow   249, 259, 275, 284, 295, 301–3, 305–6
- And Achilles   255–256, 274, 281, 281–299, 308
- And Heracles   249, 259, 261, 281, 301 f.
- And Neoptolemus   5, 248, 252 f., 256, 267, 269, 275, 280, 284, 286–288, 290, 294, 296 f., 303, 309 f.
philoi   19 f., 25 f., 28, 30, 32, 42, 68, 73, 77 f., 80, 83, 85, 92, 94, 100 f., 103, 106, 109, 133, 138, 146 f., 161, 181, 212, 257, 296, 309
philos   19 f., 23–26, 28–30, 32, 38 f., 42 f., 45, 53, 59–61, 63, 67, 72–74, 77 f., 86–90, 92, 103, 139, 156, 160, 171 f., 174, 178, 195, 202, 207, 211, 217, 238, 248, 252, 255 f., 268, 273, 275–277, 286 f., 293, 295–297, 299–301, 307–309
physis   213, 262, 277, 281, 292, 294
pity   2, 26 f., 32, 43–45, 48, 68, 97 f., 100, 103, 107–114, 116, 133–135, 137, 140 f., 143, 146, 152–158, 162–164, 169, 184, 211 f., 214–216, 219–222, 227, 229, 233, 243, 245, 250–253, 255–257, 262–272, 275, 283, 288, 291–294, 296–300, 302, 304–306
- pity and sight   261–279
- pity and sound   255, 262 f.
- seeing-and-pitying sequence   26, 32, 38, 67
poet   2, 4–10, 13 f., 18–24, 33 f., 38, 43, 45–49, 52 f., 55–61, 65–68, 70–76, 78–82, 84–89, 91, 103, 124, 147, 166, 194, 248
Polydamas   139
polyphony   284
Poseidon   26, 28 f., 81, 162
power   5, 8, 21, 28 f., 40, 66, 75, 81 f., 88 f., 91, 94, 96, 98, 101, 106, 109–112, 114–5, 117 f., 119–121, 120 f., 123 f., 127 f., 131, 133 f., 136 f., 140–142, 144, 147 f., 150, 152 f., 155, 162 f., 165–167, 170, 184–187, 189, 192–194, 199, 201, 204 f., 207, 209, 213 f., 217 f., 220–222, 226–229, 234 f., 240, 244, 248, 251 f., 261, 266–269, 273, 282, 285, 287, 297, 302–3, 306
prayer   33, 53, 80, 184, 214, 226 f.

present 8, 18f., 29f., 34, 45, 47, 55, 61, 74f., 80, 82–84, 86f., 89, 94–99, 102, 104f., 112f., 118f., 124–129, 130–132, 134, 145, 147, 148, 152, 171–173, 176f., 179, 182, 185f., 190, 193, 195f., 198, 204, 207–210, 218, 222, 227–229, 232, 234f., 289, 298, 303, 306
Priam 3, 21, 25f., 36, 40, 43, 53f., 59, 93, 249, 301, 309
pride 61, 122, 296, 299
prop 94, 124, 205, 212, 275, 279, 302, 309. *See* bow (Philoctetes'); garment; robe
prophecy 100, 127, 141, 158, 161, 168, 182, 198, 203, 249. *See* oracle
Pylades 217, 201–203, 220, 227, 230, 242, 303
Pyraichmes 63

reaction 2–4, 6–8, 12f., 19, 29, 34, 41f., 44, 57, 68, 86f., 94, 96, 98, 101, 104, 106f., 109, 114, 130–133, 136, 138, 140, 147, 150f., 157, 159, 172, 175f., 178, 182, 184f., 191, 198, 200–202, 210, 215f., 223, 228, 232, 234, 247, 250, 253–256, 261–263, 267, 269, 272f., 276, 289f., 299, 304
regret 3, 8, 56, 83, 85, 160, 212, 220f., 231f., 234, 236, 244f.
repetition 22, 85, 186, 257
respect 122, 202, 215, 243, 251, 294, 296, 303, 308
responsibility 1, 5, 8, 21, 37, 82f., 106, 113, 115f., 137–148, 154, 157, 162, 186–189, 204, 212, 236
retrospective lens 6, 9, 13, 176, 225, 237f.
revenge *see* vengeance
ritual 15, 37, 60, 62, 86, 88, 92, 125f., 185, 191, 195–197, 206, 225, 235, 286f.; *see* sacrifice
robe 27, 94, 123–127, 130, 132f., 157, 201, 204, 206f., 209f., 236, 243. See also prop, garment.
role 1f., 5–8, 10, 14–16, 18, 20, 24f., 27, 30, 34f., 37, 40, 42–45, 47–49, 54, 56, 59–61, 65, 75, 78, 81–85, 87–91, 96–99, 104f., 110, 112, 116f., 119, 121–124, 126, 130, 135, 137f., 142–144, 146, 148, 151, 153–155, 162–166, 169f., 172f., 175, 177, 182, 184, 188, 190, 194, 199–202, 207f., 212, 216–218, 225, 229f., 236, 240, 244, 247, 250–252, 254, 258f., 263–265, 274, 278–282, 285, 289, 291f., 295–298, 300, 302, 305, 308

sacrifice 37, 73, 88, 124–126, 178, 189, 191, 193, 195–197, 214, 225–227, 236, 240, 243, 274, 279
sadistic 1, 183, 198
sailors 252f., 256, 259f., 262–265, 267–273, 288, 290f., 300, 303
Sarpedon 20f., 25, 29–37, 44f., 52f., 55, 65, 68, 74, 90, 92
Schadenfreude 77, 184, 198, 219, 221
script 125, 247, 250. *See* stage, stage director, stage directions
senses 146, 263, 265. *See* eyes; gaze; sounds; vision
– pleasure 115–119, 122, 166–169, 180, 185, 187, 192–195, 202, 279, 299, 310, 312. *See* tragic pleasure
– synaesthesia 265
– touch 236–7, 259, 266f., 273, 278
shame 40, 122, 133, 139, 153, 164f., 169, 179, 210, 215, 227, 236, 238, 244f., 251, 277f., 282, 293, 293–297, 302, 304, 306
silence 12, 45, 131f., 134f., 143, 158f., 161f., 164–166, 169, 253, 266, 290, 297, 299–302. *See* sounds
song 75, 118f., 140, 143f., 169, 187–189, 214, 232–235, 258, 263–266, 268–273, 276, 287f.
Sophocles 8, 10, 16f., 94–99, 103, 105, 110, 113f., 117, 123, 127f., 133, 138, 142, 144, 155, 157, 159f., 163, 166, 168f., 172f., 177f., 191, 199–201, 206, 209–213, 215–222, 224f., 230–233, 236, 241–243, 246–249, 251–256, 264–267, 270, 272, 277, 283, 285, 289, 297, 300, 308–310
– *Ajax* 98, 110–112, 114, 116, 124, 138–140, 159, 160, 168f., 173, 266, 277, 285f., 293
– *Electra* 172, 177, 191, 199, 200, 206, 210–215, 217–222, 224–226, 228–233, 235–245
– *Oedipus Tyrannus* 100, 169

- *Philoctetes* 17, 98, 136, 157, 247–310
- *Trachiniae* 10, 16, 94–101, 110, 125, 128, 149 f., 163, 166, 170 f., 178, 305
sound 40, 86, 91, 94, 104, 125, 201, 218, 220, 237, 248, 254–268, 270–274, 282, 285 f., 289, 297. *See* silence; song
- cries 36, 40, 42, 51, 53, 64, 104, 132–134, 147, 152–3, 177, 183, 201 f., 207, 215, 217–24, 231–3, 236, 241, 250, 254–5, 257–8, 260–78, 288–9, 290–1, 297–302
- soundscape 254, 257, 259 f.
space 47, 60, 81, 201, 258, 302. *See* proximity
spectacle 5, 9, 14, 24, 26 f., 39–42, 82, 92, 94, 96 f., 101, 104 f., 108, 110–112, 116, 120, 124, 126 f., 130–132, 135 f., 138, 144, 148, 150–154, 157, 169 f., 204 f., 236, 238, 247, 249, 251 f., 254, 261 f., 279, 282, 285, 290–292, 297, 300, 302, 304–306
spectator 1–6, 8, 9 f., 10–21, 23–25, 27 f., 34, 36, 38, 42 f., 45, 53, 65–69, 71–2, 74, 76 f., 80 f., 84, 87, 89, 92–99, 101, 105 f., 108–110, 112, 114, 119 f., 124–128, 129–130–132, 134, 136, 140, 143 f., 152 f., 158, 163, 166–172, 175, 181, 184 f., 185, 200, 204–5, 207, 211, 214, 216, 218, 222, 224 f., 227, 231, 235, 237–239, 245, 247 f., 250–259, 262–3, 266 f., 269, 272 f., 275, 277, 280, 282–285, 285, 289, 291 f., 296 f., 299, 304 f., 309. *See* anonymous observer, eyewitness
stage 1, 30, 50, 73, 90, 94 f., 104, 110, 114, 118, 120, 127, 132, 135 f., 145, 147, 150–152, 154, 158, 166, 170, 176, 182, 194, 203, 205, 211, 214, 217 f., 218, 222 f., 225, 229, 233 f., 244, 247, 250, 253, 258 f., 261 f., 264, 266, 268, 272, 279, 281, 283, 285 f., 298, 300 f., 307
- offstage 1, 7, 117 f., 128, 144 f., 169, 171, 174, 176–178, 218, 222, 225, 233, 247, 264, 307
- onstage 4, 7, 14, 95, 113, 118, 132, 149, 162, 166, 171–173, 176, 182, 186, 196, 201, 208, 217, 221, 225, 233 f., 238, 247, 251, 254, 264, 266, 268, 272, 283, 285 f., 289, 302

- stage directions 124, 132, 181, 264, 289
- stage director 126 f., 152, 250, 279
- staging 124, 126, 155, 173, 176, 182, 203, 209, 222, 234, 238, 253
suggnômosynê 167–70
supplication 36, 52, 195, 204, 219, 236 f., 259, 302, 310
sympathy 45 f., 57, 59 f., 67, 72, 79, 87, 89, 102, 121, 167 f., 221, 227, 231, 241, 265 f., 273, 288, 296

Teucer 33, 140
Theseus 162 f.
Thetis 21, 31, 51, 65, 81, 83, 86, 91
time 1, 8 f., 47, 49, 79, 84–86, 100, 118, 127, 130, 147, 168, 179–182, 218, 220, 247, 281, 283, 294, 305
tragic pleasure 5, 24, 144, 221–229, 230
triple attempt scene 62–67
Trojan hero 31, 43, 53, 68 f., 72
Troy 21, 30–32, 36, 38, 40, 42 f., 52 f., 55, 64–69, 78, 80, 83–85, 88, 139, 177, 247, 249, 256, 275, 279, 281, 292, 294, 296, 300–303, 307–310
- fall of Troy 40, 45
trust 100, 162, 180, 247 f., 250, 254, 269, 278, 282, 284–286, 288, 291–295, 300, 303, 306
turning point 10, 18, 44, 55, 59, 142, 179, 215, 247, 250 f., 253–255, 272, 284, 289

utilitarianism 251, 275–6, 278, 280, 285, 292

values 8, 12 f., 42, 135 f., 158, 176, 202, 211, 225, 249, 252, 262, 267, 276, 281, 286–288, 291, 293 f., 303, 308 f.
vengeance 26, 39, 77, 82, 134, 154, 156–7, 160, 164, 172, 186, 189–90, 195–7, 207–9, 211, 213, 220–1, 225–230, 304 f.
victim 3, 19, 35, 43–45, 56 f., 69, 88 f., 92, 98, 116, 122, 127, 131, 134, 137, 144, 151 f., 163, 165, 176, 178, 200, 203 f., 211, 215, 226, 231, 242, 245, 247, 250 f., 262, 267, 284, 295
violence 31, 131, 133 f., 155–157, 162, 173, 182, 184, 189, 198, 202, 208

vision   1, 2, 4, 6–14, 16, 19–21, 23, 25–29, 31f., 35–38, 40–43, 51, 57f., 64, 67, 75–78, 89, 93–95, 98, 108, 111, 100–102, 106, 108f., 113, 116, 119–121, 124f., 127–129, 131, 136, 143, 145f., 151f., 156f., 165, 168–170, 172, 175–177, 181, 184f., 188, 190f., 194f., 198, 200f204, 206f., 209f., 221–224, 226–229, 233, 235–238, 241–243, 247, 251f., 257, 261–264, 267, 272f., 279, 291, 293f., 302–304, 306, 310

voice   1, 5–7, 12, 18, 21, 33, 37, 45f., 48f., 51f., 55f., 61, 63, 65–67, 69–72, 74–76, 78–81, 84–89, 92, 99, 113, 128, 136, 143, 158, 160, 175, 189, 203f., 208, 222, 226, 231f., 237f., 244, 253, 255f., 258f., 261–270, 278, 281, 305

vulnerability   5, 18, 30, 33, 42, 47, 53, 55, 57, 59, 72, 79, 81, 88, 90–93, 96–98, 101, 105, 107, 109f., 112, 153, 169, 231, 233, 237, 266, 276

wound   19, 23–27, 29, 31, 33, 39, 45, 54, 57f., 62, 65, 67–68, 72, 77–78, 80, 114, 121, 219, 247, 249, 252, 256, 263, 274f., 278–279, 292, 296

Zeus   25–26, 27f., 29–37, 45, 52–56, 58, 68, 80f., 84, 107, 109, 119, 157, 165–170, 184, 187, 191f., 206, 208, 214, 226, 238, 310